Rūmī's Mystical Design

SUNY series in Islam

Seyyed Hossein Nasr, editor

Rūmī's Mystical Design

Reading the *Mathnawī*, Book One

SEYED GHAHREMAN SAFAVI
AND
SIMON WEIGHTMAN

FOREWORD BY
SEYYED HOSSEIN NASR

SUNY
PRESS

Published by State University of New York Press, Albany

Printed in the United States of America

Cover calligraphy by Mohammad Saeed Naghasian

For information, contact State University of New York Press, Albany, NY
www.sunypress.edu

Production by Cathleen Collins
Marketing by Michael Campochiaro

Library of Congress Cataloging-in-Publication Data

Safavi, Seyed Ghahreman.
Rumi's mystical design : reading the Mathnawi, book one / Seyed Ghahreman Safavi and Simon Weightman ; foreword by Seyyed Hossein Nasr.
p. cm. — (SUNY series in Islam)
Includes bibliographical references and index.
ISBN 978-1-4384-2795-9 (hardcover : alk. paper)
ISBN 978-1-4384-2796-6 (pbk. : alk. paper)
1. Jalāl al-Dīn Rūmī, Maulana, 1207–1273. Masnavī. 2. Sufi poetry, Persian—History and criticism. I. Weightman, S. C. R. II. Title.
PK6481.M9S228 2009
891'.5511—dc22 2008051943

10 9 8 7 6 5 4 3 2 1

Contents

Foreword

PROFESSOR SEYYED HOSSEIN NASR

It is hardly conceivable that after centuries of study of the *Mathnawī* of Jalal al-Din Rūmī, this most famous work of mystical poetry in the Persian language, it could still be possible to make a new discovery of such import and dimension concerning Rūmī's masterpiece as one finds in this book. This discovery is nothing less than the unveiling of the general structure of the *Mathnawī* to which there is no reference in earlier studies of this bible of Sufism. The book marks, therefore, a major event in the study of Sufi literature in general and of Rūmī in particular.

It is our own belief that something as essential as the intricate structure of the *Mathnawī* could not have been totally unknown to the notable authorities of the text of the *Mathnawī* over the ages but that this structure was never divulged in detail in writing. We recall a comment once made to us by a Persian master who was known as the greatest authority on the *Mathnawī* in his day, that is, the late Hadi Ha'iri. He was such an authority on the subject that scholars as celebrated as Badi' al-Zaman Furuzanfar, Jalal Huma'i, and 'Allamah Ja'fari would come to him to ask about particularly difficult passages of Rūmī. Aqa-yi Ha'iri once told us, "Do not think that the 'body' of the *Mathnawī* has no order (*nizam*). Rather, it is [the poet] Nizami who created the structured body into which Rūmī breathed the spirit (*ruh*) to create the *Mathnawī*." On reading the present work, one becomes reminded of this saying of our old teacher. It is interesting to note that the authors of this book refer to the features of parallelism and chiasmus present in Nizami's poetry. Perhaps Aqa-yi Ha'iri was alluding to the inner structure of the *Mathnawī* as revealed fully for the first time in this book. In any case the present study is the first to have described this structure with clarity for Book I of this monumental work while pointing to the presence of this structure in the other five Books.

One might ask, if over the centuries this structure had remained hidden, how did readers benefit from the *Mathnawī* and why has this work been held as the greatest opus of Sufi poetry. The answer is that the *Mathnawī* is replete with the deepest meaning at all levels echoing the Noble Qur'an and one can derive immensurable benefit from it even if one does not have a picture of the structure of the work as a whole in one's mind. Let us start with a single verse. There is many a single verse of the *Mathnawī* which is impregnated with the deepest meaning, revealing a profound metaphysical truth or containing precious practical advice. Some of these verses have become proverbial in the Persian language as for example the well-known verse from the story of Moses and the Shepherd where God admonishes Moses in these terms:

> Thou hast come to bring about union,
> Thou hast not come to cause separation.

Then there are clusters of verses that together express in the profoundest manner some spiritual reality as in sections of the exordium or *nay-namah* of the *Mathnawī* about the reality of love. After these two stages comes a whole story such as that of the King and the Slave girl where the whole story reflects profound spiritual lessons couched in the form of narrative.

Over the centuries Persian speakers, as well as those reading the *Mathnawī* in other languages from Turkish to English, have benefited immensely from the content of the work on these levels. But for nearly all of them the work as a whole has appeared as a rambling collection of narratives like a vast ocean into which one must dive deeply in order to discover the precious pearls contained therein. At last this book makes possible the appreciation of the work on one more level and that is the level of the total structure of each Book and of the *Mathnawī* as a whole, without this discovery in any way diminishing from the supreme significance of understanding the text on the level of a single verse, a cluster of verses or a single narrative or story.

To enable us to understand the total structure of the work, the authors invite us to read it synoptically, meaning together as a whole rather than separately in linear but disconnected succession, and that means to read consciously with the vision of the whole in mind. The authors in fact remind us that synoptic in Greek has the meaning of holistic consciousness. In treating the text as a whole the authors are able to reveal a remarkably ordered structure based on parallelism and chiasmus as one also finds in certain books of the Hebrew Bible such as the Book of Numbers as well as in the Avesta, in Homer and within the Islamic tradition in Nizami. To bring out the structure of the *Mathnawī*, the authors divide the work not only into verses, sections, and books as is customary, but rather into the following units:

Verse
Paragraph composed of thematically united verses
Section
Grouping of sections that they call discourse
Book

They are of the belief that Rūmī on purpose hid the headings for the discourses and the books and offers reasons for this action. In any case once the paragraphs and discourses of the book become distinguished, in addition to single verses and sections, it becomes clear that the work possesses a remarkable structure and is far from being simply a rambling collection of narratives. Furthermore, it becomes clear that this structure is based not only on parallelism and chiasmus but also on numerical symbolism.

The question of numerical symbolism invites a comparison between the *Divine Comedy* of Dante and the *Mathnawī*, each of which is the supreme poetic expression of the spiritual teachings of the civilization with gives birth to them, namely that of the Christian West and that of Islam, respectively. According to Dante himself, the *Divine Comedy* has four levels of meaning, of which the lowest is the literal and the highest the anagogical. Although there are certain obvious numerical symbols associated with the external structure of the work, such as its tripartite division into *Inferno*, *Purgatory*, and *Paradiso*, the number of *cantos* in each book and the three verse structure of each stanza, all reflecting the importance of the number three related to the Trinity, it is only on the anagogical level that the inner mathematical symbolism of the work is revealed. Now, in the *Mathnawī*, the external structure does not display an obvious numerical symbolism as one finds in the *Divine Comedy* even on the external level, but like the latter work, the *Mathnawī* also reveals its esoteric mathematical symbolism on the level of inner interpretation that would correspond to Dante's anagogical level.

In discussing the hidden structure of the *Mathnawī*, the authors also bring to light this hidden numerical symbolism, but since this is not their central concern, they merely refer to it. Considering how important mathematical symbolism is in Islamic esotericism as in many other traditions, it is our hope that a separate work will be devoted to this subject in light of this discovery of the inner structure of the work as a whole and the numerical symbolism associated with it.

'Abd al-Rahman Jami called the *Mathnawī*, "the Qur'an in the Persian language" and in the deepest sense the *Mathnawī* is a commentary on the Sacred Scripture of Islam. Moreover, in the same way that the Noble Qur'an is considered by those who only look at its outer form not to possess a noticeable structure as a whole, likewise the *Mathnawī* had been seen until now to lack a coherent structure. But the Qur'an *does* possess the most profound harmony and structure that belong, however, to its inner dimension and cannot be detected outwardly. One can turn to the *Futuhat al-makkiyyah* of Ibn 'Arabi, the middle part of which contains 114 chapters based in reverse order on the 114 chapters of the Qur'an, to see how various parts of the Qur'an are integrated into a remarkable connected structure. Moreover, there is an unbelievable mathematical order that accompanies the letters, words, verses, and chapters of the Sacred Book. Of course, the Qur'an is the Word of God and the *Mathnawī* a human work, but one written by a sage who had reached the highest level of human perfection and attained the highest degree of sapiental knowledge and could therefore compose a work that reflects many qualities of the Sacred Text of which the *Mathnawī* is a profound commentary that also emulates to a certain extent structurally the Word of God.

The present work covers only the first Book of the *Mathnawī*. Already a similar type of analysis has been carried out for Book II and analyses based on the same methodology outlined in this work are planned for the other four Books. But this book concerns also the whole of the *Mathnawī* in that its methodology is concerned with not only Book One but also with the whole text. In any case the present book is a seminal work and a major contribution to the study of Rūmī and in fact mystical literature in general.

Before concluding this preface, it is of interest to point out the many contributions made by the class of '*ulama*' and *hukama*' in Iran, of which Dr. Safavi is a member, to the study of Rūmī and especially his *Mathnawī*. One need only recall the commentary of Hajji Mulla Hadi Sabziwari on the *Mathnawī*, the keen interest in it by Mirza Abu'l-Hasan Jilwah, and the composition of the poem *Taqdis* ("The Royal Throne") based closely on the *Mathnawī* by Mulla Ahmed Naraqi—three of the great *hakims* of the Qajar period who also belonged to the class of the '*ulama*'—and more recently the voluminous commentary of 'Allamah Muhammad Taqi Ja'fari. Dr. Safavi belongs to this illustrious tradition and demonstrates through this work the continuous vitality of this tradition in our own day. His work is one more illustration of the existence of the profound nexus between Shi'ism in its gnostic aspect and classical Sufism of which Rūmī was one the supreme authorities.

In conclusion, we must congratulate Dr. Safavi and his thesis adviser at the University of London Professor Simon Weightman, for the composition of this work. We look forward to the day when the methodology outlined in this book will be applied to the whole of the *Mathnawī*, that celestial symphony composed of eternal melodies echoing the mysteries of the day of our preeternal covenant with God (or as Rūmī would say *asrar-i alast*).

Preface

SEYED GHAHREMAN SAFAVI AND SIMON WEIGHTMAN

The *Mathnawī-ye Ma'nawī* of Jalāl al-Dīn Rūmī is one of the world's truly great works of spirituality. Before working together, between us, we must have been reading this spiritual masterpiece sporadically for over seventy years, mostly in part, but several times in its entirety. From the time that we began to study it seriously together, we began to make discoveries, and we were soon obliged to acknowledge that up till that point we really had not known how the book should be read. As our discoveries mounted up we at last began to appreciate more fully both how extraordinary was the achievement of its composition and how potent was its transformative effect on the reader. We had been in a fine multistoried building and thought it had only a ground floor, or at most a ground floor and a basement. From the commentaries on it and the scholarship about it, it was clear that we were not alone in thinking this. We have written this book to share our discoveries with spiritual seekers, literary connoisseurs, scholars, and the general reader alike. We have written it as the book we wished we had had prior to and alongside our reading of this great spiritual poem, as an explanatory study and as a reader's guide.

Our discoveries are largely about uncovering the hidden inner organization of a work that has hitherto been regarded as disorganized. In so uncovering, we have been able to see the rationale behind the work as a whole and its various phases and the contexts within which each passage is articulated. This has permitted a fuller and more significant interpretation to be given to larger wholes within the work. But one thing must be made clear at the outset: we make no claim to completeness. What we have offered here is not the last word on the structure of the *Mathnawī*, but rather the first, given that the consensus view was that there was no structure at all. We hope very much that others will find what we have discovered useful and will use it to advance the appreciation and understanding of this great spiritual masterpiece. Since this is a work of great richness, there are certain to be many things we have missed that others of greater spiritual understanding and experience than ourselves will notice and recognize.

We owe the new approach we have adopted to the *Mathnawī*, that of a synoptic reading, largely to the work which Professor Mary Douglas has done on the biblical Book of Numbers and on Leviticus. In acknowledging the source of our methodological inspiration, we would also like to thank her for her continued encouragement in our endeavors and for her questioning and challenges. We lament her passing.

We must also acknowledge with gratitude the Department of the Study of Religions at the School of Oriental and African Studies in the University of London, where this work was born and nurtured. Many are the colleagues there who have either knowingly or unknowingly contributed in some way to the final emergence of this book.

There are three scholars in particular whose advice and encouragement we wish to record in gratitude. The first is the doyen of Islamic and Iranian Studies, Professor Hossein Nasr, who has kindly written a foreword to this work, and to whom all in this field owe an immense debt. The second is Professor William Chittick, whose contribution to the study of Islamic spirituality is enormous and notable for its clarity and depth of understanding. The third is Professor James Morris, whose enthusiasm and advice on many points has ensured that the work reaches the reader in as useful a form as possible. Finally we thank Nancy Ellegate and her colleagues at SUNY Press and Cathleen Collins and her production team for converting a difficult manuscript into this finished book with complete professionalism and benign tolerance. While thanking all whose help we have acknowledged, and the many we have failed to mention, we must further add the absolution. It is we alone who are responsible for any defects or mistakes occurring in this book. For these we apologize and seek the reader's indulgence.

The striking calligraphy on the cover is the work of Mohammad Saeed Naghasian, to whom we are indebted. It is based on the verse with which we conclude this book, where it is translated, and a note to that verse explains the conception of the calligraphy.

Introduction

Jalāl al-Dīn Rūmī, who was born in 1207 CE and died in 1273, will henceforth in this book be referred to by the name Mawlānā, Our Master, one of the two honorific titles by which he is most commonly known in Muslim lands (the other being Mawlawī, My Master). The name Rūmī, by which he is widely known in the West, is a toponym referring to the fact that he lived in the province of Rūm (Anatolia), the country now known as Turkey. Mawlānā is here preferred simply because it comes most naturally to the authors. Similarly, the title of this great work will be shortened from *Mathnawī-ye Ma'nawī*, which means the Spiritual Couplets, to just the *Mathnawī*.

Later, it will be necessary to contextualize both Mawlānā and the *Mathnawī* in terms of history, of religious and spiritual tradition, and of literary genres and antecedents; but here, at the outset, the reader is due some guarantee of the relevance to her- or himself of a long thirteenth-century poem written in Persian by a former preacher and Muslim jurisprudent in the town of Konya in central Anatolia. While some initial justification is due for our claim to greatness for both author and work, it is not enough just to establish greatness, for there have been many great writers and works. What the reader is entitled to know is why it will be worth their while to give their time and effort to this particular author and this particular work. The short answer is because Mawlānā was a man who had attained to Reality, and who deliberately designed his *Mathnawī* to enable his readers and hearers to become real themselves. But for the *Mathnawī* to be transformative, it is necessary to know how to read it, which is the purpose of the present volume. Mawlānā often addresses the reader directly as a prospective spiritual traveler: sometimes he thunders, sometimes harangues, sometimes beguiles, sometimes entertains, sometimes inspires with flights of soaring mystical vision, and sometimes he is deliberately insulting, even vulgar. It can be a bewildering work, but if readers are prepared to work on the *Mathnawī*, they may be assured that the *Mathnawī* will work on them, whether or not they can read it in the original Persian. This many have experienced in working on the *Mathnawī*, and there must be very few books which will reward the effort needed in quite this way. To add weight to this, it will be helpful to examine some credentials.

Mawlānā Jalāl al-Dīn Rūmī was an acclaimed poet even during his own lifetime, and his reputation and the appreciation of his poetry has grown over the last 700 to 800 years to the point of what has been called "Rūmī-mania" in contemporary America. The current enthusiasm derives from two sources of inspiration. The main source is translations into English of some of Mawlānā's mystical lyrics taken from the large collection of his shorter poems entitled the *Dīwān-e Shams-e Tabrīz*. The second source has been visits to America and performances there of the Dervish turning, to the haunting and poignant music of the *nay*, the reed-pipe, by members of the Mevlevi Order of Dervishes, of which Mawlānā was the eponymous founder. There are two discontinuities here: the first is translation, since the English re-creations, which are clearly effective, are, in some cases, of questionable accuracy in terms of Mawlānā's original meaning and intentionality; the second is that the Mevlevi Order, along with other Sufi orders in Turkey, was abolished in the 1920s and the present troupes are a modern reconstitution. Nonetheless, in spite of the discontinuities, enough of Mawlānā's poetic power, the authenticity of his mystical experiencing and his authority as a major spiritual teacher and leader have come through to create the present effect, even after more than seven centuries. Those able to read the original Persian poetry readily attest to his supreme command of the poetic art. As a poet, he has astonishing control and seems able to produce in the reader almost any effect that he wishes. What this present book will show is that his literary achievement is even more remarkable than has hitherto been realized.

Two distinguished Western scholars, R. A. Nicholson and A. Bausani, both of whom were professors of Persian, at Cambridge and Naples respectively, have assessed Mawlānā as the world's finest mystical poet of any age. His poetic credentials have been referred to above, so what of the "mystical"? "Mystical," "mystic," and "mysticism" are all slippery words. Up to about 1900 CE, mysticism was generally understood to be the theory and practice of the contemplative life, but from the publication of William James's Gifford Lectures, *The Varieties of Religious Experience*, in 1901–1902, a modernist construction began to supplant the traditional interpretation of mysticism. In this, mysticism became personal, subjective, and experiential, open to all states that transcend our everyday mundane consciousness, however they are derived. The modernist construct appears to lump together states that are phenomenologically similar, states given by Grace in response to a life of prayer and the surrender of one's soul to God, with those deriving from the surrender of one's mind to drugs and chemicals, or those that arise from clinical forms of madness. Within the spiritual tradition in which Mawlānā was brought up, a distinction is made between *ḥāl*, a temporary, sometimes momentary, state, and *maqām*, a station, a permanent transformation of part of one's being. The Sufi path, like the Christian mystical path, is primarily concerned with inner transformation rather than with the attainment of transcendent states. For the paradigmatic mystics of both traditions the principal issue was the extirpation of egoism and the surrender of the will to Almighty God, and Saint Teresa of Avila, for example, warns against attaching importance to transcendent states, which she regards merely as "consolations." Mawlānā was, as will be seen, educated externally in the Muslim sciences of his day and followed his father in becoming a preacher. Inwardly, he was trained in ascetic and spiritual disciplines by a spiritual mentor appointed by his father, so that by the time he met with the man who was to transform his spiritual nature even further, the dervish Shams-e Tabrīz, he was probably already a spiritual director himself, albeit a somewhat reluctant one, with a profound understanding of human nature, of himself, and of the spiritual path. What experiences Mawlānā had as a result of his association with Shams-e Tabrīz he refused to speak about directly, but it seems he was given access experientially to the transcendent spiritual world in a way he had never known before. There is also a new and deeper experience and understanding of the power and potency of Love. Mawlānā's spirituality, therefore, combines both perspectives: from below looking up, and from above looking down, which makes him one of the most authentic of spiritual guides, fully meriting one's attention. From the lyrics of the *Dīwān-e Shams-e Tabrīz*, at least from those currently re-created, it might appear that Mawlānā's concern is solely with the transcendent spiritual world, and hence that he is deserving of the categorization of mystical poet, but when the *Mathnawī* is also taken into account, a fuller picture emerges, of a spirituality as concerned with how to live spiritually in this world as with how to attain access to the transcendent world. As Mawlānā constantly reminds his readers, Almighty God is Lord of both worlds, *rabb al-'ālamayn*, and his glorification of the Creator is matched by his appreciation of and gratitude for creation and his deep understanding of the problems and dilemmas of his fellow creatures. It might then be better to regard Mawlānā as a great poet of the spiritual in its broadest sense rather than as an exclusively mystical one.

Coming to Mawlānā's *Mathnawī*, it has to be said that its genre is like nothing to be found in Western spirituality. In scope, scale, and conception it also far transcends its own antecedents, and these were considerable enough. Its very first sentence begins: "This is the Book of the *Mathnawī*, which is the roots of the roots of the roots of Religion, in respect of its unveiling the mysteries of attainment (to the Truth) and of certainty, which is the greatest science of God." There are then three depths of roots. The last of the roots, that is, the ones least deep and nearest the surface, are taken to refer to the *Sharī'ah*, which means a clear broad highway to a watering place, and is used to refer to the canon law of Islam that prescribes the duties and obligations that must be observed by every Muslim. This outer side of Islam also includes inter alia the sciences of theology, jurisprudence, and scriptural hermeneutics. The intermediate roots are taken to refer to the *Ṭarīqah*, the spiritual path of Sufism, *Taṣawwuf*, which is the narrower path of the spiritual traveler, the *sālik*. Finally the deepest roots are the level of *Ḥaqīqah*, Reality, the watering place itself. The attainment of Reality, then, through the general *Sharī'ah* and the more specific spiritual path of the *Ṭarīqah* is, in Mawlānā's opening words, the greatest science of God.

The *Mathnawī* reflects these three levels in its design. Design is a crucial notion, since it combines the shape and structuring of a product with its rationale and purpose, which is why it has been chosen for the title of this book. In communication theory, semantics is the science of how words connect with the world through the relationship of meanings. Pragmatics is the science of how words and meanings are used to do things with, to effect a change in some part or state of the world. The organization of a literary work from the point of view of pragmatics, of what it is trying to accomplish, is called its rhetorical structure. Mawlānā's purpose in writing the *Mathnawī* was to make it possible for its readers and hearers to transform, to change inwardly in the direction of reality, a task that he had conducted in person for many years as a spiritual director on the Sufi path.

A crucial specification of Mawlānā's design for the *Mathnawī* was clearly that its literary form should embody in its structure his own experience and understanding of reality. One of the most fundamental assumptions of his worldview is that the world of appearances, the plurality which is accessible to the senses, is not the whole of reality; there is also a hidden all-encompassing spiritual world, which is transcendent, beautiful and a unity. Humanity stands between these two worlds and is able to participate in both, in the actuality of the physical world by means of the body, senses, mind, psyche, and selfhood, and in the spiritual world through the spirit, intellect, love, and a purified and receptive heart. It is human nature to be drawn into this mundane world, even to the point of losing contact with one's own spiritual nature and the spiritual world. For those who are not satisfied with living an entirely worldly life, who aspire to retain, or regain, contact with their own spirituality, there exists the spiritual path, in this case, the Sufi path. It is the aspiring traveler on the spiritual path, the *sālik*, to whom the *Mathnawī* is largely addressed. Mawlānā has then designed his *Mathnawī* simultaneously to reflect these three levels: this mundane world, the spiritual world, and, between these two, the Sufi path. How he has accomplished this within a single work makes the *Mathnawī* of exceptional interest not only for its rich spiritual content, but also for its literary form, which fully deserves the attention of those engaged in comparative literature.

It is not difficult to see how these three levels in the *Mathnawī* correspond to the three kinds of roots described above. The literal surface verbal level, and the edification derived from it, represent the roots nearest the surface, the outer side of religious life, the *Sharī'ah*, the clear broad path open to all, which prescribes the duties and obligations incumbent on all Muslims when living in this world. Hidden within the surface text is the symbolic level of the spiritual path of the Sufi *Ṭarīqah*, the narrower path of the spiritual seeker and traveler, which represents the intermediate roots. This assumption of an outer and an inner, of the exoteric and the esoteric, is shared by most Muslims, since in the Holy Qur'ān God is described both as the Outward, *al-ẓāhir*, and as the Inward, *al-bāṭin*. It would have been expected, therefore, that Mawlānā's *Mathnawī* would have an outer literal, surface, verbal level, but that there would also be hidden within it an inner, symbolic level pertaining to the spiritual path. In order to discern and understand this symbolic level, the reader would have to become an active and intelligent seeker. Much of the symbolism in the parables and stories is conventional or else is explained or implied by Mawlānā. But symbolism is multivalent; it has as many levels of reference as there are levels of understanding and being in the reader. No single understanding or interpretation can exhaust the potential analogies or correspondences present within the symbol, especially one given by someone as spiritually advanced as Mawlānā. The effect of the symbol, when well founded, is to lead one ever upward because it is open-ended. Symbolism is then a characteristic feature of the second intermediate level of the *Mathnawī*, as will become apparent later.

It is the third level of the text, the deepest roots in the opening image, which pertains to and represents the spiritual world. Here Mawlānā has done something quite exceptional. As he constantly stresses in the *Mathnawī* people are unaware of the spiritual world because they are habituated to form and, further, God wishes the spiritual world to remain unseen. Yet the spiritual world is infinitely richer than this world, it is a unity, in it all opposites are reconciled and transcended, it contains all meaning and purpose and is the source of all primary causation, since, in the shadow play of this world of opposites, there are only secondary causes. So effectively has Mawlānā hidden this level, that almost nobody has realized it is there, or, at least, nobody has written about it as far as is known. Rather than following the imagery of the roots and burying this level deeper still than the symbolism of the Sufi path, he conveys the spiritual world in the macro-compositional structure of the entire work, in the overarching organization of the *Mathnawī*, and he does this using a quite distinct and unexpected literary technique.

The first level, that of the surface literal text of lines and verses, has a linear structure; one verse follows another and one section succeeds the previous one. This sequentiality is particularly suitable because it is the direction of "time's arrow" which is a determining condition of life in this world. Further, being verbal, this level shares in the characteristics of the world of forms. The poetry is superb and has verve and variety; however, scholars have criticized the work for being rambling and lacking in orderliness, and certainly the self-presentation of the *Mathnawī* is one of planlessness, of extempore and spontaneous instruction and exhortation. Rather like life in this world, the work is episodic and at this level one never really knows what is coming next.

If this world is represented by the line, symbolizing time and space, the spiritual world is represented by the circle, the symbol of eternity. The literary form Mawlānā has used to portray the unseen spiritual world is ring composition. Ring or annular composition will be explained and demonstrated fully later, for now it is enough to show how it works in comparison with sequential ordering. Ring composition is when, for example, seven segments of text are arranged A [1], B [2], C [3], D [4], C* [5], B* [6], A* [7], where there is a particular correspondence between A and A*, B and B*, C and C*. The correspondence between a pair of segments is termed "parallelism." Parallelism was ideal for Mawlānā's purpose because it permits nonlinear and nonlocal relationships, thus allowing him to meet two of the criteria for the spiritual world, that of unity or unicity, in that every part of the poem is interconnected, and that of the reconciliation of opposites, in that opposites can be held in parallel for them then to be transcended at a higher level. As will be shown later, he has organized the whole of the *Mathnawī* by means of three levels of ring composition but stopped short at a point somewhat above the level of the verses so that the naturalness and sequentiality of the actual verses is unaffected. This overarching organization contains the rationale and purpose of the various levels and parts of the work and thus is the primary cause of what occurs, although secondary causation is to be found in the actual text itself, such as in the unfolding plot of a story he is telling. In this way, ring composition enabled Mawlānā to represent the unseen spiritual world in the organization and literary structuring of his masterpiece in such a manner that it was to remain seemingly undetected for centuries, thus confirming his constant assertion that those habituated to the world of form will rarely if ever be aware of the spiritual world.

Intermediate between the world of form, the surface textual level, and the spiritual world, represented in the overarching circular organization of the entire work, is the symbolic level of the spiritual traveler, the *sālik*, struggling along the spiritual path, to whom the *Mathnawī* is most often addressed. The spiritual traveler participates in both worlds, so it is appropriate that the literary form of this level combines the characteristics of each of these worlds. There is progression in that the various stages of the spiritual path proceed successively, but each stage is treated in a distinct discourse that is organized by ring composition. Perhaps the idea of a spiral would not be too far-fetched as a description. Certainly this level of the spiritual traveler has about it the quality of recurrence, of returning to where one started but, it is hoped, each time starting slightly higher up and with a different perspective. This is the level at which Mawlānā is most demanding, of the spiritual traveler and hence of the reader. He has not marked the discourses, so readers have to become seekers to find them for themselves. The ring compositional structures of these discourses are often complex and highly sophisticated, each one different, and all the parallelisms have to be explored and pondered. Then there is the symbolism of each discourse to be identified and reflected on, and allowed to do its work within at whatever level. These tasks could not possibly be performed in a single sequential reading; recurrent reading, work, and reflection are necessary, but each new reading will lead to a new realization at some level.

This then is how Mawlānā has designed and executed the *Mathnawī* to shame, inspire, awaken, guide, and transform. Each of the three levels makes different demands and offers different rewards. The first level is the poetic text itself which requires a sequential reading. Here there is the impact of immediacy. There are constant variations in voice, in pace and urgency, in theme, and in the density of imagery. Stories and anecdotes are told sometimes at length, sometimes with astonishing brevity. The text presents itself as spontaneous, extempore, directly pointed at the aspiring Sufi traveler and the reader. So rich and controlled is the poetry that interest rarely flags: sometimes the instruction is explicit, sometimes the moral is implicit; sometimes Mawlānā shows himself as storyteller and entertainer, sometimes as preacher or spiritual guide, sometimes as mystical poet with flights of high mystical vision, sometimes as a supplicant before God with prayers of gratitude and glorification. It would have to be a very dull reader indeed who was not captivated, edified, and inspired to change by such a text as this. It has about it the feeling that it comes from some very high place but through the mediation of a profound and compassionate understanding of the human condition, and certainly through the voice of a true master of the poetic art.

The second level, that of the spiritual Sufi path, requires recurrent readings and for the reader to become an active seeker. The demands it makes on the reader are considerable and have been already mentioned: to identify larger discourses, to grasp their structures, to identify and ponder the symbolism, and to explore and reflect on all the parallelisms and their implications. In the first level Mawlānā is met as the master poet; at this level he is encountered as a master architect, since the variety and sophistication of the discourse structures reveal him as the virtuoso of ring composition. Quite apart from the astonishing and hitherto unnoticed craftsmanship, at this level the contexts are larger than the first level. In sequential reading the context is "the passage," the size of which is determined by the extent of the reader's short-term memory, whereas, at this second level, the context is the "discourse," which has its own larger structure, scale and proportions. The result is to enlarge the present moment of the reader. Each discourse deals with a separate stage on the spiritual path, and this is done far more systematically and autobiographically that has hitherto been recognized. Here Mawlānā is encountered as the Sufi Shaykh, the spiritual guide who has been through each stage himself and shares his insights. The contemplation and reflection on the discourse, the search to uncover the hidden rationale and the exploration of the shapes, forms, inner connections, and perspectives within which it is articulated, result in what may be called realization. The reader makes the form, shape and content of what has been read and worked on her or his own. In so doing, as it enters deeper into the reader's consciousness and understanding, it becomes transformative and part of their reality. This level of the *Mathnawī* is designed to "sink in" and to be realized within the reader. Most books that people read simply add to their "acquired" or "secondhand" knowledge, which diminishes as the memory fades. Here is a work so designed that, with a reader's sincere effort and searching, it can become a real and permanent part of themselves on their path to Reality.

Finally, there is the third level, that of the unseen spiritual world, which is represented in the overarching organization by ring composition of the entire work. There are, in fact, three levels of ring composition: the level of the discourse, the level of the book and the level of the work as a whole. Starting with the work as a whole, there are six books, naturally ordered 1–6. But the organization, rather than the order, of these books, is ring-compositional A, B, C, C*, B*, A*. The parallelisms indicate that Book One is reflected in Book Six, Book Two in Book Five, Book Three in Book Four, but in reverse order and at a higher level. Thus the first discourse in Book One is thematically parallel with the last discourse in Book Six, the second discourse in Book One is thematically parallel with the penultimate discourse in Book Six and so on. The first half of the *Mathnawī* is thus the mirror image of the second half and vice versa. As will be seen, the notion of the mirror has very great importance in the *Mathnawī*, not only in symbolism and imagery, but crucially in spiritual practice, so it is entirely appropriate that Mawlānā has given a spatial representation of the mirror in his overall literary form. Nor is this all, for he has hinged the mirror so that the two sides can reflect one another, and the hinge is a story begun at the end of Book Three and concluded at the beginning of Book Four. This is the only example of two books being so joined, and it occurs precisely in the center of the work. In ring composition, both in Mawlānā's usage and elsewhere, the crux, crisis, or real inner significance is given at the very center. This story, which acts as the hinge of the two halves of the mirror, or the binding holding the two halves of the *Mathnawī* together, is a story of love. Love is the crux of the *Mathnawī*, as it is of the spiritual path, and the *Mathnawī*, in every sense, hinges on love.

Not only is the work as a whole organized by ring composition, but so are the discourses in a book, and the sections within a discourse, as will be seen later. Readers' attention can only be in one place at a time, so until they know the discourse they are reading really well they will miss the parallelisms within that discourse; and until there is full familiarity with the whole of the book in which that discourse is located, they will miss the parallelisms with other discourses in that book; and until the entire work is thoroughly known, they will miss the parallelism with other discourses in other books. It is then unsurprising that this level of overarching organization has remained undetected for so long. A good example of parallelism between discourses occurs in Book One, in which there are two "Lion" discourses in parallel. In the first discourse the lion is all ego, the great "I am" par excellence, pure self-centeredness; in the second the lion is without ego and has been granted the true individuality that lies beyond ego. Both lions are fierce, but the first is ineffective and the second a true master. In placing these two lions, ego and nonego, in parallel, Mawlānā is making use of a contrastive parallelism which is aesthetically neat, intellectually satisfying and spiritually apposite, but he is also offering the reader the opportunity to hold the two together and reach up beyond them both to their transcendent origin. As an example of interbook discourse parallelisms, there is in the final discourse of Book Two a discussion of the spiritual symbolism of the duck in which it is praised for being able to travel both on land, this world, and in water, the spiritual world, thereby being able to live in both worlds. The parallel discourse at the beginning of

Book Five also deals with the duck, but this time as a symbol of greed, since it spends its life with its beak in the mud looking for food. These two contrasting views of the spiritually symbolic potential of the duck are held together in parallelism and invite the reader to that place in the imaginal world where everything can be seen as a symbol of something higher and charged with spiritual significance. The full importance of this level of the *Mathnawī* will only become apparent when the entire work has been thoroughly thematically mapped, for the moment it is enough to know that it is there.

It is possible to read, enjoy and benefit from the *Mathnawī* without even being aware of this level of spiritual organization let alone being familiar with its particularities, as countless reader and hearers have proved throughout the centuries. Equally, it is possible to live in this world and enjoy oneself without any awareness of the spiritual world. But many of those readers will have brought to their reading their own conviction of the existence of such a world and would have felt that the *Mathnawī* derived from some such realm even if they did not know how the *Mathnawī* was designed. For the contemporary reader, coming new to the *Mathnawī*, to know that what is being read is connected through a network of correspondences with other parts of the work within an overarching unseen organization of significances, is to extend the present moment, to enhance consciousness and to open a dimension of transcendence, which is itself training to live spiritually in this world. When later, through increased familiarity with the work, the opportunity can be taken to reflect and meditate on Mawlānā's parallelisms and where they are contrastive to seek to reach beyond the contraries to the place where they are transcended and reconciled. This process is itself spiritual training, while at the same time returning the *Mathnawī* to the place from whence it came. To do this, interestingly, is not to leave the text behind, because the extension upward of the present moment brings about an equal extension downward, so that there is a new awareness of the very sounds or letters of the lines but, this time, not externally but from within. All of this is possible and much more, because this is how Mawlānā designed and executed his *Mathnawī*.

The present book aims to facilitate the processes just described for readers of the *Mathnawī*. Mawlānā did not do things by half-measures. He constantly asserts that one really should keep secrets, especially about spiritual matters. He therefore has hidden the inner, spiritual organization of his poem in what, even in his time, must have been an unexpected and highly sophisticated way. He provokes the reader or hearer to search, and he left clues and indications and, no doubt, intelligent seekers nearer his time were able to grasp what he had done. There is evidence to suggest, however, that the contemporary reader, whether of the original Persian or in translation, will no longer be able to pick up the clues and uncover the hidden spiritual organization unaided. This is most unfortunate, particularly for readers, since it means they are missing perhaps the most important dimension of this extraordinary work and its possible transformative effect. But it is also unfortunate for the author, because it is in the hidden superstructure of the work that Mawlānā displays a hitherto unsuspected degree of mastery of architectonic skills and literary craftsmanship.

It is hoped that the above brief introduction to Mawlānā Jalāl al-Dīn Rūmī and his *Mathnawī* has proved sufficient recommendation to the reader, both on account of the poem's great literary interest and for its rich spiritual content. Those already familiar with the *Mathnawī* may well be surprised, even startled, by this description of its design, just as were the authors of this work when they began to realize what Mawlānā had done. There is, however, nothing in this description that will not be demonstrated, it is hoped fully convincingly, later in this book. This volume deals with Book One of the *Mathnawī*, which is concerned with the spiritual path and the development and transformation of the selfhood at the various stages on that path. Those readers coming from a Christian background will find much in this work familiar from St. Teresa of Avila's *Way of Perfection* and the *Interior Castle*, although cast in a different idiom and put over in a strikingly different manner. For the general reader there is an introduction to the life of Mawlānā, his religious and spiritual position and his literary antecedents in Chapter 1. Chapter 2 identifies ring composition as the major structuring principle in the *Mathnawī*, explains the various features of this macro-compositional style and the need for a synoptic reading. Chapter 3 is the necessary reader's guide to the text of Book One. It gives a synoptic reading of the whole of Book One, providing summaries of the text, analyses of the various structures and offering spiritual interpretations from a synoptic point of view. In Chapter 4 there is an analysis of Book One as a whole, the identification of its rationale and an indication of how Book One can also be seen as a fully integrated part of the *Mathnawī* as a whole. Chapter 5 draws conclusions from what has been revealed and discusses how Mawlānā must have planned the *Mathnawī*, how he must then have composed it and the purpose of his design, which lies in his wish to transform the natures of his readers and share with them his experience of reality.

What does the reader of the *Mathnawī* need? First, he or she needs the text of the work itself. There are several excellent editions, the most reliable of which are given in the Bibliography, but fortunately the textual tradition is excellent and there are not very great differences between the editions. This work has used the Nicholson text, so if the reader is using another edition they will need to be aware of this and make the necessary adjustments for all references. If the reader cannot read the Persian—and it is well worth learning Persian solely to read the *Mathnawī*—then they will need to read it in translation. There exist translations of the whole of the *Mathnawī* in English (R. A. Nicholson), French (Eva de Vitray-Meyerovitch), Turkish (Gölpınarlı), Hindi (V. C. Pandey), Arabic (Ibrahim al-Dasuqi Shita), Urdu (Muhammad Gulshanabadi), Swedish, Italian, and Spanish. These translations vary in their accuracy, their elegance, and their completeness. Nicholson's English translation is extremely close to the original, but some find it awkward and dated. He reverts to Latin when he encounters passages that he feels might offend "good taste"; he even spent time developing his Latin for this particular task. Fortunately two excellent new English translations of Book One have recently been published by Jawid Mojaddedi in the Oxford World's Classics Series, and Alan Williams, in Penguin Classics.

These are certainly the recommended reading for the first encounter with Book One. But putting a translation into verse comes at a price, an inevitable loss of completeness. For the further study of Book One, the fullness of Nicholson's translation will also be needed.

The translations often include notes and explanations of difficult or unfamiliar items or references, and Nicholson has produced two volumes of commentary in addition to his text and translation. None of the commentaries, however, of which there are many, deal with what is offered in this book, a synoptic reading, simply because it was not hitherto realized how Mawlānā had organized his work. Two other important works should be mentioned for someone embarking on the serious study of the *Mathnawī*: Franklin Lewis's compendium to Rumi studies, *Rumi, Past and Present, East and West* (Oxford, One World Publications, 2000) and William Chittick's excellent systematic treatment of the spiritual teachings of Mawlānā, *The Sufi Path of Love: The Spiritual Teachings of Rumi* (Albany, SUNY Press, 1983). Both of these works can be treated as works of reference for present purposes and need not be read sequentially from beginning to end. They both have an excellent table of contents at the beginning and a fine index at the end so that one can see immediately what these works contain and can find the references at once.

Chapter One

Contextualizing the *Mathnawī*

Mawlānā's Life—An Outline

Mawlānā was born in 1207 in Central Asia, possibly in Balkh in Khorasan, possibly in Vakhsh in Transoxania, some 160 miles southeast of Samarqand.[1] His father, Bahā al-Dīn Walad, following the family tradition, was a preacher and religious jurist. Originally from Balkh in Khorasan, he had moved to Vakhsh probably in about 1204 to further his vocation. Vakhsh, however, proved to be a backwater and eventually Bahā al-Dīn realized that, on account of a dispute between himself and the Qazi, he needed to move on and search out a pious patron elsewhere. He moved first to Samarqand around 1212 and was certainly there with the five-year old Mawlānā when it was besieged by Khwarazmshah. Accepting that his opportunities would be few anywhere within Khwarazmshah's dominion, in 1216 he set out with his family for Baghdad. It is now considered possible that the reason he came westward was his own personal decision and not flight from the Mongols as traditional accounts suggest, since it seems probable that the family had already left before any Mongol threat became apparent. Further, it is no longer believed that he visited the great Sufi poet Farīd al-Dīn 'Aṭṭār in Nishapur on this journey, since there is no mention of this supposed meeting until 200 years after it was said to have taken place, and then only in an unreliable source.

The stay in Baghdad was short, little more than a month, because they then set off to perform the Hajj at Mecca in the spring of 1217. This huge journey from Khorasan in itself must have been an amazing experience for the ten-year-old Mawlānā, but then to witness and be part of the great religious pilgrimage of the Hajj was to add an altogether new dimension. But the traveling was not yet over; from Mecca they traveled north to Damascus and then on to Malatya in eastern Turkey, which they reached in the summer of 1217. They did not stay long in Malatya, leaving between November 1217 and March 1218 for Akshahr, a town no longer existent by that name about halfway between Sivas and Erzincan in northeastern Turkey. Bahā al-Dīn had found a patron, 'Ismati Khātun, the wife of Fakhr al-Dīn Bahrāmshāh, the Prince of Erzincan.[2] Bahrāmshāh built a religious college in Akshahr for Bahā al-Dīn, where he lived and at which he taught general subjects for four years. It has been suggested that it was more a Sufi center than a college, but that is unlikely, because, although Bahā al-Dīn was mystically and ascetically inclined, he did not identify himself formally as a Sufi but rather as a preacher and educator. His personal decision to leave the East clearly included the intention of performing the Hajj, but that must have been within his overall resolve to dedicate the rest of his life to God's work rather than to further his own advancement, so that straight after the pilgrimage he went to what was effectively the Islamic frontier in terms of religious affiliation. Anatolia was very diverse ethnically but largely Christian, while those Turks and Turkmen who were resettled there were only recently converted Muslims. There was much missionary work to be done therefore for a deeply pious Muslim preacher and teacher in bearing witness to Islam and in teaching its fundamentals. For those of his pupils so inclined, he also became their spiritual director, since, wherever he was, he soon gathered around him a group of committed spiritual disciples.

The deaths of Fakhr al-Dīn Bahrāmshāh and of 'Ismati Khātun his wife, brought an end to Bahā al-Dīn's time in Akshahr in 1221, since the college had apparently not been permanently endowed. His patrons' daughter, Saljuqi Khātun, was married to 'Izz al-Dīn Kay Kāus I in Konya and it is perhaps through this connection that the family now headed southwestward toward Konya. But it was not to Konya they went initially, so it is thought, but to Lārende, the modern Karaman, which is about sixty-five miles south of Konya. Here Amīr Mūsā, the local Seljuk governor, provided a college building for Bahā al-Dīn's use in the center of the town. The family was to stay here for seven years, and during this period Mawlānā's mother, Mu'minah Khātun, must have died, since her grave has been found in Karaman. Also during this period, in 1224, when he was seventeen, Mawlānā was married to Gawhar Khātun, the daughter of one of Bahā al-Dīn's principal female disciples who had been with the family since Samarqand. They produced two sons; the eldest, 'Alā al-Dīn, was probably born in 1225, and the second son, Sultan Walad, in 1226.

In 1229, the Seljuk Sultan 'Alā al-Dīn Kay Qobād invited Mawlānā's father, Bahā al-Dīn, to Konya, where he was accorded a warm welcome and accommodated in the Altunpā Madrasah. It must have been there that he preached and taught until his death just two years later in February 1231, when he was just short of being eighty years old. He was buried in the Sultan's rose garden with a fulsome inscription on his tombstone, since he had been a respected spiritual guide to a large group of disciples and an inspiring preacher. Bahā al-Dīn did not write a book but he kept a spiritual journal. This has been published under the title *Ma'ārif*, Intimations, but a new edition is much needed. It shows Bahā al-Dīn to have had a rich inner life: he had many varied and vivid mystical visions; his personal *dhikr* (repetition, remembrance of God) was *Allāh Allāh* repeated continually; and his constant concern was with the Presence of God. In his view, God was both totally transcendent yet also immanent, as in the Qur'ān: "Truly We created man, and We know what his soul whispers to him, for We are nearer to him than his jugular vein" [50:16]. God is completely Other, yet is also intimately near to creation. This nearness Bahā al-Dīn sought to discern in both the inner and the outer world, not intellectually but through capturing the "taste," the direct experience of the Presence and Communication of God. He did this through occupying himself with the Qur'ān and its levels of meaning, through ascetic practice and self-deprivation, through meditation and contemplation and through prayer and outer observance. Many of the subjects, assumptions and attitudes in Bahā al-Dīn's writings are to be found in Mawlānā's *Mathnawī*, although they are expressed in his own characteristic way and from his own perspective and understanding. It can be imagined how hard hit Mawlānā must have been by the loss of such a father, and it seems he withdrew from Konya and returned to Lārende.

One year after Bahā al-Dīn's death, one of his first disciples and Mawlānā's godfather, Sayyid Burhān al-Dīn Muḥaqqiq, arrived in Konya and sent for Mawlānā. He gathered the former disciples of Bahā al-Dīn and assumed the role of their shaykh or spiritual director. With Mawlānā he laid out plans for the future. Mawlānā spent the next four years, 1233–1237, advancing his formal education in religious law and the religious sciences with good teachers and schools in Syria, probably mainly in Aleppo but also in Damascus. On his return from his studies, Burhān al-Dīn then trained him inwardly with a regime that would almost certainly have included fasting, seclusion, (*khalwat*), and the intensive study of and meditation upon Bahā al-Dīn's writings. This lasted for nearly five years, until Mawlānā was thirty-five, at which point Burhān al-Dīn withdrew to Kayseri, where he died, probably in 1241. Like Bahā al-Dīn, Burhān al-Dīn also kept a sort of journal covering the last ten or so years of his life. He, like many teachers, taught the need to "die before you die," to wrestle with the lower parts of one's nature, and to seek the Beloved. His favored means of self-mortification was fasting. The importance of the saints or Friends of God is also stressed, especially the *quṭb*, the spiritual *axis mundi*, who is present at all times. Burhān al-Dīn was fond of poetry and particularly the poetry of Sanā'ī. Many of the quotations from poets, the Qur'ān, from the traditions of the Prophet and even the choice of stories in the *Mathnawī* could well have had their immediate origins in Burhān al-Dīn's writings and addresses.

It is not known for certain when Mawlānā took up his father's old position. Certainly during Burhān al-Dīn's lifetime he was already known as Mawlānā. He could well have started teaching in the college soon after he returned from Syria with his education completed, but it is unlikely he would have assumed the role of spiritual director for the disciples until Burhān al-Dīn had left for Kayseri. In 1242 or 1243, Mawlānā's wife Gawhar Khātun died, by which time it is thought the two sons had already been sent off to Damascus to receive a proper education. Mawlānā married again, this time to a widow, Kirrā Khātun, who bore him a son, Muzaffar al-Dīn Amīr 'Ālim Chalabī (died 1277), and a daughter, Malikah Khātun (died 1303–1306), both born in the 1240s. What is apparent is that, like his father before him, Mawlānā was a truly inspiring preacher and he had a considerable following among merchants and artisans as well as from both Armenian and Greek Christians, some of whom he converted to Islam. This then was Mawlānā's situation: he was a respected and qualified jurist and teacher, an inspiring preacher and a spiritual guide to a group of devoted disciples, but on November 29, 1244, there arrived in Konya the man who was to revolutionize his inner and outer life forever, the sixty-year-old dervish, Shams al-Dīn of Tabriz.

Shams al-Dīn of Tabriz, or Shams-e Tabrīzī, will, for the sake of brevity, just be referred to as Shams, which means "sun" in Arabic. Shams was born, as few are, with unusual spiritual abilities and sensibilities. As a child he felt in contact with the spiritual world and experienced overflowing love for God and estrangement from the empirical world and his family. He tells of feeling a lethargy descend on him every four days or so when he would not be able to eat, and just before puberty the experience of spiritual love was so strong he could not eat for thirty or forty days. Often for such rare people puberty brings the loss of this contact, which can only be restored later in life through spiritual training. It is not known whether this happened with Shams or not. Certainly he speaks of receiving divine promptings throughout his life. Tabriz, when Shams was growing up, was rich in every kind of spiritual figure: pirs, shaykhs, dervishes, and holy men, some learned and educated, some barely literate. It is not known precisely with whom he received either his outer or his inner education. He had studied the main legal texts books of the Shāfiʿī school of religious law and read widely; when he came to Konya he was educated and very knowledgeable in a number of the religious sciences and other disciplines. His favored way of learning was through debate and discussion and he must have exhausted countless teachers and fellow-students in the course of his lifetime. With regard to his inner education, he certainly had had a shaykh, probably several, and had taken part, no doubt on many occasions, in the mystical dances and whirling of the *samāʿ* with various groups, but he had high expectations and was very demanding both of himself and of others, so he must often have been disappointed and moved on from a succession of teachers and groups. It would seem he spent his life wandering in search of a true saint, a *walī*, a real "friend of God." He would earn enough for his meager needs from doing various jobs, including teaching children the Qur'ān, and would put up at caravanserais pretending to be a merchant and keeping his spiritual state hidden. Shams was a spiritual loner, striving constantly to follow the precepts and precedents of the Prophet Muḥammad and receiving his spiritual guidance and illumination directly from above. He was also spiritually lonely, and prayed to God to allow him to be the companion of a saint. In dreams he was told he would be made a companion of a saint who lived in Anatolia, but the time was not yet ready.[3] So it was that, when the time was ripe and Shams was sixty, this spiritually advanced, highly intelligent, learned, articulate, severe, and demanding old wandering dervish came to Konya.

It has been calculated that Shams remained in Konya on this occasion for fifteen months and twenty-five days, mostly in the company of Mawlānā, whom he had seen and listened to some sixteen years earlier in Damascus. At that time he had been impressed both by what he heard and also by Mawlānā's spiritual potential, although he was not then ready for Shams to approach him. It is difficult to categorize the nature of their relationship, and Shams himself in his discourses was not sure how to describe it. On the one hand, Mawlānā was of a similar disposition, and Shams was tired of himself and longed for a companion with whom he could be without pretense and who would understand what he said. Further, he recognized in Mawlānā a high spiritual station and he derived various benefits from being in his presence. On the other hand, he could see that Mawlānā was not inwardly awakened to his station and a transformation was required, which he knew how to effect. In this respect, then, Shams had to assume the role of the master. The revolution he effected in Mawlānā was to turn him from being an *ʿālim*, a learned divine, into an *'āshiq*, a lover, and an *'ārif*, a gnostic who saw directly and received intelligence from the spiritual world. Everyone agrees that this really took place. Precisely how it was done is another matter.

It seems that first he deliberately wore him out in endless discussion about matters of religious learning, which no doubt Shams would have enjoyed as an intellectual game, but it had the desired effect of enabling Mawlānā to realize that spiritual development was not about knowledge and knowing, but about being and direct experience. Shams certainly forbade Mawlānā to read his father's writings, and may even have suggested that he stop reading altogether, as some shaykhs do. Shifting the center of gravity from thinking in the head into experiencing in the heart at the center of the chest is a necessary preliminary in several spiritual paths. The heart is the principal spiritual organ for development in Sufism but it first needs to be cleansed by some form of purification such as ascetic practice. Mawlānā's heart, though neglected, would already have been pure and his spiritual, psychic, and nervous systems strong from his ascetic disciples and piety. He was ripe for Shams to awaken his heart and set it on fire. It would be presumptuous to speculate precisely how Shams did it; it is enough that he did.[4] The resultant continual outpouring of some of the most beautiful mystical poetry the world has ever heard is evidence of an extraordinary influx of creative energy and the even higher energy of spiritual love. It is clear from the poetry that during this period Mawlānā had many transcendent mystical experiences and ecstasies, but also that he had the greatest difficulty experientially in distinguishing Shams from God, or at least from a manifestation of God, as the object of his love and yearning. This second point suggests that his absorption in Shams, their spiritual union, had reached the point of what is called in Sufi terminology *fanā fī shaykh*, annihilation in the spiritual guide. From his discourses it appears that this was not a role that Shams had sought or desired, but it was probably inevitable. It is also known that Shams encouraged Mawlānā to stand and then spin and later to join in *samā'*, the collective *dhikr* or Remembrance of God, which may include chanting, poetry, music, and the whirling dance. This Mawlānā did, to the surprise of many and the consternation of a few; their sober, deeply pious ascetic preacher and spiritual guide had turned into a "drunken" Sufi, an ecstatic mystical poet and a whirling dervish. But Shams had not finished with Mawlānā. In order to get Mawlānā to the station beyond spiritual drunkenness, to experience the even more powerful transformative effect of the pain and suffering of love in separation, and to transfer Mawlānā's annihilation and absorption in himself to annihilation and absorption in God, Shams did what he must have known he would have to do from the outset, without warning he disappeared and left Konya.

While the transformation described above is almost classical in its conformity to the model of spiritual transformation followed by many shaykhs and traditions in the Sufi path of love, in this case there was something unusual: Mawlānā was not a raw novice, he was already a person of considerable outer and inner standing. Inwardly this meant he was already far more prepared than is usually the case, and, in consequence, the depths, heights, and breadth of his receptivity and experiencing must have been exceptional in their extent as his spiritual potentiality began to be realized. Then there is the poetry. It is easy enough, glibly, to attribute the origin of the poetry to the great influx of creativity and inspiration, but where did the poet come from? There is craftsmanship in these lyrics, and some consider he might in fact have already been developing these poetic skills privately prior to the arrival of Shams, which would make sense given the complexity of Persian meters. But it was the outward situation that least corresponded to the traditional model. Mawlānā was himself a shaykh, a spiritual director of a reasonably large group of disciples; he was also a professional preacher and teacher; finally he was a family man, with a wife, two older and two younger children, not to mention other relatives and retainers for whom he was responsible. In each of these three domains, Mawlānā's prolonged preoccupation with Shams would have created tensions. The hagiographies of Mawlānā, which in some matters are the only extant sources, exaggerate by definition, but they all suggest there were jealousies among both the disciples and some members of the family. There is no doubt that Shams could be severe, demanding, and dismissive, and his expertise was in the spiritual plane and not in social niceties, so he could not have been an easy person to have around. Shams himself explains that those who enter his company lose their appetite for being with others.[5] If this had happened to Mawlānā there would certainly have been a number of very disappointed and jealous people in Konya. But to suggest, as the hagiographies do, that it was these jealousies that drove Shams away is to misunderstand Shams's purpose. He went because Mawlānā needed to suffer from the pain of separation; had Mawlānā been a disciple of the ordinary kind, he would have been sent away from the shaykh at this point. Since Mawlānā could not leave Konya, it was Shams who had to go.

Suffer Mawlānā did, but far from seeking consolation in the company of others, inconsolable, he withdrew almost totally, and in his seclusion his poetry also dried up. It is not known for how long this lasted, certainly more than six months, possibly a year, until, at some point, a letter arrived from Shams. Sultan Walad, the second son, was sent with a party to bring Shams back, armed with some poems from Mawlānā. They found him either in Damascus or Aleppo in Syria, and persuaded him to return to Konya. Mawlānā, greatly relieved, resumed composing poetry and participating in the *samā'*. That Shams was aware of the jealousy he had previously provoked is apparent since he spoke about it on his return.[6]

The scholar M. A. Muwaḥḥid, who edited Shams's discourses under the title of *Maqālāt-e Shams-e Tabrīzī*,[7] has suggested that Shams left in order to force Mawlānā to choose between his love for Shams and his desire to please his disciples and maintain his position and reputation. This has certain merits because in the *Mathnawī*, Mawlānā describes how position and reputation (*jāh*) is a cage from which one must escape before one can progress spiritually, so it is a well-established function of a shaykh to break any attachment a disciple might have to position and reputation as part of the spiritual training. It is highly likely that this may have formed part of the reason for his departure, but that it was not the primary reason is clear from one of Shams's discourses, which appears to be addressed to Mawlānā, in which he speaks of the transforming, refining, and maturing power of the suffering of separation, how he went solely for the sake of Mawlānā's development, and how he hoped that Mawlānā would follow his instructions and that this one departure would be enough.[8]

Shams had left Konya in March 1246 and probably returned in April 1247, giving Mawlānā almost a year of intense personal suffering. Shams and Mawlānā resumed their close spiritual companionship on his return, and in the autumn Shams was married to a girl who was a disciple of Mawlānā's and part of his household. Sadly she fell ill shortly afterward and died. Tensions and jealousies, meanwhile, began to build up again and late in 1247 or early in 1248, Shams left Konya forever, as he had threatened to do. Mawlānā, with some of his disciples went to Syria in search of Shams but failed to find him. No credence, it seems, can be given to the suggestion that Shams was murdered. Mawlānā, a little later, went on a second journey to Syria in a search that lasted months, maybe a year or two, but by around 1250 it seems he finally accepted he would never see Shams again. It is not possible to be certain, but the most probable of the suggestions about what happened to Shams is that when he left Konya he set out, not for Syria, but for Tabrīz, and that he died not long after at Khuy on the road from Konya to Tabrīz, since there is a site there that has been associated with the name of Shams-e Tabrīz since at least 1400. No doubt Shams died as obscurely as he had lived and it may have been quite a long time later that Mawlānā learned that he had died.

In contrast to the first departure, this second disappearance did not result in Mawlānā ceasing to compose poetry. It is not possible to establish a chronology of the poems in Mawlānā's *Dīwān* since they are all undated, but there are some eighty poems that are addressed to or dedicated to Ṣalāḥ al-Dīn rather than to Shams. This Ṣalāḥ al-Dīn is Ṣalāḥ al-Dīn Farīdūn Zarkūb who came to

Konya from a nearby village to become a goldsmith, and who, like Mawlānā, had been a disciple of Burhān al-Dīn. When Burhān al-Dīn left for Kayseri, Ṣalāḥ al-Dīn had retired to his village, but he returned to Konya around 1242 and became close friends with Mawlānā having heard him preach the Friday sermon in the Bu al-Fazl mosque. In all the upheaval caused by the comings and goings of Shams and the consequent indisposition of Mawlānā, it was Ṣalāḥ al-Dīn who had held things together both in Mawlānā's household and with the disciples. Mawlānā named Ṣalāḥ al-Dīn as his successor and deputy, which meant that he preached and acted for Mawlānā as a shaykh to the disciples. No doubt he also helped Mawlānā in other practical ways. Spiritually, with the loss of Shams, Mawlānā regarded Ṣalāḥ al-Dīn as his new spiritual axis, as the focus of his inner concentration and the mirror both of his own state and one through which he contemplated the Divine, hence the eighty poems dedicated to Ṣalāḥ al-Dīn. But Ṣalāḥ al-Dīn was no Shams, personally impressive as he was and favored by Mawlānā in this way. There was much whispered criticism of Ṣalāḥ al-Dīn and feelings ran so high that there was even a plot to murder him, which Mawlānā heard about and was obliged to defuse. One measure to improve relations was the marriage of Mawlānā's second son, Sultan Walad, to Fātimah Khātūn, the daughter of Ṣalāḥ al-Dīn, who was one of Mawlānā's most advanced female disciples. Ṣalāḥ al-Dīn continued to fulfill his various roles until his death in 1258 after a long and painful illness.

If Ṣalāḥ al-Dīn acted as a possible conduit for the local Turkish- and Greek-speaking working classes to make contact with Mawlānā's spiritual circle, his successor, Ḥusām al-Dīn Chalabī, provided a similar connection to the youth guilds and fraternities that were highly influential among the mercantile, artisan, and military classes in Anatolia.[9] Ḥusām al-Dīn had grown up in one such fraternity. Ḥusām al-Dīn had for some years been in charge of Mawlānā's financial affairs and those of the college and the household, and also functioned as his secretary, but on the death of Ṣalāḥ al-Dīn, Mawlānā appointed him his own designated successor (*khalīfa*) and his deputy (*nā'ib*). Ḥusām al-Dīn's practical responsibilities were considerable but he discharged them with Mawlānā's full authority. Spiritually he must have had responsibilities for the disciples, as a shaykh acting for Mawlānā, and Mawlānā also treated him as he had Shams and Ṣalāḥ al-Dīn, as the focus of his own spiritual energies, his spiritual axis and as a mirror both of his own inner state and one through which he could contemplate the Beauty of the Divine. But it was not so much in lyrical poems in which he adulated Ḥusām al-Dīn, but in the *Mathnawī*, which he refers to as the "Book of Ḥusām." He invokes Ḥusām al-Dīn as his muse at the beginning of each of the six books. Convention required that the person to whom a book is dedicated should be praised in somewhat extravagant terms, and this Mawlānā duly does in the Preface to Book One of the *Mathnawī*, but then, as will be seen later, he follows this fairly soon afterward with a dialogue between himself and Ḥusām al-Dīn, in which he makes it quite clear, when speaking of Shams, that Ḥusām al-Dīn was far from Shams's level of spiritual attainment. In terms of levels, Ḥusām al-Dīn is treated as an excellent shaykh on the spiritual path to Reality, but Shams is treated as part of Reality Itself. But if this appears to diminish the standing of Ḥusām al-Dīn, it should not, because Mawlānā continually insists that everyone, no matter who they are, needs a shaykh, among other things, to keep spiritually honest, and he cites the Prophet's saying that even 'Alī his own son-in-law needed a shaykh. That Mawlānā considered Ḥusām al-Dīn to be an excellent shaykh is evidenced by a letter he wrote to the Sultan recommending Ḥusām al-Dīn for appointment as shaykh to a particular Sufi lodge.

But it is, above all, for his part in the creation and production of the *Mathnawī* that Ḥusām al-Dīn deserves the gratitude of posterity. Ḥusām al-Dīn was Mawlānā's amanuensis; he wrote down every verse that Mawlānā composed, recited it back to him and suggested any revisions. Sometimes, as is apparent from the text itself, these sessions went on all night long until dawn. Given that the *Mathnawī* contains over 25,000 verses, this was a huge and demanding undertaking for both of them. It seems likely that the *Mathnawī* was started around 1260, and the first book was completed in 1262. Then there was a two-year hiatus because Ḥusām al-Dīn's wife had died and he had withdrawn to be alone with his sorrow, during which period Mawlānā ceased to compose. They resumed the work in 1263–1264 and continued until all of the six books of its design had been completed, probably not long before Mawlānā's death in December 1273.

While Ḥusām al-Dīn, as amanuensis, was the practical means whereby the *Mathnawī* came into being, there is also a tradition that he was the immediate cause for its composition, since it was seemingly on his suggestion that Mawlānā came to compose it at all.[10] There is another sense too in which Ḥusām al-Dīn can be regarded as a source of inspiration for the *Mathnawī*, and that is in his capacity as "audience." Every writer or speaker addresses his target readers or hearers and seeks to speak to their needs and answer their questions, whether these are spoken or unspoken. Since Ḥusām al-Dīn had been Mawlānā's disciple since he was a very young man, Mawlānā would have witnessed every stage in his spiritual development and seen what was needed at each stage. Since Mawlānā addresses much of the *Mathnawī* to the spiritual traveler or Sufi novice, the *sālik*, it could well have been that Ḥusām al-Dīn served as his model *sālik*, his model "reader," although the degree to which this might have been the case in unquantifiable. Nevertheless, in those composing sessions lasting over ten years Ḥusām al-Dīn was Mawlānā's sole and actual audience and this must have had its influence. It is known, however, that passages from the *Mathnawī* were recited and discussed among the spiritual disciples of Mawlānā's circle while it was being composed, so Mawlānā would have had some wider indication of how it was being received.

Although most of Mawlānā's poetic energies were directed to the production of the *Mathnawī* in the later years of his life, he still occasionally produced short lyrical poems: some to mark special occasions, some for particular people, and some for use in the collective sessions of the *samā'*. The full collection of his shorter lyrical poems is known as the *Dīwān-e Shams-e Tabrīzī*. In Furūzānfar's ten-volume critical edition there are well over 3,000 separate poems, amounting to around 40,000 lines of verse.[11] The *Mathnawī* in Nicholson's critical edition has just over 25,500 verses.[12] This is an astonishing poetic output by anybody's standards and amounts in total to some 65,000 lines. In addition to the poetry, there is the collection of some seventy-one talks and discourses by Mawlānā entitled *Fīhi mā fīhi*, which literally means "In it is what is in it," that is, it is a miscellany.[13] It is not known who recorded these talks or edited the collection, but it is thought it was produced after Mawlānā's death. These discourses are informal in style and of great interest and are considered to be fully authentic. Probably from an early stage in Mawlānā's life, that is, before Shams, there is also a collection of seven of Mawlānā's sermons titled *Majālis-e sab'ah*, or Seven Assemblies.[14] Finally, there are his collected letters, which, as Chittick notes, in contrast to the collected letters of many Sufi masters, hardly mention spiritual matters.[15] They are largely addressed to statesmen, kings, or nobles seeking their assistance in economic or social affairs on behalf of disciples or family members or recommending particular people for positions of various kinds. Mawlānā had become highly respected in Konya circles and, although he did not participate in its social life he was far from being a recluse, since these letters show him to be in touch with the world and active in working for his household and community.

It is not known precisely when the *Mathnawī* was completed, but there is no reason to think that its "unfinished" appearance was anything other than deliberate, for the subject matter at that point was ready to move to a domain beyond words. Mawlānā himself died on December 17, 1273, after a life rich in spiritual achievement and experience and leaving behind a legacy of such creativity that it resonates to this day. The community and disciples continued to be looked after by Ḥusām al-Dīn until his death in October 1284. There is some uncertainty about what happened immediately after that. Sultan Walad, Mawlānā's son, seems to have become the titular head of the disciples but he himself describes a Shaykh Karīm al-Dīn b. Baktamur as the guide to the community. Karīm al-Dīn was a man of spiritual attainments and Sultan Walad regarded him highly as his shaykh, but he was unobtrusive and is ignored by some chroniclers. Karīm al-Dīn died probably in May 1291, and Sultan Walad then became the leader in every sense. It was Sultan Walad who organized the community, expanded it, and established it as a Sufi order with many of the rituals, traditions, and institutions which that required. Some twenty years after the death of Mawlānā, the Mawlawiyya or Mevlevi Sufi Order was born.

There is a somewhat cynical but perceptive view among sociologists that, as a general rule, religious institutions succeed and survive precisely to the extent that they frustrate the wishes and intentions of their eponymous founders.[16] It will be interesting to conclude the summary of Mawlānā's life by testing this rule in the case of the Mevlevi Order. First, in Book Three of the *Mathnawī*, Mawlānā makes clear his disapproval of elaborate shrines for people of sanctity on the grounds of the sheer inappropriateness of this type of worldly show for those whose achievements were not of this world.[17] In particular, during his lifetime he declined to erect an elaborate shrine for his father. After Mawlānā died, Sultan Walad, during the leadership of Ḥusām al-Dīn, had just such a shrine erected. A visit to Konya to see the considerable Mevlevi shrines will quickly reveal the extent to which the Order has ignored the guidance of its eponymous founder in this respect. Second, Mawlānā chose three people not of his family as his *khalīfa* (his successor), Shams, Ṣalāḥ al-Dīn, and Ḥusām al-Dīn, maybe on the model of the early history of Islam. When his son Sultan Walad attained the leadership, the Headship of the Order became hereditary. Third, it would be an anachronistic mistake to consider that Mawlānā ever saw himself as a Sufi shaykh and his community as an order, since, as Lewis points out, he did not enjoin or observe the rituals typical of most Sufi orders, such as the bestowing of ceremonial cloaks and so forth.[18] Mawlānā, in fact, had all the necessary credentials and the right circumstances to be a shaykh and to found an order, but he chose not to, preferring to remain as invisible as he could to escape from the cage of rank and reputation,[19] referring his disciples to his designated deputies, Shams, Ṣalāḥ al-Dīn, and Ḥusām al-Dīn. He also has much to say about the need to go beyond outer form to the reality of inner content. In spite of Mawlānā's quite explicit example, under Sultan Walad the community became a Sufi order with all the usual Sufi ceremonials and rituals and institutions eventually being established. Finally, Mawlānā frequently warned against association with kings and of the danger of wealth and power for those on the spiritual path.[20] In spite of these warnings, the Mevlevi Order was founded by Sultan Walad with state patronage. As it expanded beyond Konya, it cultivated the local aristocracies and governors and built Mevlevi lodges with charitable endowments. The Order thus gradually moved away from its popular roots in the mercantile and artisan classes and cultivated the elite and the powerful. It reached the point that there were eventually fourteen large Mevlevi lodges, *tekkes*, in the cities of the Ottoman Empire, with a further seventy-six minor lodges in provincial towns. Lewis argues that it was state patronage that actually kept the Mevlevis, whose shaykhs often wielded considerable power and influence, subordinate to the government. Thus the Grand Chelibi's choice of who was to be appointed as shaykh to each of the Mevlevi *tekke*s had to be approved by the Shaykh al-Islam and the Ottoman Sultan.[21] The Mevlevi Order clearly had achieved very great success; the question is, however, whether Mawlānā, in whose name the order was founded, would have considered it "success."

The above four examples are adduced not in any sense of criticism of the Mevlevi Order, simply to demonstrate that this case complies with the general sociological rule as stated. That the whole enterprise, together with the other Sufi orders in Turkey, was brought to a shuddering halt by Atatürk's decree in 1925, was the result of the exigencies of history not of its own internal entropy. The Mevlevi Order was the "road not taken" by Mawlānā, who took instead "the one less traveled by, and that has made all the difference." The "road" of the Mevlevi Order was the characteristic way of external expansion; the "road" Mawlānā took, "the one less traveled by" was the way of inner transformation. The account above has shown how he was guided, cajoled, even compelled, to transform by Shams. They both knew to do this he needed to become inconspicuous, which to some extent he managed to achieve through appointing deputies. He also stopped preaching and teaching. He had Ḥusām al-Dīn manage finances, and sometimes refused to accept donations so that wealth did not constitute an inner hazard. His transcendent experiences convinced him that the spiritual world was far richer than the mundane world around him and the great energies released that were not absorbed by the process of transformation found their outlet in poetry. He was not a professional poet, so there is no ego or affectation in his poetry. Indeed, he played down his poetic skills, regarding the process of versifying laborious. His creativity was both quantitively and qualitively astounding. The shorter poems must have just poured out at certain stages in his life. But it is in the *Mathnawī* where all his creativity, skills, knowledge, understanding, experience, and his receiving from above come together; it is the culmination of the "less-traveled" way he had taken. The *Mathnawī* is almost certainly far more autobiographical than has yet been acknowledged; it is the real account of Mawlānā's life, his inner life, and from this it derives its authenticity. The *Mathnawī* is also far more systematic in its design than has yet been allowed, as will be shown later, both practically in terms of its effects and theoretically in terms of the unfolding of the Sufi path of Love. There are then two surviving legacies of Mawlānā: the Mevlevi Order in his name, which has undoubtedly contributed to the spiritual development of many over the centuries and which still exists in a much attenuated form; and the poetry, particularly the *Mathnawī*, not only in Mawlānā's name but also in his voice, which is Mawlānā's *Ṭarīqah*, his own chosen means of passing on to others the pathway of Love and inner transformation.

Mawlānā's Religious Outlook

It might seem unnecessary to state that Mawlānā was a Muslim, but it can serve as a reminder that in the Konya of his day there were Jews and several types of Christians: Greek, Armenian, and Syrian Christians being the most typical.[22] Further, in the Eastern provinces from which he had come, there were Buddhists and probably Hindu and even Zoroastrian merchants. Certainly Mawlānā shows an awareness of people of other faiths in the writings, although the non-Muslim characters he introduces tend to be used for his own symbolic purposes rather than as individuals. But it was in a deeply pious Muslim family that he grew up; he came from a line of pious and ascetic Muslim preachers and teachers of canonical law, and his own higher education was in the Islamic sciences. He too was a deeply pious and ascetic preacher and teacher, and there is no more effective way of mastering a subject totally than to teach it. But for Mawlānā it is not just a question of what one knows, but the manner of one's knowing.

There is a parable in Book Two of the *Mathnawī* that tells of a peasant going out in the dark to stroke his ox in a stall, little realizing that what he is stroking is the lion that has eaten his ox. Mawlānā allows the lion to reflect for a moment on what the peasant might feel if he realized: "If the light were to become greater, his gall-bladder would burst and his heart would turn to blood." The reader laughs at the stupidity of the peasant. Then Mawlānā turns on the reader: "God is saying, 'O blind dupe, did not Mt. Sinai fall in pieces at My Name? You have heard this (God's Name and Religion) from your parents; in consequence you have embraced it without thinking. If you become acquainted with Him without *taqlīd*, blind imitation, by His Grace you will become without self-existence, like a voice from Heaven.' "[23] While Mawlānā is saying here, as he does elsewhere, that people do not value, nor are grateful for, that which they inherit, particularly from their parents, that is very much secondary to the primary distinction being made here between that which is known at "secondhand" and that which is known "for real." Most of what a person knows has been acquired through *taqlīd*, imitation; a second process, *taḥqīq*, realization, is needed for something to become real. *Taḥqīq* is more than making something one's own, and more than verification, although both are part of the process of realization; it is to make direct contact with the *ḥaqq*, the reality, of something for oneself. To practice religion without *taḥqīq* is simply *taqlīd*, imitation, which is like stroking one's own familiar ox and feeling comfortable; but to have realized for oneself the reality behind religion would be to live in an almost permanent state of awe at God's Might and Majesty.

In the pre-Shams era of Mawlānā's life, as has been shown in the biography, he was obliged to absorb enormous quantities of information about religion and the religious sciences, and his spiritual mentor Burhān al-Dīn even required him to read his father's writings a thousand times. One of the first thing Shams required of him was that he was not to read his father's writings at all in preparation for the extraordinary transformation he was to effect in Mawlānā. The change in emphasis from secondhand knowledge to direct experience, from *taqlīd* to *taḥqīq*, was a crucial element in the transformation. But it must not be thought that mystical experience necessarily undermines or challenges the religious tradition within which it arises. Mysticism is as much conservative of the tradition as it is innovative.[24] There are two particular areas in which the "mysticism" of both Shams and Mawlānā can be seen to be "conservative" and supportive of the tradition: the Qur'ān and the Prophet Muḥammad.

When the mystical poet Jāmī described the *Mathnawī* as "the Qur'ān in Persian" he was making a statement on a number of levels. At the most obvious level, there are many direct quotations from the Qur'ān in the *Mathnawī*—one estimate is 528 verses of the Qur'ān alluded to or quoted and then commented on—as well as many less obvious and less easily detected resonances. Many too are the references to personages, episodes, or stories occurring in the Qur'ān. Not only are these references and quotations used as part of the explicit teaching and edification of the poem, but the style of the *Mathnawī* itself was also designed to be reminiscent of the Qur'ān, as is apparent from a passage in Book Three. In this passage there is a wretched fellow who does not have a high opinion of the *Mathnawī* because it is just the story of the Prophet, it consists of imitation and it does not treat the spiritual path systematically from asceticism to union with God. Mawlānā's reply is that this is just what the unbelievers said when the Qur'ān was revealed: that it was just legends and tales; that it lacked profound inquiry and lofty speculation; that little children could understand it; that it was just a list of "dos and don'ts" with accounts of Joseph and his curly hair and Jacob and Zalikha; that it was simple so anyone could follow it, and it was not intellectually challenging. To this critic God replied: "If this seems so 'easy' to you, then just you compose one Sūra in a style as 'easy' as the Qur'ān, or even just one verse!" In this episode Mawlānā is deliberately underlining the correspondence in style between the two works.

The above passage is followed by an entire section devoted to the Qur'ān but from a quite different viewpoint and level. "Know that the words of the Qur'ān have an exterior sense, and under the exterior sense there is an overpowering inner sense; and under that inner sense is another inner sense in which all intellects become lost; and under that sense, there is a fourth sense which none have perceived but God, who is without equal and incomparable" [Book Three 4244–4245]. When Mawlānā states in the Arabic preface to Book One that one of the functions of the *Mathnawī* is to be an expounder of the Qur'ān, it has to be understood as the Qur'ān in its fullness, in all the senses described above except, of course, the last one. As Steven Katz writes: "There is an almost universal Sufi concern with *ta'wīl*, the spiritual exegesis of the Qur'ān which also functions as profound, mystical self-interrogation. *Ta'wīl* is the dialectical complement of *tanzīl* (transmitting downwards): one brings the Qur'ān from above, the other returns the Qur'ān to its transcendent source. According to a classic text: 'He who practices *ta'wīl* is the one who turns his speech from the external (exoteric) form towards the inner reality, *ḥaqīqat*.' "[25] It is important to realize that mystical exegesis is not the same as scriptural hermeneutics; it is not the pursuit of meanings; it is rather the raising of the Qur'ān by mystical means back to its source: Allāh. Katz continues: "In other words, it is only the Sufi who knows the true depth of the Qur'ān; he alone is aware of the full reality it reveals. At the deepest level, the mystic becomes conscious, as must we, that there is no secret *above* or *behind* the sacred text: the text *is* the secret!—if only one knows how to 'read' it."[26] Mawlānā is scathing of attempts by people to "interpret" the Qur'ān using their ordinary human reason, especially when what they produce is simply what they want it to mean anyway. For Mawlānā, to expound the Qur'ān is to express in his own way the realities that were directly revealed to him mystically through the Qur'ān. This he does in the *Mathnawī*, and the correspondence he makes between the Qur'ān and the *Mathnawī* implies that the *Mathnawī* too requires the opening of the mystical consciousness to meet with the realities, the *ḥaqīqah*, which are contained therein.

Sufism, or Islamic mysticism, evolved organically from two sources: meditation on the Qur'ān was the first; obeying and following the example of the Prophet, the Messenger of God, was the second. Both Shams and Mawlānā were totally dedicated to both, and in addition to the 528 verses from the Qur'ān that are explicitly referred to in the *Mathnawī*, there are no less than 750 traditions (*ḥadīth*) relating to or deriving from the Prophet similarly to be found there. Mawlānā and Shams both shared the mystical veneration of the Prophet that had become virtually universal among Sufis of their time, regarding him as the Perfect Man, the exemplar of the highest spiritual perfection attainable by human beings, and sometimes going even further and considering him as light from the uncreated Divine Light that preceded creation.

It is now necessary to examine the word Sufi as it might have been understood in Mawlānā's time. There are now many excellent accounts of Sufism in general and monographs treating of individual orders or particular Sufis, so it is no longer necessary to repeat material readily available elsewhere. If Sufism is considered as a particular way of life for a Muslim, a life dedicated totally to God and surrendered to God's Will, then Mawlānā was a Sufi. If to be a Sufi means to belong to an Order, to swear allegiance to a shaykh, and to follow the rites, rituals, and practice of that Order, then Mawlānā was not a Sufi. The foundation of Orders began from about 1150 onward but in Mawlānā's lifetime the institutionalization of Sufism was not universal by any means. There were still many individuals, like Shams, who were highly developed spiritually, but who were free spirits not belonging to any particular Sufi Order. Equally, there were many groups of disciples, gathered round spiritual figures, who trod the spiritual path but who had no wish to institutionalize. Mawlānā would have identified himself and Shams as Sufis in the general sense but not in the institutional sense. Earlier in this chapter it was suggested that the institutionalization of his group into an Order was an option for Mawlānā, but it was one he rejected, choosing instead to pass on his guidance through his poetry in the *Mathnawī*.

There was one requirement above all others that Mawlānā considered vital for spiritual development, and that was the need for every spiritual aspirant to have a shaykh, whether or not within the context of an institutional Sufi Order. He had had his own father, Burhān al-Dīn and Shams as his shaykhs, and even when his own transformation had been effected by Shams, he still respected this need and considered as his shaykh, first Ṣalāḥ al-Dīn and then Ḥusām al-Dīn. Often he warns in the *Mathnawī* against attempting to tread the spiritual path alone. There are many passages, even entire discourses, underlining the need to have a shaykh. The reasons are: first, because the opposition in the form of the deviousness of one's own selfhood, the *nafs*, inspired by Iblīs, Satan, is so strong one would quickly be overcome without one; second, because one cannot see oneself and need to have the shaykh as a mirror in which to see one's true state and in which to find the reflections of Divine mysteries; third, only a shaykh who had died to self would have the spiritual insight and disinterestedness to require from the aspirant the efforts and sacrifices necessary for spiritual progress at each particular stage.

While the shaykh, or *pir* as he is also known, remains the central spiritual focus for the aspiring Sufi, Mawlānā also speaks of the saint, the *walī*, the friend of God, of whom there are various grades, with the *quṭb*, or spiritual axis, being responsible for the spiritual welfare of the world at any particular time. Another term Mawlānā uses is the Perfect Man, *insān al-kāmil*, which refers to someone who has attained the highest degree of spiritual perfectibility achievable for a human being. Mawlānā often also speaks of the prophets and of the angels. Saints and prophets derive their spiritual receiving from the Universal Intellect or Intelligence, *'aql-e kullī*, although not all necessarily to the same degree. The intellect or intelligence, *'aql*, inherent in an ordinary human being is termed *'aql-e juzwī*, or partial intellect, because it is veiled from the Universal Intellect by the murky clouds of selfhood, the *nafs*. One of the tasks of the spiritual path is to disperse these clouds of selfhood so that the *'aql*, the intellect, which is an attribute of the spirit, *rūḥ*, may begin to receive indications from the *'aql-e kullī*, the Universal Intellect. Since this is one of the themes developed in Book One and Book Two, however, there is no need to anticipate it further here.

Mawlānā's Literary Antecedents

It is perhaps unnecessary to stress that, wherever he was born or lived, Mawlānā's culture was through and through Persian. His language was Persian, his sensibilities were Persian and his literary inheritance was Persian. As the third leg in this contextualization of the *Mathnawī*, therefore, it will be helpful briefly to examine its literary antecedents.[27]

The *mathnawī* is a literary form that is thought to be of purely Persian origin in spite of its Arabic name.[28] It was used as the vehicle for didactic and narrative works in Persian from the tenth century CE. It was the preferred vehicle for long poems, presumably because, with the rhyme being internal to the verse *(bayt)* and therefore changing with every verse, it was far less demanding on the poet's resources. The first major work in this form is the *Shāhnāmah* (The Book of Kings), the Persian national epic, which was written by Firdawsī in Ghazna around the year 1001 CE.

The Persians have a long history of didactic moralizing literature stretching back to pre-Islamic times that produced an "Advice" or "Wisdom" (*Ḥikmat*) tradition. The ancestors of the Persians, the Indo-Iranians, like their cousins the Indo-Aryans who went to India, clearly felt the need for such a tradition, not so much for the ordinary populace, but particularly to educate nobles, kings, and princes in appropriate standards and behavior so that they would treat their subjects, advisers and, above all, their poets, justly and generously. This tradition produced the Mirror-for-Princes genre in Persian literature, which mixed moral and practical homilies with parables, and the *Nīti* genre in Indian literature. The *Nīti* tradition in India, which was largely about "King-up-man-ship," whereby a king remained on top through a wide variety of tricks, stratagems, and devices, made great use of animal fables. One large collection of such animal fables, the Sanskrit *Pancatantra*, was translated into Pahlavī, the Middle Iranian literary language of pre-Islamic Sassanian Iran, and was then rendered from Pahlavī into Arabic within the mirror-for-princes genre by Ibn al-Muqaffaʿ in the ninth century, with the title *Kalīla wa Dimna*. Mawlānā refers to this work as the source for several of the many animal fables within his *Mathnawī*.

The first person to use the *mathnawī* for spiritual purposes was the poet Sanāʾī.[29] Sanāʾī was born in Ghazna in the second half of the eleventh century and died there in 1131. He tried but failed to become a court poet and found his patrons instead among religious scholars, judges, and preachers, mainly in Khurasan. It was probably because of the nature of his patrons that Sanāʾī's poetry was mainly homiletic, but this moralistic didacticism was also used by him as a vehicle for the expression of Sufi ideas. In his collected works there are odes (*qaṣīdas*) lyrics (*ghazals*), and the longer narrative poems (*mathnawīs*). The two spiritual *mathnawīs* are the *Sayr al-ʿibād ilāʾl-maʿād* (The Journey of the Servants to the Place of Return), and the *Ḥadīqat al-ḥaqīqa wa sharīʿat al-ṭarīqa* (The Garden of Reality and the Law of the Path).

The *Sayr al-ʿibād ilāʾl-maʿād* is a short work of just short of 750 verses. The poet relates his growth from birth to the spiritual maturity that enables him to recognize his ideal, the religious jurist, his patron, who is the Chief Justice of Sarakhs. At the same time, there is a description, of a more general application, of the successive stages of life, each being guided by one of three personifications: the nurse, representing the vegetative soul guiding physical growth, a tyrannical king, representing the animal soul, and finally an old man representing the *ʿaql-e faʿʿāl*, the intellect in man which is open to the Universal Intellect. With the guide, the narrator, the poet makes a journey through various levels of the universe in each of which he encounters allegorical equivalents of the forces in his nature, until, finally, at the Universal level, he recognizes the Place of his Return. This *mathnawī* provided the model for later allegories of the spiritual journey.

Quite different from this is the *Ḥadīqat al-ḥaqīqa wa sharīʿat al-ṭarīqa*, about which it is difficult to speak with any great certainty because it exists in several early versions, each of different sizes. The oldest version is divided into three parts: an introductory section, which deals with the Creator, the Qurʾān, the Prophet, and so on; the second section, which deals with a wide range of topics relevant to somebody on the spiritual path, with warnings about the power of the selfhood to obstruct spiritual progress, the dangers of this world and the inevitable approach of death; the third section, which begins as a panegyric to Bahrāmshāh, the Sultan of Ghazna, quickly reverts to ethical and moral instruction for the king in the manner of the Mirror for Princes genre. The work then is didactic, homiletic and wide ranging in its subject matter. It is also known by two other names: the *Fakhrī-Nāmeh*, after Bahrāmshāh to whom it is dedicated, and the *Ilāhī-Nāmeh*, the name by which Mawlānā refers to it in the *Mathnawī*.

In imitation of Sanā'ī, the poet Niẓāmī of Ganja (1141–1209) wrote a *mathnawī* entitled *Makhzan al-Asrār* (The Treasury of Secrets) in honor of his patron Bahrāmshāh of Erzincan in Eastern Anatolia who, it will be remembered, was also later the patron of Mawlānā's father and the family. Because of the family connection, and because it is known that Mawlānā was particularly fond of Niẓāmī's poetry and urged his disciples to read it, it will be worth looking at this *mathnawī* in some detail.[30] The structure of the poem is set out below.

1. In Praise of God [55]
2. First Prayer: On Punishment and the Wrath of God [40]
3. Second Prayer: On the Bounty and Forgiveness of God [22]
4. In Praise of the Prophet Muḥammad [25]
5. On the Ascension [68]
6. First Eulogy to the Prophet [23]
7. Second Eulogy [33]
8. Third Eulogy [27]
9. Fourth Eulogy [41]

10. In Praise of King Fakhr al-Dīn Bahrām Shāh [28]

11. On Audience to the King [36]
12. On the honor and dignity of this book [43]
13. On the excellence of speech [27]
14. The superiority of poetry to prose [66]
15. Describing the night and cognizing the heart [85]
16. The first seclusion [75]
17. The fruit of the first seclusion [30]
18. The second seclusion [55]
19. The fruit of the second seclusion [46]

Twenty moral and spiritual discourses, each with an exemplary story.

20. On the ending of the book. [28]

It will be noticed that there are twenty sections that constitute the introduction and the conclusion of the poem: nineteen as introduction, and one as conclusion. In between come the twenty discourses, each with its own exemplary story. The main body of the work, therefore, alternates homily, narrative, homily, narrative. The first nineteen sections are of particular interest in terms of their structuring. The emphasis in this kind of rhetorical structure is given by the central point, which is Section 10, the eulogy in praise of the King-patron. On either side of this section are two blocks of nine sections, and, again, the central point of each nine-section block, that is 5 and 15, respectively, contain the main emphasis, that is the Prophet's ascension, his night journey to the Throne of God, in the first block, and the description of night and cognizing the heart in the second block. These two Sections, 5 and 15, are each the longest in their respective blocks, further emphasizing their central importance. There is an obvious correspondence between the two blocks, which could be stated: just as the Prophet was the spokesperson for God, so is the poet for the King Bahrām Shāh. There is also a more subtle pattern of correspondences between the sections of each block of a kind that will be examined in the next chapter, but for now it is notable, for example, that the Prophet's night journey to God and the poet's night journey within his own heart are placed in parallel in Sections 5 and 15. Such parallelism does not in any way imply a claim to similarity or equality; it simply suggests a correspondence, a night journey, without any need to explain that there were prodigious differences of scale and context between the two, because that would be understood by any reader. Although not shown here, the range of the stories is interesting: kings, sages, Sufis, animals of all kinds, shopkeepers, barbers, farmers, historical or legendary personages, and the like are all participants. A similar variety will be found in Mawlānā's masterpiece.

Nizāmī could be called a poet's poet. His poetry is sophisticated and mannered, rather like the Elizabethan poets in English literature. In addition to the early didactic poem just described, he also wrote four other *mathnawīs*: *Majnūn and Laylā*, a traditional story of self-denying love, and three dealing with subjects from the legendary history of Iran, the *Haft Paykar*, *Khusraw and Shīrīn*, and the *Iskandar-Nāmah*. The *Haft Paykar*, which has been beautifully translated into English verse and carefully analyzed by Meisami, will be discussed in the next chapter.[31] It is difficult to establish to what extent these four poems can be called Sufi; they have a potential spiritual dimension, but they are predominantly the product of secular court culture, a culture that was essentially analogical so it would be a mistake to argue they were exclusively Sufi or exclusively court poems. Morality and wisdom there certainly is, and observance of the pieties, but you will not find in Nizāmī the flights of mystical imagination nor the profound spiritual understanding that is found in Mawlānā.

The true forerunner of Mawlānā in terms of spiritual and mystical content is the poet of Nishapur, Farīd al-Dīn 'Aṭṭār, who probably died around the year 1220.[32] Little is known of his life except that he worked as a pharmacist in the bazaar at Nishapur. His poetic output was extraordinary, even when one ignores the many works which have been wrongly attributed to him. From this extensive corpus there are four spiritual *mathnawīs* that are undoubtedly authentic: the *Manṭiq al-Ṭayr* (The Parliament of the Birds), the *Ilāhī-nāmah* (The Book of the Divine), the *Muṣībat-nāmah* (The Book of Affliction), and the *Asrār-nāmah* (The Book of Mysteries).[33] The first three are set within an allegorical frame story.

The *Parliament of the Birds* tells of the birds, under the leadership of the Hoopoe, undergoing a long pilgrimage in search of the mythical Sīmurgh whom they wish to make their king, an allegory of souls on the spiritual path seeking union with God. Many birds were too frightened even to start the journey, which in fact proved so arduous that only thirty birds completed it. They had to pass through seven valleys named respectively: Search, Love, Illumination, Detachment, Unity, Bewilderment and Poverty, and Nothingness. These names indicate they are certain stations on the spiritual path, but they are also, horizontally, the route through the desert to be followed on the pilgrimage to Mecca, and, vertically, the ascent through the Ptolemaic spheres that was traditionally understood as the ascent through the different levels of being to perfection. When finally the thirty birds (*sī murgh*) reach the moment of union with the Sīmurgh, they realize that the pun is the reality, that they and the Sīmurgh are one. That is the frame story, but the poem itself contains many stories and anecdotes illustrative of the spiritual points being made at the time. Sometimes these stories are straightforward and their import easily accessible, but at other times they can seem obscure and puzzling, deliberately so, because the reader is then obliged to search and struggle and ponder until realization dawns as to the intended purpose of the anecdote in the context in which it occurs. This requires an active reader, an intelligent seeker, not someone who expects to be entertained passively. The benefit to the reader, however, is considerable, not just in terms of the enhanced memorability deriving from the struggle, but from the potentially transformative effect of the process itself on him- or herself. This technique is one that Mawlānā was to use in his own masterpiece, and for this he is certainly indebted to 'Aṭṭār.

There is one particular story that illustrates the point just made. It occurs at the very end of the work. The thirty birds have united with the Sīmurgh, and, after an indefinite period of total Nothingness, they have their individuality restored and are heirs to eternal life. This clearly represents, first, *fanā*, total annihilation of the selfhood, followed by *baqā*, eternal subsistence in God. Then comes this story of a king who had a very wise vizier. The vizier had a son who was excellent in all respects and had become a very special favorite of the king. One day the son fell in love with a lovely girl of the court and they spent the night together. The king finds them together and is furiously angry in his jealousy and has the son imprisoned. The vizier visits the son and arranges with the warder to have a convicted murderer executed and to pretend it is the son, whom the vizier takes to a place of hiding. The king, still angry, comes to visit the prisoner and is very pleased with the warder when he explains he has been executed. The king returns to the palace and slowly the anger subsides only to be replaced by an increasing sadness and sense of loss. When his suffering reaches crisis point, the vizier brings his son in and they are united again in deep and lasting happiness. At this point the poem ends; but what is the purport of the story?

The first question is whether the story is a continuation of the allegory of the birds. It could be from its context a symbolic representation of *baqā*, subsistence in God. What argues against such an interpretation, however, is the anger and jealousy of the king. There is no reason why there should be Divine Anger with souls who have been naughted and endowed totally with God's attributes. If not explanatory of *baqā*, then of what is it explanatory? The symbolism is characteristically Sufi. The king will be symbolic of God; the vizier symbolic of the Universal Intellect, the *'aql-e kullī*; the son symbolic of a human spirit, *rūḥ*; the warder symbolic of the shaykh; the girl symbolic of the attractions of existence or of the world; the convicted murderer symbolic of the selfhood, the *nafs*; and the execution symbolic of the naughting of the selfhood, *fanā*. Sufi symbolism is multivalent; it can apply on as many levels as there are modes of understanding and being to apprehend it. Certainly the story can be read as a clarification of *fanā*. It provides the reassurance that the annihilation of the selfhood is only a pretended death: that the death of egoism, the false "I," is not death at all, but the clearing of the way so that true individuality may be granted by God. That reading makes contextual sense, but another reading could be that it is a summing up of the human situation in relation to the Divine and hence it can also be considered a general statement applicable to all. It is almost certainly both, and probably more besides, but this last reading, as a general statement, J. W. Morris rightly observes, is the precise point at which Mawlānā begins his *Mathnawī*, so this could be another intertextual act of homage by Mawlānā to his acknowledged predecessor.

There is another debt that Mawlānā owes to 'Aṭṭār which has to do with the second *mathnawī*, the *Ilāhī-nāmah*. In this case the frame story is of a Caliph who had six sons whom he asked to tell him their deepest wishes. The first wishes to marry the daughter of the king of the fairies; the second wishes to control magical powers; the third wishes for Jamshīd's world-revealing cup; the fourth seeks to find the Water of Life; the fifth desires the Ring of Solomon; and the sixth wishes to learn the secrets of the alchemist. In his introduction, 'Aṭṭār indicates what the sons respectively represent: the first son, the selfhood (the *nafs*); the second son, the Devil (*Iblīs*); the third son, intellect (*'aql*); the fourth son, knowledge (*'ilm*); the fifth son, spiritual poverty (*faqr*); and the sixth son, Unicity or the Realization of the Uniqueness of God (*tawḥīd*). The Caliph fulfils the desires of each son, but not in the manner they initially expected. Through the medium of a set of stories, he transforms the aims of each son from a worldly to a spiritual purpose. The Caliph, 'Aṭṭār makes clear, is the human spirit, the *rūḥ*. Mawlānā's debt to this work is that he designed his great *Mathnawī* to have six books and the overall subject of each book is that which is represented by each of the six sons above. Such intertextuality is not to be regarded in any sense as plagiarism but rather as an act of homage to a master mystical poet and an acknowledgment by Mawlānā that he stood on the shoulders of giants. It was also a statement by an author indicating precisely within which tradition he was locating himself.

The *Muṣībat-nāmah* is another journey allegory with a meditating subject being taken to different parts of the universe, first a descent from the transcendent realm to the material worlds and then the ascent back again. But it is the *Asrār-Nāmah* that proved to be influential with Mawlānā in that he refers to it by name and uses several of the stories, with his own modifications, in the *Mathnawī*. The *Asrār-Nāmah* is not an allegorical narrative, and has no frame story. It is divided into chapters, but no headings are given to the chapters to indicate what the central ideas being treated are, a precedent Mawlānā was to follow. It covers a number of different spiritual subjects, seemingly without apparent order or rationale, and in this respect follows the model of Sanā'ī's *Ḥadīqat al-ḥaqīqa wa sharī'at al-ṭarīqa*. In his discussion of this poem, De Bruijn, having paraphrased some thirty lines from the beginning of Chapter 6, concludes:

"As this paraphrase of a passage of no more than thirty lines shows, the dense use of imagery, word-play and a few illustrative tales enable the didactical poet to express a connected line of profound mystical thoughts quite effectively within a very small compass. The great art of this homiletic style lies not so much in the attractiveness of the narratives, which are usually very short indeed, but in the flashing movement of the poet's discourse from one theme to another. It was this style as it is exemplified in the *Asrār-Nāmah* which characterizes both the didactic poetry of 'Aṭṭār's predecessor Sanā'ī and that of his successor Mawlānā Jalāl al-Dīn Rūmī."[34]

This completes the literary contextualization of the *Mathnawī*. It is now time to look at the poem itself and consider how it can best be read.

Chapter Two

Reading the *Mathnawī*

The *Mathnawī* as Given

The *Mathnawī* consists of six untitled books. Each of these six books begins with a short introduction. The introductions to Books One, Three, and Four are in Arabic; those to Books Two, Five, and Six are in Persian. Following the introduction in each book is a proem, a sequence of verses that acts as a preface to that book. These proems are of varying lengths: Book One, 35 verses; Book Two, 111 verses; Book Three, 68 verses; Book Four, 39 verses; Book Five, 30 verses; and Book Six, 128 verses. The total number of verses in each book, that is, including the proem, again varies. In Nicholson's edition of the text, Book One has 4,002 verses; Book Two has 3,810; Book Three has 4,810; Book Four has 3,855; Book Five has 4,238; and Book Six has 4,916. This gives a grand total for the entire work of 25,631 verses.

The verses of each book are broken up by headings (*'unwān*), such as "The story of the king's falling in love with a handmaiden and buying her" (after line 35, Book One), or "The first to bring analogical reasoning to bear against the Revealed Text was Iblis" (after line 3395, Book One). While it is not uncommon for editors and scribes to add headings of their own to works of this kind, or to omit existing headings, in this case there are good reasons to assume that these headings were the work of the author himself. The first reason is that the transmission of the text is good, and the headings as found in Nicholson's edition correspond, for the most part, with those of the earliest manuscript, dated 1278 CE, which is almost contemporary with the finishing of the work.[1] The second reason is that some of these headings could never have been inserted by anyone other than the author, since they are either too bizarre, unconnected with what follows, or in some way or another improbable for anyone else to have produced them. A scribe or an editor would only put in what he imagined would simplify the text, not seek to complicate it. The third and final reason is that these headings effectively divide the books up into sections, and each section is almost invariably foreshadowed in the verses that immediately precede the heading, thereby giving that heading, at least as a section marker, validity from the text itself. Because of their importance, the word "section" will henceforth be used in this study as the technical word for those verses that are contained between two headings, and constitute a discrete portion of text marked and identified by the author as such.

Sections vary considerably as to their length, the shortest being only two verses long, the longest well over a hundred verses. In Book One there are 173 sections; in Book Two, 111 sections; in Book Three, 220 sections; in Book Four, 137 sections; in Book Five, 174 sections; and in Book Six, 140 sections. This gives a grand total for the work as a whole of 948 sections. The work then has 25,631 verses, divided into 948 sections, divided into six books, which together constitute the *Mathnawī.* The text as given therefore may be said to have four levels of organization marked by the author: the level of the *verse*; the level of the *section*; the level of the *book*; and the level of the *work*.

The Question of Structure

The *Mathnawī* is an acclaimed masterpiece, and has been for most of the 700 or 800 years of its existence. It has been very thoroughly studied and, across the centuries, the subject of many commentaries, analyses and appreciations by scholars, devotees and men of letters from East and West. It is widely known and is often quoted and many people know lines or even longer segments of its text by heart. That most fundamental method of literary analysis, the close reading, has often be applied to it by people of great erudition and literary and spiritual experience, but so far it has failed to yield a structure, a principle of organization that determined why one particular passage should appear where it does. It will be helpful, then, to see how scholarship has viewed the *Mathnawī.*

Edward Granville Browne addressed not so much the structure as the content when he wrote: "It contains a great number of rambling anecdotes of the most various character, some sublime and dignified, others grotesque and even (to our ideas) disgusting, interspersed with mystical and theological digressions, often of the most abstruse character, in sharp contrast with the narrative portions, which, though presenting some peculiarities in diction, are as a rule couched in very simple and plain language"[2] Similarly, William Chittick uses the word "rambling," although he applies it, quite correctly, not to the anecdotes themselves but to the totality: "the *Mathnawi* is a rambling collection of anecdotes and tales derived from a great variety of sources, from the Qur'ān to the folk humor of the day."[3] Arthur Arberry, having quoted with approval Reynold Nicholson's proposition that "The poem resembles a trackless ocean," goes on to say: "Written sporadically over a long period of time, without any firm framework to keep the discourse on orderly lines, it is at first, and even at repeated readings, a disconcertingly diffuse and confused composition."[4] It is the French who make a virtue of this lack of order and account for it in terms of inspiration. Baron Bernard Carra de Vaux writes: "The composition of the Mathnawi is, it must be granted, very disjointed; the stories follow one another in no order, the examples suggest reflections which in their turn suggest others so that the narrative is often interrupted by long digressions; but this want of order seems to be a result of the lyrical inspiration which carries the poet along as if by leaps and bounds, and if the reader yields to it, the effect is by no means displeasing."[5] From Eastern Europe, Rypka writes: "Our amazement at his vast power of imagination, is somewhat modified by the lack of balance in the material."[6] Annemarie Schimmel, who has written extensively on Mawlānā and his work, writes of the *Mathnawī*: "The book is not built according to a system; it lacks architectural structure; the verses lead one into another, and the most heterogeneous thoughts are woven together by word associations and loose threads of stories."[7]

But it is interestingly Reynold Nicholson, who knew the work better than almost anyone else after his thirty-five years' work editing, translating, and commenting on it, who felt there was much more going on than appeared on the surface, although he never himself quite identified or explained what it was. He writes at the end of his great task: "Anyone who reads the poem attentively will observe that its structure is far from being as casual as it looks. To say that 'the stories follow each other in no order' is entirely wrong: they are bound together by subtle links and transitions arising from the poet's development of his theme; and each Book forms an artistic whole."[8] Then, tantalizingly, he continues: "The subject cannot be discussed here, but I may refer the reader to an excellent analysis and illustration of these technicalities by Dr Gustav Richter which has been published recently."[9] Richter's study, now republished in English translation,[10] proves, however, to be a valuable and suggestive analysis of Mawlānā's style in the *Mathnawī* rather than of its structure; it is more micro-compositional than macro-compositional, although it does in places touch lightly on structural implications. In discussing Richter's essays, Franklin Lewis writes: "Richter shows how the *Mathnawī* follows the paradigm of the Qur'ān in integrating stories, parables, ethical exhortations, and didactic philosophy, which may at first glance seem randomly digressive, but when regarded more deeply resolve into an intricate pattern, like a Persian carpet."[11] He then quotes the distinguished Iranian scholar Foruzanfar from the Introduction to his commentary to the work (*Sharḥ-e Masnavī*, l:ii): "The *Masnavi* is not divided into chapters and sections like other books; it has a style similar to the noble Qur'ān, in which spiritual insights, articles of belief, the laws and principles of faith, and exhortations are set forth and mixed together according to divine wisdom. Like the book of Creation, it has no particular order."[12] On the question of structure, or rather of the absence of structure, then, Iranian and Western scholars are united.[13] None of the many commentaries written on the *Mathnawī* even mentions structure, being concerned wholly with the meaning of words or lines, with the origin of stories, anecdotes and quotations, and with possible Sufi symbolic or allegorical interpretations.

One scholar, Julian Baldick, takes issue with Nicholson concerning his assertion that each book is an artistic whole, on the grounds that a story is begun at the end of Book Three and is completed at the beginning of Book Four.[14] This particular story plays an important role as will be shown later, but Baldick's most valuable observation is that the overall subject of each of the books of the *Mathnawī* corresponds precisely with one of the six sons in the *Ilāhī-nāmeh* of Farīd al-Dīn ʻAṭṭār, as was seen in the previous chapter. The *Mathnawī* and the *Ilāhī-nāmeh* share the same overall plan. Book One of the *Mathnawī* deals with the *nafs*, the self-hood; Book Two deals with *Iblīs*, the Devil; Book Three deals with *ʻaql*, intelligence, intellect; Book Four with *ʻilm*, knowledge; Book Five with *faqr*, poverty, and Book Six with *tawḥīd*, unity or unicity. Baldick then rejoins the scholarly consensus, when he writes: "It would be wrong, however, to lay stress upon the plan of the *Mathnawī*. It is unlikely that here, or in the case of ʻAṭṭār, attempts at structural analysis would add anything once the obvious has been pointed out."[15]

Any reader of the *Mathnawī* would be able to concur with this consensus view held by these scholars from across the world. This is how the *Mathnawī* appears to be, this is its self-presentation. Mawlānā, however, had almost complete poetic control, so, if this is how it appears to Iranian and Western scholars alike, that is exactly how Mawlānā intended it to appear; its appearance and self-presentation are precisely what he sought to produce, they are part of his design. Some of those referred to above have seen in the apparent randomness of the *Mathnawī* the working of inspiration. If they are right, and it must be initially accepted that they could be, then the only principle of organization is the outpouring of the creative process. That is not satisfactory for many reasons, the most cogent of which is that the work itself constantly emphasizes that creation is highly intelligent and, could the reader but see it, wonderfully ordered. It would be a most curious irony if Mawlānā were to have denied to his masterpiece the very intelligence and order he urges his readers to find in themselves and in the universe. In the Introduction it was affirmed that there is indeed an inner spiritual organization to the work, but that Mawlānā has hidden it in a highly sophisticated and unexpected way. Before showing how he did this, it is necessary to have regard to some further analytical considerations.

Some Further Considerations

Four levels of organization marked by the author have been identified in the *Mathnawī* as given: the levels of the verse, the section, the book, and the work. Which is the level that lacks structure? It is neither the level of the verse, nor in the way the verses are grouped to form sections; although there are sometimes sudden transitions of theme within a section, these are made to seem natural and logical. People love the lines of Mawlānā's poetry, they appreciate the high flights of mystical outpouring, the earthy anecdotes, the amusing stories, the ironies and the insights, even if they really cannot see where it is going. In fact, by lack of structure, people usually mean that they cannot see any level of organization at what is here called the level of the book. Often there is no apparent reason why one section should come where it does; the sections at times appear to be almost random in their order. A story will start in one section; then come two sections of teaching; then comes the start of a second story in the following section; then another section of teaching; then a return to the first story; then more sections of teaching, then the second story is continued, and so on. It is the apparent lack of any rationale for the way the sections follow one another that has led to the accusations of a lack of structure. If this is the level that is problematic, it is the most likely level at which to seek for what Mawlānā has hidden. The quality of the poetry, the high level of spiritual and moral insight, and the mystical flights, in most people's eyes, more than compensate for this structural deficiency, but in reinforcing the highly questionable proposition that inspiration and the mystical are necessarily irrational, the present situation is more than unsatisfactory.

If close reading, sequentially, following the given levels of verse, section, book and work, has failed to reveal an organizing principle and structure, then the work must be read differently. The method applied here is to concentrate on two unmarked intermediate levels: thematically united passages within sections and the groupings of sections. The first, in English prose, would be described as a paragraph, and, for want of a better word or technical term, the word "paragraph" is used in this study as a technical term to refer to a passage of thematically linked verses. The level of the paragraph is intermediate between the verses and the sections. The second intermediate level is between the sections and the book. In English prose, this could be thought of as a chapter, but since in English prose the whole work would be thought of as a book, and the *Mathnawī*'s books as chapters, another word seems to be required. It has been decided for the purposes of this study to use the word "discourse" as the technical word to designate a group of sections. "Story" would not be a particularly satisfactory word, in that it would suggest that the sections are united narratively, which is only sometimes the case, so "discourse" is preferred here since it encompasses both narrative and teaching sections. In fact, "discourse" is particularly apt because it reflects the Arabic word *maqālah,* often used in works in precisely the sense that is intended by the word "discourse" here. Mawlānā could easily have divided his sections up into *maqālah*s by grouping the sections together into marked identifiable units and called such a grouping of sections a *maqālah*, a discourse, as other writers have done; he could even have given each *maqālah* a name such as "Discourse on Pride," or "Discourse on not seeing Reality," for example. But he chose not to do so. This decision not to mark the subwholes into which sections are grouped within a book is the first way in which he has hidden his inner organization. Now it is necessary to examine the units of these two intermediate levels.

It is one of the contentions of this study that Mawlānā's poetry is so rich, the verses so seductive, that the reader is drawn to the level of the line almost to the exclusion of other levels. A "close" reading, under these circumstances, such as that made by commentators, will only detract further from the clues and linkages that might constitute an organizing principle and structure. To find such a structure it is necessary, at least initially, to stand away from the actual lines, their language and imagery. To find structure, what is needed is not a "close" reading but a "distant" or "detached" reading. It is very fortunate that Nicholson's translation is so accurate and literal. Working from Nicholson's English translation, in fact, permits one to identify and summarize paragraphs, that is, the units of thematically related verses that constitute the building blocks or bricks of the thematic structure, without being drawn into the level of the line by the attractive power of Mawlānā's Persian poetry. This procedure of summarizing the paragraphs is one of the main methodological procedures used in this analysis and it has been found to be of considerable heuristic power. With translation, it has been said, what you lose is the poetry, which is precisely why it is used here initially. No reference will be made to the rich poetic features of the work, or the many changes of voice and tempo; anything which might detract from the single-minded search for the underlying structure and organizing principles, has been deliberately excluded. When it is known where one is going, then it is safe to return to the poetry. Seven hundred years of commentaries that are silent about structure, confirm this is the right way around.

There is a famous section of 18 verses in Book One (lines 2835–2852), entitled "The Story of what passed between the Grammarian and the Boatman." which can serve as an example of what constitutes a paragraph. This section has three paragraphs, according to this analysis, each of six lines. The first tells the story of the exchange between the grammarian and the boatman; the second puns *maḥw* (self-effacement) and *naḥw* (grammar) in the first line and again in the last line and draws a conclusion from the story; while the third returns to the story of the Bedouin and foreshadows the section to follow. A full summary of this section will be given later at the appropriate place. It has to be said that not all paragraphs are as clear as these three, and it is fully recognized that "paragraphs" are subjective analytical constructs. Nonetheless, they have proved crucial in arriving at an understanding of the thematic and rhetorical structure of the work and they constitute a major part of this analysis.

If the paragraph is the thematic building block, the section is the room and the discourse is the building. In Book One, it is fairly straightforward to identify a discourse from its narrative unity, which was clearly Mawlānā's intention, but later in the work it is made more difficult, with fewer clues. The first nine sections of the work, for example, clearly constitute one discourse, that of the King and the Handmaiden, while verses 900 to 1,389 in Book One, form another discourse, that of the Lion and the Beasts. There is no doubt that the decision of the author not to tell his readers which sections to take together as a given unity but to require them to find out for themselves, has been one of the major factors contributing to the accusations of randomness and lack of structure. When the unity of the sections in a discourse has a narrative basis, it is easy enough to see where one discourse ends and another begins. When, however, the unity of a discourse is thematic rather than narrative, only an appreciation of the themes under examination by the author enables one to identify which sections belong to which discourse. Sometimes the unity is narrative, sometimes thematic, often both together. Readers are therefore required to be both active and intelligent, entirely in keeping with Mawlānā's overall purpose. One of the major tasks of the analysis here undertaken is the identification of the discourses and an examination of their structure.

A discourse is made up of a number of sections. The number of sections varies with each discourse, the shortest being five sections, the longest over forty sections. What, however, emerges surprisingly from this examination of Book One is that, in fact, the discourses, and the sections they organize, have to be read "synoptically" and *not* "sequentially." Perhaps the major discovery of this study, confirmed by this analysis, is that the organization of the sections in a discourse is not sequential; the primary relationships between sections in a discourse are organized by "parallelism" and "chiasmus." This is the second way in which Mawlānā has hidden his inner spiritual structure. Of course, sections follow one another in sequence, but which section comes where is determined by the higher order organization of the discourse, just as where a particular discourse comes is determined by the even higher organization of the book, as will be shown later. The realization that Mawlānā was using parallelism and chiasmus to organize the higher levels of his work has been a major surprise. The recognition that the organization of the sections is nonsequential and based on parallelism and chiasmus, reveals discourse structures that are elegant, symmetrical, and beautifully balanced, and of great variety and intricacy: in short, fitting testimony to an inspired master architect. But these discourse structures are not just aesthetically satisfying; they reveal patterns of significance and meaning as well as disclosing the distribution of emphases. The methodology used here to analyze the structure of the discourse, is to apply the principles of parallelism and chiasmus to the sections as units using their thematic and narrative contents as summarized by the paragraph analysis to detect the parallels. Sometimes it is only the parallelism that permits identification of the discourse's beginning and end. Before showing how Mawlānā used these two literary techniques, it is first necessary to look at recent work on synoptic reading, and the two literary principles of parallelism and chiasmus, sometimes known as ring composition, since they may not be familiar to everyone.

Synoptic Reading and the Principles of Parallelism and Chiasmus

"Synoptic," from the Greek, means seeing together, seeing as a whole. To read synoptically is to be aware of the organization of the whole as one reads. It is to read consciously, since "consciously" is the Latin equivalent of the Greek "synoptically." The familiar way of reading is sequential: the attention is split between the unfolding sequence of new material, on the one hand, and the larger developing contexts of structure, plot, or argument, on the other. Each new discrete element successively encountered is briefly allowed its own self-identity before surrendering it as the element itself becomes part of the enlarged context for the next element. In a number of premodern works, however, additional and particular significance, sometimes the rationale of the work itself, was embodied in the macro-compositional structure, that is, they were designed and composed synoptically, as organic, organized wholes. This higher organization is not usually sequential; it makes use of various types of nonlinear relatedness, and it requires a synoptic reading. Recent studies have begun to reveal that works so designed were far more common than had hitherto been suspected.[16]

A recent study of the Old Testament book of Leviticus by the prolific anthropologist Mary Douglas, who had for many years struggled to understand the answers to certain questions raised by this book, has shown convincingly that the macro-compositional structure of the book is modeled on the shape of the Tabernacle, which in turn is considered to be modeled on the holy Mount Sinai.[17] The Tabernacle has a large area open to the public, then a much smaller priestly area, and finally the Holy of Holies, which belongs to God, just as the summit of Mount Sinai was the abode of God, the cloudy region below that only Moses could enter, and below that on the lower slopes the people awaited. Further, the description of the various bodily parts of sacrificial animals follows the same analogy, and certain parts are assigned to the public, certain to the priests, and certain parts to God. The analogous spatial areas of the sacrificial body, the Tabernacle and Mount Sinai provide the model for the proportionality and segmentation of the text of the book of Leviticus and determine the content of each segment, with a large open section, a smaller priestly section and the holiest section for God. Mary Douglas had read this book many times over several decades; Hebrew scholars and rabbis had studied it for centuries and written learned commentaries; countless others had perused it as part of the Bible; yet until now nobody had realized the design of its compilers, why it is structured as it is. The reason nobody saw it before is because it is not obvious from sequential reading, nor was it expected; only Mary Douglas's persistent synoptic interrogation, together with certain clues others had provided, finally brought it to light. But to read Leviticus now, knowing its design and rationale, is to read it quite differently. The meanings become more precise, and they become that much more significant from the reader knowing where he or she is, where the emphases lie, and the full extent and implications of the contexts, enriched and sanctified by the multiple layering of the analogies. This is to read synoptically.

A previous study by Mary Douglas produced a synoptic reading of another major book of the Old Testament, the book of Numbers. While it is neither possible nor necessary to give a full account of this complex study here, it can be used to introduce the literary principles that are of present concern.[18] First, the book of Numbers, which is a significant work in Judaism because it is part of the Pentateuch, has been regarded by many as lacking in unity or coherence. Douglas's study shows that Numbers is in fact highly structured but that it requires a synoptic reading and the recovery of a lost genre. The first feature of this macro-compositional genre is alternation, in this case the alternation of narrative and law. The transitions between the two mark thirteen sections of the text overall. There are seven sections of narrative alternating with six law sections. These sections are arranged in a ring of a kind shown in the diagram in fig. 2.1 to which the reader is here referred.[19]

Fig. 2.1. A Twelve/Thirteen Term Ring Compositional Scheme

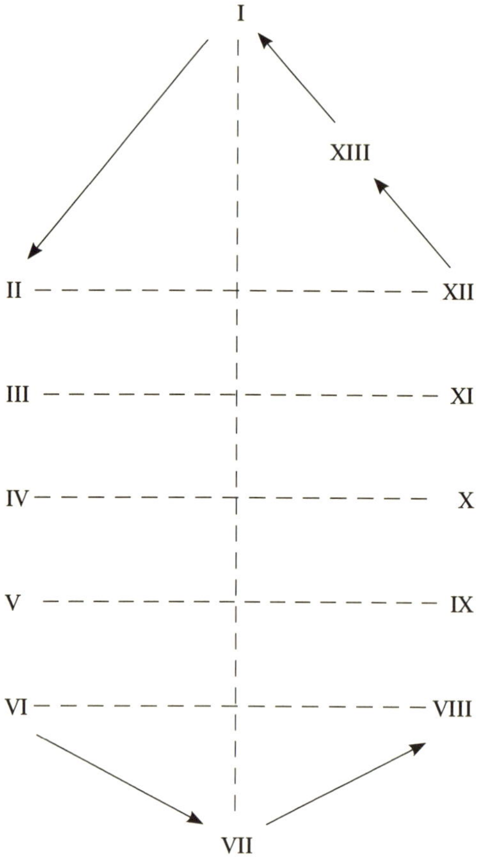

This type of arrangement is known as annular or ring composition, of which there are different forms found. In this twelve-section model, I and VII are in parallel as are II and XII, III and XI, IV and X, V and IX, and VI and VIII. Section XIII acts as a latch connecting the end of the ring to its beginning. This structure is apparently similar to literary forms well-known in the Mediterranean region from the eighth to the fifth centuries BCE. Another very beautiful example of a twelve/thirteen ring composition, although without the alternation, is the well-known story of Noah in Genesis.[20]

The way that the Noah story fits the scheme given in fig. 2.1 is as follows. At I, Noah was a righteous man who walked with God. He had three sons. God saw the earth had been corrupted by all flesh. At II, God told Noah he had decided to destroy all flesh but made a covenant with Noah that he, his wife, and his sons and their wives should go into the Ark with two of all living things to be kept alive. At III, the Lord said to Noah that he should take with him seven pairs of clean animals and birds, and two of unclean animals and birds, for he was going to destroy all flesh with a flood. At IV, the flood of waters came and two of all living things went into the Ark with Noah. At V, the flood began and, with everyone and two of every living thing on board, the Lord shut them in. At VI, The flood continued for forty days and destroyed all life apart from those on the Ark. At VII, God remembered Noah and the inhabitants of the Ark and so he caused the waters to recede. At VIII, after forty days Noah opened the window and sent out birds until he knew that it was dry by their nonreturn. At IX, God told Noah they could all come out, since it was dry. At X, Noah built an altar and made burnt offerings of clean animals and clean birds to the Lord who was so pleased He vowed never again to destroy all flesh. At XI, God blessed Noah and his sons and told them to fill the earth, allowing them to eat meat provided it is not with its blood. At XII, God made another covenant with Noah that He would never again destroy all flesh and made the rainbow the sign of this covenant. The latch section XIII says the three sons then peopled the earth, thus connecting the end to the beginning of the ring.

When these terms are fitted on the diagram at fig. 2.1, the parallelisms across the ring are obvious. II and XII are parallel in respect of the two covenants and being the beginning and the end of the episode. At V the waters begin and they go into the Ark and God shuts them in, while in the parallel IX the waters had dried and God let them out. At VI the waters prevailed and at VIII the waters receded. The vertical parallelism between I and VII is also clear in that in I Noah was righteous and walked with God, and in VII the turn comes when God remembered Noah. This leaves III, IV, X, and XI, which form a particularly interesting feature, because the parallelisms are not horizontal but diagonal. This means that III is parallel with X, and IV is parallel with XI, thereby creating a cross in the middle of the ring. The reason is clearly because, whereas all the other sections deal with God and all life on earth, the four sections creating the cross are cultic rather than universal. Only in III is the number seven used of clean animals and birds, elsewhere it is two by two. Why is seven used there? It is because in the parallel Section X that Noah built an altar and made offerings. Had there only been two of a kind, he would have destroyed a species. Section IV reverts back to two by two and has Noah and his wife and sons and daughters-in-law all in the Ark with all living creatures. In XI God tells them to multiply and releases them from cultic vegetarianism and permits them to eat any of these creatures provided it is without its blood. This rather beautiful cross in the middle of the ring is therefore used to mark out the specifically cultic material from the ancient flood story with which they are combined in this very effective ring. The use of such a cross is found in the earliest Iranian poetry and Mawlānā uses it at the very beginning of the *Mathnawī*.

Once one has recovered the genre, it is possible to see both Noah and Numbers as beautifully integrated and structured works of considerable sophistication and elegance, but that is only synoptically. When read sequentially, ring composition and parallelism and the abrupt transitions required to mark the sections off from one another, can produce the very effect of disorder, repetition, randomness and incoherence about which their detractors complain. The message from this is that whenever a work of some significance is universally criticized for being badly constructed, it is probably because it is not being read correctly and its genre is not understood. Once Douglas had established the genre and the rhetorical structure, she was able then to lay bare the rationale of the whole book. Ring composition adds precision and fullness to the meaning of the words, and it recaptures the significance of the meanings through the provision of context and relatedness, thereby greatly enriching the reading and interpretation of the work.

The nonlinear relationship of correspondence between two segments of text in the genre just discussed is termed parallelism. It was first named thus in the eighteenth century and for long was regarded as a feature solely of Hebrew poetry, but it is now recognized as being almost universal in literatures throughout the world.[21] Parallelism is not a literary doctrine, simply the literary exploitation of correspondence, and, since there are many ways that literary elements can correspond—phonologically, lexically, semantically, and thematically, for example—the range of usage covered by the term is exceptionally wide. Thematic parallelism, sometimes aptly referred to as "thought rhyme,"[22] in its ideal form in Classical Hebrew poetry used to be described as the relationship between two elements of the kind: Given X, how much the more Y? Nowadays it is recognized that even in classical Hebrew literature, the second element can repeat, complete, affirm, contradict, develop, echo, mimic, pun, and so on, the first element, and that, in some cases, parallelism means little more than "and." It all depends on the case in point and the genre in which it is used. In a genre like the one discussed above, where the second half of a ring is at a higher level than the first as a result of some transforming crisis at the crux, then certainly it is often found that the second element has the sense of "how much the more." Countless examples of parallelism will be encountered from now on in this study, so it is not necessary to attempt to characterize its wide range of techniques at this juncture. More fruitful will be to consider the example of Psalm 67 in the Bible, which is given below.

Psalm 67

1 May God be gracious to us and bless us
And make his face to shine upon us,

2 That thy way may be known upon earth
Thy saving power among all nations

3 Let the peoples praise thee, O God;
Let all the peoples praise thee.

4 Let the nations be glad and sing for joy,
For thou dost judge the peoples with equity
And guide the nations upon earth.

5 Let the peoples praise thee, O God;
Let all the peoples praise thee.

6 The earth has yielded its increase;
God, our God, has blessed us.

7 God has blessed us;
Let all the ends of the earth fear him.

In this well-known psalm from the Revised Standard Version of the Bible, Verse 1 is in parallel with Verse 7, in that the first line of 1 is fulfilled in the first line of 7, and the second lines of each verse are respectively how we ask God to be toward us, and how we should be toward God. Verse 2 is in parallel with Verse 6 in that both are about the state of the earth: in the first how we pray it could be, in the second how it has become through God's blessing. Verses 3 and 5 are clearly in parallel by virtue of the repetition, but it moves from the earth to how the peoples should behave. Verse 4 is not in parallel with anything. This psalm not only illustrates parallelism, it also demonstrates the second literary feature being discussed here, chiasmus. Chiasmus is a replaying of a sequence but in reverse order, as for example. A, B, C, C*, B*, A*. The last three are the mirror image of the first three, but often at a higher level. In the Psalm above, the sequence is A, B, C, D, C*, B*, A*. This type of arrangement happens whenever there is an odd number of verses or elements in the sequence, and the tradition or convention is that, it is the middle element that contains the real inner content of the whole, the central message, which, in a sense, the other chiasmic and parallel elements simply frame and protect. In psalm 67 above, the two outermost verses are about God, the next two in are about the earth, and the next two in are about the peoples of the earth. In the middle Verse, 4, these three, God, the earth, and the peoples, are brought together in the central message that God is the totally fair judge who guides the peoples on the earth, for which they should be glad, but whom they should also fear. It is the central verse that introduces the main information, sums up what has gone before, and foreshadows and explains what is to come.

Chiasmus is a rhetorical scheme named after the Greek letter Chi, written as "X," which it resembles. There are many varieties and, as yet, the technical vocabulary for the different types has not become settled. Accordingly, throughout this study the terms "chiasmus" and "chiasmic" will be used to include all arrangements of this general nature without making further differentiations. Jacob Milgrom in his commentary on the book of Numbers insists that "chiasm," which he prefers to "chiasmus" used here, refers only to a pair of items that reverses itself, like the *ut tu*—that you—which occurs so frequently in Augustine's *Confessions.* When the series has more than two members, he uses the term "introversion." He argues that the two types must be distinguished because chiasm, with two members, is purely an aesthetic device, whereas introversion, with more than two members, can have didactic implications. He gives the example A, B, X, B*, A*, and points out, as has been seen above, "that the central member frequently contains the main point of the author, climaxing what precedes and anticipating what follows."[23] Another usage, at odds with Milgrom's, reserves "chiasmus" for only a particularly sophisticated chiasmic type, which has just been seen in the Noah story where there was a cross formed by diagonal parallelisms. These two usages for the term "chiasmus" illustrate the unsettled state of the terminology in what is, astonishingly after two and a half thousand years, a relatively new field of enquiry for most, and justifies the simplification proposed here.

This concludes the brief but necessary introduction to synoptic reading and the two literary conventions of parallelism and chiasmus. Examples have been given of both parallelism and chiasmus in action, and of a macro-compositional genre involving annular or ring composition. Ring composition, which is essentially no more than the outcome of the application of chiasmus and parallelism within certain conventions, has been used sparingly as a term because it has acquired associations largely with oral literature, whereas what has been considered here is too cultivated, developed and sophisticated to have arisen from either a bardic or a priestly need to have aids to memorization, or from the need in performance to mark the opening and the closure of digressions. On the contrary, what has been suggested here is that it was the transition from bardic and priestly repertoires, from which selections were made to suit the occasions of performance, to established and authorized versions of works, that is to say, the process of textualization, which led to the cultivation and development of these macro-compositional genres and conventions. Whatever their motivation, editors and compilers rather than authors and poets were responsible for the shape of many works that exist today. They brought together the ancient materials, doubtless adding some more that was new, and they organized it all in such a way that the text could be read sequentially quite innocently and meaningfully, if at times somewhat awkwardly, while synoptically, at the macro-compositional level, they embodied in the overall structuring the rationale of the work through the nonlinear patterning of significances. The rationale and patterning of significance was rarely ever neutral, since it was, in a sense, a commentary on the sequential material, and this provided the scope for a stance to be embodied, be it political, philosophical, moral, or religious. It was quite possible, for example, when textualizing an ancient epic about a war, to appear quite jingoistic at the sequential textual level, but to have, at a macro-compositional level, embodied within it a stance that proclaimed the futility of war and the irresponsibility of the gods and goddesses of the pantheon. Although an oversimplification, this probably, in fact, happened with regard to both the *Iliad* in Greece and the *Mahābhārata* in India, although much more work needs to be done for these hypotheses to be conclusive. But this is why it is appropriate to call the synoptic macro-compositional design of a work, its rhetorical structure.

Rhetorical Latency

There is a problem that all working in this field have to confront. In a short work, such as a psalm, it is not difficult to recognize its structure as one reads. In larger works, and especially very long works like epics, even though they are divided into separate books, it is not possible to grasp a macro-compositional structure of the kind described here through sequential reading, no matter how impressive one's memory span. The reason is that parallelism is nonlinear and requires the attention to be in two, often widely separated, places at the same time. The only way such a structure can be uncovered is by constant rereading or by mapping the whole work thematically, and then, by examining the map, to discern the patterns. The evidence of this is that these works have been read for sometimes as long as 2,000 years and only today are their structures being uncovered. If rhetoric is about persuasion, what is persuasive about an unseen and undetected structure?

Significant works were not, as today, read sequentially once, then finished with. Those who could read, would read and reread, study and reflect, and maybe memorize or meditate on such works, especially one by an author of prestige and authority. More and more of the parallels and correspondences would become apparent at every reading, and the analogies would have their effect, since analogies have implicit power to awaken the understanding and charge the microcosm with significance. These rhetorical structures can have power, not from the persuasiveness of the entailments of their logic, but from the potentially explosive implications of their analogies.

But there is another way to reach the rhetorical structure of a work of this kind: that is to know its style and genre, which would then inform the reader's expectations and awareness. If works such as the Homeric epics and the books of the Pentateuch were being structured by parallelism and chiasmus at a macro-compositional level, that is because there was, at the time, a prestigious and well-known genre and style within which the compilers were working. If it was known to them, it would be known to others who might read or listen to the works. All works have some kind of a plan, and the editors charged with the awesome responsibility of putting together the text of a Homeric epic or a sacred book of Hebrew scripture would plan it to the very highest standard possible, using the most appropriate and most prestigious style and genre available to them and to their contemporaries. The readers who recognized the genre and style would know the sort of thing to look for, but equally they would know they would not find it in a first sequential reading; rather, they would have to reread, reflect and ponder to reach the full depths and potency of the work.

Two Iranian Exemplars

Two Iranian works, at least 2,000 years apart, have now to receive attention. The first is a collection of seventeen poems, called *Gāthās* or hymns, by the poet-priest Zarathushtra (Greek, Zoroaster), who, in addition to being the eponymous founder of the Zoroastrian religion, must also be considered the earliest Iranian poet whose works are extant. Dating Zarathushtra is fraught with difficulty, but scholars currently consider around 1000 BCE to be the most plausible. But the problems do not end with dating, there are difficulties with the meaning of a number of words and therefore with the interpretation of some of the verses. But enough is understood with certainty for present purposes, and two scholars in particular have been responsible for discoveries that are of interest here, Hanns-Peter Schmidt and Martin Schwartz.[24]

It is thought that the Iranian peoples to whom Zarathushtra belonged were probably located somewhere in southern Central Asia. They had an established mature culture, part of which dated back to the even older Indo-Iranian culture that existed before the Indo-Aryans moved south into India. There were families of hereditary poet-priests who retained in their memories a corpus of hymns to a variety of deities which were performed, probably in a "re-created" form, in connection with the sacrificial fire cult. These cultic gatherings, it is known from Indian materials, included an agonistic element. The poet-priests had to compete one with another, certainly in poetry or hymn competitions, probably in theological and philosophical debates, and maybe in other ways too. What the poet-priests were competing for was essentially patronage. The princes and leaders, who were the potential patrons, looked for priests who could ensure them divine favors and poets who could make their names immortal. Zarathushtra was clearly a winner in this agonistic culture, but one cannot separate the priest from the poet. This was a preliterate society and the literary culture was oral, but it must not be thought primitive. It was mature, long-established and highly sophisticated, to the point that Schwartz refers in the title of one of his articles to the "outer limit of orality," so far had it been cultivated. In this very elaborate oral literature, Zarathushtra was a master, and he certainly made his patron's name immortal. As a priest, he attacked the reigning polytheism and introduced the dualism for which he has become famous. What matters here, however, is that, thanks to the labors of these two scholars, it is now realized that the organizing principles of the *Gāthās* of Zarathushtra were parallelism, ring composition, and chiasmus.

Unfortunately, there are only seventeen hymns extant in the corpus of the *Gāthās*, but of these only one is not organized by ring composition. Since the hymns are not very long, it is impossible to see how larger works might have been structured. Further, since the convention was of performance and the parallelisms had to be heard, many of them were phonological and lexical, although there is semantic parallelism as well. Despite these limitations, the principles of their structuring is clear. An illustration of the parallelism in Y.50 is provided in Schwartz's study.[25]

In all of the hymns, the central stanzas are the most significant and contain the main points. Schwartz, in his study, also gives in diagrammatic form the Gathic types of symmetrical compositions he discovered.[26] Two of these structures illustrate that type of chiasmus, discussed briefly above, where two sets of stanzas are in parallel diagonally and not horizontally, thereby forming a cross. To register such patterns while listening to an oral performance would require a wide attention span, and considerable experience of the genre. But the demands that Zarathushtra makes on his hearers did not stop there. Schwartz writes: "As I have tried to prove from attention to recurrences of lexic, semantic and phonic clusters, his poetry features not only ambiguous syntax, elaborate and subtle word-play, words within words, anagrammatic scrambles and symbolic alliteration, but even features, in connection with the word for 'bliss,' a preliterate acrostic and an elaborate theological symbolism of sound combination."[27]

So far attention has only been directed at the parallelism and chiasmic structure of these hymns individually, but Schwartz further demonstrates that there are similar correspondences and relationships *between* hymns, so that there is intertextual parallelism and chiasmus. He writes of "the striking technique of composition based on a stanza-by-stanza recasting of material of an earlier of the poet's hymns *remembered backwards*, whereby the bulk of hymn Y.32 derives from Y.46, and Y.32 in its own turn produces, again through reversed recollection, the basis of Y.48."[28] This technique foreshadows a similar situation with regard to some of the books of the Pentateuch, where one book can be a guide to reading another as Douglas demonstrates with regard to the book of Genesis and the book of Numbers.[29]

A recent scholarly study by Almut Hintze of the literary structure of the *Older Avesta* is persuasive that the entire *Older Avesta* is structured by ring composition, that is, by parallelism and chiasmus.[30] She demonstrates its structural design and unity, and argues that the totality might well, therefore, be the work of a single person, namely Zarathushtra. This is interesting because it moves the situation away from oral hymn competitions, the context in which Zarathushtra no doubt won his spurs and attracted his patrons, to a more settled courtly environment in which he was, say, the chief priest, and was able to develop his work, through a process not dissimilar to that of textualization, by establishing a unified liturgical corpus for worship. When, in later times, more texts were added, they retained, at the exact central point of the enlarged *Yasna*, the self-same text which Zarathushtra had placed at the center of the liturgical corpus of the *Older Avesta*, and which he had most probably composed. What matters here, however, is that the various scholarship just reviewed has demonstrated that the literary styles and conventions of ring composition, of parallelism, and of chiasmus, were not simply present in the poetry of Zarathushtra, the first Iranian poet whose works are extant, to a large extent they constituted it.

The second Iranian exemplar is the *Haft Paykar*, a work by Nizāmī Ganjawī (1140–1202 CE), which was completed about four years before his death. Since this work also exemplifies ring composition and the two principles of parallelism and chiasmus, the question naturally arises as to what happened to these features in Iranian and Persian literature in the two thousand years between the *Older Avesta* and the *Haft Paykar*. The answer is that noone knows, quite simply because, as far as one can tell, nobody has looked. As has been shown again and again above, works so structured do not announce it to the world; the rhetorical structure remains latent, unperceived. It requires an eye experienced in these texts, that knows what clues to look for, and a persistence amounting to obsession. It also, crucially, requires edited texts that are faithful to their authors' original versions. Given all this, the Pahlavi books in Middle Persian are an obvious first place to look, and then the Mirrors for Princes in classical Persian, since they have always operated by analogy. But these questions are for other to solve; in the case of the *Haft Paykar* the identification of the structural principles has already been made by Meisami in her excellent study of Persian court poetry.[31] In the chapter on romance as mirror, she provides a diagram showing the rhetorical structure of the work, to which the reader is now referred.[32]

Meisami's analysis identifies three structuring principles in the work which is itself designed to reflect the design of the cosmos. The first is the linear pattern showing the movement through time and space. The second is alternation, just as in the book of Numbers, although here the alternation is between Kingship and Adventure whereas, there, it was between Law and Story. The alternation overrides the section divisions: some alternate segments contain several sections, and Section 52 contains two alternating segments. There is further alternation in the seven tales, although here it is between the moral faculties of concupiscence and irascibility as dominant motivating impulses for the action. As in the usage in Hebrew texts, the convention has no regard to proportionality, in that a short segment of text can alternate, or be in parallel with, a very long one. The third structuring principle is ring composition, with the circle, the symbol of eternity, being the overall unifying pattern of the whole poem.

Meisami draws attention to how these structural patterns "evoke spatial and numerical symbologies echoed throughout the poem."[33] She shows how Nizāmī, with his references to lines and points and circles and spatial configurations, follows Sanā'ī in affirming "the principle that 'intellectual geometry' provides the means of passing from material to spiritual understanding, which can lead to the understanding of human justice and divine wisdom."[34] Coupled with geometry in the King's education is astronomy, "whose purpose is to purify the soul and instill in it the desire for celestial ascent."[35] Astrology also plays an important part throughout the poem, but, as in many medieval works, the primary symbology is that of number, to which Meisami rightly devotes particular attention: "Like the created universe itself, the Haft Paykar is a work of art through which knowledge of the Creator may be achieved through the truth of number."[36]

No more need be said here about the *Haft Paykar* because Meisami's excellent translation, analysis and appreciation of the poem, which is both detailed and perceptive, is readily accessible. There is, however, one larger matter which does need to be discussed. Both Meisami, in the context of medieval Persian court poetry, and Douglas, in the context of Leviticus, address the question of analogical thinking. Douglas devotes an entire chapter to the subject, differentiating between the rational ordering deriving from Aristotelian logic, with which the West is familiar, and the "correlative," "aesthetic," or analogical ordering, such as, for example, is found in Han cosmology in China, which is neither based on dialectical principles of noncontradiction nor on the linear sequence of the syllogism, but rather on analogical association. Both authors refer to the microcosm/macrocosm as the primary exemplar of analogical thought, and both argue that it was the analogical mode of thinking which led to the development of the rhetoric and poetics of analogy, with its extensive use of parallelism and correspondence. Both authors are replete with examples and rich references for readers who wish to pursue this topic. Meisami's entire study is based on the proposition that medieval court literature in Persian was through and through founded on the poetics of analogy, and her various chapters illustrate this within the different genres.

The poetry of Nizāmī Ganjawī has brought to an end this long excursus into ring composition, parallelism, and chiasmus, which has crossed 2,000 years and touched on numerous exemplars, and finally leads back to Mawlānā. It will be recalled that when Mawlānā's father, Bahā al-Dīn, had completed the pilgrimage he went to Malatya in eastern Anatolia where he found a patron in 'Ismati Khātūn, the wife of Fakhr al-Dīn Bahrāmshāh, the Prince of Erzincan. It was under Fakhr al-Dīn's patronage that the poet Nizāmī of Ganja (1141–1209) had written his didactic spiritual *mathnawī*, the *Makhzan al-*

Asrār, the Treasury of Secrets, a connection that cannot have failed to be made known to Mawlānā's family during their four-year stay in Akshahr. Doubtless this family association resulted in Mawlānā feeling an indirect but personal attachment to the works of Nizāmī, of which he was known to be fond. Whether or not Nizāmī was the sole source of the usage of parallelism and chiasmus by Mawlānā, or whether similar usages are to be found in the works of Sanā'ī and 'Aṭṭār, remains to be seen when the textual position of these last two poets becomes more certain. For the moment, Nizāmī can provide a temporary answer to the question of immediate origins, with the *Haft Paykar* discussed above displaying a number of important literary features that were to occur again in the *Mathnawī*.

The Synoptic Reading of Book One of the *Mathnawī*

The next chapter, Chapter 3, gives a synoptic reading of the whole of Book One. This serves a number of purposes, the primary one of which is to produce a reader's guide to a text in which it is all too easy to lose one's way. Experience suggests this is necessary for those already familiar with the *Mathnawī* as well as for those coming newly to it. A second purpose concerns the structure and inner organization of the work, which Mawlānā has hidden so successfully, as is apparent from the survey of scholarly comment given earlier. The only way to show conclusively that the structure identified is truly there in Mawlānā's own words and poetry and not some analyst's theoretical construct projected on to it, is to demonstrate it throughout the text. This has the additional benefit of revealing an unsuspected aspect of Mawlānā's poetic craftsmanship. But the overall purpose is to remove those obstacles which can prevent readers from having a full exposure to the experiences Mawlānā has embodied in the design of his spiritual masterpiece to advance their inner progress. Before embarking on the next chapter some explanation is necessary as to both the form and nature of what is presented there and also of the spiritual context of Book One.

The reader will find in Chapter 3 a complete summary of Book One, the identification of the separate discourses, as well as a detailed structural analysis and an interpretation of each discourse. Each section of verses, that is, those occurring between two headings, has been divided up into paragraphs—groups of thematically linked verses—and summarized in English. A paragraph is not a formal unit but a subjective analytical construct that permits a thematic mapping of each section. It is possible that other people would have established different paragraphs, but this does not matter provided that the thematic mapping is more or less the same. Each verse has been read in both Persian and in Nicholson's English translation, usually many times. Commentaries have been consulted to ensure the meaning and references have been understood, and limited notes have been included as part of the reader's guide, but in no sense is this a full commentary.

The sections are grouped into what is believed to be Mawlānā's own discourse divisions. These divisions are arrived at by combining narrative and thematic unity with a new criterion of structural unity, since it soon becomes clear that Mawlānā has given his discourses distinctive spatial and architectural configurations that can be recognized. These are structures of sections, varying in shape and form, each producing its own internal relationships between sections, always using parallelism and chiasmus, but in many different ways. Sometimes Mawlānā uses blocks of sections, for instance, with parallelism and chiasmus internal to a block but not across blocks; at other times he runs the parallelism and chiasmus across blocks of sections. In this spatial and structural organization Mawlānā shows great versatility and variety, producing structures of great beauty, elaboration, and symmetry. Whether a discourse was identified through its narrative or thematic unity first, or by its structural unity, is immaterial; what matters is that they should coincide. The combination provides a double check on the validity of the discourse divisions. The analysis identifies twelve discrete discourses and three link sections.

After the summary of the sections in a discourse, there is an analysis of the structure of the discourse in which all of the parallelisms between sections are identified and discussed. As with the spatial shapes of the discourses, Mawlānā shows great variety in his use of parallelism: sometimes the second section completes the first, sometimes it shows an analogous situation, sometimes it produces the opposite of the first, sometimes the parallelism is that both sections are in the form of question and answer, sometimes it is verbal or the same person is being spoken about. While not at odds with the high seriousness of the work, there is about the parallelism a lighter note, as if, in this hidden realm which he rightly anticipated few would penetrate, he was able to give free rein to his creativity and enjoy himself unseen. Sometimes, alongside the primary parallelisms of the main structure, there are secondary parallelisms, which have been noted where they are recognized. Tertiary parallelisms, such as images that recur in several sections, are more stylistic than structural and have not been recorded. The analysis also discusses the use of blocks of sections within the overall structure of a discourse, and the way in which chiasmus is utilized.

After the analysis, which is largely structural and thematic, there comes what is perhaps overambitiously called an interpretation. Space does not permit giving a full interpretation of every discourse, even if such a thing were possible for any one person, given the open-ended nature of analogy. No one interpretation can conceivably be sufficient. But what these rhetorical structures do, is to define significances and to distribute emphases. Each discourse has its own rationale, often apparent in the design of the discourse. It is hoped that the so-called interpretations will give at least the salient points of the discourse's rationale as revealed by the analysis. It must be for others of greater spiritual awareness and erudition to give a full account of the implications of these extraordinary discourse structures. What is given here are no more than preliminary pointers to what such an interpretation might contain. As they stand, the interpretations included here in all too brief a form are themselves condensations of many pages in which the views of various commentators are recorded and attempts are made to match these to the newly emerged rhetorical design.

At the beginning of each discourse, comes a diagrammatic representation of the discourse in question. Great importance is attached to these visual representations since they really do permit a synoptic view of the whole discourse, showing the total rhetorical and thematic structure, the relationships that pertain and the processes at work. To read the *Mathnawī* is to journey along the spiritual path. For such a journey, travelers need a map to see where they are, especially with regard to the total geography of the area. Such is provided by these synoptic diagrammatic representations of the discourses.

This, then, is the nature, form, and purpose of what is to come in the synoptic reading of the next chapter, but what is the spiritual context and content? The overall subject of Book One is the *nafs*, translated here as the selfhood and elsewhere variously as the fleshy soul or the ego.[37] Broadly, Mawlānā means by *nafs* in much of this book, the body with its desires and appetites and its animal nature, which, coupled with egoism, constitutes the major obstacle to any kind of spiritual progress. In order to make spiritual progress, the *nafs* needs to be transformed, although it is almost impossible to transform one's own *nafs* without help: help from God, the Universal Intellect or from Love, help from the prophets and saints, the friends of God, or from a shaykh or *pir*, a spiritual guide. Following the Qur'ān, the Sufis often refer to three stages in the transformation of the *nafs*: the *nafs-e ammārah*, the selfhood that commands to evil, is the starting point, then comes the *nafs-e lawwāmah*, the selfhood that blames itself, until finally one reaches the *nafs-e muṭma'innah*, the selfhood at peace with God. The spiritual path which Mawlānā traces in Book One is broadly the progressive transformation of the selfhood, the *nafs*, following this tripartite division.

The *nafs* as the selfhood stands in contrast to the *rūḥ*, the spirit. The spirit comes down from the spiritual world at the Command of God and its coexistence with the selfhood, the *nafs*, within a human person, constitutes the human spiritual dilemma. This is often expressed by the image of the *nafs* being form and the *rūḥ*, the spirit, meaning; sometimes this image is accompanied by the proverb that things are made clear by the opposites. It is the spirit that animates a person at all levels and one of its attributes is *'aql*, intellect, intelligence, the property of discernment that can distinguish good from evil, for example. Within an untransformed human being the *'aql* is manifested as discursive reason, but because of the clouds and clutter of the *nafs*, it is limited in its view of Reality and is often referred to as the *'aql-e juzwī*, the partial intellect. When a transformation of the *nafs* has taken place, the *'aql* is informed by the *'aql-e kullī*, Universal Reason or Universal Intellect, and then has direct access to Reality and the spiritual world, as well as the overwhelming experience of Love. Love and the powers of the Universal Intellect, the *'aql-e kullī*, have the ability to order and transform the selfhood, the *nafs*.

There is one other spiritual component of a human being, the heart, which is the very center of one's spiritual consciousness. The heart is neither the same as the physical heart, although it is located level with it but in the center of the chest, nor the same as the reacting emotions, which are experienced mainly in the solar plexus. Spiritual transformation in Sufism requires the awakening, purging, and purification of the heart, emptying it of all that is other than God's, so that it can become the unsullied mirror that reflects back the Beauty of God. It is the purified and awakened heart that can have a direct contact with Reality since it has an eye, the eye of the heart, which receives from the Universal Intellect.

This brief and somewhat oversimplified picture of the human spiritual situation should be sufficient to contextualize what is to follow.[38] The spirit comes from God and longs to return to God from the prison of this world. This is Mawlānā's starting point and the beginning of the spiritual traveler's journey. In order that the first contact should be with Mawlānā, it is recommended at this point that the reader reads the first 247 verses of the *Mathnawī*, either in the original Persian or in one of the English verse translations, before beginning Chapter 3.

Chapter Three

A Synoptic Reading of Book One of the *Mathnawī*

The Arabic Preface
The Proem (verses 1–35)

Discourse One	The Story of the King and the Handmaiden (36–246)
Link Section	The Greengrocer and the Parrot (247–323)
Discourse Two	The Jewish King Who Used to Slay Christians (324–738)
Discourse Three	The Story of the Second Jewish King (739–899)
Discourse Four	The Story of the Lion and the Beasts (900–1389)
Discourse Five	The Story of the Ambassador of Rum (1390–1546)
Discourse Six	The Story of the Merchant and the Parrot (1547–1877)
Central Link Section	"Whatever God Wills, Comes to Pass" (1878–1912)
Discourse Seven	The Story of the Old Harper (1913–2222)
Link Section	The Prayer of the Two Angels (2223–2243)
Discourse Eight	The Story of the Bedouin and His Wife (2244–3012)
Discourse Nine	The Story of the Lion, the Wolf, and the Fox (3013–3149)
Discourse Ten	The Story of Joseph and the Mirror (3150–3499)
Discourse Eleven	The Story of Zayd's Vision (3450–3720)
Discourse Twelve	The Story of 'Alī and the Infidel Knight (3721–4003)

The Preface

Summary

The *Mathnawī* is the roots of the roots of the roots of the Religion with regard to the unveiling of Truth and certainty, which is the greatest science of God. It is more brilliant than the sunrise and spiritual travelers consider it a Paradise for hearts, and the mystically developed and those blessed by Grace consider it the best spiritual resting place on the Path. In it, the righteous and the long-suffering can eat, drink, and be joyful, but to the unrighteous and the unbelieving it offers only grief. It is a curer of souls, a reliever of sorrows, an expounder of the Qur'ān, a giver of generous gifts, and a cleanser of dispositions. Because God observes it and watches over it, falsehood cannot approach it. Muḥammad ibn Muḥammad ibn al-Ḥusayn of Balkh declares that: I have labored to compose this Poem in rhymed couplets, which incorporates unusual stories, rare sayings, valuable discourses and precious indications, which traces the path of ascetics and offers a garden for devotees, and which, though brief in expression, is rich in meaning, at the request of my master, the inestimable Shaykh Ḥusām al-Dīn Ḥasan ibn Muḥammad ibn al-Ḥasan, whose lineage is of great spiritual excellence. May it ever be thus. Amen. Glory be to God and blessings on Muḥammad and his pure and noble kin.

Comment

The very first sentence is much discussed in the various commentaries, and the consensus view is that the last of the roots, that is, the ones least deep, refer to theology; religious law and exegesis, and so on; the sciences of Islam; and that this level, the literal level, broadly represents the *Sharī'ah*, the clear broad path to a watering place that is used to refer to the canon law of Islam. The second level, the intermediate roots, are taken to refer to the inner level representing the *Ṭarīqah*, the level of Sufism, the narrower path of the *sālik*, the spiritual traveler. Finally the deepest roots are the level of *Ḥaqīqah*, Reality, the watering place itself. Nicholson, perhaps influenced by his observation that in one key manuscript, one of the "roots," the least deep, is added by another hand, in his commentary treats only of two levels, the outer, "theological" level and the inner Sufi mystical level.[1] This is unfortunate because, while Nicholson's commentary on this Preface is both perceptive and illuminating, particularly on the relationship with the Qur'ān, it leads him to equate Ḥusām al-Dīn, who has to be taken as representing the highest station on the Sufi path, with Shams, who is represented much more as belonging to the deepest level of *Ḥaqīqah*, Reality. The evidence for this comes very early on in the *Mathnawī*, in a conversation between Mawlānā and Ḥusām al-Dīn on the subject of Shams (Book One, verses 125–143), in which it is clear that they are on two quite different levels; indeed, the difference is almost portrayed as that between the Sufi shaykh and God, the Friend. Although Nicholson conflates the three levels into two in his commentary, his edition of the text and his translation both have three levels of roots. Ḥusām al-Dīn, as the inspiration for Mawlānā's writing the work, is praised as an excellent Sufi shaykh, but in relatively modest terms for the genre.

Proem (35 lines)

Summary

Listen to the reed pipe (*nay*) as it tells its story, complaining of separation, saying: "Ever since I was taken from the reed-bed my lament has caused men and women to moan. I need a heart torn by separation to which I can unfold the pain of love. Everyone taken from their source wishes back the time of their unity, so everyone to whom I uttered my lament, happy and unhappy, became my friend but for their own reasons, not for my secret, which is not far from my lament in fact, but is still un-apprehended like the soul. The noise of the reed is fire, the fire of love, for the reed is the comrade of all parted lovers; it is both poison and antidote, both sympathizer and longing lover. It tells of the Way, full of blood, and of the passion of Majnūn, but only the senseless can apprehend; the tongue has no customer save the ear. Our days have passed in burning sorrow; but let them go. Only You remain, Who alone are holy, but whoever is not a fish becomes sated with Your Water. None that is raw understands the ripe, so I shall be brief. Farewell.

Oh son, how long will you be in bondage to gold and silver? The eye of the covetous is never satisfied. Only he who is rent by a mighty love is purged from covetousness and all defects. Hail, O Love that brings us good gain—you that are the physician of all our ills, the remedy of our pride and vainglory, our Plato and our Galen! Through Love the earthly body soars aloft, the mountain began to dance and Mount Sinai became drunk. Were I not parted from one who speaks my language, I could tell all. The Beloved is all, the lover a veil; the Beloved living, the lover dead. When Love has no care for him he is helpless. Love wills the Word should be known, but the mirror of the soul does not reflect it because the rust is not cleared from its face. Hear then this story which is the essence of our inner state.

Commentary

These thirty-five verses are much commented on, and deservedly so, because they must be one of the most beautiful and striking openings to any mystical work.[2] Indeed, the mystical poet Jāmī comments only on these verses out of the entire *Mathnawī*. Technically this proem, or at least the first eighteen verses, resembles and functions as a *nasīb*, the exordium of a *qaṣīda* (purpose-poem or elegy), which sets the tone or "establishes the value system relative to which the poem as a whole must be interpreted."[3] In the *nasīb* the poet often "complains of the force of his passion, the pain of separation, and the excessiveness of his longing and desire, so as to incline hearts towards him and attract interest, and gain an attentive hearing."[4] While it perhaps goes too far to suggest, as some have, that the *nasīb* "generates" the meaning of the whole poem, certainly it usually foreshadows what is to come, and is often linked to the poem that follows by thematic parallelism. A similar usage is illustrated here by the verse quoted above about Love as the physician of all our ills, which foreshadows the first discourse in which a Divine doctor appears who solves the problem presented. As for setting the tone, certainly the proem establishes the two main perspectives from which it is written: first, in the first eighteen lines, like the *rūḥ*, spirit, descending '*az bālā*' from above, *sub specie aeternitatis*, from the viewpoint of eternity; second, in the remaining seventeen verses, that of a Sufi shaykh who is himself both an adept and an experienced spiritual director addressing a novice who seeks to re-ascend on the Sufi path. The proem also establishes the peculiar spiritual situation that humankind finds itself in, and, above all else, the centrality of Love, which further serves to identify and define Mawlānā's particular path. The proem, then, acts as a *nasīb*, which might have been a suggestive model.

The principal issue for commentators has been what or who is symbolized by the '*nay*,' most accepting that it symbolizes a *rūḥ*, spirit, sent down through the various level of being into a human person, which longs to return to its preexistent state and close relationship with God, the Beloved, and whose plaintive notes are expressive of this yearning and the pain of love in separation. As to the question of whose spirit is intended, the change found in manuscripts of the second word of the text from '*īn*' (this) in the earliest manuscript to '*az*' (to) in later manuscripts, which avoids a specific identification with the author and leaves the identity nonspecified, assuming it was made by Mawlānā himself, means it was to be deliberately left open. Accordingly it could be the spirit of a *walī*, a saint or friend of God, of a shaykh, the Perfect Man, Ḥusām al-Dīn, or Mawlānā himself: that is, any spirit which fits for the readers or hearers in question, *including their own*, since the implication must be that if people could but see it consciously, every spirit is lamenting its separation and is yearning to return to its origin in God. At another level, however, what it is the hearers are requested to listen to is the *Mathnawī* itself, composed by Mawlānā, which stands in analogical relationship with the *nay* and its lament.

What none of the commentators have mentioned, however, is that these verses need to be read synoptically as well as sequentially. There are strong reasons for claiming this. The first reason is that Mawlānā has made a clear break after Verse 18, approximately the midpoint, at which point there is a change of addressee, perspective, and voice. Hence the Proem is in two nearly equal halves. The number 18 has a special significance for Mawlānā and the Mevlevi Order, so the number of verses in the second part had to be less than this in order not to challenge the sacred completeness of the first eighteen verses.[5] The second reason is that lines 1 and 35, the first and the last verses, are in parallel in that they both contain the words "listen" and "story." The third reason is what happens in the middle. The four lines either side of the midpoint form two sets of four verses in contrastive parallelism. The set that completes the first half describes the problem of the adept, the "*pokhtah*" (cooked, mature, transformed), which is permanent grief and burning longing, whereas the set that begins the second half is addressed to "son," the raw, inexperienced, undeveloped novice, whose problem is enslavement to wealth and covetousness. The image of water and the sea further relates both sets, since the adept always wants more of the water of God's grace, while the eye of the covetous is never satisfied since it is like a pitcher into which the sea is poured but can only hold so much. To the adept, Love is the cause of grief; to the novice Love is the solution to his covetousness. The fourth reason is that, to these very clear, almost formal, parallelisms, can be added lines 10 and 27, both nine verses from the midpoint in their respective halves. In Verse 10 *'ishq*. Love, the main theme of the second half, appears for the first time as the fire that is in the *nay*, while in parallel Verse 27, Mawlānā as *'āshiq*, lover, would reveal all, like the *nay*, the main theme of the first half, if only there were someone who could understand him. The fifth reason requires a diagrammatic representation to demonstrate.

Below, in fig. 3.1, the two halves are represented by two vertical parallel lines, with Verse 1 at the top left and Verse 35 top right. As has been shown, these two verses are linked by formal lexical parallelism as well as being the beginning and the end of the proem respectively. The bottom four verses of each column are similarly formally joined in parallel, and now there are Verses 10 and 27, which interconnect both halves with one another at the middle. To these parallelisms, it is now necessary to add two more, between the set of three Verses 2–4 and the set 30–32, and between the set 5–7 and the set 33–35. The reason for doing this is because, after the first line of the Proem, the next six, 2–7 are the reed's own complaint: three verses, 2–4, about wishing to return to its origin from which it was torn, and three verses, 5–7, about the lack of interest, in whatever company, in seeking the reed's secret. On the other side, the proem ends with six verses which also constitute two sets of three. The first set, Verses 30–32, introduce, for the first time, the Beloved, beside whom and without whom the lover is nothing. The final set of three, 33–35 speak of Love willing that this word be made known, but the mirror of the addressee (novice/hearer/representative human-being) is rusty and cannot reflect. There are two parallelisms here, the first is that the origin of the *nay*, for which it yearns, is the Beloved; the second that this word which Love wills to be made known is the unsought secret of the *nay*. These two sets of three verses on either side are in diagonal parallelism and form a chiasmic cross. In this way the parallels across the divide answer the questions raised: What is the origin of the *nay*? The Beloved. Why don't people seek the *nay*'s secrets? Because their hearts are like rusty mirrors. To read the proem again knowing Mawlānā's rhetorical structure, adds to the significance of what is said. But that one can do for oneself.

The synoptic view of the proem just given reveals clear use of parallelism and chiasmus of the most sophisticated kind within a beautifully integrated

Fig. 3.1. The Rhetorical Structure of the Proem

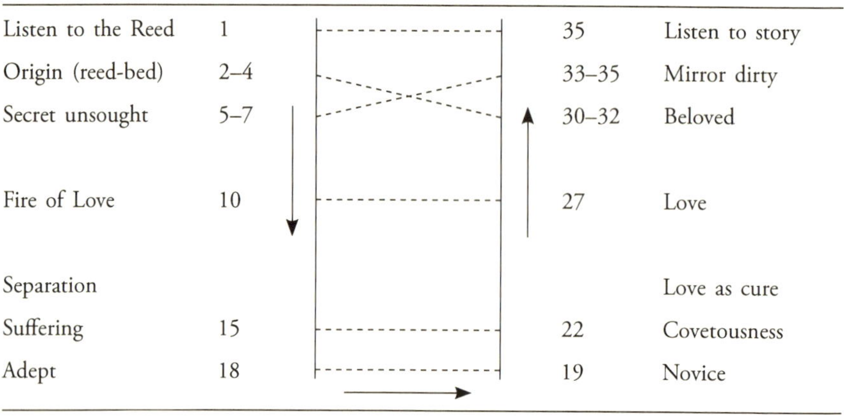

ring composition. It was to have been expected that Mawlānā would somehow indirectly indicate how the *Mathnawī* was to be read at the outset of the poem, and now it has been shown that he did. The proem reads well sequentially so the rhetorical structure remains latent, hidden yet potent. The technical brilliance of Mawlānā lies in his integration of the sequential and the synoptic to give the total effect. There is an obvious analogy between the story of the *nay* and the writing of the *Mathnawī*, and the *nay* has a secret that is in fact "not far from its lament." Is this a hint given by Mawlānā that the *Mathnawī* too has secrets which are also not far from the text? Hearing or reading the proem, and reflecting on its shape and analogical structure, must have made clear to alert and responsive hearers and readers alike just what Mawlānā was likely to do in the main body of the poem itself.

Discourse One:
The Story of the King and the Handmaiden

Summary of the Narrative and Thematic Content

SECTION 1 36–54 (19) *The story of a king falling in love with a handmaiden and buying her.* (a) [36–39] There was a king of both temporal and spiritual power out hunting who saw and fell in love with a handmaiden, whom he then bought. (b) [40–50] Through Destiny or bad luck (*qaḍā*) she fell ill; if things can go wrong, they will. The desperate king turned to doctors who said they would use their intelligence (*'aql*) but, in their arrogance, they didn't say: "If God Wills"—not that just saying it is any use if your heart is

Fig. 3.2. A Synoptic View of Discourse One

Sec. 1	King falls in love and buys girl who falls ill and doctors can't cure
Sec. 2	King prays and is told in dream of the coming of a Divine Doctor
Sec. 3	May God make our behavior seemly and avert unseemliness
Sec. 4	King greets the Doctor who knows all our secrets and solves problems
Sec. 5	Doctor diagnoses love, love human and divine; Shams, Ḥusām al-Dīn
Sec. 6	Doctor examines girl, learns her secret and promises not to tell anyone
Sec. 7	Doctor tells king to beguile goldsmith with gold and robes of honor
Sec. 8	Girl wedded to goldsmith who is then poisoned; he dies, girl set free
Sec. 9	The man was slain by Divine Command, not greed; no crime; analogy

not in it—and so their cures didn't work. (c) [51–54] Through bad luck or Destiny, she gets worse.

SECTION 2 55–77 (23) *How it became obvious to the king that the physicians were unable to cure the handmaiden, and how he turned his face to God and dreamed of a holy man.* (a) [55–60] The king, seeing they were useless, went to the mosque and wept copiously. Coming out of *fanā* (here an intense state or unconsciousness) he prayed to God for help. (b) [61–65] He cried out from the bottom of his soul and while weeping he fell asleep and in a dream was told his prayers were answered and a Divine physician would come next day from God whose remedy was absolute magic. (c) [66–77] The stranger arrived the next day, as a phantom (*khayāl*), and the king himself went to meet him and greet this guest from the Invisible. Their souls swam together and the king told him that it was he, not the girl, who was his beloved in reality, although in this world deed issued from deed; he was to the king as Muḥammad and the king pledged to serve him as ʿUmar served Muḥammad.

SECTION 3 78–92 (15) *Beseeching the Lord who is our Helper to help us to observe self-control in all circumstances, and explaining the harmful and pernicious consequences of indiscipline.* (a) [78–79] Prayer to God to help us to exercise self-control (*adab* = seemliness) since there is danger to all from one who is without *adab.* (b) [80–87] A table of food came down from heaven without its recipients' efforts, but the people of Moses demanded garlic and lentils as well, so it was withdrawn. Then Jesus made intercession and God again sent sustenance, which again was withdrawn because of irreverence and greed and insolence. Showing suspicion, greed, and ingratitude at the Lord's table closed their gate to Divine Mercy. (c) [88–92] Withholding the poor-tax produces drought; fornication, the plague; whatever grief befalls is the consequence of irreverence and insolence, and he who shows irreverence in the path of the Friend is a robber and no man. Through *adab* heaven filled with light and the angels became holy, but through irreverence Iblīs (Satan) was turned back at the door.

SECTION 4 93–100 (8) *The meeting of the king with the divine physician whose coming had been announced to him in a dream.* (a) [93–100] The king received him like love into his heart, and questioned him about his home and the journey. The king said he had obtained a treasure by being patient, hailing him as a gift from God, and the meaning of "Patience Is the Key to Joy." His face is the answer to every question and problems are solved without discussion. He can interpret what is in the heart and helps all sufferers. The King welcomed him as the chosen one, the approved one, who is the protector of people, and those who do not seek him, go to perdition.

SECTION 5 101–143 (43) *How the king led the physician to the bedside of the sick girl to see her condition.* (a) [101–109] The king took him to the girl whom he examined. He said the remedies prescribed would not have worked but were themselves destructive. He saw her pain was because she was heartsick from being in love, but he did not tell the king. (b) [110–115] Love's ailment is separate from other ailments, since Love is the astrolabe of God's mysteries. Love human and Divine, both lead us yonder. Any explanation is inadequate; intelligence is helpless; only Love itself can explain love and lover-hood. (c) [116–123] The sun is proof of the sun; but what of the spiritual Sun. It is peerless, beyond imagination; when Shams was heard of, the sun of the 4th heaven hid its face. (d) [124–143] This is a conversation, seemingly between Mawlānā and Ḥusām al-Dīn, who asks Mawlānā to tell him of the ecstasies he enjoyed with Shams. Mawlānā says he is still out of himself and they are indescribable; so please leave it for now. Ḥusām al-Dīn says: "I am hungry, feed me now; Sufis do not say tomorrow." Mawlānā replies it is better the secrets of the Friend are not divulged but disguised and told, as in this story, through the words of others. Ḥusām al-Dīn says: "No, tell it openly." Mawlānā says if God revealed Himself "openly," that would be the end of him. If the Sun gets too near the earth, all will be consumed. Do not seek trouble and turmoil and bloodshed; speak no more of Shams. Let's return to the story.

SECTION 6 144–181 (38) *How the saint demanded of the king to be alone with her to discover her malady.* (a) [144–145] The physician makes sure the house is empty of all but he and the girl. (b) [146–157] He puts his hand on her pulse and gently questions her. If a thorn in the foot is hard to find, a thorn in the heart is harder. When a thorn is stuck into a donkey, it jumps. The physician, thorn-remover, was an expert. (c) [158–169] In his questioning about home and friends, he came to Samarqand and she jumped, from which eventually he learned that she had been parted from a goldsmith there and that was the cause of her grief and woe. (d) [170–181] He told her he knew her secret and would perform magic, but she was not to tell anyone, since you attain your desire more quickly through not speaking about it. His promises and soothing words set her free from worry. There are true promises and false promises, one is sterling coin, the other leads to anguish.

SECTION 7 182–184 (3) *How the saint told the king the diagnosis.* (a) [182–184] The physician advised the King to bring the goldsmith there as a cure, and to beguile him with gold and robes of honor.

SECTION 8 185–221 (37) *How the king sent messengers to Samarqand to fetch the goldsmith.* (a) [185–196] Two messengers lured the goldsmith with gold and robes of honor and greed brought him to the King, little realizing what lay in store for him. (b) [197–201] The King honored him, and on the advice of the physician, wedded him to the handmaiden who was fully restored to health after six months. (c) [202–215] Then the goldsmith was gradually poisoned so that he began to lose his beauty, then became ugly, and little by little she ceased to like him. The peacock's plumage is its enemy. He called out that he was a victim, who was killed for something other than himself, and his blood would be avenged. (d) [216–221] He dies and the girl was purged of pain and love, because love for the dead does not endure. Choose the love of the Living One and approach the King. Do not say, "We have no admission to that King." Dealings with the generous are not difficult.

SECTION 9 222–246 (25) *How the slaying and poisoning of the goldsmith was at Divine suggestion not from sensual desire and wicked thinking.* (a) [222–246] This man was slain, not for hope or fear; the physician waited till the Divine command came. If one who gives spiritual life should slay, it is allowed. It was not a crime. The king was a good king and elect of God. He takes half a life and gives a hundred. Do not give judgment by analogy with yourself. Consider well.

Analysis of Discourse One

This discourse occupies the first nine sections of Book One, which form a unity both narratively and thematically. Only Section 3 on the subject of seemliness and unseemliness (*adab* and *bi-adabī*) is purely homiletic; the other sections in some way either advance the narrative or, in the case of Section 9, justify it. Because the narrative develops sequentially there is no need at the end of a section for specific foreshadowing of the next, although each section has been narratively prepared for. The entire story, however, has been foreshadowed in the Proem, particularly in last seventeen verses of the Proem, and specifically in Verses 22–24, where Love is hailed as the true physician.

Analysis of the discourse shows both chiasmus and thematic parallelism. The overall structure is in the form ABCDEDCBA, with the inner emphasis being given to E, that is, Section 5, which is also the longest. The parallelism between Section 1 and Section 9 lies, first, in that Section 1 provides the setting that begins the story and Section 9 the conclusion that completes the story; second, Section 1 begins with the king and the last section, Section 9, ends with the king, although the king here could be God or the Perfect Man (*insān-e kāmil*), so this parallelism could be considered developmental; third, the contrastive use of *qaḍā* in 1 where it just means bad luck or chance, with, in 9, action brought about by Divine inspiration and command; finally, there is a contrastive parallelism between the doctors who fail, symbolic of partial intelligence (*'aql-e juzwī*), with the doctor who succeeds, symbolic of Universal Intelligence, (*'aql-e kullī*). The parallelism between Sections 2 and 8 is that of fulfillment, because in 2 the Divine physician is described as one whose remedy is magic and in whom there was the Might of God and in Section 8 we find this promise being fulfilled. Additionally, the first lines of Section 2 are about the king turning to God for help with tears and the last lines of 8 are about choosing to love the Living One and "Do not say we have no admission to that King. Dealings with the generous are not difficult." The parallelism between Section 3 and Section 7 is that 3 introduces the need for self-control, *adab*, especially over greed, and the dangers of its absence *bī-adabī*, and warns that awful things are due to irreverence and ingratitude. In Section 7 it is precisely greed that the physician relies on to lure the goldsmith from Samarqand, although even his trap is polite. The parallelism between Sections 4 and 6 is that, in Section 4, the Divine physician is described as the knower of secrets and the solver of problems, and, in Section 6, he exercises both of these faculties in his discovery of the girl's secret. There are therefore four parallel and chiasmically arranged sections framing Section 5, which is clearly the most significant in that it introduces Love and the Perfect Man, and Shams and Ḥusām al-Dīn. It also makes clear that on matters of Love and the highest spiritual states one must speak in parables and through the words of others, thus explaining Mawlānā's methodology in the work. It should also be noted that whereas the story proceeds sequentially from 1 to 9, the inner "protected" purport is in Section 5, which looks both ways: it speaks of ordinary human love first, looking back to the problem of the king and the handmaiden, then it speaks of spiritual love, looking forward to the second half.

It is possible to detect additional parallelisms that neither detract from nor add to the primary chiasmic structure but rather that strengthen and integrate it further. These could be termed secondary parallelisms. Between Sections 1 and 3 there is a parallelism of *bī-adabī* in the example given in line 48 of the doctors: "In their arrogance they did not say 'If God Wills,' therefore God showed unto them the weakness of man." This case of irreverence receives a fuller more general explanation in Section 3. Sections 2 and 4 are parallel in that they are both part of the initial meeting between the king and the Divine physician. Sections 6 and 8 have the secondary parallelism of the promises given between the girl and the Divine physician in 6 and their being kept in 8. Finally there is a delicate parallelism between Sections 7 and 9. In Section 7 the Divine physician proposes the arrangement that the goldsmith be beguiled with gold and robes of honor, which is taken by any reader, and by the goldsmith as understood from his dying words, to be a trap to murder him unjustly. But the parallelism here connects the arrangement with Verses 242–243, where he is led "to fortune and the best estate," entirely to his real benefit in spiritual terms. It should be noted that Section 7 is one of the shortest sections in the entire work. The three verses could equally well have been added to Sections 6 or 8 without in any way weakening the narrative. It is here argued that the need to have a separate section was structural and not narrative and lends further support to the synoptic approach advocated here.

Interpretation of Discourse One

As the very first story in the *Mathnawī* and one that Mawlānā announces as "the very essence of our inner state," this discourse is necessarily of great importance.[6] At the literal level, the story is clearly told, without too many interruptions, and need not be repeated here, since the summary is above. At the allegorical level, while the commentators disagree over certain points of detail, the general structure of the allegory is agreed. As Nicholson, after Anqirawi, says, the king represents the *rūḥ* (spirit) and the handmaiden the *nafs* (selfhood) with whom the *rūḥ* falls in love.[7] The *nafs* is already secretly in love with a goldsmith who represents either the world (*dunyā*), or worldly pleasures (*ladhā'idh-e dunyawī*). Either by bad luck or through fate, *qaḍā*, she falls ill but the doctors, representing *'aql-e juzwī*, personal and partial intelligence, fail to cure her, because they are too arrogant to say "If God Wills." This, then, is the human dilemma. The spirit has come from God and is destined to return but has formed an attachment to the selfhood with which it is necessarily associated, and the selfhood is attached to the world. The king is out hunting, symbolic of being in search of spiritual realities. This strains the selfhood, which falls ill through being pulled in two directions. This is a realistic spiritual diagnosis of humanity, a condition in which one is subject to the laws of fate and which one's own arrogant intelligence cannot solve. It is also the condition of the *sālik*, the Sufi traveler, at the very beginning of his Path.

The next stage for the king, the *rūḥ*, and for the *sālik*, is to turn to God in prayer and weeping and to ask for help. To receive a dream, as did the king, is of great significance in Sufism and indicates communication from the Unseen world. The Divine physician is variously identified by the commentators as the Perfect Guide, *murshid-e kāmil* or Universal Intelligence, *'aql-e kullī*. Equally he could be the Perfect Man, *insān-e kāmil*, which, if the story is read as autobiography, would mean Shams. If the story is read as an allegory of the Sufi path he could be the shaykh, and, if read with regard to the Proem, he could be Love itself, there described as the physician of all our ills. Any or all are possible and intended to be possible. Mawlānā himself later refers to him by the general term *walī*, saint or friend of God, thereby indicating the status but leaving the identification open. When they meet the next day, the physician, like a *khayāl*,—indicative of the *'ālam-e mithāl*, the imaginal world of similitudes, of which everything in the sensible world is but a copy—displays the Divine attribute of Divine Beauty, *jamāl*, which leads the king to say: "You were my Beloved not she." The king, *rūḥ*, and the saint can be united because they are both spirit and that is why the king asks about the physician's home and journey, which is his own destination and his path back.

The following section, the homily on *adab* and *bī-adabī*, seemliness and unseemliness, is about how one should receive God's gifts with reverence and gratitude or everyone suffers. Whatever awful happens to one is due to irreverence and ingratitude. Nicholson in his commentary explains *adab* and suggests that this subject, which is so important for novices in Sufism, was suggested by the way the king treated the physician. Another property besides *adab* that is highlighted at this stage in section 4 is *ṣabr*, patience, self-control, self-discipline. In addition, the properties of the Divine physician, to be able to answer every question without discussion and to interpret what is in the heart, are reminiscent of the qualities one hopes to find in one's shaykh.

The structural analysis above disclosed that it is in Section 5 where the major inner significance of the story is to be found. This section is primarily about Love. Human love, *'ishq-e majāzī*, metaphorical love, is contrasted with Divine Love, *'ishq-e ḥaqīqī*, real Love, but "both lead us yonder." It is a clear affirmation that Mawlānā's Sufism is the path of Love, *'ishq*, not the path of asceticism, *zuhd*. After discussing the sun and the spiritual Sun, Mawlānā comes to Shams and appears to be about to speak of him when he is interrupted by, presumably, Ḥusām al-Dīn, formally his shaykh and the named inspiration of the *Mathnawī*, who asks him to speak of the ecstasies he enjoyed with Shams. There follows an extraordinary conversation between the two. On the face of it, Ḥusām al-Dīn emerges not so much as a Perfect man, more as the spiritual inferior of both Mawlānā and Shams, whose secrets he can never share. He is shown as being unaware of Mawlānā's state through asking him to speak when he had not fully returned to sensible consciousness; as being importunate and impatient; of wanting to be told directly of matters that should only be conveyed indirectly through the words of others; and of wanting to experience what was beyond his capacity to endure. Although Ḥusām al-Dīn is not named—the two words *nafs-e jān* are used—the commentators all consider this to be Ḥusām al-Dīn. There is a well-established literary convention that when you address a work to someone, you praise them in the most extravagant terms, as Mawlānā has done in the Preface, but it is not usual then to put them down, let alone so early in a work. There is little doubt that this dialogue, indeed the whole story, reflects Mawlānā's own spiritual biography and, by putting it as he has, he is reassuring the reader that what he writes is fully authentic, deriving from his own personal spiritual experience. Not only does Mawlānā thereby establish his own authority and credentials to write about these matters, but he, at the same time, explains why he has to write as he does through parables, and why there are limits to what can be said. Why then does Ḥusām al-Dīn appear as he does? It could be that it was never Mawlānā's intention that he should, and that it should not be read this way. It could be that Mawlānā simply needed another character with whom to have the dialogue to make his points. It could also be read, however, as referring back to the three levels in the Preface, the literal external level, the inner Sufi esoteric level, and finally the level of reality, *ḥaqīqah*. If that is the context in which the dialogue is to be taken then Ḥusām al-Dīn is assigned a high place on the Sufi level, and Shams is assigned a place on the level of reality, a level so awesome that Ḥusām al-Dīn is advised to keep away from it.

In the following sections the symbolism continues the Sufi path. The house, *jism* (body), is made empty, producing *khalwah* (seclusion), in which the physician makes an examination (*muḥāsabah*) of the *nafs* (selfhood). From the pulse he learns her secret, which leads to the importance of keeping secrets (*rāzdārī*), and the giving of promises. The cure is to lure the goldsmith by means of wealth and rank. The *nafs* is reunited with worldly attractions and recovers, thereupon the goldsmith is given poison and loses his attraction to the *nafs* and dies cursing that he has been killed for something other than himself. What the poison is can be deduced, since worldly attachments cannot survive either severe asceticism, *zuhd*, or strong mystical experiences of the spiritual world, *'irfān*, especially the overwhelming experience of mystical Love. It is unlikely in the context of this discourse to be the former, since mystical Love rather than asceticism is Mawlānā's own methodology. Love of the dead does not endure, so love the Living One. The physician only killed him on Divine Command; the king was upright and elect. One benefits from being slain by such a king, that is, the *rūḥ*, but the king here could equally be the physician or God. In this way the *nafs-e ammārah* (the self that commands to evil) is transformed into *the nafs-i muṭma'innah* (the self at peace with God) and all the promises given, even those to the goldsmith, are fulfilled.

Discourse One is both a general introduction to the work, and to Book One. It delineates the human condition, having a spirit in association with a selfhood, and provides a general introduction to the Sufi path, setting out the various procedures and methods of the Way of Love. It is also clearly autobiographical, introducing the author and his credentials. It gives particular emphasis to the two major themes of the *Mathnawī*, the Saint or Perfect Man, and Love, but here Love seen as purifier in its relation to the *nafs*. The discourse fully illustrates the line of the Proem which foreshadows it: "He (alone) whose garment is rent by a (mighty) love is purged of covetousness and all defect" (verse 22).

LINK SECTION: THE STORY OF THE GREENGROCER AND THE PARROT

Summary of Narrative and Thematic Content

LINK SECTION 247–323 (77) *The story of the greengrocer and the parrot and the parrot's spilling the oil in the shop.* (a) [247–262] A greengrocer had a talking parrot that spilled a bottle of oil on a bench, which its master then sat on. Furious, the greengrocer hit the parrot, who then became bald and refused to speak. The greengrocer was repentant because he had damaged his own livelihood. Three nights later a bald-headed dervish passed by and the parrot cried out: "Hey, bald-pate, what happened? Did you spill oil too?" Everybody laughed because it thought the dervish was like itself. (b) [263–276] Do not measure the actions of holy men by analogy with yourself. It is for this reason that saints and prophets are not recognized; people say they are men like themselves whereas there is an infinite difference that they do not see in their blindness. From one species comes a sting, from another honey; from one deer comes dung, from another musk; one reed is empty, another full of sweetness. There are thousands of similar examples: one eats and produces only filth, another eats and becomes entirely the Light of God; one eats and produces avarice and envy, another eats and produces only love for God; this soil is fertile, that brackish; this one an angel, that one a devil. They resemble each other externally but only someone with inner discernment knows the difference. Find such a person. (c) [277–298] The ignorant think that magic and the miracles of prophets are both founded on deceit, but the rod of the magicians was followed by God's curse while the rod of Moses was followed by God's mercy. The unbelievers aped the prophets thinking no one could tell the difference in their action, but the prophets act by the command of God and the apish imitators from quarrelsome rivalry. In religious matters the hypocrites practice competitive observance but in the end the believers triumph. Each goes to his proper destination according to the name; hypocrite has the taste of hell, not because of the letters, but because of their meaning. (d) [299–310] You cannot tell the difference from your own judgment but only if God has put the touchstone in your soul. When someone alive eats rubbish, he ejects it. The worldly sense is this world's ladder; the spiritual sense, the ladder to heaven. Well-being depends on the doctor for the first, the Beloved for the second. The first depends on a flourishing body; the latter on the body's ruin.

Spiritually one ruins the body and then restores it to prosperity; ruin the house for the treasure, then with the treasure, rebuild it; cut off the water and cleanse the riverbed, then let drinking water flow. (e) [311–323] Who can describe the action of God? Sometimes it is like this, sometimes not; it is bewildering. Not bewildered through not looking at God, rather through drowning in God and being drunk with the Beloved. The face of the spiritual looks to God, the worldly at himself. Look long at every face so that by serving Sufis you will come to know the face of a saint. Since many devils wear the face of Adam, don't give your hand to everyone, for the vile steal the language of Sufis to deceive the simple. The work of the holy is light and heat; that of the vile is trickery and shamelessness.

Comment

This section is considered a link section because it comes between two discourses and its function is to link them thematically.[8] This it does by telling the parrot anecdote, the gist of which is that we should not judge others by analogy with ourselves, especially holy men such as the Divine Doctor, since there is a world of difference between them and ourselves, and then, through several phases, coming to vile deceivers in order to foreshadow the next story. Analysis suggests that there are three such links sections in Book One. Since this section is mainly homily there are no problems with its overall interpretation. It should not be thought, however, that, since it acts as a link section, it is any less important for that. There is a very strong autobiographical element here, since this is precisely what some of Mawlānā's disciples did with regard to Shams: they judged him and reacted to him as if he were like themselves. Although generalized to encompass the situation of all humanity, the first discourse can also be read autobiographically. It was Mawlānā who was the king, entangled with the handmaiden of his selfhood, which was sick because it was still attached to the world. It was Mawlānā who had prayed to God and to whom was sent the Divine Doctor, Shams, whom he treated with great reverence and respect (*adab*). It was Mawlānā's selfhood which was submitted to close examination in the months of their seclusion together and whose worldly attachments were burnt off in the ecstatic and mystical experiences of Love he enjoyed as a result of Shams's training. The disciples who caused trouble did so because they could not see who or what Shams really was, nor that what he was doing was to the great benefit of their master, because they, just as everybody else habitually does, assumed Shams was like themselves and judged him by their own standards. The consequence of this blindness is developed in the second discourse. This human failing, though, is universal.

Discourse Two: The Story of the King who Liked to Kill Christians and His Vizier

Summary of the Narrative and Thematic Content

SECTION 1 324–337, (14) *Story of the Jewish king who for bigotry's sake used to slay the Christians.* (a) [324–326] There was a Jewish king who destroyed Christians. Although it was Jesus' turn and Jesus and Moses were one soul, the king was squint-eyed and saw them as separate. (b) [327–332] A master

Fig. 3.3. A Synoptic View of Discourse Two

Sec. 1	Jewish King; squint-eyed; didn't see Moses and Jesus as one; killed Christians
Sec. 2	His guileful vizier had a plot; mutilate me as a Christian and I'll confuse them
Sec. 3	I'll say I'm a secret Christian and true guide; the King obliged, expelling him
Sec. 4	He deceitfully won them over; hard to tell true from false; self-interested piety
Sec. 5	Many snares; destroy devotion; God puts senses to sleep at night; saint awake
Sec. 6	Laylā awake to spirit; cling to the Perfect Man; beware of envy like the saint [*hasad* (envy)]
Sec. 7	Vizier was born of envy and had no spiritual sense; only outwardly a guide
Sec. 8	The spiritually discerning saw his guile but the unwary became his slaves
Sec. 9	Messages between King and vizier; the time now to sow discord among them
Sec. 10	There were twelve tribes of Christians and twelve emirs all slaves of the vizier
Sec. 11	The vizier wrote twelve scrolls one for each emir all contradicting one another
Sec. 12	The vizier could not see the Unity of Jesus; God is Bountiful and Miraculous [*waḥdat* (Unity), *kathrat* (Multiplicity) and the Might of God]
Sec. 13	The vizier did not see he was up against the Inevitable; God is All Powerful
Sec. 14	The vizier tried a new plot, secluding himself; all pleaded with him to stop
Sec. 15	He refused; enslaved by words they should retreat within and cultivate silence
Sec. 16	They are not ready; his words are their life; to be with him better than Heaven
Sec. 17	He says not to bother him since he is engaged with inner experiences; he stays
Sec. 18	His seclusion is not *jabr* because it is without humility; don't say it is *jabr* [*jabr* (compulsion)]
Sec. 19	He says Jesus had told him to go into seclusion and they should eschew talk
Sec. 20	He then gave each of the emirs a scroll and secretly made each his successor
Sec. 21	He shut himself up for forty days then killed himself; a month of mourning
Sec. 22	Prophets are vicars of God but one with God; give up form or God will do it
Sec. 23	The emirs with their scrolls claimed the succession and many killed in war
Sec. 24	Some saved by the name of Aḥmad; if the name is so great, what of the man?

tells a squint-eyed pupil to fetch a bottle and he sees two. The master tells him to stop squinting and then says break one. He breaks one and there are none left. (c) [333–335] Anger and lust, self-interest, and bribery taken by a Qadi produce squint-eyedness. (d) [336–337] The Jewish king became so squint-eyed he killed thousands of Christians claiming to be the protector of the religion of Moses.

SECTION 2 338–347, (10) *How the vizier instructed the King to plot.* (a) [338–341] The King had a vizier who was guileful and a deceiver who told the king that killing Christians was useless because they simply hid their religion deeper, outwardly agreeing, inwardly disagreeing. (b) [342–343] The King asked what the best plan was so that no Christians remain either openly or in secret, (c) [344–347] The vizier said cut off my ears, nose, and hands and bring me to the gallows so someone can intercede. Do this in public, then banish me to a distant land where I can cause confusion among them.

SECTION 3 348–362, (15) *How the vizier brought the Christians into doubt and perplexity.* (a) [348–354] The vizier continues: "I will say I am secretly a Christian and the king learned of it and sought to kill me not believing my pretence. Had it not been for the spirit of Jesus he would have torn me apart. (b) [355–360] I would have given my life for Jesus but I know his religion well and it seemed a pity it should perish among those ignorant of it. I am a true guide who has escaped from Jews and Judaism. It is the time of Jesus, listen to his mysteries." (c) [361–362] The King had him mutilated in public and drove him away to the Christians where he began to proselytize.

SECTION 4 363–370, (8) *How the Christians let themselves be duped by the vizier.* (a) [363–365] Christians gathered around the vizier and outwardly he preached but inwardly he was a snare. (b) [366–370] The Companions of Muḥammad, because it is difficult to tell the true from the false, asked him about the deceitfulness of the ghoul-like selfhood (*nafs*) and how it mixed self-interest into worship and piety. They became adept at recognizing the deceitfulness of the fleshy self.

SECTION 5 371–406, (36) *How the Christians followed the vizier.* (a) [371–373] The Christians in blind conformity gave their hearts to him and regarded him as the vicar of Jesus when he was really the Antichrist. (b) [374–386] Oh God, how many are the snares and bait and we are greedy foolish birds. Every moment a new snare from which every moment You free us. We put corn in our barn but a deceitful mouse has made a hole and eats the corn. Oh soul, avert the mischief of the mouse, then help garner the corn. A *ḥadīth* says, "No prayer is complete without presence." If there is no mouse, where is the corn of forty years' devotion? Many stars are born of merit but a hidden thief puts them out. (c) [387–396] In spite of the many snares all is well when You are with us. Every night You set the spirits free from the cage and snares of the body so there is no thought or imagination of profit or loss. This is the state of the mystic (*'ārif*) day and night, asleep to the world, a pen in the Lord's hand. All share this state to some degree through the sleep of the senses. (d) [397–402] Then He leads them back on a tether to the body at dawn and makes them pregnant again with thoughts and actions. (e) [403–406] Would that God guarded the spirit as He did Noah and saved the mind and ear and eye from the flood of wakefulness and consciousness. There is an *'ārif* beside you, in converse with the Friend, but your eyes and ears are sealed.

SECTION 6 407–436, (30) *Story of the Caliph's seeing Laylā.* (a) [407–408] The Caliph asks Laylā if it is she for whom Majnūn is distraught, since she seems so ordinary. She says: "You are not Majnūn." (b) [409–416] To be awake to the material world is to be asleep to the spiritual. When not awake to God, wakefulness is like closing the door on God. To be preoccupied with the world prevents the soul from journeying heavenward. Asleep to spiritual things, one has hope of fantasies and talks with them. (c) [417–428] The bird is flying on high, it shadow speeds on earth and a fool exhausts himself chasing the shadow. He doesn't know it is a reflection, nor its origin, but fires arrows at it till the quiver of his life is empty. When the shadow of God is his nurse then he is freed from fantasy and shadows. The shadow of God is he who is dead to this world and alive in God. Cling to him, the saint; obtain a sun not a shadow. Cling to Shams, and if you don't know how, ask Ḥusām al-Dīn. (d) [429–436] But if you are seized by envy, that is a characteristic of Iblīs, since envy is at war with felicity. Envy is a real obstacle and the body is the house of envy, though God made it pure. If you practice envy and deceit you stain your heart black. Be hard on envy like the men of God.

SECTION 7 437–445, (9) *Explanation of the envy of the vizier.* (a) [437–438] The vizier was born of envy and cut off his ears and nose from vanity so that his envy could reach the Christians' souls. (b) [439–443] Anyone who cuts off their nose is unable to apprehend spiritual things. Someone who does catch a spiritual scent should give thanks or ingratitude will devour his nose. Give thanks and be a slave to those who give thanks. (c) [444–445] Do not be like the vizier and lead people from ritual prayer. He appeared as a guide but had craftily put garlic in the almond cake.

SECTION 8 446–454, (9) *How the sagacious among the Christians perceived the guile of the vizier.* (a) [446–448] The spiritually discerning Christians tasted his sweet words mixed with bitterness. He seemed to say be diligent but actually said be slack. (b) [449–451] What on the surface is white can still blacken your hand. Lightning is luminous but it can blind. (c) [452–454] The unwary Christians were captive of his words and, over six years, surrendered their souls and religion to him.

SECTION 9 455–457, (3) *How the King sent messages in secret to the vizier.* (a) [455–457] Messages passed in secret between the King and the vizier: the King said the time has come, and the vizier replied that he was preparing to cast discord into the religion of Jesus.

SECTION 10 458–462, (5) *Explanation of the twelve tribes of the Christians.* (a) [458–462] The Christians had twelve emirs in authority over them and each party was devoted to their own emir out of desire (for worldly gain). They and the emirs were slaves of that vizier and would have given their lives for him.

SECTION 11 463–499, (37) *How the vizier confused the ordinances of the Gospel.* (a) [463–464] He prepared a scroll for each emir, each scroll contradicting the others. (b) [465–496] One urged asceticism and hunger; one generosity. One urged trust and submission; one outer acts of worship and service. One urged that Divine commands were to show our weakness so we recognize the power of God; one said that weakness is ingratitude and we should regard our power for it is from God. One said whatever is seen is a sign of dualism; one said do not put out the candle of sight for it is a guide to concentration. One said put out the candle of sight; so that the candle of the spirit is increased. One said we should accept everything God has given us gladly; one that it is wrong and bad to comply with one's nature since religion is meant to be hard. In one he said only spiritual food should be the life of the heart. One said seek a teacher; one be a man and your own master. One said all this multiplicity is one; another that it is madness to say a hundred is one. (c) [497–499] How should all these contradictory doctrines be one, they are as poison and sugar. Only when you pass beyond the duality of poison and sugar will you reach unity and oneness. Twelve books in this style were drawn up by that enemy of the religion of Jesus.

SECTION 12 500–520, (21) *Showing how this difference lies in the form of the doctrine, not in the real nature of the Way.* (a) [500–511] He had no perception of the unicolority of Jesus, nor was he dyed in the vat of Jesus, which would make a hundred colors as simple and one-colored as light. It is like fishes and clear water: though there are many colors on dry land, fishes are at war with dryness. Where is God in this simile? Myriad seas and fishes in the world of existence bow down before that Bounty. How many rains have produced pearls in the sea, how much sunshine has taught the sea to be generous. The sunbeams of wisdom have struck the earth so that it becomes receptive of seed. The earth derives its faithfulness from God and the soil shows its secrets only in the spring. (b) [512–516] The Bounteous One informs the inanimate, but His wrath makes men blind. Who can understand? Wherever there is an ear his alchemy transforms it to an eye, a stone to a jasper. He is an alchemist and giver of miracles, what is magic compared to this? (c) [517–520] My praise is really the absence of praise, since in the presence of His Being we should be not-being.

SECTION 13 521–548, (28) *Setting forth how the vizier incurred perdition (by engaging) in this plot.* (a) [521–526] The vizier was ignorant and heedless like the king and didn't realize he was up against the eternal and inevitable. God is so mighty He can bring hundreds of worlds to existence from nonexistence. This world is vast, but to Him only an atom. This world is the prison of your soul, go forth yonder. This world is finite, that one infinite; image and form are the barrier to Reality. (b) [527–539] Moses' staff versus Pharaoh's lances; Galen's arts versus Jesus' breath; books versus Muḥammad's illiteracy; with a God like this how can you not die to self? He uproots minds, so sharpening the intelligence is not required, but being broken in spirit is. God turned the wicked woman into Venus, so turning yourself into clay isn't much. Your spirit was moving heavenward but you went to earth. (c) [540–548] You sought the (material) stars not the heavens and though a son of Adam you did not recognize he was the manifestation of God. You want to conquer a world and fill it with yourself, but God could with one spark lift the sin of a thousand viziers, turn that false imagination into wisdom, make that poison a drink, turn doubt into certainty and hatred into love.

SECTION 14 549–564, (16) *How the vizier started another plan to mislead the (Christian) folk.* (a) [549–556] The vizier hatched another plot and went into seclusion and the people became desperate and pleaded that he was their nurse and they needed his protection. He said his soul was near those that loved him but he was not allowed to come out. (b) [557–564] The emirs and disciples came and pleaded that they were orphaned, that they were in distress while he was pretending, and they missed his sweet discourse. They asked him to come to their aid.

SECTION 15 565–577, (13) *How the vizier refused the request of the disciple.* (a) [565–577] "You are enslaved with words," says the vizier, "block the senses so you can hear within, for our journey is interior. Cultivate silence."

SECTION 16 578–590, (13) *How the disciple repeated their request that he should interrupt his seclusion.* (a) [578–584] "This is too much for us since we are young birds not yet ready to fly and liable to be caught by a cat. (b) [585–590] When you speak we are filled with intelligence, with you earth is better than heaven. Compared to you what is this heaven, since you are the essence of sublimity."

SECTION 17 591–594, (4) *The refusal of the vizier to interrupt his seclusion.* (a) [591–594] The vizier tells them to be quiet and heed his advice. If he is trustworthy and perfect, why is he being so molested. He will not leave seclusion because he is engaged with inner experiences.

SECTION 18 595–642, (48) *How the disciples raised objections against the vizier's secluding himself.* (a) [595–611] "We are not being quarrelsome, but weeping like a babe for its nurse. You are the mover and we are the moved. You are the painter and we the picture; how could the picture quarrel with the painter? Do not look at us, look at your own generosity. We did not exist, but your grace called us into existence." (b) [612–620] Before Omnipotence people are helpless; He makes the picture, now the Devil, now Adam, now grief, now joy. God said: "You did not throw when you threw." We are the bow. God is the archer. That is not *jabr* (compulsion) it is *jabbārī* (Almightiness). Humility is evidence of necessity, our guilt evidence of free will. If there were not free will, why this shame and confusion? Why this argument between master and pupils? Why this changing of the mind from plans already made? (c) [621–629] If you say God's compulsion is ignored when free will is asserted, the answer is the humility and remorse when falling ill, for illness is a time of consciousness of one's sins when one prays to God for forgiveness. That illness has given you wakefulness, the more wakeful, the more full of suffering; the more aware of God, the paler the countenance. (d) [630–636] If you are aware of His *jabr*, where is your humility? How can a captive act like one free? If you consider you are shackled do not act the tyrant to the helpless. Since you do not feel His compulsion, do not say you are compelled. What you want to do, you feel able to perform. When you don't want to do it, you are a necessitarian, saying this is from God. (e) [637–642] Prophets are necessitarians to this world, unbelievers to the next. Free will for prophets belongs to the next world, but for unbelievers, to this. Every bird flies to its own congener, it follows its spirit, the prophets to heaven, the unbeliever to Hell. Return to the story.

SECTION 19 643–649, (7) *How the vizier made the disciples lose hope of his abandoning seclusion.* (a) [643–649] The vizier cried out Jesus had given him a message to be in seclusion and to have nothing to do with talk. "I am dead so that I may sit with Jesus at the top of the fourth heaven."

SECTION 20 650–662, (13) *How the vizier appointed each one of the emirs separately as his successor.* (a) [650–662] He summoned all the emirs one by one and told them separately that he was the vizier's successor and no one else was. He was not to tell anyone while the vizier lived, and to each he gave one of the contradictory scrolls.

SECTION 21 663–667, (5) *How the vizier killed himself in seclusion.* (a) [663–667] The vizier then shut the door for forty days, then killed himself, and there was mourning for a month.

SECTION 22 668–695, (28) *How the people of Jesus—on him be peace—asked the emirs, "Which one of you is the successor?"* (a) [668–673] In as much as God is out of sight, prophets are His vicars. (b) [674–685] No, it is wrong to think of God and the prophets as two, they are one if you escape from form. Ten lamps in one place differ in their form but their light is indistinguishable. In matters spiritual there is no division and no number. Sweet is the oneness of the Friend and His friends, form is headstrong. Do away with form or God will do it for you since He shows Himself to our hearts and unites Himself with the mystic. (c) [686–695] We were one substance once like the Sun. When that Light took form, it became many in number like the shadows of a battlement. Raise the battlement that difference disappears. I would have explained more strongly but weak minds might stumble, so I sheathed the sword. Now to complete the tale.

SECTION 23 696–726, (31) *The quarrel of the emirs concerning the succession.* (a) [696–705] Each emir advanced with his scroll and sword and claimed the succession. They fell to fighting and hundreds of thousands of Christians were slain and there were mounds of severed heads. The plan of the vizier had worked. (b) [706–716] The walnuts of the bodies were broken; those that had a kernel had fair spirits. On death those that had reality were manifest, those that were rotten were put to shame. Strive after reality, Oh worshiper of form, for reality is the wing on the body of form. Be with followers of reality; the spirit devoid of reality is like a wooden sword in the sheath, it seems valuable until taken out, then is fit only for burning. Don't go into battle with a wooden sword. The sword of reality is the weapon of the saints, associate with them. (c) [717–726] The *'ārif* (gnostic) is a mercy; when you buy a pomegranate, buy it when it is laughing so that you know its seeds. Unblessed is the red anemone from whose laughter (openness) you see the black heart. The laughing pomegranate makes the garden gay like the company of saints. Rock becomes a jewel when you reach the heart of a saint. Give your heart to the love of those whose hearts are glad. Don't go to despair: there are hopes; don't go to darkness: there is light. The heart leads to the saint, the body to the prison of earth. Feed your heart with talk from those in accord with it and seek advancement from the advanced.

SECTION 24 727–738, (12) *How honor was paid to the description of Muṣṭafā (Muḥammad), on whom be peace, which was mentioned in the Gospel.* (a) [727–738] The name of Muṣṭafā (Muḥammad) was in the gospels with descriptions, and a party of Christians kissed the name when they saw it. They were secure from the plotting of the vizier and had the protection of the name of Aḥmad (Muḥammad), so they multiplied. The others held the name of Aḥmad in contempt but they themselves became contemptible from their dissension and their religion was corrupted. If the name of Aḥmad was such a protection, what then of his essence?

Analysis of Discourse Two

The discourse has twenty-four sections, and the totality is framed and held together by Providential History, that is, the history of God's interventions in human life by means of the prophets. The first section, 1, introduces Moses, and is in parallel with the final section, 24, which introduces Muṣṭafā (Muḥammad). Sections 2 and 23 are also in parallel as conception and conclusion, and deal with Christians and Jesus, as do most of the intervening sections. In the Providential History of the time, Moses stood for *kathrat*, multiplicity, and this world. He was followed by Jesus who stood for *waḥdat*, unity and the next world. He was followed by Muḥammad who stood for *jāmi'īyat*, multiplicity in unity and unity in multiplicity and for *'ālamayn*, the two worlds.

The structure is first exemplified in four blocks of six sections each. Block 1–6 can be characterised as the conception in which the initial situation is introduced together with the three main characters: the squint-eyed King, the vizier and the Christians; block 7–12 can be characterized as preparation; block

13–18 as implementation; and block 19–24 as conclusion. Each block reveals a further development of the vizier's plotting. In the first block he pretends to be a Christian, in the second he introduces multiplicity of doctrine, in the third he resorts to seclusion and silence and in the fourth he relies on his different successors to effect the destruction of the Christians after he has killed himself. Each block is connected to the next block, the first to the second by the idea of envy; the second to the third through the Might and Power of God; the third to the fourth through *jabr* (compulsion), which is dealt with explicitly in Section 18 and is used by the vizier when he claims he was acting under instruction.

In terms of parallelism there are three parts over which it is operative. The first twelve sections, that is, the first half of the story, form the first part; blocks three and four are the second and third parts. In the first part, Sections 1 and 12 are in parallel through the contrast between multiplicity in 1 and unity in 12. Sections 2 and 11 are in parallel through the idea of confusion being announced by the vizier in 2 and his putting confusion into effect in 11 through producing a multiplicity of doctrines. Sections 3 and 10 are in parallel in that in 3 he announces how he will win over the Christians and in 10 he has made all twelve tribes his slaves. Sections 4 and 9 are in parallel in that in 4 the vizier as deceitfulness had duped the Christians, and in 9 he tells the king he has done this and all is ready. Sections 5 and 8 are in parallel in that 5 begins with the Christians being taken in by the vizier, and 8 ends with the Christians being taken in, but in both cases there are exceptions. In 5 snares are discussed and how everyone is caught by them except for the *ʿārif*, the spiritually aware gnostic who is in contact with God. This is demonstrated again in 8, but with the similar exception of those who are spiritually discerning. Sections 6 and 7 are in parallel through the concept of envy, but also in the contrastive parallelism of the Perfect Man in 6 and the opposite, the vizier, in 7.

The second part across which there is parallelism is block three, that is, Sections 13–18. Sections 13 and 18 are in parallel in that in 13 the vizier is described as wrestling with the Eternal and Inevitable and in 18 there is the discussion of *jabr*, compulsion, necessity, and *jabbārī*, Almightiness. Sections 14 and 17 are in parallel through the concept of seclusion. Sections 15 and 16 are parallel through the notions of silence and discourse. The third parallel part is formed by block four, Sections 19–24. Sections 19 and 24 are in parallel through the two prophets, Jesus and Muhammad. Sections 20 and 23 are in parallel through the appointment of the successors in 20 and their quarrel in 23. Sections 21 and 22 are in parallel through the death of the vizier and the succession.

Interpretation of Discourse Two

While the narrative element of this discourse is clear, there is disagreement among commentators as to the salient points this discourse makes.[9] For example, Foruzanfar sees its central point to be that the prophets are one, with one another and with God. Hamid Dabashi, in a perceptive and thoughtful essay on these twenty-four sections, which he rightly identifies as a discrete *maqālah*, finds the moral discourse to be theological and concerned with theodicy—the origin of evil—and free will and predestination.[10] Nicholson, following Ānqirawī, finds it to be concerned with the nature of the *nafs*. In a synoptic reading, such as that being given here, account is taken of the different levels of organization of the work as a whole, that is, the full design of the *Mathnawī*. It could then be argued that Dabashi is right about the literal surface level of the text and its subtexts; Nicholson right on the Sufi level; and Foruzanfar right on the spiritual level.

With these matters in mind, an interpretation can be offered. Starting with the Jewish king, symbolically he is generally accepted as being the *nafs*, and quickly Mawlānā makes clear that he is not just the *nafs* in general but a particular variety of the *nafs-e ammārah* known as the *nafs-i sabu'ī*, the "wild-animal self," which is driven by *khashm*, anger, *ḥiqd*, rancour and hatred, and *ḥasad*, jealousy and envy, even to the point of killing people. These properties, together with other properties of the *nafs* such as greed, desire, and so on, lead a person to lose the potential for seeing reality and unity so that they become *aḥwal*, squint-eyed, seeing double. This had happened to the king, who became a tyrannical zealot in consequence. Since the time was that of Jesus in the prophetic cycle of providential history, his targets were the Christians. The vizier represents an instrumental crystallization of part of the *nafs-i ammārah* that was formed out of *ḥasad*, jealousy or envy. He is very cunning and a master of deceit, *makr.* His mutilation meant he was devoid of any spiritual awareness or spirituality. The Christians represent the spiritual powers or faculties, at one level, and the Sufi *sālikān* or spiritual travelers on another. The various types and varieties of the *nafs* and its properties as understood in Islam, and particularly the accumulated Sufi wisdom on the subject, was all brought together by Al-Ghazzalī in his *Iḥyā'Ulūm al-Dīn*, which may well have been a source known to and referred to by Mawlānā.

This discourse is foreshadowed at the end of the Link Section, which warns about being taken in by clever but evil impostors. In the first three sections, the vizier proposes his hypocritical impersonation (*nifāq*), and the king implements his mutilation and banishment. In the fourth section, the Christians are duped by the vizier, which at another level means the spiritual powers were taken in by the *nafs*, as is confirmed by the attached explanation of how the Companions of Muḥammad, concerned about the mingling of self-interest in their worship, were taught by the Prophet to recognize the *makr-e nafs-e ghūl*, the deceitfulness of the ghoul-like selfhood. In the following section, the Christians took him to their hearts, which is followed by a passage addressed to the novice about how presence is needed in prayer or the *nafs* will erode the benefit, and how, only in sleep is there freedom from snares. This is a reminder that this discourse also serves as a training module in the early stages of a disciple's training. Section 6, the final section of the first block, starts from being asleep to the material world and to the spiritual world respectively, moves on to the need for a refuge and guide like Shams or Ḥusām al-Dīn, and culminates with a warning about jealousy. The use of the word "jealousy" so soon after these two names makes clear that there is a strong autobiographical element intended here. It was jealousy from the disciples of Mawlānā which, if it didn't drive Shams away, at least created all sorts of problems, and the vizier was born of jealousy. Precisely what happened will probably never be known, but it is not unlikely that jealousy split the group of disciples into factions and that they lost their collective togetherness outwardly and their inner collectedness also, in consequence of which they deteriorated spiritually. The appearance of the names of Shams and Ḥusām al-Dīn in the final section of the first block, must be taken as indicating that, when there is a block of six sections, its is the sixth which has a special emphasis. This is further confirmed by the high tone and content of Sections 12, 18, and 24. This first block, then, is concerned with being deceived and taken in by false impostors: narratively, by the vizier; outwardly, by false shaykhs and "leaders"; inwardly, by the *nafs*, the arch-impostor.

The importance of envy and jealousy is not solely autobiographical, as Mawlānā emphasizes in verses 429–430, where he points out that envy is particularly associated with Iblīs, Satan, so that it is not simply a primary destructive source of evil, it is also the most Devilish. Section 7, which begins the second block, is presumably addressed to the novices, since it deals with envy eroding the spiritual sense, a sense for which one should be grateful and give thanks. The reference to not turning people away from ritual prayer, could refer to an actual situation that took place amongst the disciples of Mawlānā, as well as indicating in general a particularly heinous spiritual crime that must be avoided. Section 8 explains how the vizier was able to say one thing outwardly but produce exactly the opposite effect inwardly, so that all but the wary and discerning fell under his spell. Section 9 demonstrates the king, the *nafs-e ammārah*, actually commanding to evil, in this case the spreading of confusion. Section 10 explains there were twelve main divisions of the

Christians, each with a leader under the influence of the vizier. In Section 11, the twelve scrolls—sixteen, in fact—which the vizier wrote to produce confusion, are detailed. Dabashi is interesting here. He argues that Rumi's purpose in enumerating conflicting doctrines is to make subtextually evident the inaccessibility of "truth" to reason. If reason can produce equally persuasive and yet contradictory positions, then there is something fundamentally wrong with the notion of the rational attainment of the "truth." He writes: " 'Truth,' then, has a reality for Rumi independent of its possible rational attainment. By producing multiple and contradictory narratives, Rumi parodies not only the mystical but also the juridical, theological, and philosophical doctrines and discourses in search of the truth."[11] But Mawlānā's purport is perhaps made evident by the important Section 12, the final and most significant section of the second block, in which he states the vizier could do this only because he was unaware of the "unicolority" of Jesus, whereby a "hundred colors would become as simple and one-colored as light." This is followed by a further compelling example, that of God's Bounty, which, though multiple in manifestation in the phenomenal world, is a unity in the real spiritual world. This discourse is written from the perspective of the *nafs*, the selfhood, for whom the divergence of views represents an opportunity to exploit differences. What the vizier was relying on to cause confusion were multiplicity, division, and contradiction. The second block, and especially its final section, ends with a foreshadowing of the next section on the subject of the Might of God.

The third block opens with a statement that the vizier, in his ignorance, was "wrestling with the eternal and inevitable," after which there is much about the Might of God, about wondering how the addressees, the spiritual novices, had chosen to go down instead of up and yonder, and about the Omnipotence of God. In Section 14, the vizier begins a new plot: having lured the Christians, won them over, and made them seemingly totally dependent on himself, he goes into seclusion. There is an interesting contrastive parallelism between blocks two and three. Although not fully implemented until the fourth block, in the second, the vizier prepares to confuse the Christians externally through doctrinal contradictions, whereas, in the third block, by his act of seclusion, the vizier seeks to confuse them internally through dependence then deprivation. In the second block, when he seduced them with his speech, they were passive and fully trusting; in the third block, when he went into seclusion, they reacted and accused him of pretence and of making excuses. In both cases, the vizier sought to destroy *jam'iyat*, togetherness, but in the second block it is the collective togetherness, and in the third block the internal collected-ness of individuals. Through having the vizier act as he does in the third block, Mawlānā demonstrates to the novice that even the most venerable

Sufi disciplines, such as seclusion, silence, and awareness of spiritual states and experiences, can be used by the *nafs* for its own selfish purposes.

There is one major theological or metaphysical question raised in the third block and touched on at the beginning of the fourth, that of predestination, *jabr*, and free will, *ikhtiyār*. This is a subject to which Mawlānā returned again and again. Apart from this discourse, Nicholson lists twelve other places in the *Mathnawī* where the issue is brought up and discussed, sometimes at length, so that it appears in every book except Book Two. It comes up first in verses 470–473 where it appears as two of the contradictory doctrines the vizier incorporated in his scrolls, and again in Section 18, where it seems, at least initially, to be put in the mouths of the distraught Christians, but very soon Mawlānā's own voice takes over. In full flow, Mawlānā comes very close to being a necessitarian, but quickly says: "This is not *jabr* it is the meaning of Almightiness, *jabbārī*. The mention of Almightiness is for the sake of inspiring humility within us. Our humility is evidence of necessity, but our sense of guilt is evidence of free-will." In this way Mawlānā retreats back to what Nicholson calls the orthodox *via media* between *jabr* and *ikhtiyār*, between Predestination and free will. But the vizier, in addition to using the issue in his scrolls, claims it was a Divine Command, or, at least, a Prophetic command, that required him to enter seclusion. In Section 19, his claims to a high spiritual level are extreme, but it is obvious, in view of the foregoing discussion, that his lack of humility gives the lie to any claim to be acting under Divine compulsion.

Having given the scrolls to the twelve Christian emirs, the vizier kills himself. Narratively, this is to precipitate the confusion and killing that will follow over his succession, but spiritually it is because jealousy is so potent a source of evil that it is self-destructive. It should be noted that, neither here, nor in the first discourse, is the *nafs* itself killed, the handmaiden and the king remain alive. It is the goldsmith and the vizier, representative of the misplaced forces acting on the *nafs*, who are destroyed. The request to the emirs to appoint the successor occupies the first six verses in Section 22, but this is followed by an exposition of one of the major themes of this discourse, the Prophets are one with God, and only the worshiper of form sees the Prophet and God as two. "In things spiritual there is no division and no numbers; in things spiritual there is no partition and no individual." Block four, therefore, answers back to block one in parallelism. It completes the plot there conceived narratively and it answers the *aḥwal* king. In Section 23, after the battle of the Christians, Mawlānā urges the novice to "consort with the followers of reality and plant love of the holy ones within the spirit" in contrastive parallelism with the undiscerning Christians and the vizier. Finally, Section 24 brings in the Prophet Muḥammad to complete the symmetry with Moses in the first block, to give the exemplar of the holy for the novice to plant in their spirit as advised in the preceding section, and to introduce the notion of *jāmi'īyat*, unity in diversity and diversity in unity, as the reconciling view symbolized in the Prophet Muḥammad between the multiplicity symbolized by Moses and the unity symbolized by Jesus. It was the Prophet's other name Aḥmad which acted as a refuge for a party of spiritually aware Christians, who were saved from the disaster described in the story. At the very end of this section, those who held the name of Aḥmad in contempt became themselves reviled, but this is a foreshadowing of the next discourse.

Discourse Three: The Story of the Second Jewish King Who Sought to Destroy the Religion of Jesus

Summary of the Narrative and Thematic Content

SECTION 1 739–768, (30) *The story of another Jewish king who endeavored to destroy the religion of Jesus.* (a) [739–742] A second Jewish king followed the evil ways of the first. (b) (743–750) The evil turn to the evil (congener), but the righteous inherit the sweet water of the Qur'ān. The seeker's longings are rays deriving ultimately from the Light of Muḥammad and go toward it. (c) [751–758] A person's affinities are to the planets at his birth, but beyond these material stars are spiritual stars, moving in another heaven, born under which a soul burns the unbelieving in driving them off. (d) [759–762] God gives his light to all but only the saints catch it in their skirts of love. (e) [763–768] The particular is set toward the universal. Everything is going whence it came. Our souls leave the body their motion mingled with love.

Fig. 3.4. A Synoptic View of Discourse Three

Sec. 1	Second evil Jewish king; evil to evil, good to good; part returns to its whole
Sec. 2	He set up idol of self to which all must bow or sit in fire; self is hell; flee body
Sec. 3	A child cast into the fire told all to come in; fire beats world; King shamed
Sec. 4	Man mocked Aḥmad but he was ridiculous; weeping attracts Divine Mercy
Sec. 5	Fire still fire but the sword of God who commands the elements; higher cause
Sec. 6	Hūd and shepherd protected believers; know God and fear not fire of lust
Sec. 7	King got worse; fire blazed killing Jews; of fire to fire; each to his own kind

SECTION 2 769–782, (14) *How the Jewish King made a fire and placed an idol beside it saying, "Whoever bows down before this idol shall escape the fire."* (a) [769–771] The second king set up the idol and required those who would not bow down to it to sit in the fire. He set up the idol because he had not controlled the idol of his *nafs.* (b) [772–778] The idol of the self is far worse than an actual idol. It is a fountain whereas an actual idol is the black water. It is easy to break an idol, but never the self. (c) [779–782] The self is Hell, always sowing trouble; seek refuge in God and Aḥmad, flee the body.

SECTION 3 783–811, (29) *How a child began to speak amid the fire and urged the people to throw themselves into the fire.* (a) [783–790] The king took a child from its mother and threw it into the fire. The mother having lost faith was about to bow down when the child cried out he wasn't dead but was happy because the fire was only fire in appearance to hide the truth. It really had the quality of water and was evidence of God and the delight of His elect. (b) [791–795] When he left the womb it seemed like death, but afterward the womb seemed like a prison and the world was pleasant. Now the world seems a prison since in that fire all is the breath of Jesus, a world seemingly nonexistent beside our own existent one, but the real situation is just the opposite. (c) [796–802] Come in Mother and all true believers, do not miss the chance. (d) [803–806] The people were all entering the fire out of love for the Friend till the king's servants had to hold them back. (e) [807–811] The king was disgraced and the people became more ardent and firm in *fanā.* The Devil's plot had caught him, and the Devil himself was disgraced. All the shame he sought to rub into the faces of the people accumulated in his face, while they were untouched.

SECTION 4 812–822, (11) *How the mouth remained awry of a man who pronounced the name of Muḥammad, on whom be peace, derisively.* (a) [812–816] A man mocked the name of Aḥmad and his mouth stayed awry. He asked for forgiveness saying he was stupid to ridicule, and it was he who was ridiculous. When God wishes to shame someone he causes them to ridicule the holy and when he wishes to hide someone's blame he causes them not to blame the blameworthy. (b) [817–822) When God wishes to help somebody he causes them to weep. Blessed the eye and heart that weep for Him for the outcome is laughter. Where water, there greenery; where tears, there Divine Mercy. If you desire tears, have mercy on the weeper; if mercy, show mercy to the weak.

SECTION 5 823–853, (31) *How the fire reproached the Jewish king.* (a) [823–828] The King asked the fire why it was not burning and whether it had changed its nature, (b) [829–833] The fire replied it was still the same fire but was in fact the sword of God. (c) [834–839] If the fire of your nature gives pain or joy, that is from God. The elements are His slaves, fire ever waiting to do His Will. (d) [840–853] Stone and iron produce fire, they are causes. But beyond them are higher causes that the prophets know of and which they can make operative or not. Do not mistake the two types of cause. God commands the elements. From Him come the water of mercy and the fire of wrath. He informed the soul of the wind, which distinguished believer from nonbeliever in the people of 'Ād.

SECTION 6 854–868, (15) *The story of the wind which destroyed the people of 'Ād in the time of (the prophet) Hūd, on whom be peace.* (a) [854–859] Hūd drew a line around the believers and the wind destroyed all but those. Shaybān a shepherd drew a line round his sheep when he went to pray and kept the wolf out. The concupiscence of sheep and wolf were barred by the circle of the man of God. (b) [860–868] Examples: Men who know God fear not the wind of death; fire did not burn Abraham, and the religious were not burnt from the fire of lust, and so forth. Your praise of God comes from water and clay and becomes a bird of paradise through your sincerity. Mount Sinai seeing Moses became a Sufi and began to dance.

SECTION 7 869–899, (31) *How the Jewish king scoffed and denied and would not accept the counsel of his intimates.* (a) [869–876] The king ignored his advisers and bound them and behaved even worse until the fire blazed up and consumed those Jews. Fire was their origin and to fire they returned as particulars toward the universal. (b) [877–886] The mother seeks the child as the fundamentals pursue the derivatives. Thus our breath and good words rise up to God and His mercy descends. (c) [887–892] The attraction comes from whence comes our delight and the delight comes from our own kind (congener) and certainly the part is drawn to the universal. Water and bread are not our congeners but become such from their outcome and come to resemble the congener. (d) [893–899] If we delight in what is not homogenous, it will resemble the congener, but as a loan that has a time limit. Do not be taken in by impostors or vain imagining will cast you into the well as in the next story.

Analysis of Discourse Three

The rhetorical structure of this discourse is almost paradigmatic. If further confirmation of the synoptic nature of the *Mathnawī* were needed, this discourse supplies it, since it has the same form as Psalm 67, that is, ABCDCBA, with special emphasis therefore given to Section 4, which stands alone, but, because it has the name of Aḥmad in its title and deals inter alia with ridicule, it also connects with the foreshadowing final section of Discourse 2, in which those who held the name of Aḥmad in contempt, themselves became contemptible. Section 1 states that the particular returns to the universal, and everyone is drawn to their own kind, their congener. Section 7, in parallel with it, shows how those whose origin was of fire perished in fire and further elaborates on congeners. Sections 2 and 6 are in parallel because both of them are concerned with the differentiation and division of different types of people. In Section 2 the king sets up the idol of selfhood and says those who do not worship the self will perish in the fire, while, in Section 6, the prophet Hūd sets up a line dividing the believers, who will not be destroyed by wind, from the nonbelievers, who will; and the shepherd draws a line to protect the sheep from the wolf. Sections 3 and 5 are in parallel because both are concerned with the fire. Section 3 shows that the child in fact achieved *fanā* and not destruction in the fire, and Section 5 explains that the fire remains the same, but is ever ready to do the Will of God. These parallel sections move from the universal law of return to one's congener, to the division between people, to the instrument of God's action, the fire which effects the division. This all leads to the inner protected Section 4. Section 4 begins with five verses that show how ridicule toward a man of God returns to its producer and makes them ridiculous. The remaining six verses explain how, to attract the Mercy of God, one must weep, but in order to be able to weep, one must be merciful to the weepy and the weak. Section 4 is the inner "meaning" of the discourse: Section 7 the external climax.

Interpretation of Discourse Three

This discourse also deals with a king who kills, and Mawlānā indicates he is of the same kind as the previous king, whose path of evil he followed.[12] This means that he too must be regarded primarily as that extreme kind of *nafs-e ammārah* referred to as *nafs-e sabu'ī.* As with the vizier in Discourse Two, the king is killed by his own excesses. Here, though, it is not envy and jealousy but rather anger and hatred which seem the primary characteristics of this king, whose nature was obviously fiery because he returned to fire in his destruction. Verse 809 twice refers to him as devil: once as *shayṭān*, and once as *dev.* It is impossible to tell whether this is to be taken as "the Devil" or as "a devil." Either would fit, but perhaps the latter reading is to be preferred, since

Mawlānā locates the source of evil in forces within the *nafs*. Indeed, in Verse 779 he equates the *nafs* with Hell. Mawlānā is careful always to associate Iblīs, Satan, with the *nafs*, never allowing the Devil to be considered as an independent principle of evil in creation like Ahriman in dualistic Zoroastrianism. The fire is both the natural element and a force within one's nature, which can, on the one hand, fire anger, but, on the other hand, it is also what in India is called *tapas*, the intense inner heat engendered by asceticism. The idol is one's selfhood, the *nafs*. It is tempting to think of egoism in this connection, but that is not quite sufficient because what the king was seeking to elicit from people was not so much *khūd-parastī*, self-worship, as *nafs-parastī*, worship of the selfhood, in its widest sense, contrasting with the worship of God. It is more like total self-indulgence, of which egoism is a significant part.

The first section connects this king back to the previous king through their evil natures, thus demonstrating the universal law that every nature is drawn to its own congener, *jins*. The righteous have inherited the Qur'ān and their vibrations are drawn to the "substance of prophet-hood." Evil is drawn to evil, good to good, each to his own congener. God and the men of God can direct the forces of nature, because above natural causation there is spiritual causation, just as there are spiritual planets beyond the actual planets that determine men's character. God has scattered his Light—possibly the Light of Muḥammad—over all spirits, but only the fortunate receive it, whereafter they turn their faces away from all but God. The second universal principle is that the particular is returning to the whole. The question then is what is the nature of the particular concerned. The spirits of the righteous are returning to God; no destination is given for the spirits of the wicked. This, then, is the universal situation the novice Sufi must confront and understand according to Mawlānā. In Section 2 he sets up the criterion which distinguishes one kind of nature from another, the idol of the *nafs*, before which one must bow or be thrown into the fire. An idol is nothing a little iconoclasm can't remove: the real problem is the *nafs*, whose horrors and hellish nature are detailed. The child in Section 3, who was thrown into the fire by the king to be destroyed, cries out that it is alive, that is, that *fanā*, dying to self, is not death and that self-mortification is only fire in appearance, being in fact the gateway to a freer, richer and happier world. For the king as the *nafs-e ammārah*, however, self-mortification would be death, so his mistake, which leads to his being shamed by the very shame he sought to inflict on others, was, at least, understandable.

Section 4 does precisely what a central section conventionally does: it sums up what has gone before, with the example of ridicule toward a man of God being reflected back on to its producer; it introduces something entirely of its own, the great importance of weeping; and it foreshadows what is to come, namely examples of the Mercy of God. The messages to the novice Sufi accumulate: do not ridicule the Shaykh or it will rebound on you; be merciful to the weak and those that weep; learn to weep yourself, since that will attract the Mercy of God.

Section 5 sees the fire explaining to the complaining king that its nature is still the same, but that it and the other elements are the servants of God, ready to do His Will, as moved by the spiritual causation that lies beyond natural causation. For the novice there are some memorable verses on pain (834–837) as well as the prediction that, when he is fully awake, he will see that "from God too are the water of clemency and the fire of anger" (852). This leads in Section 6 to several examples being given of God's Mercy in protecting the believers, and of His anger in destroying the unbelievers, the agents of God being wind, fire, water, and earth, together with the prophets, Hūd, Abraham, Jesus and Moses, and so on, who effected the discrimination between the two categories of people. In the final Section there is the external climax when the Mercy of God, or his Anger if the two are to be separated, causes the fire to swallow up the king and his fellow Jews. The fire was their origin, to which they returned in the end. "That company was born of fire: the way of particulars is to the universal." (874–875) But at this point Mawlānā adds a further principle: The mother of the child is always seeking it: the fundamentals pursue the derivatives (878). This means that God actively draws the soul to Himself and there is a continual ascent of prayer and descent of Mercy. There then follows a short discussion on attachments to what is not homogenous, before a short foreshadowing of the next discourse. This discussion does not seem to go anywhere in particular, that is, until the parallel discourse on the Mouse and the Frog toward the end of Book Six, which deals with precisely this situation.

Discourse Four: The Story of the Lion and the Beasts

Summary of the Narrative and Thematic Content

SECTION 1 900–903, (4) *Setting forth how the beasts of the chase told the lion to trust in God and cease from exerting himself.* (a) [900–903] Some beasts were being harassed by a lion who ambushed them and carried them off and this made their valley unpleasant. They plotted to make their valley pleasant again and said to the lion that they would give him a fixed allowance to keep him fed but he should not hunt.

Fig. 3.5. A Synoptic View of Discourse Four

Sec. 1	Lion harming beasts, who offer an allowance
Sec. 2	Lion agrees but fed up with fraud; *nafs* worse
Sec. 3	They say, trust in God best; don't fight Destiny
Sec. 4	Lion says trust in God but tie up camel; earner loved
Sec. 5	They put trust before effort; bad vision the trouble
Sec. 6	Limbs are God's signs; free will gratitude, *jabr* not
Sec. 7	Schemes fail but God's decree stays; effort fancy
Sec. 8	Man saw Azrael but died in India fleeing from death
Sec. 9	Holy work for next world; wealth for religion good
Sec. 10	Lion argued till deal agreed; hare reluctant to go
Sec. 11	Beasts tell hare to go quickly or lion furious
Sec. 12	Hare says let me be so my nous can save us all
Sec. 13	They say donkey stay hare-size; boast is conceit
Sec. 14	God gives speciality to each; heed spirit not form
Sec. 15	Hear hare with inner ear; his plot; form and spirit
Sec. 16	Tell us the plan; good to take counsel with trusty
Sec. 17	Don't tell secrets; not safe; wise don't and win
Sec. 18	Hare late; lion angry; seek wisdom, lose desire
Sec. 19	Divine help needed not opinion; opinion useless
Sec. 20	Lion's ear tricked him; words skin; meaning spirit
Sec. 21	Intellect hidden; form visible; spirit unseen; renewal
Sec. 22	Lion angry at hare's delay; says: Listen to my roar
Sec. 23	Hare apologizes and tells story of the other lion
Sec. 24	Set off says lion to his nemesis; Destiny can blind
Sec. 25	The hoopoe claims to see water underground
Sec. 26	Crow says he lied or he would have seen snare
Sec. 27	Hoopoe says it no lie but Destiny put him to sleep
Sec. 28	Divine Destiny caused Adam to slip in same way
Sec. 29	Hare turns pale which is God's sign of fear; nervous
Sec. 30	Hare explains it's because of the lion in the well
Sec. 31	Side by side they see a lion and a hare; lion jumps in
Sec. 32	Happy hare tells beasts the hell-hound was in hell
Sec. 33	To their praise says it was God's help; he's only hare
Sec. 34	Lion outer foe; inner the *nafs* only God can defeat

SECTION 2 904–907 (4) *How the lion answered the beasts and explained the advantage of exertion.* (a) [904–907] The lion agreed provided they were not frauds. He was fed up with fraud and spite, but worse than that was the

nafs within waiting to attack. He had taken to heart the Prophet's saying: "The believer is not bitten twice."

SECTION 3 908–911, (4) *How the beasts asserted the superiority of trust in God to exertion and acquisition.* (a) [908–911] The beasts said forget precaution, it is no use against Divine Decree. Trust in God is better. Don't quarrel with Destiny or it will quarrel with you. Be dead in the presence of the Decree of God.

SECTION 4 912–914, (3) *How the lion upheld the superiority of exertion and acquisition to trust in God and resignation.* (a) [912–914] The lion said: "All right, but the Prophet said trust in God but tie up the knee of your camel. Remember the earner is beloved of God and do not neglect the ways and means."

SECTION 5 915–928, (14) *How the beasts preferred trust in God to exertion.* (a) [915–920] The beasts dismissed acquisition (work) saying there was nothing better than trust in God. "We run from trouble into more trouble. Man devises something which then becomes his own trap and locks the door when the foe is in the house. Pharaoh slew babies when the baby he sought was in his own house. (b) [921–928] Our foresight is defective, so let it go and follow the sight of God. Children are safe when they make no efforts; it's when they do later they get into trouble. Our spirit flew free before they had bodies, then they were trapped in anger and desire. We are the children of the Lord. Who gives rain can also give bread."

SECTION 6 929–947, (19) *How the lion again pronounced exertion to be superior to trust in God.* (a) [929–937] "The Lord set up a ladder and we must climb it; to be a necessitarian here is foolish. You have hands and feet so why pretend you don't? When a master puts a spade in a servant's hand this is a sign. Follow the sign and you will fulfill His will. Follow His commands and you will see mysteries, burdens will be lifted and He will give you authority and favor you until you will attain union. (b) [938–947] Free will is to thank God for his beneficence; necessitarianism to deny it. Necessitarianism is to sleep on the road amid highwaymen. If you reject His signs you will lose what understanding you have. Ingratitude is a sin which leads to Hell, so trust in God and sow."

SECTION 7 948–955, (8) *How the beasts once more asserted the superiority of trust in God to exertion.* (a) [948–955] "Millions have schemed and acted but apart from what was predestined they got nothing. Their plans failed and only the decree of God remains. Exertion is only vain fancy."

SECTION 8 956–970, (15) *How 'Azrā'il (Azrael) looked at a certain man, and how that man fled to the palace of Solomon; and setting forth the superiority of trust in God to exertion and the uselessness of the latter.* (a) [956–960] A man ran to Solomon saying he had been looked at by Azrael the angel of death in such a way that he wanted Solomon to get the wind to take him to India so his life might be saved. (b) [961–970] People flee from poverty and become prey to covetousness and striving, which are like India in this story. Solomon did what he was asked and then met Azrael and asked him why he had looked so angrily at the man. "That was not anger," said Azrael, "it was surprise, because God had asked me to take his spirit in India and I couldn't see how." From whom should we flee? From ourselves? Oh absurdity! From God? Oh crime.

SECTION 9 971–991, (21) *How the lion again declared exertion to be superior to trust in God and expounded the advantages of exertion.* (a) [971–978] "Yes but consider the exertions of the prophets and believers, they were all excellent and no one has suffered through following them. Work is not against Destiny but according to it. (b) [979–986] Plots for things of this world are useless, for the next, inspired by God. The best plot is for the prisoner to dig a hole out of prison. The world is a prison and we are prisoners; dig a hole and let yourself out. What is this world? To be forgetful of God: not money and women. Wealth for religion is good, like water that can sink a boat when inside, but a support when underneath. Since Solomon had cast out desire for wealth from his heart, he called himself "poor." (c) [987–991] The stoppered jar floats because its wind-filled heart is empty; so does the heart filled with poverty. Seal your heart and fill from within. Exertion is real."

SECTION 10 992–997, (6) *How the superiority of exertion to trust in God was established.* (a) [992–997] The lion went on producing proofs like this till the beasts gave up and made the agreement whereby he got his daily ration without further demands. Each day the one on whom the lot fell would run to the lion, until it came to the hare, who cried out: "How long shall we suffer this injustice?"

SECTION 11 998–999, (2) *How the beasts of the chase blamed the hare for his delay in going to the lion.* (a) [998–999] "We have sacrificed our lives in troth and loyalty so don't give us a bad name. Lest he be angry, go quickly." Thus replied the beasts.

SECTION 12 1000–1004 (5) *How the hare answered the beasts.* (a) [1000–1004] The hare said: "Friends grant me a respite so my cunning can save you and safety will be the heritage for your children." Thus spoke every prophet who had seen from Heaven the way of escape. Though in their sight he was small as a pupil of the eye, how great was the real size of that pupil.

SECTION 13 1005–1007 (3) *How the beasts objected to the proposal of the hare.* (a) [1005–1007] The beasts said: "Oh Donkey, keep yourself within the measure of a hare. What a boast is this that your betters have not thought of. You are self-conceited or else Destiny pursues us."

SECTION 14 1008–1027 (19) *How the hare again answered the beasts.* (a) [1008–1011] The hare said: "Friends, God gave this weakling wise counsel. Lions and elephants do not know what the bee and silkworm were taught by God. (b) [1012–1017] Adam learned knowledge from God and taught the angels to the confusion of Iblīs for whom God created a muzzle so he had no access to the knowledge of religion. The intellectual sciences are a muzzle for the man of the senses but into the heart God gave a jewel which he gave to nothing else." (c) [1018–1027] How long will you worship form? Hasn't your soul yet escaped from form? The form may be fine but it lacks the spirit, that rare jewel.

SECTION 15 1028–1040 (13) *An account of the knowledge of the hare and an explanation of the excellence and advantages of knowledge.* (a) [1028–1034] Listen to the story of the hare, not with your asinine ear but with a different one. How he made a plot to catch the lion. Knowledge is the spirit and the whole world is form; by virtue of knowledge all creatures are helpless before man. (b) [1035–1040] Man has many secret enemies who strike him every instant. Wash in a river and there is a hidden thorn you will come to know because it will prick you. Likewise the pricks of Satan and angels and many others can only be known when your senses are transmuted and then you can see who is prompting you.

SECTION 16 1041–1044 (4) *How the beasts requested the hare to tell the secret of his thought.* (a) [1041–1044] They said: "Hare, tell us your plan. The mind is helped by other minds and counsel gives understanding, as the Prophet said: 'Oh Adviser, take counsel with the trustworthy, for he whose counsel is sought is trusted.' "

SECTION 17 1045–1054 (10) *How the hare withheld the secret from them.* (a) [1045–1049] You should not tell forth every secret; if you breathe words on a mirror it becomes dim for us. Do not speak of your death, your gold or your religion for there are enemies in wait if you do. Anyway, tell one or two people and you might as well have published it. (b) [1050–1054] A wise man gains his object without betraying himself, like the Prophet, who took counsel cryptically, and his companions would answer without knowing his true meaning. He would express himself in a parable and get the answer without anyone knowing the question.

SECTION 18 1055–1081 (27) *The story of the hare's stratagem.* (a) [1055–1058] He waited and arrived late so the lion was very angry. The lion cried: "I knew their promise was in vain and their talk has duped me. How long will this world deceive me?" (b) [1059–1067] The road is smooth but under it are pitfalls, no meaning in the words. Seek real wisdom, so that the guarding tablet of your heart which preserves the lessons of wisdom can become a Guarded Tablet, an inviolable source of Divine knowledge. When the understanding is transformed by the spirit it becomes the pupil of the soul and knows it cannot go further. (c) [1068–1075] Whoever through heedlessness is without thanksgiving and patience has to resort to *jabr.* But to plead necessity is to feign illness and pretended illness leads to death as the Prophet has said. *Jabr* is to bind up a broken foot; you have not broken yours, but one who does through effort on the path is the acceptor of Divine commands and is accepted. (d) [1076–1082] Until now he follows the King's command, now he delivers them to the people; he was ruled by the stars, now he rules them. Refresh faith you who have secretly refreshed your desire. While desire is refreshed, faith cannot be, since desire locks the gate of faith against you. You have interpreted the word of the Qur'ān, interpret yourself not the Book. You have interpreted the Qur'ān according to your desire and degraded its sublime meaning.

SECTION 19 1082–1090 (9) *The baseness of the foul interpretation given by the fly.* (a) [1082–1087]] A fly on a straw on a pool of ass's urine interpreted the urine as the sea, the straw as a ship and himself as the pilot. (b) [1088–1090] The false interpreter of the Qur'ān is like the fly, who, if he left off interpreting following opinion, would be transformed. One who receives Divine indications is not a fly; his spirit is not analogous to his form.

SECTION 20 1091–1106 (16) *How the lion roared wrathfully because the hare was late in coming.* (a) [1091–1095] The hare is an example of one whose spirit is not analogous to his form. The Lion was furious saying that his ear had blinded him. Their tricks had tied him up and he would never again listen to their palaver which was designed to deceive like the cry of demons. He would tear them to pieces and rend their skins for they were nothing but skin. (b) [1096–1098] Skin is specious words lacking continuance. Words are skin and meaning the kernel; words are form and meaning the spirit. The skin hides a bad kernel and also guards the secrets of the good kernel. (c) [1099–1106] When the pen is of wind and the scroll water, it quickly perishes. The wind in men is vanity and desire; when vanity and desire go, there will be a message from God that will not perish. Kings and empires change, only the insignia of the prophets endure. The pomp of kings is from vanity, the prophets are from God. The names of kings are removed from coinage; the name of Aḥmad, which is the name of all the prophets, is stamped forever.

SECTION 21 1107–1149 (43) *Further setting forth the stratagem of the hare.* (a) [1107–1108] The hare delayed while thinking about his plots. (b) [1109–1113] How wide is the ocean of intelligence on which our forms move fast, like cups on the surface that float until they are full, then sink. Intelligence is hidden and only the phenomenal world is visible; our forms are its waves or its spray. Whatever the means our form makes to approach Intelligence, the ocean uses the same means to cast us away. (c) [1114–1120] The heart does not see the giver of conscience; the arrow does not see the Archer, just as a man thinks his horse is lost though he be speeding along the road on it. He should come to himself. The spirit is lost to view because it is so manifest and near. (d) [1121–1135) How can you see colors if you don't first see light? But since the mind is absorbed in the color it doesn't see light. The colors act as a veil of the light. There is no seeing color without external light, equally with the color of inner fantasy—outer light is from the sun, inner light is from the reflection of beams of glory. It is the light of the heart that give light to the eye, and the Light of God that gives light to the heart. At night it is dark and there is no color. Light is made manifest by its opposite and pain was created so happiness may be known. So are hidden things known, and since God has no opposite, He is hidden and cannot be made manifest, so our eyes do not perceive Him. (e) [1136–1141) Form springs from spirit, and voice and speech from thought, but you don't know where the sea of thought is, only that it is noble. When the waves of thought sped from the ocean of wisdom they were given the form of voice and speech. The form was born of the Word and died, withdrawing back to the sea. The form came from Formlessness and returned for "Verily unto Him we are returning." (f) [1142–1149] You are dying and returning every moment: every moment being renewed and life arriving anew, but in the body it seems continuous. The continuity comes from its swiftness; the swift motion caused by the action of God appears as duration. Even if you are learned and seek this mystery, ask Ḥusām al-Dīn, who is a sublime book.

SECTION 22 1150–1156 (7) *The hare's coming to the lion and the lion's anger with him.* (a) [1150–1156] The furious lion saw the hare coming along boldly and confidently since he thought it would be less suspicious if he was bold rather than humble. When he was near the lion shouted: "Villain, I have destroyed oxen and vanquished fierce elephants, what is a half-witted hare to disregard my behest. Give up the hare's heedlessness and slumber, give ear, Oh donkey, to the roaring of this lion."

SECTION 23 1157–1180 (25) *The hare's apology.* (a) [1157–1161] When the hare asked for mercy and sought permission to excuse himself, the lion replied that fools were short-sighted and their excuse worse than the crime. Was he ass enough to give ear to an excuse devoid of wisdom? (b) [1162–1166] The hare replied that it would not diminish his bounty to listen to one oppressed. The lion said he would give bounty where it was due. (c) [1167–1180] The hare then told his story of how he and another hare had set out after breakfast to come to the lion, when another lion attacked them. He told that lion that they were slaves of the King of Kings but that lion had dismissed his king as a loony and forbade their going on. The hare asked to take the news to his king but had to leave his friend as a pledge of his return. The road is blocked, our agreement ended, and if you want the allowance, clear the way and repel that irreverent one.

SECTION 24 1181–1201 (20) *How the lion answered the hare and set off with him.* (a) [1181–1187] The lion said: "Come on, let's find him. Go in front if you speak truly, that I may punish him, or you if you are lying." The hare was the guide to the deep well he had made a snare for the lion. The hare was like water under straw; water carries away straw, but can straw carry away a mountain? His guile was a noose for the lion. What a hare with a lion as his prey. (b) [1188–1193] Moses draws Pharaoh into the Nile, a gnat cleaves Nimrod's skull; just look at the state of those who listened to the enemy Satan. The enemy speaks in a friendly way as a snare. Regard his candy as poison and if he is kind to your body, it is cruelty. (c) [1194–1201] When Divine destiny comes you see only appearances and won't distinguish friends from enemies. Because of this begin supplication, lamenting, fasting, and praise now. Ask God who knows the hidden not to crush us beneath contrivance. May the creator of the lion not set the lion on us if we behave badly; may he not make sweet water fire. When God makes us drunken with the wine of his wrath, it is to pervert our senses so we cannot see reality.

SECTION 25 1202–1220 (19) *Story of the hoopoe and Solomon, showing that when the Divine destiny comes to pass, clear eyes are sealed.* (a) [1202–1213] The birds came to Solomon who spoke their language and when they stopped twittering they became clear and articulate. To speak the same tongue is kinship and affinity, not to, is to be in prison. Many Turks who speak the same language are strangers; others, who don't, do so in fact because the tongue of mutual understanding is different, and to be one in heart is even better. The birds were telling Solomon their respective talents to gain access to him, as a slave gives a good account of himself if he wants to be bought, but a bad one if he doesn't. (b) [1214–1220] The Hoopoe said he had only one talent. When he was at the zenith he could see water at the bottom of the earth so it would be useful when the army needed to camp. Solomon accepted him as a good companion in waterless places.

SECTION 26 1221–1226 (6) *How the crow impugned the claim of the hoopoe.* (a) [1221–1226] The crow said out of envy that the hoopoe lied about his keen sight, otherwise he would have seen the snare beneath the earth and would not have gone into the cage. Solomon asked the Hoopoe if he had been lying and bragging.

SECTION 27 1227–1233 (7) *The hoopoe's answer to the attack of the crow.* (a) [1227–1233] The hoopoe said that Solomon should kill him if he lied but urged him not to listen to his enemy who does not believe in Divine Destiny and is really an unbeliever. He, the hoopoe, can see the snare unless Divine Destiny muffles his intelligence and puts wisdom to sleep. It is not strange to be deceived by Divine Destiny, indeed, it is Destiny that an unbeliever does not believe in it.

SECTION 28 1234–1262 (29) *The story of Adam, on whom be peace, and how the divine destiny sealed up his sight so that he failed to observe the plain meaning of the prohibition and to refrain from interpreting it.* (a) [1234–1237] Adam was given knowledge of the names of the real nature of everything for all time. Nothing he named changed its nature for all time. (b) [1238–1245] Hear about the name of everything and its mysteries from the knower: with us the name is the outer appearance, with God the inner nature. For God Moses' staff was a dragon, the idolater 'Umar, a believer, and seed was you beside me. The seed was a form in nonexistence with God, and was exactly how it turns out to be, so what we are is our name with God. That name is our final state, not the state He calls a "loan." (c) [1246–1248] As Adam saw with Pure Light, the soul and innermost sense of the names were obvious to him and the angels bowed down in worship. I cannot praise this Adam enough. (d) [1249–1254] All this Adam knew, but when Divine Destiny came he was at fault on a single prohibition, not knowing whether it was to be obeyed or was open to interpretation. He veered toward the latter and his nature went toward the forbidden fruit. As he slipped, Satan carried off the goods from the shop. He cried, "I have sinned" and Divine Destiny became the cloud which covered the sun. (e) [1255–1262] If the hoopoe did not see the snare when Divine Destiny came, he was not alone. Divine Destiny knocks you in various ways in order to stand you up. It is God's loving mercy that first He terrifies you, but only in order to make you more secure. The subject has no end: return to the story of the hare and the lion.

SECTION 29 1263–1296 (34) *How the hare drew back from the lion when he approached the well.* (a) [1263–1266] Coming near the well the hare hung back, and when the lion asked why, he replied that he was terrified as his pale color showed. (b) [1267–1272] The eye of the gnostic is on the signs, since God called the signs informative. Color, smell, and sound all give knowledge. The color of the face gives knowledge of the heart: a red complexion thankfulness, a pale one patience and need. (c) [1273–1275] "I am affected by that which takes away my physical strength, my color and all outward signs; that destroys everything it reaches; that defeats the material, vegetable, animal and human kingdoms. (d) [1276–1288] These are only parts, wholes too are subject to Destiny: the world is now patient, now thankful; the garden now green, now bare; the sun now red, now pale; stars burn up and the moon diminishes; the earth is agitated by earthquakes and mountains become grains of sand; the air conjoined with spirit becomes foul and water the sister of spirit turns yellow when Destiny comes; the sea is in constant agitation and the heavens ever whirling containing stars now fortunate, now unlucky. (e) [1289–1296] You are a part made up of wholes so why should you be not afflicted when wholes suffer grief and pain, especially when you are made up of contraries, earth, water, fire and air. Life is the peace of contraries, death when they are at war. Since the world is sick and a prisoner, it's not surprising that I am passing away and hung back."

SECTION 30 1297–1303 (7) *How the lion asked the reason of the hare's drawing back.* (a) [1297–1303] "Yes," said the lion, "but what is the particular cause of your malady since that is my object." The hare told him it was the lion who lived in the well. Those wise ones live in wells because spiritual joys are attained in solitude, and the darkness of the well is better than the dark shades of the world. "My blow will subdue; let's see if he is in," said the lion. The hare replied: "I am afraid of his fieriness so come beside me so I dare to open my eyes."

SECTION 31 1304–1338 (34) *How the lion looked into the well and saw the reflection of himself and the hare in the water.* (a) [1304–1307] Side by side they looked into the well and the lion saw his own reflection with a plump hare beside him. Seeing his adversary he jumped into the well. (b) [1308–1316] The lion fell into the well which he had dug and his iniquity was coming back on his own head. The iniquity of evildoers is a dark well, the more iniquitous the deeper. If you are digging a well for others you are making a snare for yourself, so don't make it too deep. Do not consider the weak to be without a champion, remember *When the help of God shall come.* The weak attract help and you will suffer. (c) [1317–1328] The lion saw himself in the well and thought his own reflection was his enemy. Many iniquities you see in others are your own nature reflected, and when you hit them you are hitting yourself. If you could see the evil in yourself you would hate yourself. When you reach the bottom of your own nature you see the vileness is from you, just as the lion saw at the bottom of the well the enemy was his own image. Do not run away from yourself, the faithful are mirrors to one another. (d) [1329–1338] You held a blue glass to your eye and the world turned blue, but the blueness came from yourself. To the true believer things appear plainly through the Light of God, but if you see through the Fire of God you cannot tell good from evil. Bit by bit put water on your fire. Oh Lord put water on the world-fire that it may become light. Everything is under Your control and deliverance from evil is Your gift.

SECTION 32 1339–1356 (18) *How the hare brought to the beasts of chase the news that the lion had fallen into the well.* (a) [1339–1348] The hare, delighted to be delivered from the lion, ran happily along to the other beasts. The boughs and leaves were singing thanks to God like spirits who had escaped from clay and dance in the air of Divine Love. (b) [1349–1356] The hare put the lion in prison. Shame on the lion for being beaten by a hare. Oh lion at the bottom of the well, your hare-like *nafs* has shed your blood. The hare ran crying: "Rejoice, the enemy of your lives—his teeth have been torn out by the vengeance of the Creator. The Hell-hound has gone back to Hell. He who smote many heads with his claws—him too the broom of death has swept away."

SECTION 33 1357–1372 (16) *How the beasts gathered round the hare and spoke in praise of him.* (a) [1357–1364] The joyful animals gathered round the hare and praised him as the Azrael of fierce lions. They asked him to explain how he had used guile to wipe out the ruffian so that the tale could be a cure and salve since the iniquity of that tyrant had inflicted many wounds on their souls. (b) [1365–1372] The hare replied that it was God's help since he was just a hare. God had given him power and light in his heart. God raises up and also brings low in due course and turn, doubters and seers alike. Do not exult in a kingdom given in turns; you are a bondsman to vicissitude do not act as if you were free. There is a kingdom beyond vicissitude where the kings are everlasting. Cease from drinking worldly pleasure for a brief lifetime and you will sip the drink of Paradise.

SECTION 34 1373–1389 (17) *Commentary on (the Tradition) "We have returned from the lesser Jihād to the greater Jihād."* (a) [1373–1385] Oh Kings, we have slain an outward enemy but within there is a worse enemy. The inward lion is not overcome by a hare, reason and intelligence. The *nafs* is Hell and Hell is a dragon not subdued by oceans of water. However much food, it is unappeased until God asks if it was filled and it said no, there is still burning. It swallowed a whole world and asked for more until God puts his foot on it and it subsides. This *nafs* of ours is part of Hell and parts have the nature of the whole. Only God has the power to kill it. Be a straight arrow and escape from the bow, for the arrows of the *nafs* are bent and crooked. (b) [1386–1389] I turned from outer warfare to inner warfare, returning with the Prophet from the lesser *jihād* to engage in the greater *jihād.* I pray God will grant me strength and aid and success. Think little of the lion who breaks the ranks of the enemy, the true lion is he who conquers himself.

Analysis of Discourse Four

The structure of this discourse, which has thirty-four sections, is constituted by four blocks of sections arranged 10, 7, 7, 10. The first ten treat of the beasts and the lion and their argument over effort versus trust in God. The first section gives the beasts' offer of a fixed allowance and the tenth rounds off the block by having them all agree the arrangement. The next block of seven sections is the conversation between the beasts and the hare about his plan, which he refuses to divulge. The third block of seven sections is between the lion and the hare and ends with them setting off together. The final block begins with four sections showing how Divine Destiny can blind us as it did the hoopoe and Adam. The rest finish off the story with the destruction of the lion and the hare telling the beasts it is over. The final section points out that the lion is only the outer enemy; the inner enemy, the *nafs*, only God can destroy. The story also has two equal halves: the first seventeen sections create the situation and the second seventeen resolve it.

Just as the blocks are arranged chiasmically, so is the entire story, with the first seventeen sections sequentially, parallel with the second seventeen sections in reverse order. Section I is parallel with Section 34 through the discussion of the lion as outer enemy and the *nafs*, the selfhood. Section 2 is parallel with Section 33 through the notion of *makr*, fraud, guile, plotting. In the first section the lion says he is fed up with being cheated by cunning and fraud, *makr*, although the selfhood, the *nafs*, is worse, and in the parallel section the hare is praised as the Azrael of lions who used his cunning, *makr*, although the hare denies it saying his light and power came from God. Section 3 warns the lion not to grapple with Destiny lest Destiny pick a quarrel with him and Section 32 parallels this with the hare's announcement that their enemy had had his teeth pulled out by the vengeance of his Creator and this fulfils Section 3. Section 4 is parallel to Section 31 in that in Section 4 the lion is urging the importance of action and effort and in 31 he acts only to destroy himself in so doing. Section 5, in parallel with Section 30, has the beasts stating that when man devises something his device becomes the snare that traps him. In Section 30, the lion says come on to the hare so he can find the lion to destroy him with his blow, thus demonstrating Section 5. Section 6 and Section 29 are strongly parallel in that both deal with the signs of God. Section 7 and Section 28 are parallel in that in the first section the beasts declare that, despite man's scheming, only that which is predestined comes to pass, whereas in the second it is Divine Destiny which determines that Adam falters. Section 8, which gives the story of the man who saw the angel of death and fled to India only to be taken there by Divine Destiny, is in parallel with Section 27, where the hoopoe discusses Divine Destiny causing him not to see the snare, and the need to believe in Divine Destiny. Section 9 has the lion further expounding on the need for efforts and endeavor in parallel with Section 26 in which the crow, addressing the hoopoe, although illustrative too of the lion, says if he was so sharp how did he not see the snare and end up in the cage? Section 10 has the beasts making their covenants with the lion when it comes to the hare's turn, in parallel with Section 25 in which the birds are in conversation with Solomon and then it comes to the hoopoe's turn. The section by section parallelism of these last eight sections, 7–10 and 25–28 is less convincing individually than as two blocks taken together. The first block overall stating that in spite of one's efforts one cannot escape Divine Destiny and the second block illustrating how it is Divine Destiny that blinds us, however worthy we might be, for its own purpose.

The middle sections begin with Section 11 and Section 24 in parallel in that in both the hare is urged to set off; in the first by the beasts so that he can be killed by the lion, in the second by the lion so that he can kill the second lion, but really so that the hare can kill him. Section 12 is in parallel with Section 23 in that in the first section the hare pleads with the beasts to let him explain his plan and in the second section the hare pleads with the lion to let him tell his story. Sections 13 and 22 are in parallel in that in both the same pun is used giving "Oh donkey, (*khar*) listen (*gūsh*)" out of the word for a hare (*khargūsh*). Sections 14 and 21 are strongly thematically parallel in that both deal with intelligence and spirit hidden in form. Sections 15 and 20 are in parallel in three ways: the first is the need to listen to the hare with the inner ear and the lion complaining his ear had blinded him; the second is the notion of knowledge as spirit and the world as form repeated as "words are skin and the spirit meaning"; and finally the idea of secret hidden enemies. Section 16 is in parallel with Section 9 in that in the first the hare is urged to "seek counsel from the trustworthy," and in the second this is clarified showing that only Divine inspiration is trustworthy and that to follow opinion in interpretation is to be like the fly on the pool of ass's urine who thought it was the sea. Sections 17 and 18 are parallel in that in the first there is a warning about sharing secrets and how the wise gain their ends without revealing their purpose, just like three birds tied up together who look defeated but are in secret consultation. This is reflected in Section 18 in which the lion is furious at being deceived especially by words and names that are devoid of meaning. It is of course the beasts, in captivity to him like the three birds, which have been in secret discussion with the hare.

This sequence of seventeen different parallelisms shows a wide range from the verbal pun of "Listen, Oh donkey," through situational parallelism to full thematic parallelism where the second illustrates, develops or fulfils the first. Some sections are demonstrably more parallel than others. The first and the last sections and the middle fourteen are particularly tightly parallel while in some of the others it seems a looser parallelism was felt to be acceptable.

Interpretation of Discourse Four

Almost certainly, the lion in this story symbolizes the *nafs-e ammārah*, of which, in this particular instance, the predominant characteristics are pride, (*kibr*), anger, and a large ego.[13] Mawlānā's emphasis here is clearly on the egoism that fills the selfhood. The beasts are generally taken to be the various spiritual powers and faculties, and the hare is understood to be *'aql*, the intellect, intelligence, certainly *'aql-e ma'āsh* empirical intelligence or discursive reason, but on occasions able to access *'aql-e ma'ād*, transcendental intelligence or Universal Reason. Nicholson's suggestion that the hare represents Universal Reason itself is perhaps improbable given Verse 1374, which states that the inward lion is not subdued by the hare. It is more a question here of the intellect (*'aql*) being able to receive Divine inspiration when the situation demanded it. The *nafs*, or perhaps better, the egoism filling the selfhood, is causing serious interruptions to the spiritual powers' peaceful grazing, so they devise a scheme to provide it with a regular supply of sustenance from their own number, which means the spiritual powers would become severely weakened, or, at another level, more of the spiritual faculties would be swallowed by egoism. It is to this scheme that the hare, *'aql*, objects, and in response to which he devises the plan to destroy the lion before he himself is swallowed too. The animal fable comes originally from the Indian *nīti* tradition, works of advice and instruction to kings, often in parable form, to enable them to stay on top.

In the first ten sections, the beasts and the lion debate the issue of *tawakkul*, trust in God, leaving everything to God including one's "daily bread," versus effort, action, and personal initiative, bringing in a range of arguments to support their respective stances. The spiritual powers, of course, urge *tawakkul*, their natural predisposition, and the lion, action and effort, for which the *nafs* is designed to be the instrument and for which its ruling ego takes the credit. Nicholson's commentary on these sections is full and clear, so rather than repeat its points, it will be useful to consider this passage as instruction for the spiritual novice and as a characterization of his situation.[14] The Sufi novice will be given tasks and exercises and disciplines to develop his spiritual faculties, but pride, belief in his own efforts and the like all contrive to erode his spiritual powers. He is still the prey of his own selfhood and ego, which is rightly suspicious it is under attack. In the early months, maybe years, of his training, all of the arguments and attitudes expressed in these first ten sections will have at one stage or another been entertained for a while, only to be replaced by a counterargument or attitude, until out of sheer exhaustion the novice will come to some accommodation with the *nafs* of the sort symbolized here. It is perhaps more fruitful to see this as a perceptive analysis of the spiritual psychology of the novice than as a theological debate, although it is, of course, both. In terms of the argument, as Nicholson remarks on Section 9, Mawlānā sums up in favor of the lion; in terms of the spiritual situation of the novice, however, this is only the beginning of the story, for the tyranny of the *nafs* and its egoism remains.

Into this situation, from Section 11, *'aql*, intervenes, to the initial exasperation of the spiritual faculties, who regard his claim to be able to see a way to escape from the tyranny of the *nafs* as conceit. The hare asserts that God had given him inspiration, whatever his size and form. In Section 14, according to Nicholson's inverted commas, that is all the hare says; the rest is Mawlānā. God has given special knowledge to every part of creation, particularly to Adam, to whom was given the knowledge of religion which was kept from Iblīs. But to Adam and his descendants God gave something he gave to no other, the spiritual heart. It is spirit and the spiritual essences within that are crucial, not the outer form. The whole world is form, knowledge is the spirit.[15] But the spiritual heart is prompted in secret from many different sources, and it will only be when one's nature is transmuted that one is able to recognize where each prompting comes from. The spiritual faculties wanted to know the hare's plan but he refused. Here, at Section 17, at the very center of the discourse, the place to seek its real inner message, is the affirmation of one of the most firmly established principles of Sufism, that of *rāz-dārī*, the keeping of secrets, especially those which come from a high spiritual source, *even from oneself*, given the context. That the hare was eventually successful was because he kept to this fundamental principle, and the message to the Sufi novice is clear.

The second half of the discourse begins with Section 18. The hare is deliberately late in reaching the lion, thus successfully ensuring that the lion is very angry, and hence less inwardly perceptive as to what is about to happen. The lion cries out that the beasts' promises were empty and their talk had deceived him, but then Mawlānā's voice takes over. "Words and names are too often empty of meaning and reality yet they absorb much of one's life. The seeker after wisdom can become a fountain of wisdom. His intelligence and understanding can be enriched by the spirit so that it becomes a source of Divine knowledge, after which his understanding which was his teacher becomes his pupil; or like the Prophet who went from being the commanded to become the Commander." This possible evolutionary transformation from *'aql-e ma'āsh* to *'aql-e ma'ād* is held out to the Sufi novice, but at the price of asceticism, prayer and thanksgiving, with no excuses. To interpret the Qur'ān, whose origin is from Divine knowledge, by means of opinion and the discursive reason (*'aql-e ma'āsh*) is to act like the fly in Mawlānā's parable, although, as Nicholson notes, Section 19 was probably referring specifically to the way the expression "The moon was cloven asunder" had been interpreted. The parallelism between Section 16 and Section 19 is that in both cases discursive reason and opinion sought inappropriately to comment on wisdom derived from the *'aql-e ma'ād*. Section 20 again shows the furious lion, still waiting and even angrier at being deceived, anxious to "rend their skins for that is all they are."

Then Mawlānā's voice takes up the subject of skin, since words are skin, and meaning the kernel; words are as form and meaning as spirit; the skin hides the defects of a bad kernel and the secrets of a good one. The written word perishes swiftly; only when desire, self-will and vanity have been abandoned, will one receive messages from the *'aql-e ma'ād*, which will endure like those of the prophets. Section 21, after two verses on the hare only now just beginning to set off for the lion, then gives itself fully to *'aql* as Universal Intelligence or Universal Reason, rightly appreciated and commented on by Nicholson for this is a fine sustained passage of mystical vision. It concludes with the name of Ḥusām al-Dīn, further indicating that it has a special significance. In fact, this section is the climax of a block of eight sections, four either side of the very center of the discourse, that deal in detail with *'aql*, both particular and universal, the central subject of this discourse, as love was for the first discourse. There is much in Section 21, but one side issue worth noticing is that Verse 1130–1131 gives Mawlānā's view of theodicy: "God created pain and sorrow for the purpose that happiness might be made manifest by means of this opposite. Hidden things are manifested by means of their opposite; since God has no opposite, He is hidden." This confirms what has been said before, that there is no independent principle of evil in Mawlānā's view of creation. The lion and the hare are kept waiting until this treatment of *'aql-e ma'ād* is completed, but their story resumes in Section 22 when the hare finally reaches the enraged and roaring lion. In Section 23 he makes his excuses and explains about the other lion and hare. In Section 24 the lion sets off behind the hare who leads him toward his snare, with comments on snares and enemies in Mawlānā's voice. From Verse 1194, there is a foreshadowing of the next block of four sections, with the warning that when Divine Destiny comes to pass, one sees only the outer appearance, and cannot tell friend from foe.

Sections 25–28 tell the story of Solomon and the hoopoe, and how he was made unseeing of the snare by Divine Destiny. Just to prove that this can happen to the best of us, the hoopoe cites the parallel example of Adam. The positive aspect of Divine Destiny is emphasized in the penultimate five verses of Section 28. Section 29 is largely about the different "signs" that are informative and should be given attention, beginning with the pale and trembling hare as indicative of terror, or, at least, of feigned terror. The Qur'ān has at Sūra 41:53: "And we shall show them Our signs in the horizons and in themselves" and urges believers to seek out these hidden signs. Toward the end there is a discussion of the contraries contained within a person: sheep and wolf, lion and onager, which are usually taken as referring to the *rūḥ* and the *nafs*. "Life," says the hare in giving counsel, "is the harmony of contraries; death, war between them," thereby highlighting the choice the lion has.

Section 30 has the hare telling the lion that the other lion lives in the well, safe from harm's way. Mawlānā then adds that everyone who is wise should choose the bottom a well, because spiritual joys are best attained in solitude, and there is no salvation in following on the world. In Section 31, the lion duly does his leap into the well to destroy the lion he saw reflected in the water, and Mawlānā draws the inevitable moral required in animal fables, that the lion jumped into a well of his own making, and so forth, and that one should never assume the weak are without a champion. But having honored the ethical requirements of the *nīti* genre, Mawlānā then produces a spiritually and psychologically penetrating seventeen verse passage—addressed to the reader, and to the man of sorrow—in which he points out that the evil seen in others is really the evil of one's own nature, just as the lion realized at the bottom of the well that the lion he thought he saw, was in fact his own image. The section concludes with a prayer addressed to God. Section 32 is unashamedly triumphalist about the victory of the hare over the lion, and in Section 33 the animals gather round to praise him and to ask how he did it. "It was with God's help, for I am only a hare," he explained, "God gave me power, and light in my heart, and the light in my heart gave strength to hand and foot." Then comes Mawlānā's voice warning not to put one trust in the changeable and cyclical, but only in the kingdom beyond change. The final section, Section 34, compares the war against the *nafs* to the greater *jihād*, a war not winnable by the hare, reason or intelligence. Since the *nafs* has the nature of Hell, only God has the power to conquer it. The true lion is he that conquers himself.

Reflecting on this discourse as a whole, it resembles more the first discourse than the second or the third. In the first, it is the goldsmith not the handmaiden who is killed; the *nafs* is redeemable with the help of the Divine Doctor and Love. In the second and third discourses, there is naked evil, and the *nafs* is beyond redemption. Certainly in this discourse the lion is slain, but by God's giving the hare an inspiration, that is, by enabling the *'aql-e ma'āsh* to access the wisdom of the *'aql-e ma'ād.* What was the inspiration? It was so to arrange things that the *nafs-e ammārah*, or perhaps better here the ego, sees itself and does not like what it sees. Mawlānā has made the lion a far more lovable and sympathetic character than either the evil vizier or the evil Jewish king. He wins the argument in the first ten sections, and piously not hypocritically; though angry at the delay, he doesn't simply eat the hare but listens to its obsequious deceit; he is the victim of trickery. Of course, his own pride and egoism rather than the hare's cunning cause his demise, but to the reader, and to the *sālik*, he feels redeemable. But more than that, he feels well worth redeeming, well worth transforming into a faithful instrument of action, different from, but in harmony with, the spirit. And Mawlānā explains how it can be done: through cleansing the eye of the heart so that it can receive from the *'aql-e ma'ād*, the Universal Intellect, from which perspective there can be nothing but dissatisfaction with the picture shown of one's self and its dominant ego. This dissatisfaction is the real beginning of the path. It would be possible to interpret the self-induced death of the lion in the well as *fanā*, the annihilation of the ego, but to do so is arguably premature, it would be to set *fanā* too low, and certainly would be out of sequence within Mawlānā's careful unfolding of the Sufi path. For this discourse it is enough that the novice becomes aware of egoism and how it swallows up a person's spiritual potentialities, and that he becomes dissatisfied. The next discourse shows the beginning of the solution.

Discourse Five: The Story of the Ambassador of Rūm and the Caliph 'Umar

Summary of the Narrative and Thematic Content

SECTION 1 1390–1414 (25) *How the ambassador of Rūm came to the Commander of the Faithful, 'Umar, may God be well-pleased with him, and witnessed the gifts of grace with which 'Umar was endowed.* (a) [1390–1395] The ambassador of Rūm went to see the Caliph 'Umar and asked where his palace was. He was told 'Umar had no palace except an illumined spirit, which the ambassador could not see because he had hair grown over the eye of his heart which first needed to be purged. (b) [1396–1407] A spirit purged of desire will see the Divine Presence and Porch, like Muḥammad, who saw everywhere the Face of God, which you cannot, being subject to Satan's promptings. God

Fig. 3.6. A Synoptic View of Discourse Five

Sec. 1	Ambassador finds 'Umar has no palace, only spirit; heart needs purging to see
Sec. 2	As a seeker, he finds 'Umar asleep; feels love and awe; self-questioning; he waits
Sec. 3	'Umar relaxes him; speaks of stages of spirit; times precreation; seeker eager
Sec. 4	God sent spirits to earth; gave man riddle; *jabr* and free will *khayāl*; *jabbārī*
Sec. 5	Our acts caused by God's acts; only God sees both; Adam; intellect and spirit
Sec. 6	Knowledge, ignorance, sleep, waking, etc. God's; only He alone is; we are nothing
Sec. 7	Why spirit trapped like meaning in a word; for benefit; don't deny God benefit
Sec. 8	Ambassador's *ḥāl* became *maqām*, alive, free; follow Prophets; escape the cage

is as manifest as the sun or moon to every open heart. Put fingers on your eyes and you see nothing yet the world is still there, so the fault lies with the fingers of your evil self. Take off the finger and see what you wish. Man is eye, the rest is skin; sight is seeing the Beloved, otherwise the eye is better blind. The ordinary beloved is better out of sight. (c) [1408–1414] The Ambassador became even more full of longing hearing this and sought him everywhere having now become a seeker. He was told 'Umar was asleep under a tree.

SECTION 2 1415–1426 (12) *How the ambassador of Rūm found the Commander of the Faithful 'Umar sleeping under the palm tree.* (a) [1415–1426] He saw 'Umar asleep and felt in his heart the contraries of love and awe. He had a question and answer session within himself. Why do I, a hero, feel such awe for one unarmed and asleep? This is awe of God not of a dervish. Everyone, man and jinn, is afraid of one who is afraid of God and makes that his religion. He waited reverently till 'Umar woke up.

SECTION 3 1427–1445 (19) *How the ambassador of Rūm saluted the Commander of the Faithful.* (a) [1427–1432] 'Umar returned the ambassador's salaams and removed his fear and put him at ease. (b) [1433–1438] He spoke then of the Friend, of His loving kindness, and of *ḥāl* and *maqām*. *Ḥāl* is the unveiling of a beautiful bride which all nobles may witness; *maqām* is when the king is alone with the bride in the bridal chamber. *Ḥāl* was common for Sufis but *maqām* rare. (c) [1439–1445] He spoke of the stations on the Path and the journeys of the spirit and the time before creation when the spirits enjoyed the bounty of Divine grace; he found the ambassador eager for mysteries. 'Umar as a shaykh found him adept and with a capacity to receive good guidance, so he sowed good seed in good soil.

SECTION 4 1446–1479 (34) *How the ambassador of Rūm questioned the Commander of the Faithful.* (a) [1446–1450] He asked 'Umar how the spirit came to the earth, how the infinite bird got into the cage. 'Umar replied God recited spells over the nonexistences and they danced joyously into existence and then he recited another spell and they rushed back into nonexistence. (b) [1451–1455] God spoke to the rose that it should laugh; to the stone that it be a cornelian; to the body that it be spirit; to the sun first to be radiant and then to eclipse; to the cloud that it should weep and to the earth to remain regardful and silent. (c) [1456–1462] To man's ear God has spoken a riddle so that he is perplexed: should he do what God commands or the opposite. God determines for each the most likely choice he will make. If you seek not to be in this perplexity use the spiritual ear and eye which can receive *waḥy*, inspiration other than through sense-perception, reason, and opinion. (d) [1463–1479] I am fed up with the way they use the term *jabr*, compulsion; this is not compulsion but union with God. They alone know its true meaning whose spiritual eyes are open; their free will and compulsion are quite different since they can transform a drop into a pearl. For you free will and compulsion are simply ideas, fancy; for them it becomes the Light of Majesty.

SECTION 5 1480–1508 (29) *How Adam imputed that fault (which he had committed) to himself, saying, "Oh Lord we have done wrong" and how Iblīs imputed his own sin to God, saying, "Because You have Seduced me."* (a) [1480–1487] There are our manifest actions and the actions of God which brings our actions into existence. Reason cannot see both at the same time, only God comprehends both. (b) [1488–1495] Satan hid his own act by blaming God; Adam knew of God's action but blamed himself. After Adam's repentance God said it was my Fore-ordainment so why take the blame? Adam said: "I was afraid, so I maintained respect." God said: "As I have to you, for reverence begets reverence." (c) [1496–1508] A hand may tremble involuntarily and it can shake because you knock it, but even though God creates both actions, they are not comparable. You are sorry for having knocked his hand but he too is sorry for his tremor. This is an intellectual quest; the spiritual quest is quite different. In the first, the intellect and senses deal with effects and secondary causes; the spiritual comes from illumination and has no concern for premise, conclusion, argument, or proof.

SECTION 6 1509–1514 (6) *Commentary on "And He is with you wherever you are."* (a) [1509–1514] If we come to ignorance, that is His prison; to knowledge, His Palace; to sleep, His intoxication; to wakefulness, His protection. Weeping is His bounty; laughter His lightning; war, His might; peace, His love. What are we in this complicated world where nothing is single but He? Nothing at all.

SECTION 7 1515–1528 (14) *How the ambassador asked 'Umar, concerning the cause of the tribulation suffered by spirits in these bodies of clay.* (a) [1515–1516] The ambassador asked what was the wisdom in imprisoning the spirit in this dirty place, binding spirit to bodies. (b) [1517–1528] 'Umar said your profound question traps meaning in a word for a benefit, but you don't see the benefit of God. He is the Author of benefit so He must see the benefit for us. You are a part whose act of speaking is beneficial, so why do you deny benefit to the Whole? If speech is not beneficial, be silent; if it is, give thanks, which is a duty for all. The meaning in poetry has no direction; it is like a sling, not under control.

SECTION 8 1529–1546 (18) *On the inner sense of "Let him who desires to sit with God sit with the Sufis."* (a) [1529–1534] The ambassador became beside himself and distraught at the power of God. He arrived at this *ḥāl* and it became a *maqām*. When the torrent reached the sea, it became the sea; he became alive, endowed with knowledge, filled with light and knowledge, (b) [1535–1540] Happy the man freed from himself who unites with one alive, and alas for those who consort with the dead. Flee to the Qur'ān of God and mingle with the prophets who are the fishes in God's holy sea. Accept it and read of the prophets and the bird, your soul, will be distressed in its cage. (c) [1541–1546] If the bird in the cage does not seek to escape, it is from ignorance. Prophets are those who have escaped and tell us how to do it. They tell us the way to escape so that you should not be wretched to be let out of the cage of worldly reputation, which is like a chain of iron.

Analysis of Discourse Five

The structure of this discourse is of eight sections in parallel arranged chiasmically. Section I tells of the ambassador who becomes a yearning seeker on hearing about 'Umar, the Perfect Man, who has no palace but an illumined spirit. Section 8 has this *ḥāl* become *maqām* in a permanent transformation of his nature. Also parallel is the expectation of the ambassador that someone as famous as 'Umar must have a palace and the final part of Section 8 about the "cage of reputation" which both parallels Section 1 and also foreshadows the next discourse. Having become a seeker in Section 1, in Section 2 the ambassador is full of questions, seeing 'Umar asleep, and has a question and answer session with himself. In the parallel Section 7, 'Umar is awake and the question and answer session continues with 'Umar answering and using the question itself as an illustration of the answer about trapping meaning in the form of words for benefit in the same way that spirits are imprisoned in bodies. Sections 3 and 6 are parallel in that 3 introduces the topic of the spirit's journey before becoming embodied, and this is developed in 6, since this is the "tale" to which 6 explicitly states it returns. In 3 the ambassador is "eager for mysteries," and in 6 there is given one of the greatest mysteries of all for a human being. Finally 4 and 5 are in parallel through the theme of *jabr* and free will and the two levels of causation. It can finally be noted that the final section contains exactly eighteen verses, a very important and spiritually significant number for Mawlānā and the later Mevlevi Order, arranged in three "paragraphs" of precisely six verses each, so it is to be expected that it carries a special emphasis. It can also be noted that Section 6, with a heading from the Qur'ān, has exactly six verses.

Interpretation of Discourse Five

The first thing to note about this discourse is that it is totally different from the first four in both tone and subject matter: the *nafs-e ammārah* is no longer the predominant theme.[16] This discourse belongs to the early Muslim period of 'Umar and its literal surface subject is about a distinguished non-Muslim meeting the Caliph. Its symbolic subject, as a number of commentators suggest, is the first encounter of a potential spiritual seeker with his future spiritual guide and teacher, his shaykh, a *walī*, saint, or the Perfect Man. This is foreshadowed in the last verse of the previous discourse when it says: "The true lion is he who conquers himself."

Section 1 starts from the ambassador's arrival in Medina with his horse and baggage, looking for the Caliph 'Umar's palace; it ends with horse and baggage forgotten, with the ambassador full of yearning, *shawq*, set only on finding 'Umar. The change was produced by hearing that 'Umar had no physical palace, only an illumined spirit, graces that he would not be able to see because the eye of his heart had first to be purged of the desires and defects of his selfhood, the *nafs*. He wonders how there could be a man of such graces in the world, yet hidden like spirit from the world. This awareness of one's own defects and the yearning to find a true friend of God, as exemplified in the ambassador, is the prior condition for a potential seeker to find his Sufi shaykh. When he finds 'Umar asleep he stands quietly at a distance. Sleep here could well symbolize that 'Umar was asleep to this world but awake to God. The ambassador experiences the contraries of love and awe, and wonders why he, a hardened warrior and familiar of kings, should be trembling in the presence of one asleep. He decides that it is awe, not for this dervish, but of God, since everyone fears someone who is afraid of God and makes that fear his practice. In Section 3, 'Umar takes away this fear and then gives spiritual instruction: about God, the Friend, and His loving kindness; about *ḥāl* and the rarer *maqām*, the stages of the soul and the journeys of the spirit; and of the time before existence. Mawlānā says: "The shaykh was adept and the disciple eager." The shaykh has found in the potential *sālik* (novice) the capacity to receive guidance. Section 4 sees the ambassador ask 'Umar how the spirit came into the world from above. In a wide-ranging answer, 'Umar tells how God cast spells to bring everything from nonexistence into existence; how a person is perplexed because He presents the choice: to do what He says, or not; but how He also gave each such person an inclination to do one of the two; how those who have cleared their spiritual ear to apprehend God's mysteries and Will, can receive *waḥy*, inspiration, which is beyond sense perception, discursive reason and opinion; how to follow the Will of God in this way is not compulsion but union; how those in whose hearts God has opened the spiritual eye have different qualities, vision and perspectives; how for them free will and compulsion are the dawning of God's light but for others it is only an intellectual matter; and how great is the Power of God. In all of this the shaykh is awakening the new pupil to what inner possibilities are open to him.

In Section 5 there is an opening passage, on which Nicholson comments, concerning how God's act brings our actions into existence and how Adam and Satan handled the situation differently. After a parable demonstrating the difference between free will and compulsion, the shaykh, or Mawlānā, dismisses this as just an intellectual quest, quite different from the spiritual quest. The intellectual quest is concerned with proofs, premises and entailments, but deals only with secondary causes, whereas the spiritual quest seeks illumination and what is beyond wonder. In this way, Mawlānā places the Power and Almightiness of God at the end of Section 4 and the beginning of Section 5; then, in both sections, he moves back through the intellectual understanding of free will and compulsion, to the spiritual quest and perspective and the dawning of God's Light in the heart. Within these two sections, then, there is quite an elaborate chiasmus at the very heart of the discourse. Section 6, which is significantly six verses—another important number for Mawlānā—has a heading from the Qur'ān. As Nicholson writes: "the world itself and the soul's experience in the world are nothing but epiphanies (*tajalliyāt*) of the all-encompassing Divine Knowledge and Power, through and in which we live and move and have our being" (commentary on Verse 1509). But while that is so, what function does this play in the initial instruction to a Sufi novice? It is how he can and should view everything he experiences: everywhere the Face of God and he himself as nothing. This is something the novice can begin at once to try, if only by his lack of success to provide a future ideal to aim for. Nicholson suggests the opening reference to the "story" refers back to Section 4, which, in a way, it does, but equally it follows the heading taken from the Qur'ān, from which Mawlānā would wish to claim he had never departed. The parallelism, however, requires this section to complete, exemplify, or fulfill Section 3 and the subtle discourses 'Umar addressed to the ambassador, and it is possible to see how it does this in a number of possible matters: the holy attributes of God, His loving kindness, *ḥāl* and *maqām*, and the journeys of the spirit, for instance.

Section 7 has the ambassador asking 'Umar to explain why the spirits have to suffer in bodies of clay. 'Umar answers in terms of benefit, using the analogy of confining meaning in words to good purpose. Just because the ambassador was blind to God's good purpose in so arranging things, why should he, a part, deny benefit to the whole, especially as He is the origin of all benefit. 'Umar's final line (Verse 1524) is a characteristic shaykh's way of concluding his discourse: "If there is no benefit in speech, do not speak; if there is, leave off making objections and give thanks." The first thing to note is the importance attached by Sufis to being aware of and carefully controlling one's speech. The second point is that objecting to the tribulations of the spirits is to deny Divine Providence and Wisdom, as Nicholson comments. The third point is the need to give thanks, not just to God for so arranging things, but also to 'Umar for a wonderful exposition and preparation of the ambassador novice. It is the first lesson in *adab*, seemliness to God and all of creation. Mawlānā's voice then joins in on the subject of giving thanks and not disputing, and concludes with a final verse amounting to: poetry can not fully express this; live it to find the meaning. The parallelism of this section is with Section 2. As proposed in the analysis, both are in the question and answer mode, which examples elsewhere in the *Mathnawī* suggest constitutes an accepted mode of parallelism. There is contrastive parallelism also, in that in the first section the ambassador was questioning silently to himself, whereas in this section the interlocutor is 'Umar and the questions and answers are, appropriately, in speech. Finally, in the first section the ambassador feels awe at seeing this great spirit in a sleeping body, so, when he objects to this arrangement, he is rightly told to be grateful. Section 8 says so much just in its heading to confirm that this discourse is about the first meeting with a shaykh. The ambassador had certainly taken in all that had been said about the Power of God, but, as Mawlānā foreshadowed in the final line of the previous section, he lived it too in experience to the point that he became beside himself and experienced a spiritual mystical state which is not infrequent at the first meeting with one shaykh or afterward, say, in a dream. Verses 1535–1536 conclude this discourse strongly and lead on to the foreshadowing of the next discourse. The Qur'ān contains the states of the prophets, the spirits who have escaped from their cages, who tell of the way to escape. Reading it will make the bird of one's soul distressed in its cage. The way to escape from the cage of reputation is to make oneself ill and wretched. In this it is both a looking back to 'Umar, who in the first section had clearly escaped from reputation through his inner and outer poverty, and a looking forward to the parrot in the next discourse.

Discourse Six: The Story of the Merchant and the Parrot

Summary of the Narrative and Thematic Content

SECTION 1 1547–1574 (28) *The story of the merchant to whom the parrot gave a message for the parrots of India on the occasion of his going there to trade.* (a) [1547–1554] A merchant had a parrot whom he asked what present he wanted the merchant to bring him from India. The parrot said: "Please tell the parrots there about my plight, that a parrot here is in prison by Divine destiny and yearns for you. She greets you and asks for justice and guidance. (b) [1555–1563] She says, is it right that I should die in grief in separation from you; that I should be imprisoned while you are in the rose garden? Remember this poor bird and drink a cup in my memory. (c) [1564–1570] What of the covenant and promises? If you have forsaken your servant because of inadequate service, your cruelty is in fact sweet. I am in love with the contraries of violence and gentleness. (d) [1571–1574] If I escape from this thorn and enter the garden of joy, I shall moan like the nightingale. What a nightingale that eats thorns and roses together; it must be a dragon since it make unsweet things sweet because of its Love. He is a lover of the Universal and himself the Universal; in love with himself, and seeking his own Love."

Fig. 3.7. A Synoptic View of Discourse Six

Sec. 1	Parrot's message to Indian parrots seeking guidance to escape cage
Sec. 2	Indian parrots as free spirits and Divine Intelligences
Sec. 3	Indian parrot dies; dangers of the tongue; speak without desire
Sec. 4	Only saints can do without abstinence; seekers should be careful
Sec. 5	Be silent; listen; have a master; weep; deal only with the lawful
Sec. 6	Merchant tells what happened; remorse for tongue; saints can correct
Sec. 7	Parrot also falls dead; merchant laments; separation; God transcends
Sec. 8	God is jealous and transcends all speech and contraries; Perfect Man
Sec. 9	The merchant on fire; thrashing like drowning man; exert yourself
Sec. 10	Dead parrot flew off; message was to act dead; captivity from voice
Sec. 11	Parrot gives advice; flies off as free spirit; merchant converted
Sec. 12	Body is cage; through praise and blame it deceives soul; be meek

SECTION 2 1575–1586 (12) *Description of the wings of the birds that are Divine Intelligences.* (a) [1575–1586] Such is the parrot of the soul, but where is the confidant of the spiritual birds? When he moans, without thanksgiving or complaint, and says: "Oh My Lord," then from God comes a hundred cries of "Here am I." To God his backsliding is better than obedience; his infidelity better than all faiths. Every moment he has an ascension to God. His form is on earth and his spirit is in 'No place' beyond all imaginings. He has control over place and No place. But stop explanation—God knows best—return to the bird and India and the merchant who accepted the message to her congeners.

SECTION 3 1587–1602 (16) *How the merchant saw the parrots of India in the plain and delivered the parrot's message.* (a) [1587–1589] In India, the merchant saw some parrots on a plain and gave voice, delivering the message, whereupon one of the parrots fell over and died. (b) [1590–1592] The merchant repented and said he had killed the parrot, who must have been a relative to his, two bodies and one spirit. Why had he killed this parrot with his speech? (c) [1593–1597] The tongue is like a stone that produces fire, so don't strike iron against it to tell a story or boast. You can't see the cotton ready to burn, but a single word can set a whole world on fire. Wicked are those who speak blind to the consequences. (d) [1598–1602] Spirits have the breath of Jesus, but in bodies one breath is a wound, another a plaster. If the bodies were removed every breath would be like the Messiah's. If you wish to utter sweet words, refrain from desire, do not eat this sweetmeat. The intelligent seek not the sweetmeat children crave, but patience and self-control, so that they may reach Heaven.

SECTION 4 1603–1614 (12) *Commentary on the saying of Farīd al-Dīn 'Aṭṭār—"You are a Sensualist, Oh heedless one, drink blood (mortify thyself) amidst the dust (of thy bodily existence). For, if the spiritualist drink a poison, it will be (to him as) an antidote."* (a) [1603–1614] A saint can drink poison because he has spiritual health so that he doesn't need abstinence, but the seeker is still in a fever. The Prophet said: "Oh Seeker, beware of taking on one who is sought for guidance." If you can't swim don't dive into the sea boastfully. The saint fetches pearls from the bottom of the sea; he turns earth into gold. The imperfect turns gold into ashes. The saint is hand-in-hand with God, the imperfect with the Devil. The saint turns ignorance into knowledge; the imperfect knowledge into ignorance. Whatever an ill man takes becomes illness, but for the saint infidelity becomes religion. If you are on foot don't contend with a horseman or you will lose your head.

SECTION 5 1615–1648 (34) *How the magicians paid respect to Moses, on whom be peace, saying, "What do you command? Will you cast down your rod first, or shall we?"* (a) [1615–1620] The magicians contended with Moses but let Moses go first. He said they should cast down their tricks first and in doing so won them to the religion. (b) [1621–1631] To the saint every mouthful, every saying, is lawful but if you are not perfect do not eat or speak. You are an ear and God told ears to be silent. A newborn baby is silent, it is all ear, until it learns to speak. In order to speak one must first hear, since there is no speech independent of hearing, except for that of the Creator who is the Originator and needs no master. The rest need a master and a pattern. (c) [1632–1637] If you can hear this discourse become a Seeker and shed tears because, by means of tears, Adam escaped from blame, and tears are the speech of the penitent. Adam came to earth to weep, so if you are from him, then seek forgiveness. The garden blooms from the heat of grief and the water of tears. (d) [1638–1648] But what do you know of tears, you bread lover? Empty of bread you will fill with jewels. Wean your soul from the Devil's milk and consort with the Angel. If you are gloomy it is from the Devil; light comes from what is lawful. From the lawful morsel comes wisdom and love, from the unlawful envy and ignorance. The morsel is seed whose fruit is thoughts; the morsel is sea, thoughts are its pearls. From the lawful morsel is the inclination to serve God and go yonder.

SECTION 6 1649–1690 (42) *How the merchant related to the parrot what he had witnessed on the part of the parrots of India.* (a) [1649–1657] The merchant returned from India and gave out his presents, but the parrot wanted to know what had happened. The merchant said he was full of remorse for delivering such an inconsiderate message, since on hearing of its pain one parrot trembled and died. He was sorry he had said it, but what was the use in repenting afterward. (b) [1658–1668] A word from the tongue is like an arrow from a bow, unrecoverable. It leaves its source, which should have been stopped, and lays waste the whole world. Our actions bring forth unseen results that are in fact from God, though they are attributed to us. Zayd shot 'Amr and he was in pain for a year before he died. God created the pain, but call Zayd a murderer and impute the pain to him. It is like this with sowing and speaking and laying snares and sexual intercourse; their results are determined by the will of God. (c) [1669–1680] But the saints can turn back an arrow that has been fired, with power from God. When a saint repents he can make what has been said forgotten, as in the Qur'ān: "They made you forget." These miraculous actions depend on their mystical seeing and understanding. But I must not say more, the Perfect One prevents me. (d) [1681–1690] Recollection and forgetting depend on that Perfect One and every night he empties hearts of good and evil thoughts while by day he fills the heart with pearls. All skills and thoughts return next day to their owners, good to good and evil to evil, just as on the day of Resurrection. At dawn the skills and thoughts return to their owners bringing useful things from other cities than their own.

SECTION 7 1691–1762 (72) *How the parrot heard what those parrots had done, and died in the cage, and how the merchant made lament for her.* (a) [1691–1693] When the parrot heard what the Indian parrot had done it trembled and fell over cold. The merchant sprang up and beat his breast. (b) [1694–1716] "Oh alas for my sweet-voiced friend and confidant who I gained so cheaply and quickly turned away from. Oh tongue, you have done me great damage, you are both a treasure and a disease without remedy. You have made my bird fly away. These cries of alas are caused by the idea of the Beloved and my state of separation. It was the jealousy of God against which there is no device. Where is there a heart not shattered by God's Love? Alas for my clever bird that interpreted my thoughts and consciousness and told me what should come to me so I might remember." (c) [1717–1726] That parrot is hidden within you whose voice is inspired and was before creation. She takes joy and gives joy. You were burning the soul for the sake of the body, but I am burning with love. How can such a moon be hidden beneath the clouds? I am burning with separation that is like a lion too great for the meadow. (d) [1727–1734] I am thinking of rhymes but my Beloved says think only of Me. Words I will throw into confusion to speak with you. I will tell you the word I did not tell Adam or Abraham, which Gabriel did not know nor Jesus spoke. (e) [1735–1741] I found individuality in nonindividuality. All kings are enslaved to their slaves, all loved ones to their lovers. Water seeks the thirsty as the thirsty seek water. (f) [1742–1750] He is your lover so be silent. Dam the flood of ecstasy. He who is drowned in God wishes to be more so, but it is wrong to distinguish joy and woe. It is lawful for Him to slay the whole world. We gained the price and the blood-price and hastened to gamble our soul away. (g) [1751–1762] The life of lovers consists in death. I sought to win His heart but he put me off saying I held Him in disdain because I had bought Him so cheaply and he that buys cheaply gives cheaply. I am drowned in love but have told it briefly otherwise you and my tongue would be consumed. I am sour-faced out of sweetness, silent out of fullness of speech, and I have told but one of a hundred mysteries.

SECTION 8 1763–1813 (51) *Commentary on the saying of the Hakīm (Sanā'ī): "Anything that causes you to be left behind on the Way, what matter* *whether it be infidelity or faith? Any form that causes thee to fall from the Beloved, what matter if it be ugly or beautiful?" and (a discourse) on the meaning of the words of the Prophet: "Verily, Sa'd is jealous and I am more jealous than Sa'd, and Allāh is more jealous than I; and because of His jealousy He hath forbidden foul actions both outward and inward."* (a) [1763–1772] The whole world is jealous because God is superior to the world in jealousy. The king is jealous of anyone who having seen His face, prefers the mere scent. The root of all jealousies is in God; ours is but a mere shadow. (b) [1773–1782] I will now complain of the cruelty of that fickle Beauty. I wail because He wants the two worlds to wail and I am in love with my pain. People think it is tears they shed for Him but they are pearls. My heart is not really complaining, nor is it really tormented, this is its poor pretence. (c) [1783–1792] You are the dais and I am the threshold, but not really, for where the Beloved is there is no We or I. You contrived this I and We so that You might play the game of worship with Yourself, that we should become one soul and at last be submerged in the Beloved. Do Thou come, Oh Lord of the Creative Word, You who transcends "Come" and all speech. The body can only imagine You as a body and invents sadness and joy, nor can the heart see You, relying on these two borrowed concepts. (d) [1793–1803] In the garden of Love there are many fruits other than these two; Love is greater than these. Tell the tale of the soul rent in pieces; leave the tale of the rose, tell of the nightingale that is parted from the rose. (e) [1803–1806] Our state is not caused by grief and joy, nor from fancy and imagination, but it is rare. It does not come from wrongdoing or from doing good, for these like grief and joy come into existence and everything that exists also dies. God is their heir. (f) [1807–1813] It is Dawn, Oh Supporter of the dawn, ask pardon for me from Ḥusām al-Dīn. By Your Light we drink the wine of Mansūr; what other wine could produce rapture? Wine became drunk with us not we with it. We are as bees and the body is as wax; we have made the body cell by cell.

SECTION 9 1814–1824 (11) *Reverting to the tale of the merchant who went to trade in India.* (a) [1814–1824] What happened to the merchant? He was on fire with grief and was thrashing about like a drowning man. The Friend loves this agitation, since it is better to struggle than to lie still. The King of all is never idle so exert yourself to the utmost since the King sees into the soul.

SECTION 10 1825–1844 (20) *How the merchant cast the parrot out of the cage and how the dead parrot flew away.* (a) [1825–1829] The merchant threw out the parrot and it suddenly flew to a lofty bough. The merchant was amazed and asked it what it had learned from the Indian parrot. (b) [1830–1832]

The parrot said that by her act she implied that I should abandon my voice and love for my master, because it was my voice that had put me into this cage, and I should be as dead in order to obtain release. (c) [1833–1844] A grain the birds will eat, a flower the children pluck, so hide the grain and the flower. A hundred fates await anyone who gives his beauty to auction; plots, envies, foes, and even friends take his life. Take shelter in God who will shelter the spirit, so that fire and water and stone will become your army as they did for Moses and Noah, Abraham and John the Baptist.

SECTION 11 1845–1848 (4) *How the parrot bade farewell to the merchant and flew away.* (a) [1845–1848] The parrot gave him some advice and then bade farewell. The merchant said: "God protect you, you have shown me a new way." This new way I will take, he said to himself, for it is toward the light and my soul is no less than that of the parrot.

SECTION 12 1849–1877 (29) *The harmfulness of being honored by the people and of becoming conspicuous.* (a) [1849–1877] The body is cage-like and, when it is affected by those who come and go, it is a thorn to the soul. If you are praised, it becomes the source of arrogance; if blamed, your heart will burn. Both praise and blame will last for many days and will deceive the soul. Be lowly of spirit through meekness, never domineer. Otherwise, when the beauty has gone, your companions will treat you like a ghost and even the devil will not approach you, because you are worse than a devil. Then they clung to you, now that you are like this, they fled.

Analysis of Discourse Six

This discourse is foreshadowed by the last seven verses in Discourse Five, which address themselves first to the Qur'ān, saying that, reading the stories of the prophets, the bird of your soul should seek to escape from its cage by following the prophets' way. Their way to escape from this narrow cage was to make themselves ill and very wretched in order to escape from reputation. "Worldly reputation is a strong chain; in the Way how is this less than a chain of iron?" (1546).

The discourse has twelve sections and is organized by chiasmus and parallelism. It completes the first half of Book One. The next discourse, which begins the second half, also has twelve sections. In between comes a separate link section explaining "Whatever God Wills comes to pass." This section not only links the two discourses, but it is the central point of Book One and thereby connects Discourse One with Discourse Twelve which, in their own ways, both concern the Will of God. It is interesting that this linking section has exactly the same number of verses as the opening proem of the *Mathnawī.*

In this discourse, Section 1 and Section 12 are in parallel and accord with the foreshadowing. Section 1 introduces the parrot of the soul in the cage sending a message to the parrots of India lamenting its captivity and its separation from the free spirits, followed by twelve verses in Mawlānā's voice including, "If I escape from this thorn and enter the garden, I shall moan like a nightingale." The thorn here is unspecified, but Section 12, whose heading itself accords with the foreshadowing, reads: "The body is cage-like: the body, amidst the cajoleries of those who come in and go out, became a thorn to the soul." It then goes on to elaborate on how praise and blame create this thorn and deceive the soul. Lowliness of spirit and meekness is recommended as the remedy. Section 2 speaks of the other parrots, the free spirits or Divine Intelligences, and their relationship with God. It is in parallel with Section 11 in which the parrot, now free from its cage, gives spiritual advice and then flies off to freedom, as a Divine Intelligence. Section 3 is closely parallel with Section 10. The first parallelism is that the behavior of the Indian parrot in acting dead in Section 3 is explained in Section 10 as telling the parrot to abandon his voice, which had put it in the cage, and to be as if dead in order to obtain release. The second parallelism is that the merchant's tongue apparently had killed the parrot and there is a warning in Section 3 never to be blind to the consequences of what you say or you may set the world on fire. If you want to utter sweet words, refrain from desire and practice self-control and patience so you can reach Heaven. This parallels Section 10 in that the parrot is in the cage because of its uttering sweet words and on account of its voice.

Section 4 parallels Section 9 in that the first says only a saint can do without abstinence and self-control, while the seeker needs it since he is still in a fever. As such he should not contend with the sea or fire, and so forth. In Section 9, the merchant appears as a seeker on fire with grief and thrashing about like a drowning man, with the comment that the Friend loves this agitation. It further urges effort and struggle. Sections 5, 6, 7, and 8 form a chiasmic block of four longer sections, teaching story, story teaching, climaxing with the name of Ḥusām al-Dīn. Section 5 is parallel with Section 8. Section 5 says unless you are perfect, be silent and a hearer, because only God's Word does not need a master and a pattern. Become a seeker and shed tears, eat only the lawful. Section 8 lifts to a different level, to the level of the Lord of the Creative Word, who transcends all speech, where what seem to be tears are in fact pearls, where Love transcends the lawful and unlawful and all contraries and where there is the master and pattern, the Perfect Man. It is the pattern from this level by which we make our bodies cell by cell. Section 6 is parallel with Section 7 in the most obvious sense that in 6 the merchant tells what the Indian parrot did, and in 7 his own parrot did exactly the same. In 6 the word is fired from the tongue like an arrow, unrecoverable except by the Perfect Man who can correct and cause to forget. In 7 the merchant again blames his tongue, but thereafter the section lifts to a higher level and there is further treatment of words in that Mawlānā's voice says he is thinking of rhymes but the Beloved says think only of Him, since He will throw words into confusion to speak with him, and will tell him the word he did not even tell Adam or Abraham or Gabriel. Thus the discourse makes use of parallelism and chiasmus, with the second half operating mostly at a higher level of application than the first. It can also be read as three blocks of four sections.

Interpretation of Discourse Six

The commentators agree that the parrot is the spirit or soul; the Indian parrots are free spirits, the Divine Intelligences or the Prophets.[17] The merchant symbolizes both a seeker and the *nafs-e lawwāmah*, the selfhood which blames itself. The cage is both the body, embodied-ness, but also what Mawlānā says it is, the cage of reputation, being imprisoned by what people say about one, whether praise or blame. The real difficulty with this discourse for the reader is how to situate it, especially as Mawlānā in a number of long passages soars aloft in flights of wonderful mystical imagination, vision, and explanation. In the sequence of discourses so far, four have dealt with the selfhood that commands to evil, *nafs-e ammārah*, and Discourse Five has a noble and sensitive soul meet 'Umar as Perfect Man, also representing a responsive Sufi novice meeting his shaykh for the first time, and ending in a spiritual experience of the Power of Almighty God. The context of this discourse is therefore, on the one hand, that of a Sufi novice at an early stage of his training; on the other, that of the *nafs-e lawwāmah*, the self that blames itself. Both are fully compatible one with another.

Nicholson's commentary on this discourse is extensive, full of valuable information on particular points and passages, but it never treats it as a whole; as always, it is necessary but never sufficient. Looking at the discourse from the orientation just suggested, in Section 1, the scene is set narratively and spiritually, the novice (*sālik*) being given a view of the situation of his own *rūḥ*, spirit, suffering in prison, lamenting its isolation from the spiritual world, and like a separated lover complaining of infidelity and cruelty on the part of the

Beloved, who really loves only Himself. Section 2 continues from this viewpoint of the *rūḥ*, but here it seems to be more about the spirits of saints and shaykhs, prophets and the Perfect Man, whose form is on earth but whose spirit is in "no-place" beyond all imaginings. These are the Divine Intelligences, the parrots of India, the real congeners of the *sālik's* spirit, *rūḥ*. Section 3 sees the Indian parrot fall as if dead and the merchant repenting, blaming himself for the tragedy because of what he said. This is the *nafs-e lawwāmah*, the selfhood that blames itself, coupled with instruction about the real damage the tongue can do when it speaks without regard to the consequences. The instruction to the *sālik* about guarding the tongue leads to the subject of the need for self-control and to refrain from self-indulgence. This leads on in Section 4 to a clear differentiation between what is possible for a saint and what a *sālik* can do. The *sālik* needs abstinence, and is warned not to try going beyond his limitations out of self-conceit, because he is still the imperfect man not the Perfect Man. This section is twelve verses, six of admonitions for the *sālik* and six about the Perfect Man.

The second block of four sections begins with Section 5 in which the magicians contend with Moses, the Perfect Man, and have to acknowledge defeat. This is an example of going beyond one's limitations, and failing. In the Perfect Man's mouth every mouthful and every saying is lawful, but since the *sālik* is imperfect, he should remain silent, and through silence learn how to speak. Only God follows no master, but the *sālik* should, for he has need of a pattern. He should don the dervish frock and follow Adam, weeping in a private place. He should eat only lawful food, for from that come knowledge, wisdom, love, and tenderness, as well as the inclination to serve God and ascend. Section 6 has the merchant telling the parrot what happened in India and how much he regrets what he said. Then Mawlānā's voice instructs the *sālik*, again about the damage the tongue can do, but how only the saint can correct such mistakes because he is able to control what people remember and what they forget. This completes the first half of the discourse.

The second half of the discourse begins with Section 7 in which the merchant's parrot falls down dead. The merchant is totally distraught; to self-blame for his tongue, is now added loss and great pain. His speech from Verse 1694 to Verse 1716, ranges from his sadness at losing his bosom confidant, to heaping blame on his tongue—a treasure and a disease without remedy—to the recognition that his "alas" was really for the Beloved and that it was the jealousy of God that has broken his heart, since His Love will not allow any rival. His intelligent parrot had been the interpreter of his thought and inmost consciousness. From Verse 1717 to Verse 1762, the voice is Mawlānā's addressed to the *sālik*, apart from some verses attributed to God addressed to Mawlānā. The *sālik* is told he too has a parrot hidden within, while he is burning to satisfy the body and the *nafs*. Mawlānā also is burning but from love of God in separation. He wanted to produce poetry but then God told him to think of nothing but God, for words are thorns in the hedge of the vineyard. Mawlānā is selfless and negated; he has found individuality in nonindividuality. God loves his slaves, those ready to die for Him, those who prostrate themselves before Him and those intoxicated with love for Him. Mawlānā speaks of ecstasies of love, of how he who is drowned in God, wishes to be more drowned, but there is a price, since the life of lovers consists of death, the only way to win the Beloved's heart. Mawlānā speaks of his transactions with the Beloved and that he is drowned in love. The *sālik* has been initiated into the way of Love, which dying to selfhood permits. The instruction and initiation continue in Section 8, when after an initial passage on God's jealousy, Verses 1763–1772, Mawlānā produces an outpouring of mystical love poetry that continues until dawn and Verse 1813. Toward the end of this section, which completes the second of the three blocks, comes the name of Ḥusām al-Dīn, supposedly his amanuensis, to whom he apologizes for the lateness of the hour.

The final block returns to the merchant, with Section 9 devoted to his burning grief and anguish and his terrible agitation. It is a wonderful portrayal of the *nafs-e lawwāmah*, the selfhood which blames itself. Section 10 has the merchant throwing out the dead parrot, only to be amazed when it flies up to a branch and has a conversation. It explains that the Indian parrot had sent a message: "Your voice and affection for your master keep you in the cage; become dead like me to obtain your release." Mawlānā's voice continues the explanation: if someone offers a skill or his beauty at auction, a hundred evil fates will overtake him, from enemies and even friends, so his lifetime will be taken up. Therefore flee to the shelter of God's Grace which will, in contrast, grant only blessings. Section 11 has the parrot and the merchant saying good-bye to one another, and the merchant saying the parrot had taught him a new way, which he will follow. The final section, Section 12, contains a wonderful analysis of the corrosive nature of both praise and blame and how they damage the soul, all in Mawlānā's voice. This section draws the moral from the animal fable, but not the discourse as a whole, at a spiritual and psychological level.

Finally, to consider the rhetorical structure of this discourse synoptically, it can be said that Mawlānā has woven together three threads: an animal fable warning of the dangers of reputation and how to escape from the trap it creates; the nature of the *nafs-e lawwāmah*, and the training of a fairly new *sālik*. Although all three strands are interwoven, the narrative framework of the animal fable is found predominantly in the first three sections, the last three sections, and at the beginning of the two crucial central sections. The parrot is in the cage because of its voice. The message sent by the example of the Indian parrot is to pretend to be dead to obtain release. It works, and the moral is to remain inconspicuous and meek to avoid being put into the cage of reputation. The positioning of the sections makes clear that the animal fable is the outer framing of the discourse. The *nafs-e lawwāmah* thread begins in the first half with the merchant in Sections 3 and 6 expressing great regret and remorse for having spoken as he did with its tragic consequence. But it is the second half of the discourse, in Sections 7 and 9, that the self-blame reaches fever pitch, when he thinks he has killed his own parrot: that is, he becomes aware that he might have destroyed his own soul. The third thread is that of the training of a fairly new *sālik*. Here again there is a significant difference between the first and second half. In the first half, the training is very sober. Taking up the voice theme which connects all three threads, the *sālik* is urged to prefer silence and to watch his speech very carefully. Of him, abstinence is required and the avoidance of self-indulgence. He requires a master and needs a pattern to follow: to wear the dervish frock, to weep in private, to eat and follow only what is lawful, to recognize that he is imperfect and not to strive beyond his limitations out of conceit. This is his training in the first half of the discourse, but, in the second half, the training consists of the awakening of love for God within the *sālik* by means, here, of flights of wonderful mystical love poetry and the example of Mawlānā, no doubt also augmented by the striking Mevlevi use of *samā'*. Sobriety in the first half, ecstasy in the second: two aspects of the training connected or made possible by the central point of the discourse, where the two parrots pretend to be dead. What does this mean for the *sālik*? Here there is no need to speculate, since Mawlānā explains in Verse 1909: "The meaning of dying (as conveyed) by the parrot was self-abasement, supplication, needfulness (*niyāz*); make yourself dead in supplication and poverty of spirit (*faqr*)."

There remains the autobiographical element in this discourse. Position and reputation are two of the first things a shaykh will attack in a disciple, as they constitute a major obstacle to spiritual progress. There is evidence that Shams did this to Mawlānā, because he ceased teaching and preaching, he withdrew and appointed deputies to carry out his former obligations, and he made himself as inconspicuous as he could. To escape from the cage of reputation and position, he abandoned his previous voice; it is fortunate for posterity that as a consequence he was given a new voice, as one of the world's greatest mystical poets.

Link Section and the Center of Book One

Summary

LINK SECTION 1878–1912 (35) *Explanation of (the Tradition) "Whatever God wills comes to pass."* (a) [1878–1882] We are nothing without the Favors of God; without these Favors and those of the elect, even an angel is nothing. "Oh God, Your Bounty fulfills every need and Your guidance is that no one should be mentioned but You. You have covered up many of our faults until now. May the drop of knowledge You gave us, be united with Your seas. (b) [1883–1887] Save the drop of knowledge in my soul from carnality and the body's clay, before clay and wind sweep it away. Even then You can retrieve it since a drop that vanishes into nonexistence will flee back at Your Call. (c) [1888–1895] Your Decree is drawing forth the many opposites locked in mutual destruction and caravans constantly speed from nonexistence to existence. At night, all thoughts and understanding are naught, and plunge in the deep Sea, only to surface at dawn. In autumn, leaves and boughs plunge into the sea of Death and the black crow mourns their passing, but then Your Edict requires death to give back what it devoured." (d) [1896–1908] In you there is constant autumn and spring. Look at the garden full of fresh green flowers: their scent is these words from the Universal Intelligence which guides your way and will deliver you. The scent of Joseph cures blindness and opened the eye of Jacob. You are no Joseph, so be a Jacob and grieve and weep. In the presence of Joseph don't pretend to beauty, offer nothing but the sighs and supplication (*niyāz*) of Jacob. (e) [1909–1912] The meaning of the death of the parrot was *niyāz*, supplication, self-abasement, and needfulness, so make yourself dead in self-abasement and poverty, *faqr*, of spirit so that the Breath of Jesus may revive you and make you fair and blessed. How can a rock be covered with spring flower? Become earth so multicolored flowers may bloom. You have been rock long enough: Just for a try, be earth!

Comment

This is a wonderful sustained passage in praise of the Greatness and Majesty of God and all His Bounty.[18] From God's Edict everything is constantly reborn. Universal Intelligence, *'aql-e kullī*, cures spiritual blindness and revives the spirit. The way to access it is to make oneself dead through self-abasement and needfulness, *niyāz*—the meaning of the death of the parrot—and spiritual poverty and humility. These are the preconditions for the Breath of Jesus to revive and produce spiritual resurrection. This section, at the very center of Book One, fulfills several functions: it links Discourse Six to Discourse Seven; it connects the beginning of the book to the end of the book; it acts as the gateway to the second half of the book. The link between the two discourses is made by looking back to the parrot and forward to the state of the Harper in the next discourse. In both discourses, the subject, at one level, is the *nafs-e lawwāmah*, the self that blames itself, and the theme of *niyāz*. This theme, *niyāz*, together with *faqr*, spiritual poverty, is also the gateway to the second half of Book One. Another central theme of this section is spiritual resurrection, which foreshadows at least Discourse Seven, and arguably the whole of the second half. It is interesting too that Discourse Six ends with verses about the Devil's work, and Discourse Seven begins with a section on God's Work. In between comes this section with the title: "Whatever God Wills Comes to Pass." This title, coming as it does at the very center of the book, connects Discourse One with Discourse Twelve, through the major theme of the Will of God and killing. It is astonishing how meticulous Mawlānā has been in his planning of this section so that it can fulfill all three functions at the same time. But as with the previous link section, it is important to stress that its significance should not be reduced to its functional roles. That this section is special in its own right is indicated by the fact that, like the Proem that opened the *Mathnawī* and Book One, this central section also has thirty-five verses, again divided eighteen: seventeen, the first half a prayer of gratitude and praise of God and His Works, the second addressed to the spiritual traveler, not this time referred to as "son" but as "brother," indicative more of spiritual comradeship than the hierarchical relationship of master to pupil. It would have been incongruous to emphasize the master-pupil relationship when speaking of *niyāz*, self-abasement, because "dying to self," like all death, is a great leveler. But the theme of death also holds out the hope of resurrection and this is a major emphasis of this section as it is of the next discourse.

Discourse Seven:
The Story of the Old Harper in the Times of 'Umar

Summary of the Narrative and Thematic Content

SECTION 1 1913–1950 (38) *The story of the old Harper who in the time of 'Umar, may God be well-pleased with him, on a day when he was starving played his harp for God's sake in the graveyard.* (a) [1913–1918] There was a Harper

Fig. 3.8. A Synoptic View of Discourse Seven

Sec. 1	Harper like Isrāfīl; God's voice; saints revive dead
Sec. 2	God's breath; hard to bear; thorn; Prophet; harmony
Sec. 3	Prophet; trees like interred; God in seasons; rain
Sec. 4	Clouds of Unseen world; seasonal rain; saints' breath
Sec. 5	Holy breaths like spring; don't cover up against them
Sec. 6	Rain of mercy or menace; against grief and envy; Harper
Sec. 7	Harper old; repentant soul sings to God; God's Command
Sec. 8	God's voice to 'Umar; God's Call even to wood and stone
Sec. 9	Prophet buries moaning pillar; externalists and miracles
Sec. 10	Abū Jahl's pebbles proclaim the declaration of faith
Sec. 11	'Umar gives message; Harper breaks harp and repents
Sec. 12	Harper goes beyond wailing and soul awakes

whose breath was an ornament and whose voice was so beautiful he was like Isrāfīl whose voice and song bring the souls of the dead into their bodies. (b) [1919–1924] The prophets have a note, unheard by the sensual ear, which brings life to the seeker. The peri has a note man cannot hear, but both the notes of man and peri are of this world; higher than both is the note of the heart. (c) [1925–1936] The notes of the saints say: "Oh particles of not-being, rise up from vain imaginings; your everlasting soul was not born nor grew in this world of generation and corruption." At the slightest note the souls will lift their heads up from their tombs. Listen closely for that note since it is not far off. The saints are the Isrāfīl of now who bring to life dead souls in the body's grave. They recognize this voice as different, the work of the voice of God, calling those who were dead and decayed to arise. The voice of the Friend, which calls those rotten with death inside to return from nonexistence, is from God even if from the saint's throat. (d) [1937–1942] God becomes the saint's tongue, his eye, his pleasure and his wrath, and God says sometimes it is you and sometimes it is I, but whichever, God is the illuminating Sun whose Breath removes difficulties and darkness. (e) [1943–1950] To Adam he showed the Names, and Adam showed the Names to others; it doesn't matter whether you get them from Adam or from Himself. If a lamp is lit from a candle, its light derives from the candle and from the lamp and all the lamps that have been lit from that lamp. Either derive the light from the present saints or from those who have gone before.

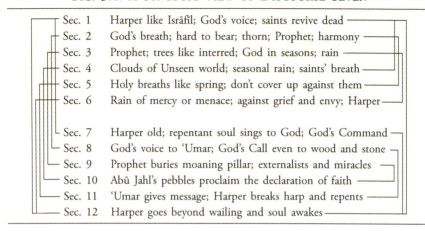

SECTION 2 1951–2011 (61) *Explanation of the Tradition, "Verily your Lord hath, during the days of your time, certain breathings: oh, address yourselves to*

receive them." (a) [1951–1959] The prophet said the Breathings of God come in these times and bring life to whom they will. Be careful not to miss them for they bring life to the dead and extinguish a burning soul. This infinite Breath is awesome and the Qur'ān says: "They refused to bear it." and "They shrank from it." (b) [1960–1971] Last night a breathing came but a morsel barred the way. Luqmān is the soul barred by *luqmah*, a morsel. Pull out the thorn from Luqmān's sole for his spirit is the rose garden of God. (c) [1972–1981] Muḥammad came to make harmony. The word for spirit is feminine but spirit is above gender. Spirit produces inner sweetness. When the lover of God is fed wine from within, reason will remain lost. (d) [1982–1985] Partial reason is the denier of Love and is naught because it did not become naught. (e) [1986–2005] The Spirit is perfection and its call is perfection as in the singing of Bilāl, who breathed the breath by which the heavens are made witless. Muḥammad was beside himself at that voice and missed his prayer on the night he kissed hands in the presence of the Bride. Love and Spirit are veiled so do not fault me for calling God the Bride. Fault is relative. The bodies of saints are pure as their spirits. The salt of Muḥammad is extremely refined and his heirs are with you, so seek them. (f) [2006–2011] Don't seek the spiritual heir before or after, these are attributes of the body. Open your vision with the pure light of God and don't be short-sighted and think you are living bodily in grief and joy. It is a day of rain; journey on, but sped by the rain of the Lord.

SECTION 3 2012–2034 (23) *The story of 'Ā'isha, may God be well-pleased with her, how she asked Muṣṭafā (Muḥammad), saying: "It rained today: since you went to the graveyard, how is it that your clothes are not wet?"* (a) [2012–2013] Muḥammad went to the graveyard with the bier of a friend and he made the earth fill the grave and quickened his seed under the earth. (b) [1214–1219] Trees are like the interred; they have lifted their hand from the earth and give a message about the earth's heart. God imprisons them in winter and revives them by means of spring and gives them leaves. (c) [2020–2026] God causes roses to grow in the hearts of His friends, each telling of the Universal. Their scent confuses the skeptics who shrink from the scent and pretend to look elsewhere but they have no eye. (d) [2026–2034] When Muḥammad returned from the graveyard 'Ā'isha said: "It rained today; how wonderful your clothes are dry." Muḥammad said: "What is on your head?" She replied: "Your old plaid." "That is why," Muḥammad said, "God showed to your pure eye the rain of the Unseen. It did not rain from your clouds today but from other clouds and another sky."

SECTION 4 2035–2045 (11) *Commentary on the verse of Hakīm (Sanā'ī): "In the realm of the soul are the skies lording over the skies of this world. In the Way of the spirit there are lowlands and highlands, there are lofty mountains and seas."* (a) [2035–2041] The Unseen world has other clouds and another sun and sky which only the elect see. There is vernal rain for nurture and autumnal rain for decay; similarly with sun, cold and wind. Even so in the Unseen world there is loss and gain, benefit and damage. (b) [2042–2045] The breath of the saints is from that spiritual springtime from which grows a green garden. Their breath is like spring rain on a tree. If there is a dry tree, don't blame their life-quickening breath. Their wind did its work and blew on; he that had a soul preferred it to his own.

SECTION 5 2046–2059 (14) *On the meaning of the tradition, "Take advantage of the coolness of the spring season, etc."* (a) [2046–2048] The Prophet told his friends not to cover their bodies from the cold of spring since it is like spring to a tree, but to flee from autumn cold, which damages the garden and vine. (b) [2049–2053] Traditionalists treat this externally but in the sight of God autumn is the *nafs* and desire; intellect and spirit are the spring and everlasting life. You have partial reason hidden in you; seek one who can make it whole so that Universal reason can defeat the *nafs*. (c) [2054–2059] The tradition means holy breaths are like spring. Do not cover your bodies against the sayings of the saints whether he speak hot or cold. The garden of spirits is living through him.

SECTION 6 2060–2071 (12) *How 'Ā'isha, may God be well-pleased with her, asked Muṣṭafā (Muḥammad), saying, "What was the inner meaning of today's rain?"* (a) [2060–2065] She asked: "Was it the rain of mercy or the rain of menace? Was it vernal or autumnal?" The Prophet replied: "It was to allay the grief on the race of Adam, since if man had to burn with such grief the world would become desolate." (b) [2066–2071] Forgetfulness of God sustains this world and intellect is a bane. Intellect is of the other world and can overthrow this world. Intellect is the sun, cupidity the ice; intellect the water, this world the dirt. A trickle of intellect is coming to restrain cupidity and envy; if the trickle grew stronger neither vice nor virtue would remain in the world. Let us go back to the tale of the minstrel.

SECTION 7 2072–2103 (32) *The remainder of the story of the old Harper and the explanation of its issue (moral).* (a) [2072–2077] That minstrel with the wonderful voice grew old and his soul-refreshing voice became useless.

(b) [2078–2081] The only thing that does not grow foul is the voice and the breath of the saint. (c) [2082–2087] When he grew old and feeble he said: "Oh God, you have greatly favored this vile wretch who has sinned for seventy years, but yet You have never withheld Your bounty. I can't earn, so today I am Your guest and I will play my harp for You." He went to the graveyard of Medina in search of God, craving from God, who accepted adulterated coin, the price of silk for his harp. (d) [2088–2095] He played a long time, then lay down and went to sleep. His soul freed from his body sang in the spiritual world: "Would that I could stay here in this garden and springtime." (e) [2096–2103] While his soul was in the huge magnitude of the spiritual world and God's Munificence, which if it were manifest would empty the material world, the Divine Command was coming to the minstrel: "Be not covetous; the thorn is out of your foot, depart."

SECTION 8 2104–2112 (9) *How the heavenly voice spoke to 'Umar while he was asleep, saying, "Give a certain sum of gold from the treasury to the man who is sleeping in the graveyard."* (a) [2104–2112] God sent 'Umar a slumber, which he recognized as having a purpose and went to sleep and dreamt that a voice came from God and his spirit heard. That voice is the origin of every sound and not just people of every race have understood it, even wood and stone as well. Every moment the call comes from God, "Am I not your Lord" and, if they are inarticulate, still their coming from nonexistence to existence is equivalent to "Yes." Listen to a story showing the awareness of wood and stone.

SECTION 9 2113–2153 (41) *How the moaning pillar complained when they made a pulpit for the Prophet, on whom be peace—for the multitude had become great, and said, "We do not see thy blessed face when thou art exhorting us"—and how the Prophet and his Companions heard that complaint, and how Muṣṭafā conversed with the pillar in a clear language.* (a) [2113–2124] The moaning pillar complained to the Prophet that he used to support the Prophet but now he used another support. He told the Prophet he wanted to endure forever, so the Prophet buried the pillar in the earth so that it might be raised like humanity on the day of Resurrection. This is to show that those called to God disengage from the work of this world. Only those who know the spiritual mysteries can truly understand the complaining of inanimate creation. (b) [2125–2140] The conformists and externalists rely on opinion and are easily swayed by a single doubt raised by the vile Devil. The logician's leg is made of wood and is infirm, unlike the steadfastness of the supreme saint, who is possessed of spiritual wisdom. The blind man's leg is a staff with which they see the way, but only under the protection of the spiritually clear-sighted without whom they would be dead. The blind produce nothing and if God did not bestow mercy, the wood of logical deduction and inference would break. God gave you the staff but it has become a weapon of attack and quarrel, even against God, so break it; bring a seer between yourself and God, lay hold of the skirt of Him who gave the staff. (c) [2141–2145] Consider Moses whose staff became a serpent and the Prophet whose pillar moaned, each proclaiming the truth of Religion five times a day. These miracles would not have been necessary if this spiritual perception were not non-intellectual, since the intellect would have agreed. The untrodden Way is unintelligible but accepted by the hearts of the elect. (d) [2146–2153] In fear of the miracles of the Prophets the skeptics have slunk away, Muslims only in name. The philosopher has not the courage to breathe a word or the true Religion will confound him.

SECTION 10 2154–2160 (7) *How the Prophet—on whom be peace—manifested a miracle by the speaking of the gravel in the hand of Abū Jahl—God's curse be upon him—and by the gravel bearing witness to the truth of Muḥammad.* (a) [2154–2160] Abū Jahl hid some pebbles in his hand and asked the Prophet to say what they were, if he was really the Messenger from God. The prophet said: "Wouldn't you rather they declare I am truthful?" and Abū Jahl agreed. Then the pebbles recited the Muslim proclamation of faith and Abū Jahl flung them to the ground.

SECTION 11 2161–2198 (38) *The rest of the story of the minstrel, and how the Commander of the Faithful, 'Umar, conveyed to him the message spoken by the heavenly voice.* (a) [2161–2166] Hear now of the minstrel who had become desperate from waiting. The voice of God said to 'Umar: " 'Umar, redeem our servant from want. A favorite servant is in the graveyard; take him seven hundred dinars from the treasury and tell him it is for the silk and to come back for more." (b) [2167–2174] 'Umar, in awe of that voice, went round the graveyard, but it was empty except for that old man. (c) [2175–2183] Finally, he sat next to him and the old Harper woke up and was terrified. 'Umar told him God had praised him and greeted him and asked how he was in his distress and sent this gold for the silk. He said spend them and come back for more. (d) [2184–2194] The old man wept long in gratitude and shame, then took his harp and broke it, accusing it of being a curtain between him and God for seventy years and bringing him disgrace before Divine perfection. Then he asked God for mercy on a life of iniquity, a life spent breath by breath in treble and bass so that in this preoccupation with the twenty-four melodies the caravan passed and the day grew late. (e) [2195–2198] God help me against this self of mine which is seeking help from You; I seek justice from this justice seeking self. I shall only get justice from Him who is nearer to me than myself. This I-hood comes to me every moment from Him; when it fails I see only Him, as when you are with someone who is counting out gold to you, you look at him, not at oneself.

SECTION 12 2199–2222 (24) *How 'Umar bade the Harper turn his gaze from the stage of weeping, which is (self-) existence to the stage of absorption (in God) which is nonexistence (of self).* (a) [2199–2208] 'Umar said to him: "Your wailing is a sign of self-consciousness (sobriety). For one who has passed beyond self-consciousness, sobriety is a sin. Sobriety arises from recollection of the past; past and future separate you from God. So abandon past and future. When you are seeking God, that is still self-consciousness; when you come home, you are still with yourself. Your repentance is worse than your sin; when will you repent of your repentance? Once you were in love with music, now you are in love with weeping and wailing. (b) [2209–2215] 'Umar was the reflector of mysteries and the old man's soul was awakened. Like his soul he became without grief or laughter, and his other soul came to life. Then a state came upon him which took him beyond heaven and earth; a seeking beyond all seeking. Beyond words and feelings and drowned in the beauty of Divine majesty; drowned beyond deliverance or recognition except by the Divine Ocean. (c) [2216–2224] Partial intellect would not tell of the mysteries of Universal Intellect were there not constant impulses requiring their manifestation. Since there are such demands Universal Intellect reaches partial intellect. The old man and his spiritual experiences have passed beyond the veil; he is beyond speech and half his tale is untold. To reach such enjoyment we must gamble away a thousand souls like the falcon and the sun of this world. The sun is life-diffusing, every moment becoming empty and refilling again. Oh Sun of Reality, diffuse spiritual life; bring newness to the old world. Soul and spirit are coming from the Unseen into human existence like running water.

Analysis of Discourse Seven

This discourse is foreshadowed in the preceding Link Section, not only in the last few lines where the foreshadowing is specific and speaks of *niyāz*, self-abasement, and *faqr*, spiritual poverty, as being the precondition for receiving the breath of Jesus, but in its entire import of being nothing without the Favors and Bounty of God. This discourse begins the second half of Book One, so it is expected that this discourse would mark the beginning of a shift to a level in some way higher than the first. This it does with its overwhelming emphasis on the spiritual world and the Mercy and Bountifulness of Almighty God. The structure of this discourse is so intricate that it has required two diagrams (shown in fig. 3.9 on page 144) to show its complex organization. Like the previous discourse, it has twelve sections, and the most noticeable division is between the two halves. Unlike the previous discourse, where there was a movement from *riyāḍat*, discipline and self-control, in the first half, to the way of Love in the second half, by way of *niyāz*, self-abasement, at the center, the two halves here are differentiated by the first being concerned with the universal, and the second half with the particular. The previous discourse was from below to above, this is from above to below, in a manner of speaking. The Harper holds the whole together by beginning Section 1 and ending Section 6 in the first half, and beginning Section 7 and ending Section 12, but transformed, in the second. Each section is clearly linked to the next, and various themes and imagery run throughout which gives continuity and integration to the totality, but the formal structure is two blocks of six sections, the first block in the form A, B, C, A*, B*, C*, and the second block A, B, C, C*, B*, A*. What is particularly interesting about this discourse is the relationship between the sections in each of the two blocks to one another. This is because, of course, it reflects the relationship between the universal spiritual world, and the particular phenomenal one of empirical existence. The parallelism and correspondences and connections between these two blocks, these two worlds, is both complex and sophisticated, so it is better to deal first with the intrablock relations first, and then examine the interblock ones.

Starting with the first block, Sections 1–6, the first parallelism that proclaims itself is that between Section 3 and Section 6, in that they are two parts of the same episode between Muḥammad and 'Ā'isha. The second parallelism is between Section 2, about the Breathings of God, which people find hard to bear because of the *nafs* within them, and Section 5, on exposing oneself to the coolness of the spring season, for that will effect revival and spiritual wholeness, as opposed to the cold of autumn which will encourage the *nafs*, selfhood, and its desires. The final parallelism is between Section 1 and Section 4. In l, there is a description of the spiritual world and its various classes, each with their own note. Section 4 is also about the unseen spiritual world, but this time in terms of it own sun and sky, clouds, and rains, each with a different characteristic and effect. These parallelisms together produce a structure that has not been encountered before here, A, B, C, A*, B*, C*, but the structure of the second block returns to the familiar chiasmus. It must have been important to Mawlānā to distinguish the two worlds in their structures. In block two, then, again there is a parallelism that proclaims itself, that between Section 8 and Section 11, since, in 8 'Umar receives God's instructions, and in 11 he carries them out. Sections 9 and 10 also are clearly parallel, both being about Muḥammad and the spiritual awareness of even inanimate objects. Finally Sections 7 and 12 are parallel because 7 begins the tale of the old Harper and 12 completes it. These parallelisms are shown in fig. 3.9 as Structure 1.

Structure 2 shows the parallelisms that link the two blocks. The first and most obvious parallelism is between Section 3 and Section 9, since both are concerned with Muḥammad burying somebody or some thing in such a way that they will them attain everlasting life on the Day of Resurrection; both also deal with skeptics. This is such an important subject, placed at the significant central position, and the parallelism is so clear, that it must be assumed that Mawlānā intended the parallelism to be horizontal and not diagonal. This suggests that the rhetorical structure of this discourse is as in the diagram in fig. 3.9, with two sets of descending sections, with various parallelisms between them, designed to be read in parallel. Such a reading will be attempted in the Interpretation below. If the structure had been a ring composition, then Section 7 would have been at the bottom of the second sequence and Section 12 at the top, and the parallelism between 3 and 9 would have been diagonal. There are diagonal parallelisms in this discourse, many of them, the most striking of which are shown in the diagram, but these have to be regarded as secondary parallelism. The primary parallelisms here are the six horizontal parallelisms, and this appropriately results in the structure of the whole discourse reflecting the nonchiasmic structure of the first half which deals with the universal spiritual world. This is further corroboration that the diagram in fig. 3.9 corresponds to Mawlānā's design.

Section 1 has several parallelisms: its primary parallelism is that it is horizontally in parallel with Section 7, in that both begin their respective halves and contain reference to the Harper, as well as the Harper praying to God—situated in 1—and God speaking to the Harper in a dream in 7. Section 1 is also diagonally parallel with Section 8, in that God speaks to 'Umar in a dream. There is also a parallelism—not shown in the diagram—between Section 1 and Section 12, as the beginning and the end of the discourse, both dealing with the Harper, but also, significantly, because in 12 the Harper enters a spiritual state that brings him into the spiritual world depicted in 1. Section 2 is horizontally parallel with Section 8, in that Section 2 requires that one seeks out one of the spiritual heirs to Muḥammad, and Section 8 is about 'Umar, who is just such an heir. Section 2 is also diagonally in parallel with Section 7 through the image of the thorn, which is explained in Section 2 and whose removal from the Harper God confirms at the end of Section 7. Sections 3 and 9 have been dealt with above, but Section 3 is also diagonally parallel with Section 10 through Muḥammad and the Declaration of Faith.

Section 4 affirms that the Unseen world has its mountains and seas and clouds and rain and so on, and Section 10, with which it is horizontally parallel, demonstrates this with spiritual pebbles hidden in the hand of Abū Jahl. It is also diagonally parallel with Section 12, because the last four lines of 4 exactly predict what happened to the Harper as the result of the presence and advice of ʿUmar in 12. Section 5 is horizontally parallel with Section 11, in that the spiritual revival and rejection of the selfhood through contact with *ʿaql-e kullī*, Universal Intellect, and the speech of saints, spoken of in 5, happens to the Harper in 11 when he meets ʿUmar. There is horizontal parallelism between Section 6, which ends the first half by Mawlānā telling himself to go back to the tale of the minstrel, and Section 12, in which Mawlānā admits that now the old man "has shaken his skirt free from talk and speech, half of the tale remains untold in his mouth." Section 6 is about the spiritual rain that takes away the soul's grief and burning by making it forgetful of God. This makes diagonal parallelisms with Section 10, since Abū Jahl was manifestly forgetful of God, and with Section 7, because the Harper in fact did remember God and was burning in his repentance, hence he, like the Prophet, did not get wet from this rain.

These parallelisms, as shown in the diagram of Structure 2 in fig. 3.9, produce a beautiful rhetorical structure, of great elegance and elaboration, demonstrating the intimate complexity of the relationship between the universal, united, unseen spiritual world and the world of the part, the phenomenal human world. Because it was Mawlānā's purpose to demonstrate the traffic and commerce between the two worlds, there are countless resonances and echoes across the divide which are more stylistic than structural, so they have not been noted here.

Interpretation of Discourse Seven

This discourse is commented on valuably at the level of detail by Nicholson, but, drawn to the part, he has not seen the whole.[19] Nor has Gustav Richter, whose essay was cited in Chapter 2. He attempts to identify Mawlānā's style with reference to parts of this discourse, and usefully draws attention to the same rich interconnectedness at the micro-compositional level which has been identified here at the macro-compositional. The discourse must clearly be read and understood first sequentially; then read synoptically as will be done here; finally being read again sequentially with the synoptic reading in view in order to complete the hermeneutic circle. Before the synoptic reading, however, it is necessary to contextualize Discourse Seven.

Fig. 3.9. The Double Structure of Discourse Seven

Structure 1

Sec. 1	Harper like Isrāfīl; God's voice; saints revive dead
Sec. 2	God's breath; hard to bear; thorn; Prophet; harmony
Sec. 3	Prophet; trees like interred; God in seasons; rain
Sec. 4	Clouds of Unseen world; seasonal rain; saints' breath
Sec. 5	Holy breaths like spring; don't cover up against them
Sec. 6	Rain of mercy or menace; against grief and envy; Harper
Sec. 7	Harper old; repentant soul sings to God; God's Command
Sec. 8	God's voice to 'Umar; God's Call even to wood and stone
Sec. 9	Prophet buries moaning pillar; externalists and miracles
Sec. 10	Abū Jahl's pebbles proclaim the declaration of faith
Sec. 11	'Umar gives message; Harper breaks harp and repents
Sec. 12	Harper goes beyond wailing and soul awakes

Structure 2

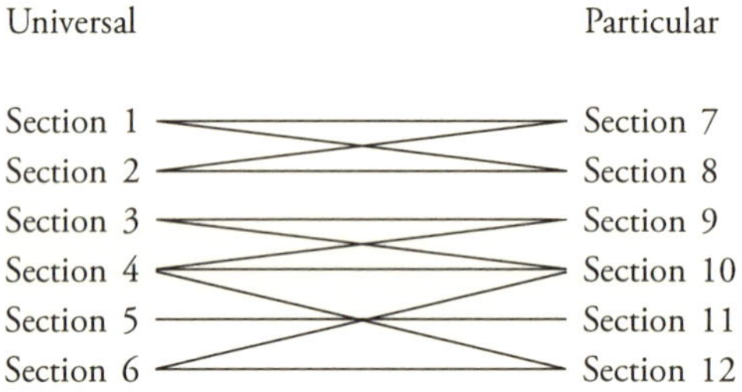

The previous discourse dealt with the *nafs-e lawwāmah*, the soul or self which blamed itself, within the parrot fable and together with two types of training for the *sālik*, discipline and self-control in the first half, and the awakening of the heart to God by means of mystical love poetry and Mawlānā's example in the second. The crucial state to pass from one type of training to the other was *niyāz*, self-abasement, supplication, spiritual poverty, and emptiness. This state, Mawlānā explains in the Link Section, is what the pretended deaths of the two parrots symbolized. The state of *niyāz* was dealt with in the Link Section at the very center of Book One, so it is also the key to the door into the second half of the book, which treats of the spiritual world and the higher stages of the selfhood, *nafs*. It is the given state of the old decrepit Harper, who is also symbolic of the *nafs-e lawwāmah*, the selfhood which blames itself. In this discourse the mode of training for the *sālik* differs from the often explicit instruction given heretofore, it is more by hint and example, by induction into spiritual perspectives, by the shape and form of situations, by feeling the spiritual realities behind the passing seasons, the clouds, rain, the sky and so forth, and reenchanting the empirical world by deciphering the signs of God. Nor should the abundant references to and quotations from the Qur'ān and the traditions be overlooked as part of the *sālik*'s training. But, in this discourse, Mawlānā uses the rhetorical structure itself and its synoptic reading to reinforce the spiritual understanding of the *sālik*, so the diagrams above should be revisited as the reading begins.

Section 1 is necessarily the starting place; it begins with the Harper, then, quickly, through the simile with Isrāfīl, the Angel of the Resurrection, it speaks of the spiritual note, *naghmah*, of prophets and of saints and others, who, like Isrāfīl, can bring the dead to life at God's Command. The theme of resurrection, the Resurrection itself in the spiritual world, the spiritual awakening of people in this world, and the analogy between the two, is sustained as a motif throughout the discourse. The saints and prophets have become one with God so they can pass on God's light and it does not matter whether this Light is received from someone past or present. From the notes and Light of God, the metaphor moves to the Breathings of God in Section 2, which should be read next. People shrink from these Breathings because of the selfhood, *nafs*, the thorn in their sole. This is a long section with too much material to summarize, but central to it is Muṣṭafā, Muḥammad, the Prophet, and his spiritual heirs. From the universal spiritual world, Section 7 should be read next, crossing the divide to the world of the part, where the Harper, the *nafs-e lawwāmah*, had become old and had lost his powers. Mawlānā writes: "What fair thing is there that does not become foul . . . except the voices of holy men in their breasts, from the repercussion of whose breath is the blast of the trumpet of Resurrection." These verses and two more on the spiritual power and blessings of the saints, make a strong parallel connection with Section 1. But the commerce between the two worlds does not end there. The desperately poor Harper in three verses, 2083–2085, expresses the most beautiful prayer of gratitude for God's Favors, repentance for a lifetime of sin, and dedication of himself and his playing to God. Here are enough hints and examples for the *sālik*: the poverty, *faqr*, both actual and spiritual; repentance, *tawbah*; dedication of oneself to God; gratitude; and, above all, *niyāz*. He then goes to the graveyard at Medina in search of God. Praying in graveyards is another Sufi practice recommended for the *sālik*, since to face the inevitability of one's own death and the certainty of the coming Day of Judgment, is a powerful corrective for an indulgent and recalcitrant self-hood, as well as the graveyard being considered an environment particularly conducive for contact with the spiritual world. The Harper asks God for the price of silk for his harp strings, plays for a long while, weeps, and falls asleep. Weeping, and dreams as one of the means of communication between the spiritual world and the human world, are further indications to the *sālik.* In his dream the Harper's soul roamed the spiritual world until the Divine Command came that he should not be covetous, since the thorn was out of his soul, and that he should return. The subject of communication with the spiritual world in dreams comes again in Section 8, which should be read next. Here it is 'Umar, symbolic of the saint or spiritual heir of Muḥammad, and also of the Sufi Shaykh, to whom God communicates His instructions.

The next four sections to be read are, in order, 3, 4, 9, and 10. These are the central sections of the rhetorical structure and are thereby given a special emphasis. The reason is clear enough: they are about the Prophet Muḥammad; burial; choosing eternal life; the Day of Resurrection; the Muslim Affirmation of Faith, the *shahādah*; the disbelief of the skeptics who rely on partial intelligence, *'aql-e juzwī,* rather than receive the wisdom of the Universal Intelligence, the *'aql-e kullī*; and the miracle of Muḥammad, made possible because behind the natural phenomena of the empirical world, mountains, sky, sea, rain, and so on, there are spiritual counterparts that obey the commands of the Friends of God in the spiritual world. In terms of communication from the spiritual world to the human world, there could be nothing more important for Mawlānā and the *sālik* than the Prophet and the Revelation he received from God, *rabb al-'ālamayn,* Lord of both the worlds. It is further to be noticed that the Prophet Muḥammad plays a leading role in sections on both sides of the divide, both in the spiritual world and in the human world.

The final set of sections, which should be read in the order 5, 11, 6, and 12, brings both sides to their conclusions, each with a twist of its own. Section 5 likens spiritual reawakening and everlasting life to the spring season and autumn to the *nafs* and its desires. The *sālik* is told he has only partial intelligence, so he should seek someone living whose intelligence is whole, since Universal Intelligence is the sure cure for the *nafs.* In parallel Section 11, 'Umar tracks down the old Harper and tells him God's message and offers him the money for harp strings. The Harper is overwhelmed and weeps from shame crying: "Oh God who has no like." In uncontrollable grief he smashes the harp and accuses it and his music of keeping him from God over his many years. He asks God for mercy. It would be difficult to find a clearer depiction of the *nafs-e lawwāmah.* Mawlānā concludes the section with a four verse prayer in which he foreshadows Section 12. The final section on the universal side, Section 6, resumes the episode of Muḥammad and 'Ā'isha in which the Prophet did not get wet from the spiritual rain. The twist given in this section is that the rain is a special rain to allay the grief of humanity that would be caused if it truly saw its own spiritual situation. It does so by making them forgetful of God, and restricting the flow of Divine Intelligence to a trickle, because without selfishness the human world would not function. No wonder the Prophet remained dry. This section precedes and foreshadows Section 7, in which the old Harper as the *nafs-e lawwāmah* experiences just that grief the rain is designed to allay. In Section 11 the last trace of covetousness—for the harp strings—has been removed and the grief and the self-blaming is even more extreme. The twist in this last section of the discourse is that 'Umar tells the Harper to stop his wailing, because it contains the very self-consciousness that keeps man from God. Through the advice and spiritual presence of 'Umar, the Harper has an experience of the Divine Ocean, at least in a temporary *ḥāl*, but maybe a more permanent transformation, *maqām*, is here indicated also, of the *nafs-e lawwāmah* to the *nafs-e muṭma'innah*, the self or soul at peace. The twist here is that weeping and wailing, one of the most marked characteristics of the *nafs-e lawwāmah*, is the very self-indulgence that prevents its further development.

Link Section: The Two Angels' Prayer

Summary

SECTION 1 2223–2243 (21) *Commentary on the prayer of the two angels who daily make proclamation in every market, saying, "Oh God, bestow on every generous person some boon in exchange! Oh God, bestow on every miser some bane (in return)"; and an explanation that the generous is he that strives earnestly in the Way of God, not he that squanders his wealth in the way of sensuality.* (a) [2223–2228] The Prophet said there are two angels who, by way of warning, proclaim: "Oh God, keep the generous fully satisfied by recompensing them a hundred-thousand-fold for what they spend, but reward the niggards with nothing but loss." Many acts of niggardliness are better than prodigality, such as not bestowing that which belongs to God except by God's Command. (b) [2229–2234] Find out the Command of God from one who is united with Him, since not every heart understands the Command, and the Qur'ān warns the heedless that their spending will be a bitter grief to them. (c) [2235–2243] The generous man should give money, and the lover should surrender his soul. If you give bread for God's sake, you will get bread in return, if life, you get life. If liberality empties your pocket, the Bounty of God will not leave you short, since when someone sows, there is no seed left, but there is goodliness in the field. If he doesn't sow, mice and so forth will devour the seed. This world is the negation of reality; seek reality in affirmation of God. Your body is empty of reality; seek it in your essence. Put the *nafs* to the sword and buy the soul which is like a great sweet river. If you can't reach the threshold of the Sublime Court, at least listen to this tale.

Comment

The meaning of this section is clear enough; use what spiritual energy you have to the full, but do not squander it heedlessly.[20] Whatever is spent rightly will be most generously replenished. The section functions as a link between Discourse Seven and Discourse Eight. It does so by looking back to the Bounty of God in the previous discourse, and forward to the next with its reference to beating the *nafs* and speaking of a great sweet river. Structurally, this link section between the first and second discourses in the second half of the book, exactly balances the link section in the first half of the book between the first discourse and the second. It should be mentioned that this section is less secure textually than the greater part of Book One.

Discourse Eight: The Story of the Caliph, the Arab of the Desert and His Wife

Summary of the Narrative and Thematic Content

SECTION 1 2244–2251 (8) *The story of the Caliph who in his time surpassed Ḥātim of Ṭayyi' in generosity and had no rival.* (a) [2244–2251] There was a most munificent Caliph whose liberality had removed poverty from the world. He was the Water of life and the Ocean of Bounty; by him Arabs and foreigners were revived.

SECTION 2 2252–2263 (11) *Story of the poor Arab of the desert and his wife's altercation with him because of (their) penury and poverty.* (a) [2252–2257] A Bedouin woman said to her husband that they were desperately poor and unhappy, that they had no bread, no water, only tears. Even the poorest were ashamed of them in such poverty and in such anxiety about food. (b) [2258–

Fig. 3.10. A Synoptic View of Discourse Eight

Sec. 1	There was a generous Caliph who relieved all poverty
Sec. 2	Arab's wife *(nafs)* complains to spouse of their poverty
Sec. 3	False shaykh is all show, but you realize too late
Sec. 4	Rarely a good pupil still succeeds; admit our poverty
Sec. 5	Husband (*'aql*) urges patience; her grief from desire
Sec. 6	She says he's all show; don't use Name of God as trap
Sec. 7	He says don't sneer at poverty; she can't understand
Sec. 8	If she could, he'd tell; try poverty; find riches; be quiet
Sec. 9	Wife cries, says sorry; wins his lonely heart
Sec. 10	Women win over wise; ignorant win over women
Sec. 11	Husband regrets his anger and asks forgiveness
Sec. 12	Pharaoh only Pharaoh here; his revolt due to Moses
Sec. 13	Rejected by saints, he lost this life and the next
Sec. 14	Ṣāliḥ's camel's (spirit) killers punished; displayed
Sec. 15	All mixed but each has own term to show fruit
Sec. 16	Solomon's strength needed to deal with this world
Sec. 17	*nafs* and *'aql* argue; both needed; see with God's light
Sec. 18	Arab agrees to take her advice from love, not a test
Sec. 19	Wife says go to the King and demonstrate need
Sec. 20	Take jug of rainwater as gift; the jug is our body
Sec. 21	She sews up jug and prays; he takes it to the court
Sec. 22	The Giver seeks the beggar as beggar seeks Bounty
Sec. 23	The lover of God and the lover of other than God
Sec. 24	God's light revealed him; he sought money now free
Sec. 25	Love the Whole and not the part
Sec. 26	The part returns to the Whole like scent to the rose
Sec. 27	Arab gives jug; God a reservoir; teacher imbues pupil
Sec. 28	Grammarian and boatman; effacement not grammar
Sec. 29	Caliph sends him off with gold via Tigris; ashamed
Sec. 30	Ḥusām al-Dīn to explain need for Pir and his quality
Sec. 31	'Alī told to take protection with a saint; endurance
Sec. 32	Qaswini's tattoo incomplete from fear of needle

2263] "Kin and stranger flee from us. Arabs are proud of fighting and giving; we are killed without fighting and have nothing to give. If a guest arrived I would go for his coat while he slept."

SECTION 3 2264–2282 (19) *How disciples (novices in Sufism) are beguiled in their need by false impostors and imagine them to be shaykhs and venerable personages and (saints) united (with God) and do not know the difference, between fact (naqd) and fiction (naql) and between what is tied on (artificially) and what has grown up (naturally).* (a) [2264–2268] Only be the guest of one who gives benefit; you are the disciple and guest of one who robs you of what you have. He is weak and can't make you strong. He makes you dark because he has no light, (b) [2269–2278] We his disciples are really poor, outwardly like the impostor's inner, dark-hearted and plausible of tongue; no trace of God, just all pretension. He uses Sufi expressions in his pretence but has no spiritual food and you get nothing from his table although he claims to be the Vicar of God. (c) [2279–2282] Some people wait for years before they see he is naught but by then it is too late.

SECTION 4 2283–2287 (5) *Explaining how it may happen, (though) rarely, that a disciple sincerely puts his faith in a false impostor (and believes) that he is a holy personage, and by means of this faith attains to a (spiritual) degree which his Shaykh has never (even) dreamed of, and (then) fire and water do him not hurt, though they hurt his Shaykh, but this occurs very seldom.* (a) [2283–2297] Exceptionally a disciple because of his illumination finds benefit from an impostor. He reaches a high degree of soul even if what he thinks is soul is in fact only body. The impostor has a dearth of soul within; we have a dearth of bread without. Why should we conceal our poverty like the impostor and suffer agony for the sake of false reputation.

SECTION 5 2288–2314 (27) *How the Bedouin bade his wife be patient and declared to her the excellence of patience and poverty.* (a) [2288–2295] Her husband said to her: "Our life is nearly past, so don't look for increase and deficiency. Whether life is untroubled or troubled is not important because it does not endure. Animals live happily without these ups and downs and anxiety. The dove, the nightingale, the falcon, and all the animals from gnat to elephant are dependent on God for their nourishment. (b) [2296–2303] All of this grief arises from our existence and desire and is a temptation. Every pain is a piece of death, to be expelled. If you can't you will die; if you can, bear the pain. God will make all sweet. Pains come from death as his messenger; do not avert your face. Whoever lives sweetly dies bitterly; whoever serves his body does not save his soul. (c) [2304–2307] It is dawn, how long my soul will you talk of gold? You were gold once, then you became a seeker of gold. You were a fruitful vine, but have become rotten as your fruit ripened when you should have become sweeter. (d) [2308–2314] You are my wife, but a married pair should match like shoes. I march to contentment with a bold heart why are you resorting to revilement?"

SECTION 6 2315–2341 (27) *How the wife counseled her husband saying, "Don't talk any more about your merit and (spiritual) rank—'why say you that which you do not?'—for although these words are true, yet you have not obtained to the degree of trust in God, and to speak like this above your station and devotional practice is harmful and 'exceedingly hateful in the sight of God.'"* (a) [2315–2317] "What pretentious nonsense," she cried, "you make reputation your religion. You speak from pride and arrogance, but look at your own acts and feelings and be ashamed. (b) [2318–2322] Pride is especially ugly in beggars. How long all this pretence and palaver? Illuminated by contentment? You hardly know the name. Contentment is a treasure but you can't tell gain from pain. Do not boast of contentment, bane of my life. (c) [2323–2326] You call me mate, but I am not the mate of fraud. You talk of grand things and then contend with dogs for a bone. Don't view me with contempt or I'll reveal your hidden faults. (d) [2327–2330] Your understanding is a shackle for mankind, a snake, and a scorpion. May it not destroy us. (e) [2331–2341] You are the snake catcher and the snake; both cast spells on one another. The charmer from greed in making his spell is not aware of the snake's spell. You used the name of God to beguile me and to trap me, but now the name of God will take vengeance on my behalf since I commit my soul and body to the name of God, not to your trap." Thus spoke the woman roughly.

SECTION 7 2342–2364 (23) *How the man counseled his wife, saying, "Do not look with contempt upon the poor but regard the work of God as perfect, and do not let your vain thought and opinion of your own penury cause you to sneer at poverty and revile the poor."* (a) [2342–2345] "Oh woman, poverty is my pride, do not reproach me. Wealth and gold are like a cap that only a bald man hides in because the man with hair is happier with no cap. The man of God is like the eye, better when unveiled. (b) [2346–2351] The slave dealer strips the slave to uncover the defects he might be hiding. The merchant is full of vice but his money hides it, because the covetous cannot see it because of cupidity. If a beggar speaks words like gold nobody hears them. (c) [2352–2356] Spiritual poverty is beyond your apprehension, do not be contemptuous of it. The dervish is beyond property but has a good portion from God. God is just; how should He tyrannize the poor, giving good fortune to one and setting another on fire. The fire is caused by having evil thoughts about God. (d) [2357–2362] You have abused me in your anger calling me a catcher of snakes. But I extract the fangs, which are an enemy to its life, to save the snake. I make an enemy my friend with this skill and never act from cupidity. (e) [2363–2364] You see things from your stance; change it. If you turn round you become giddy and the world is spinning, but really it is you that are spinning."

SECTION 8 2365–2393 (29) *Explaining how everyone's movement (action) proceeds from the place where he is, (so that) he sees everyone else from the circle of his own self-existence: a blue glass shows the sun as blue, a red glass as red, (but) when the glass escapes from (the sphere of) color, it becomes white, (and then) it is more truthful than all other glasses and is the Imam (exemplar to them all).* (a) [2365–2370] "Abū Jahl said to the Prophet that he was ugly, and the Prophet replied he was impertinent but right. Abū Bakr said to the Prophet he was a sun beyond East and West and was beautiful, and the Prophet said he was right. People asked how two such contradictory things could be both right and the Prophet said: "I am a mirror polished by the Divine hand and people see in me what there is in themselves." (b) [2371–2376] If you think me covetous rise above womanly cares since what resembles cupidity is really mercy and a blessing. Try poverty so you can find in it riches and the Light of God. Do not look sour and you will see thousand of souls through contentment plunged in an ocean of honey. (c) [2377–2382] If you were able to understand, I could unfold the story of my heart because it requires an avid and sympathetic hearer to become eloquent. (d) [2383–2393] Everything beautiful is made for those who can see it. Music is not produced for the deaf, nor musk for those who cannot smell. God made earth for those of clay and heaven for the celestials. There is no point in me producing pearls of wisdom if you are not able to receive them. If you can't stop quarreling, then go. If you can't keep silent then I shall go."

SECTION 9 2394–2432 (39) *How the wife paid regard to her husband and begged God to forgive her for what she had said.* (a) [2394–2406] The wife resorted to tears saying she little thought he would speak like that. She abased herself saying she was his dust and unworthy to be his wife. Poverty alone had made her lose patience, and it was only on his account she was upset. She would die for him and was weary of body and soul since he thought so little of her. She renounced gold and silver and if he wished to divorce her, then he must, but she pleaded against it. (b) [2407–2409] "Remember when I was beautiful as an idol and you adoring as an idolater. I matched you in ardor. No matter how you treat me I am devoted to you. (c) [2410–2417] I submit myself to you and repent. I give up opposition and lay my head on the block for you to cut it off. Do anything but divorce me since your conscience is a pleader on my behalf. I took advantage of your noble nature but now have mercy on me." (d) [2418–2424] She spoke winningly and then began to weep. She touched his lonely heart. When she whose beauty enslaves us, whose haughtiness makes us tremble, whose disdain makes our hearts bleed and whose tyranny ensnares us, resorts to pleading and entreaty, how shall we fare then? (e) [2425–2428] God so arranged it, so we cannot escape. How could Adam be parted from Eve? Rustam the great warrior was a slave to his wife, and the Prophet also. (f) [2429–2432] Fire can make water boil and water put out fire. Outwardly you may dominate your wife but inwardly you are dominated in seeking her love. This is characteristic of man alone; animals lack in love and that lack arises from their inferiority to man.

SECTION 10 2433–2437 (5) *Explanation of the Tradition, "Verily, they (women) prevail over the wise man, and the ignorant man prevails over them."* (a) [2433–2437] The Prophet said that woman prevails exceedingly over the wise and the intelligent but the ignorant prevail over woman because of their animality. They lack tenderness and kindness and affection, which are human qualities, because anger and lust, which are animal qualities, predominate. Woman is a ray of God not just an earthly beloved. She is creative, you might say, not created.

SECTION 11 2438–2446 (9) *How the man yielded to his wife's request that he should seek the means of livelihood, and regarded her opposition (to him) as a divine indication. (Verse): To the mind of every knowing man it is a fact that with the revolving object there is one that causes it to revolve.* (a) [2438–2446] The husband regretted his speech and could not understand why he had kicked his own soul. When destiny comes it dulls the intellect but after it has gone it devours itself with grief. He said to his wife that he repented and asked for her mercy; the unbeliever had now become a Muslim. When an unbeliever repents he becomes a Muslim when he asks for pardon of God who is Merciful and Bountiful. Existence and nonexistence are in love with Him as are infidelity and faith. Copper and silver are in love with that Elixir.

SECTION 12 2447–2481 (35) *Explaining that both Moses and Pharaoh are subject to the Divine Will, like antidote and poison and darkness and light, and how Pharaoh conversed in solitude with God, praying that He would not destroy his good reputation.* (a) [2447–2451] Pharaoh and Moses were both worshipers of reality, although outwardly one kept the way and the other didn't. In daytime Moses lamented to God and at midnight Pharaoh began, saying: "What a shackle I have on my neck; it is the same will that made Moses illumined and me darkened, that made Moses' face like the moon but the moon of my soul eclipsed. (b) [2452–2455] I am Pharaoh, but the acclamation of people was in fact proclaiming my eclipse. (c) [2456–2459] Moses and I are fellow servants of God, but His ax cultivates the one and ignores the other. May Your ax make my crooked actions straight. (d) [2460–2466] All night I pray and in secret I am becoming humble and harmonious, how then do I become so different when with Moses? I am whatever color He makes me; now a moon, now black." How could the action of God be otherwise; since the decree "Be and it was" we are running in Space and beyond. (e) [2467–2472] Colorlessness became the captive of color: return to your colorlessness and Pharaoh and Moses are at peace. What is strange is that since color derives from colorlessness, how come that color wars with it; the rose is from the thorn and the thorn from the rose, yet they are at war. (f) 2473–2481] Is it war or an artifice or is it bewilderment to cause you to search? Nonexistence expelled existence; the rebelliousness of Pharaoh was really caused by Moses.

SECTION 13 2482–2508 (27) *The reason why the un-blest are disappointed of both worlds, (according to the text) "he has lost this life and the life to come."* (a) [2482–2488] A philosopher thought the earth was like an egg suspended in the sky and was attracted by the sky in each direction and thus held its position. In fact the sky does not attract the earth but repels it in all directions. (b) [2489–2495] Likewise the hearts of the saints repulse Pharaohs so that they remain fixed in perdition. Rejected by this world and that, they lose both, because the saints can reject you if you turn from them. As animals are subject to man so are men subject to the saints. (c) [2496–2500] The saints are the intellect of intellects; one guide and a hundred thousand souls. What is your intellect, a camel driver, and the guide. You need an eye that can look on the sun. (d) [2501–2504] The world is dependent on the sun; yet with the guide you have a hidden sun of whom you should have no doubt. (e) [2505–2508] Each prophet came to the world alone yet within he had thousands of worlds and the power to enchant the universe. The foolish thought him weak, but how could he be who is the King's companion? Woe to the man who says: "He is a man and nothing more."

SECTION 14 2509–2568 (60) *How the eyes of (external) sense regarded Ṣāliḥ and his she-camel as despicable and without a champion; (for) when God is about to destroy an army He makes their adversaries appear despicable and few in their sight, even though the adversary be superior in strength: "and He was making you few in their eyes, that God might bring to pass a thing that was to be done."*

(a) [2509–2514] Ṣāliḥ's she-camel was outwardly a camel that the wicked tribe slaughtered for the water she shared with them, since they were ungrateful for the blessings of God. Inwardly she was God's and they rejected God, so that the blood price was an entire town. (b) [2515–2522] The saints and prophets' spirit is like Ṣāliḥ and the body the she-camel. The camel took the knocks but the spirit was with God and unable to be hurt. God attached the spirit to the body so that the unbelievers would hurt it and then be punished, and so that the saint or prophet could be a refuge for the world. Be a slave to the saint's body that you may be a fellow-servant of Ṣāliḥ's spirit, (c) [2523–2542] Ṣāliḥ said to the tribe of the town that punishment would come in three days, on the first of which their faces would turn yellow, on the second, red, and on the third, black. As a sign from him the foal of the she-camel had run to the mountains and if they caught it there would be help. None caught it. What is the foal? It is the saint's heart that can be won back. The prophecy was fulfilled and the town destroyed. (d) [2543–2560] Ṣāliḥ went to the town and hearing the lamentations he wept for them. And he talked to them and he talked to God and concluded they were not worth the mourning. (e) [2561–2569] Again he felt compassion, but his intellect was saying, Why do you waste your tears on the perverse? They conformed to their traditions and trampled on the camel of Reason, the Guide. God brought the worshipers from Paradise that he might show them the nurslings of Hell.

SECTION 15 2569–2602 (34) *On the meaning of "He let the two seas go to meet one another: between them is a barrier which they do not seek (to cross)."* (a) [2569–2572] He mixed the people of Fire with the people of Light like gold and earth in a mine but between them was Mt. Qaf. (b) [2573–2581] One half sweet and one half bitter, they appear to dash against one another, the waves of peace removing hatreds, the waves of war bringing confusion. Love draws the bitter to the sweet, and wrath the sweet to the bitter. (c) [2582–2590] Bitter and sweet are not visible except to the eye that sees the end. Many sweet as sugar conceal poison that the wise knows by its smell or when it touches the lips, though the Devil shouts "Eat." To another the throat knows, or the body, or the anus when evacuating will show what has been swallowed. To one it will be apparent in weeks or days, to another in the grave, while to a third on the Day of Resurrection. (d) [2591–2596] Every desirable thing has a period granted to it: years to a ruby, two months a vegetable, a year to the rose. God has spoken of an appointed term but this is not discourse, it is the Water of Life. (e) [2597–2602] Hear now another saying clear to mystics but not to the rest. Through Divine decree, depending on spiritual degree, even the poison of sensuality and worldliness are digestible. In one place it is injurious, in another a remedy, like the grape that can produce unlawful wine, or, as vinegar, a fine seasoning.

SECTION 16 2603–2615 (13) *Concerning the impropriety of the disciple's (murīd) presuming to do the same things as are done by the saint (walī), inasmuch as sweetmeat does no harm to the physician, but is harmful to the sick, and frost and snow do no harm to the ripe grape, but are injurious to the young fruit; for he (the disciple) is still on the way, for he has not (yet) become (the saint to whom are applicable the words in the Qur'ān): "That God may forgive you your former and latter sins."* (a) [2603–2615] If the saint drinks poison it becomes an antidote; if a seeker, a cause of darkness. Solomon said give me a kingdom it behoves not anyone after me to obtain. This was not envy from Solomon but his realization of the dangers of this worldly kingdom with all its enticements. Even with his strength he was nearly sunk, so he had compassion on all kings of the world. Hence his intercession to God to give the kingdom together with Solomon's strength so that such a person became Solomon. But to return to the tale.

SECTION 17 2616–2642 (27) *The moral of the altercation of the Arab and his wife.* (a) [2616–2621] The altercation between man and wife is a parable between your own self, *nafs*, and intellect, *'aql.* Both are necessary for the manifestation of good and evil and in this house of the world they are engaged in strife day and night. The wife wants the requisites of the house: reputation, bread, and rank, just as the flesh wishes to gratify its desires, sometimes using humility, sometimes domination, while intellect is unconscious of these worldly thoughts, having nothing but the love of God in its brain. (b) [2622–2627] This is the inner meaning, the temptation of reason by the flesh, but hear the full outward tale because if the inner meaning was sufficient, the creation would have been pointless. If love were only spiritual then your prayer and fasting would be nonexistent, but lovers' gifts, which are only forms, do bear testimony to hidden feelings of love and kindness. (c) [2628–2632] Sometimes we make a show of bearing witness ecstatically, sometimes in assiduous prayer and fasting so that the outer act, which is meant to show our inner feelings, bears false witness. Grant Oh Lord the discernment to tell the true from the false. (d) [2633–2637] How does sense perception become discerning? By seeing with the light of God you will not even need the outer signs, because the spark of love will enter and set one free from outward effect. Then there is no need of the signs of love, since love will encompass the heart. (e) [2638–2642] I could go on to details, but enough. The outer form is both near and far from the meaning; like sap and tree they are near, but essentially they are very separate. Let's leave essentials and return to the couple.

SECTION 18 2643–2683 (41) *How the Arab set his heart on (complying with) his beloved's request and swore that in thus submitting (to her) he had no (idea of) trickery and making trial (of her).* (a) [2643–2645] The man said he would do whatever she said irrespective of its potential result because he was her lover and love makes one blind. (b) [2646–2652] When the wife asked whether he was bent on discovering her secret by trickery, he replied: "No, by God who created Adam, in whom was displayed everything in the world of the spirits and at whose first instructions the angels were amazed. They gained from it more than was contained in the seven heavens so great was the range of his pure spirit. (c) [2653–2655] The prophet said he was not contained in heaven or earth but in the hearts of true believers, which is where he should be sought. (d) [2656–2667] God also said: "Enter into my servants and you shall find a paradise consisting of a vision of Me." The vast empyrean was in awe when it saw Adam, because form is nothing when confronted with reality. The angels said to Adam, before this time we knew you on earth. We were amazed that we should have this connection with dust since our nature is in heaven. But our friendship with dust was because of the scent of you whose body was fashioned from dust but whose pure light shone from the dust. We were heedless of you and argued with God, who sent us to earth. (e) [2668–2677] God replied that they should speak whatever they wished because His Mercy preceded his wrath, and in order to show this he would put into them a tendency to doubt, and He would not take offense, so that any who denied His Clemency would not dare to speak. Within His mercy there is the mercy of hundreds of mothers and fathers, who are as foam on the sea of His mercy. (f) [2678–2683] By His mercy I swear my words are true and inspired by love and not to make trial of you. But put it to the test; reveal what is in your heart and tell me what to do, and I will do what is in my power. See the plight I am in."

SECTION 19 2684–2702 (19) *How the wife specified to her husband the way to earn daily bread and how he accepted (her proposal).* (a) [2684–2688] The wife said that a sun has shone forth giving light to the whole world in the form of the Vicar of God, from whom all are happy. Gain access to that King and you will become a king. Companionship with the fortunate is like the Elixir. (b) [2689–2702] They discussed with what pretext he should go to the King, and the wife said, when in the presence of the King every inability became an ability. The heart of the matter lay in lack of means and nonexistence. The husband, however, said he needed to demonstrate his lack of means so that the King take pity, since just talk would not do. She must come up with some idea, since the King needed truth.

SECTION 20 2703–2719 (17) *How the Arab carried a jug of rainwater from the midst of the desert as a gift to the Commander of the Faithful at Baghdad, in the belief that in that town also there was a scarcity of water.* (a) [2703–2707] The wife said: "When people are entirely purged of self-existence, that is truth. There is rainwater in the jug, take it to the King saying, "This is our capital," and make it a gift, since he may have gold but in the desert water is a treasure. (b) [2708–2714] The jug is our confined body, with the briny water of our senses. May God accept this jug. The jug has the five spouts of the senses, keep them pure that there may be a passage from it to the sea and it may become of the nature of the sea, so that when you present your gift the King may find it pure and purchase it, after which its water will become without end and a hundred worlds could be filled from my jug. Stop up its spouts and fill the jug with reality." (c) [2715–2719] The husband was full of pride thinking, "Who else could have a gift like this fit for a King?" They did not know that in Baghdad there was a river full of sweet water flowing through it on which there were boats. Go to the Sultan and see those rivers beside which our senses and perceptions are as nothing.

SECTION 21 2720–2743 (24) *How the Arab's wife sewed the jug of rainwater in a felt cloth and put a seal on it because of the Arab's utter conviction (that it was a precious gift for the king).* (a) [2720–2728] The husband told her to sew up the jug in felt, for there was no water purer than this in the world. When people are used to briny water like this, how should they know of sweet water like the Euphrates, and so on? If you have not escaped from the material world, what can you know of self-extinction, intoxication, and expansion, except as words passed down the generations whose real meaning is hard to reach? (b) [2729–2743] He took the jug and set off carefully and his wife prayed that their water be kept safe from scoundrels. With his care and her prayers he brought it safely to the Caliph's palace. He found a bountiful court where both good and bad petitioners carried off donations and robes of honor. High and low, followers of form and followers of reality, those with aspiration and those without, all were quickened with life like the world at the final trumpet blast on the day of Resurrection.

SECTION 22 2744–2751 (8) *Showing that, as the beggar is in love with bounty and in love with the bountiful giver, so the bounty of the bountiful giver* *is in love with the beggar: if the beggar have the greater patience, the bountiful giver will come to his door; and if the bountiful giver have the greater patience, the beggar will come to his door; but the beggar's patience is a virtue in the beggar, while the patience of the bountiful giver is a defect.* (a) [2744–2751] A loud call was coming: Come Oh Seekers, Bounty is in need of beggars. Bounty seeks the beggars as the fair a mirror, since Beneficence is made visible by a mirror. God said, Oh Muḥammad do not drive away the beggars. Take care as the beggar is the mirror of Bounty and breath is harmful to the mirror. On the one hand, Bounty makes the beggar beg, on the other, Bounty bestows more than they sought. Beggars are the mirror of God's Bounty and united with Absolute Bounty. Everyone except these two beggars is as dead.

SECTION 23 2752–2772 (21) *The difference between one that is poor for (desirous of) God and thirsting for Him and one that is poor of (destitute of) God and thirsting for what is other than He.* (a) [2752–2756] He that seeks other than God is a mere picture of a dervish, not worthy of bread. Do not set food before a lifeless picture, for he loves God only for the sake of gain not for excellence and beauty. (b) [2757–2763] If he thinks he is in love with the essence of God, his conception of the names and attributes is not the essence, since conception is begotten and God is not. How can one in love with his own imagination be in love with God? Yet if he is sincere it can lead to him to reality. I would explain but am afraid of the feeble-minded who bring a thousand fancies with their thoughts. (c) [2764–2768] Not everyone can hear rightly; a fig is no use to a dead bird. What difference between sea and land to a picture of a fish. If you draw someone sad, the picture knows nothing of joy or sorrow, since it is free from both. But this worldly joy and sorrow are just like a picture compared with spiritual joy and sorrow. (d) [2769–2772] The picture's smile is only so that you may understand. The pictures within the world's hamāms are like clothes when seen from outside the undressing room. From outside you see only the phenomena, undress and enter the bath of reality. With your clothes you cannot enter since the body is ignorant of the soul, as the clothes are ignorant of the body.

SECTION 24 2773–2800 (28) *How the Caliph's officers and chamberlains came forward to pay their respects to the Bedouin and to receive his gift.* (a) [2773–2784] The Arab arrived and the court officers greeted him with honor, knowing what he wanted before he spoke, since they usually gave before being asked, their vision being transformed by the light of God. He greeted them humbly and said he had come from the desert to seek the grace of the Sultan. But although he had come for money, since he had arrived he had become drunken with contemplation. (b) [2785–2795] Examples like this are of Moses, Jesus, a desert Arab, a falcon, a child, and 'Abbās, who all set out to do one thing and were then transformed and became something else. (c) [2796–2800] He said he had come for money and become a chief; he had been freed like the angels from material need and moved around the court, now without any worldly object of desire. Nothing in the world is disinterested except the bodies and souls of God's lovers.

SECTION 25 2801–2804 (4) *Showing that the lover of this world is like the lover of a wall on which the sunbeams strike, who makes no effort and exertion to perceive that the radiance and splendor do not proceed from the wall but from the orb of the sun in the Fourth heaven; consequently he sets his whole heart on the wall, and when the sunbeams rejoin the sun (at sunset), he is left for ever in despair: "and a bar is placed between them and that which they desire."* (a) [2801–2804] The lover of the whole is not the lover of the part. Love the part and you miss the whole. When a part falls in love with a part, the object of love soon returns to its whole. The lover of the part became the laughingstock of another's slave, a drowning man hanging on to a powerless support. How could the loved one care for him, when he has to do his own master's business?

SECTION 26 2805–2814 (10) *The Arabic proverb, "If you commit fornication, commit it with a free woman, and if you steal, steal a pearl."* (a) [2805–2810] The meaning above refers to these two proverbs. The slave went back to its master and the lover was in misery. The scent of the rose returned to the rose and the lover was left only with the thorn, far from the object of his desire, like a hunter who grabbed the shadow of a bird while the bird itself sat on a branch amazed, thinking the fellow was mad. (b) [2811–2814] If you think the part is connected with the whole then eat thorns, since the thorn is connected with the rose. But the part is not connected to the whole really, otherwise the mission of the prophets would be pointless, since they came to connect the part to the whole, and that they could not do if they were in fact one body. But let's return to the story.

SECTION 27 2815–2834 (20) *How the Arab delivered the gift, that is the jug, to the Caliph's servants.* (a) [2815–2820] The Arab handed over the jug saying, "Take this gift to the Sultan and relieve our poverty. It is sweet water and a new jug." The officials smiled and accepted the gift because the disposition of the King had become implanted in his courtiers. (b) [2821–2824] Think of the King as a reservoir with pipes leading in all directions. When the water is sweet and pleasant to drink, all enjoy it; but if it is brackish and dirty every pipe delivers dirt. Think on this and dive deep. (c) [2825–2834] Consider how the Spirit produces effects in the whole body; Universal Reason brings the whole body to discipline, love turns the whole body to madness. The purity of the sea makes all its pebbles pearls. Whatever the master is endowed with, his pupils become the same; a theologian endows them with theology, a lawyer with law, a grammarian with grammar, a Sufi with God. Of all these sciences, on the day of death, the most useful is the knowledge of spiritual poverty.

SECTION 28 2835–2852 (18) *The story of what happened between the grammarian and the boatman.* (a) [2835–2840] A conceited grammarian got on a boat, and when the boatman said he didn't know any grammar, he told him he had wasted half of his life. This upset the boatman. Then there was a storm and the boatman asked the grammarian if he could swim. The grammarian said he couldn't, to which the boatman replied that he had wasted the whole of his life since the boat was about to sink. (b) [2841–2846] Know that self-effacement (*maḥw*) is needed, not grammar (*naḥw*). If you are dead to self, then plunge into the sea. The sea causes the dead to float but the living die. The Sea is Divine Consciousness that will raise you to the surface, while those who call others asses will flounder and the greatest scholar will behold the passing away of time and the world. This has been inserted to teach the grammar of self-effacement. (c) [2847–2852] Self-loss is the essence of law, grammar, and accidence, and the jug an emblem of a different kind of knowledge. Sure we are asses to carry a jug to the Tigris, but the Arab did not know of the Tigris. If he had he would have broken the jug with a stone.

SECTION 29 2853–2933 (81) *How the Caliph accepted the gift and bestowed largesse, notwithstanding that he was entirely without need of the gift (the water) and the jug.* (a) [2853–2859] When the Caliph saw the jug and heard the story, he instructed that the jug was to be filled with gold and he gave other donations. He said the Arab was to be taken home by way of the Tigris. When the Arab saw the Tigris he was filled with shame and wondered how the King could have accepted water from him. (b) [2860–2863] Know that everything is a jug brimming with beauty and wisdom; it is a drop of the Tigris of His Beauty that cannot be contained under the skin. It was a hidden treasure that burst forth and made the earth more shining than the heavens, like a Sultan robed in satin. (c) [2864–2869] If the man had seen even a branch of the Divine Tigris, he would have destroyed the jug of his self-existence. The jug is more perfect from being shattered, and no water is spilled but every piece is in dance and ecstasy, though reason would reject this.

In the state of ecstasy neither jug nor water is manifest and God knows what is best. (d) [2870–2877] Knock on the door of Reality and it will open, but restrain your thought which has become earthbound through eating material impressions and is devoid of understanding. You need this food because your animal soul requires it, but feed it seldom. Want of food took the Arab to the court, where he found fortune. (e) [2878–2896] When the man in love with God speaks, the scent of love springs from his mouth, so that theology turns into spiritual poverty, infidelity turns into belief, falsehood into truth. If a true believer finds a golden idol he destroys its unreal form because form waylays. You are an idol-worshiper if you worship form; leave form and turn to reality. (f) [2897–2901] This discourse is confused like the doings of lovers; it has no head since it preexisted, and no foot since it is everlasting. It is like water, each drop both head and foot but yet without either. It is not a story but my state and yours. (g) [2902–2904] We are both the Arab and the jug and the King; the husband is intellect and the wife greed and cupidity that opposes intellect. Their quarrel arose because the Whole has various parts. (h) [2905–2908] The parts of the Whole are not parts in relation to the Whole, as the scent is to the rose. The beauty of all plants is a part of the rose's beauty and the song of a bird is a part of that bird. If I discourse on this I will not be useful, so be patient. (i) [2909–2913] Abstain from distracting thoughts, for abstinence is the first principle of medicine; abstain and behold the strength of spirit. Hear. (j) [2914–2916] The diverse created things are spiritually different; from one aspect they are opposites, from another unified; one aspect in jest, another in earnest. (k) [2917–2924] The day of Resurrection is the time of supreme inspection; then the fraudulent Hindu will be exposed since he has not a face like the sun and needs night as a veil. The thorn has no leaf, so Spring is its enemy, whereas, for leafy plants, the Spring is welcome. The thorn likes Autumn when its shame and lack of beauty will be hidden; so Autumn is its Spring when you cannot tell the pebble from the pearl. (l) [2925–2933] The Gardener knows the difference even in Autumn, but his sight is the very best and he sees everything. All fair form cries out: "Here comes the Spring." Blossom is the good news; the fruit is the bounty. When the blossom is shed the fruit increases; when the body is broken the spirit lifts its head. How can bread give strength until it is broken, or grapes their wine?

SECTION 30 2934–2958 (25) *Concerning the qualities of the Pir (Spiritual Guide) and the duty of obedience.* (a) [2934–2945] Ḥusām al-Dīn, add something to describe the Pir, for though slight, we cannot see without you. Tell us what appertains to the Pir who knows the Way, for the Pir is the essence of the Way. The Pir is like summer and others like autumn. My Pir is young, yet I call him Pir for he has no beginning, nor rival, and old wine is more potent. Choose a Pir, for without one this journey is full of dangers. Without an escort you will be bewildered. Travel not alone nor turn your head from the Pir. (b) [2946–2958] If his protection is not around you then the cry of the ghoul will confuse you and entice you from the Way as Iblis did to wayfarers in the Qur'ān. Seize the neck of your ass and lead it to the Way, for he loves where there are green herbs and will stray from the Way if you let him. The ass is the enemy of the Way, so if you don't know the Way do the opposite of what the ass desires, for that will be the right way, just as the Prophet said we should consult women and then do the opposite. Do not befriend passion, since it leads you astray from God; nothing mortifies passion more than the protection of a fellow traveler.

SECTION 31 2959–2980 (22) *How the Prophet, on whom be peace, enjoined 'Alī saying, "When everyone seeks to draw nigh to God by means of some kind of devotional act, seek the favor of God by associating with His wise and chosen servant, that you may be the first of all to arrive (to gain access to Him)."* (a) [2959–2968] The Prophet said to 'Alī that he was the Lion of God, but he should not rely on lion-heartedness but seek the protection of the Sage who would keep him on the Way. His shadow is beyond all description. Of all devotional acts take refuge in the shadow of the servant of God. (b) [2969–2973] When a Pir has accepted you, surrender yourself to him and bear what he does without speaking, even though he kill a child, since his hand is the hand of God. God can kill and bring to life. What of life? He makes the spirit everlasting. (c) [2974–2980] If one has traversed the Way without a Pir, it is through the help of the heart of the Pir, since their hand is not withdrawn from those not under their authority. But if they give such bounty to the absent, what must they give to the present. When you have chosen the Pir be not fainthearted or as weak as water, since if you are enraged by every blow, think, how will you become a clear mirror without being polished?

SECTION 32 2981–3012 (32) *How the man of Qazwin was tattooing the figure of a lion in a blue on his shoulders, and (then) repenting because of the (pain of the) needle-pricks.* (a) [2981–3001] The people of Qazwin tattoo themselves in blue on the shoulders. A man asked a barber to tattoo a lion on his shoulders. At the prick of his needle the man wailed and asked him to leave out the tail and then likewise with the ears and the belly. The barber was bewildered and finally flung down the needle saying that God Himself never created a lion without a tail, belly, or head. (b) [3002–3006] Endure the pain of the lancet that you may escape the poison of your *nafs*. Sun and moon worship one who has died to self-existence, and since his heart has learnt to light the candle of love, the sun cannot burn him and the thorn becomes beautiful like the rose at the sight of the particular going toward the universal. (c) [3007–3012] To exalt and glorify God is to deem yourself despicable; to know of God's Unity is to consume yourself in the presence of the One. If you wish to shine like day, burn up your nightlike self-existence. Melt your existence like copper in the elixir into God's Being. You however are determined to hang on to "I" and "We," although this spiritual ruin is caused by dualism.

Analysis of Discourse Eight

The discourse contains 32 section arranged into four blocks of eight sections each. There is a clear progression from one block to another at the literal sequential level. The first block of eight sections deals with the altercation between an Arab and his wife over their poverty. The second block has them making peace with one another. The third block has them working together to prepare, as a gift, a jug of rainwater, which the husband then takes carefully to the court of the Caliph as part of his petition to the Caliph to relieve their terrible poverty. The fourth block has the husband's gift being accepted by the Caliph, who then fills it with gold to relieve their poverty completely.

Rhetorically, each block is internally organized by chiasmus and parallelism, and this intrablock rhetorical nonsequential level is where the primary symbolism and parallelism is located, with the wife symbolizing the *nafs*, the selfhood, and the husband the *'aql*, the intellect. The wife in the first block is the *nafs-e ammārah* at war with the *'aql* that is enforcing an ascetic regime. Here the poverty is deprivation. The second block of eight sections shows the *nafs* and the *'aql* reconciled, the *nafs* here being the *nafs-e lawwāmah*, the selfhood which blames itself. The third block of eight sections shows them working in harmony together, preparing the jug of rainwater which the husband takes carefully to the court of Bounty. The *nafs* here could also be the *nafs-e lawwāmah* prior to its final transformation, and it is she who sews up the jug of the body and who prays. The final block has the jug being delivered and filled with gold by the Caliph, God, followed by three sections on the need for a Pir and the need to be obedient and endure what he puts the disciple through. This effectively gives a further division into two sets of four sections within each block. There is another division that can be made at the halfway point, that is after Section 16, which divides the totality into two halves. The first half deals primarily with the *nafs* and shows its transformation from *ammārah* to *lawwāmah*; the second half deals primarily with the *'aql*, now in harmony with the *nafs*, which, on the point of being further transformed to *muṭma'innah*, sends the *'aql* to the court where his purpose for riches is transformed into pure contemplation. The need for self-effacement and the need, above all, to have a Pir or Shaykh are strongly emphasized.

This, however, does not end either the rhetorical structuring nor the symbolism, since there is yet another level of organization in this extraordinarily complex discourse: the parallelism between sections in one block with sections in another block, the sectional interblock parallelisms. In this level of organization the parallelisms are not chiasmic. They take the form A,B,C,D,E,F,G,H in block one in parallel with A*,B*,C*,D*,E*,F*,G*,H* in block four. The same arrangements holds between the sections of block two and block three. Although readers must judge for themselves, it certainly seems as if these parallelisms are more subtle than the intrablock ones, which sometimes have the obviousness of allegory, where wife = *nafs*, and so on, whereas these interblock parallelisms seem, on balance, to be more concerned with the spiritual world, the Real world of *Ḥaqīqah*. What is quite astonishing about this discourse, quite apart from the high spiritual understanding, is the level of sheer intelligence and technical control and skill that is displayed to produce this outcome. In identifying the parallelisms, the intrablock ones are taken first, then the interblock ones. The intrablock parallelisms are shown in fig. 3.11.

The first block of eight, after introducing the Munificent Caliph, is concerned with the altercation between the wife (*nafs*) and the husband (*'aql*) over their poverty. Sections 2, 3, and 4 are the wife's complaint, implying he is about as useful as a false shaykh and he might as well listen to her. Sections 5 to 8 complete their altercation. Section 1, about the Munificent Caliph, is paralleled in Section 8, when the husband tells her to try poverty in order to find real riches. Section 2 is the wife's lament over their poverty in parallel with the husband's response in Section 7 when he tells her not to sneer at poverty since poverty is his pride. Section 3 introduces the false shaykh, who is all pretence and produces nothing, in parallel with Section 6, her accusation that her husband, *'aql*, is also all pretence, and that he too uses the Name of God as a trap. Section 4 is the final part of the wife's complaint about their poverty, in parallel with Section 5 in which the husband tells her to be patient with regard to the poverty since her pain comes from her own desire.

The second block has Section 9 in parallel with Section 16, with the wife, *nafs*, crying for forgiveness and winning dominion over the husband in Section 9 and the wry comment that only a saint with the strength of Solomon can really handle the kingdom of this world in Section 16. Section 10 has two types of men, the wise, who have the human qualities of tenderness and affection, and the ignorant who have the animal qualities of anger and lust.

This is in parallel with Section 15, which describes how the people of fire are mixed with the people of light, each to be revealed in their own season. Section 11 has the husband repenting after destiny had dulled his intelligence and asking for mercy, an infidel becoming a believer, in parallel with Section 14 where the killers of Ṣāliḥ's camel also had their intelligence dulled but did not repent or become believers and hence were punished. Finally, Section 12 is in parallel with Section 13 through the common theme of Pharaoh and his rejection.

The third block has Section 17 in parallel with Section 24 through the theme of seeing with the light of God. Section 18 shows the *'aql* no longer in opposition to the *nafs*, which has now become transformed, and putting itself in the hands of the *nafs* out of love, in parallel with Section 23 on those in love with God and those in love with that which is other than God. Section 19 has the wife telling the husband to go to the King and demonstrate his need, in parallel with 22 on how Bounty in facts needs the beggar just as the beggar needs bounty. Finally, Sections 20 and 21 are in parallel because both deal with the jug, which is introduced in the first section and which the wife sews up in the second section.

The fourth block has Section 25 dealing with loving the whole and not the part, in parallel with the delightfully humorous Section 32 in which the man from Qazwin loved his own parts so much he could not stand the pain of the needle and as a result the whole lion was never completed. Section 26 deals with the part returning to the whole, in parallel with 'Alī being advised to return to the whole by putting himself under the protection of the shadow of God, in Section 31. Section 27 has the Arab handing over the jug of his body sewn up with the briny water in it to the Caliph's servants, followed by a description of God as a reservoir and then how the spirit of a teacher endues the disciple. This is closely in parallel with Section 30 on the need for, and qualities of, a Pir. Finally, Sections 28 and 29 are in parallel in that the themes of self-effacement, the Tigris and the breaking of the jug are introduced in one and developed in the next.

The next level of organization, which is not chiasmic, is given by the interblock parallelisms shown in fig. 3.11. These have previously been considered as secondary parallelisms, since the ones which form the actual rhetorical structure, and determine what comes where, have been regarded as the primary parallelisms. It maybe that this view will have to be revised in the light of this discourse, since the interblock parallelisms are no less a part of the rhetorical structure than the intrablock ones. They bind together blocks one and four, so Section 1 can be the starting point. Section 1 is about the Caliph, best taken as God. Section 25 distinguishes lovers of the Whole from lovers of the

Fig. 3.11. The Interblock Parallelism of Discourse Eight

Sec. 1	There was a generous Caliph who relieved all poverty
Sec. 2	Arab's wife *(nafs)* complains to spouse of their poverty
Sec. 3	False shaykh is all show, but you realize too late
Sec. 4	Rarely a good pupil still succeeds; admit our poverty
Sec. 5	Husband (*'aql*) urges patience; her grief from desire
Sec. 6	She says he's all show; don't use Name of God as trap
Sec. 7	He says don't sneer at poverty; she can't understand
Sec. 8	If she could, he'd tell; try poverty; find riches; be quiet
Sec. 9	Wife cries, says sorry; wins his lonely heart
Sec. 10	Women win over wise; ignorant win over women
Sec. 11	Husband regrets his anger and asks forgiveness
Sec. 12	Pharaoh only Pharaoh here; his revolt due to Moses
Sec. 13	Rejected by saints, he lost this life and the next
Sec. 14	Ṣāliḥ's camel's (spirit) killers punished; displayed
Sec. 15	All mixed but each has own term to show fruit
Sec. 16	Solomon's strength needed to deal with this world
Sec. 17	*nafs* and *'aql* argue; both needed; see with God's light
Sec. 18	Arab agrees to take her advice from love, not a test
Sec. 19	Wife says go to the King and demonstrate need
Sec. 20	Take jug of rainwater as gift; the jug is our body
Sec. 21	She sews up jug and prays; he takes it to the court
Sec. 22	The Giver seeks the beggar as beggar seeks Bounty
Sec. 23	The lover of God and the lover of other than God
Sec. 24	God's light revealed him; he sought money now free
Sec. 25	Love the Whole and not the part
Sec. 26	The part returns to the Whole like scent to the rose
Sec. 27	Arab gives jug; God a reservoir; teacher imbues pupil
Sec. 28	Grammarian and boatman; effacement not grammar
Sec. 29	Caliph sends him off with gold via Tigris; ashamed
Sec. 30	Ḥusām al-Dīn to explain need for Pir and his quality
Sec. 31	'Alī told to take protection with a saint; endurance
Sec. 32	Qaswini's tattoo incomplete from fear of needle

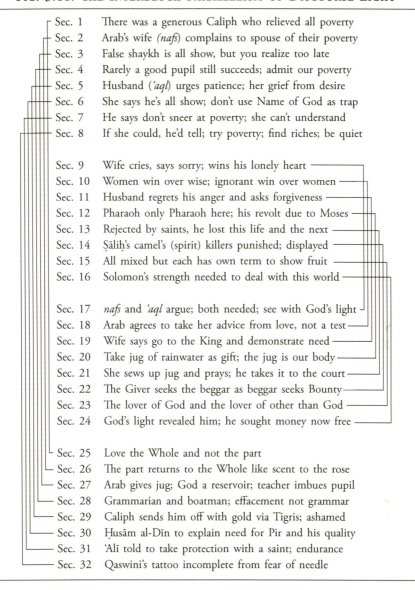

part. It is clear that the Caliph is to be considered the Whole—maybe God, maybe Universal Intelligence, *'aql-i kulli*. Sections 2 and 26 are in parallel in that in the first, the *nafs* is being deprived of its satisfactions, especially its love of the world, by a regime of self-control imposed by the *'aql-e juzwī*, the partial intellect. In the second, the folly of the love of the world is the central theme. Sections 3 and 27 are in parallel in that, the first is about false shaykhs, which is how the selfhood, *nafs*, regards the *'aql-e juzwī*, the partial intellect, and the second is about God as a great reservoir feeding in all directions, and the *'aql-e kullī*, Universal Intelligence, which brings all parts of the body into discipline. Further, it says that when a Master is absorbed in the Way, the soul of the pupil is absorbed in God. Sections 4 and 28 are in parallel in that, in the first it is possible to interpret the assertion that a disciple can, but rarely does, achieve a high spiritual state under a false shaykh, as meaning that the *'aql-e juzwī* can, but rarely does, succeed in disciplining the *nafs*. In Section 28 the grammarian, who represents the *'aql-e juzwī*, drowns because he cannot swim. What is needed is the *'aql-e kullī*, and the transition is made by *maḥw*, self-effacement. The *nafs*, therefore, was, in a sense, right to consider the *'aql-e juzwī* to be a false shaykh, since the real shaykh is the *'aql-e kullī*. Section 5, at its most obvious, is in parallel with Section 29 through the theme of gold. Lines 2304–2305 are about the tale of gold and how the wife became a gold seeker, when before she was gold itself. In 29 the Caliph fills the jug with gold, thereby restoring her to her former state. Section 6 has the wife, even in the heading, telling her husband not to speak above his station, and in Section 30 Mawlānā asks Ḥusām al-Dīn to describe the merits of a real shaykh or Pir. Section 30 also has the advice of the Prophet to consult women and then do the opposite. Section 7 is in parallel with 31 situationally: in 7, the *'aql* sings the praises of deprivation to the *nafs*, who should accept it just as a disciple must accept whatever a Pir does for his spiritual benefit in 31. Even 'Alī was advised to seek the protection of a Pir. Sections 8 and 32 are similarly parallel to the preceding in that the first urges the *nafs* to accept poverty as the way to riches, and the second urges the *sālik* to accept the pain given by a Pir for the sake of spiritual gain, using the analogy of the tattooist's needle and the complete tattoo.

Sections 9 and 17 are in parallel in that in 9, the wife has suddenly changed her mode of operation and become humble, and in 17 there is a full explanation and discussion of this tactic and of the relationship between the *nafs* and the *'aql*. Sections 10 and 18 are also clearly parallel, with the theme of women prevailing over the wise common to both. Sections 11 and 19 are in parallel in that in the first the husband yields to the wife and in the second she tells him what to do. Sections 12 and 20 are in parallel in a more subtle and interesting way. In 12 Pharaoh and Moses are seen to be both equally servants and creatures of God, but the contrast in their natures arises only from the existential relationship they have vis-à-vis one another. The section needs to be read taking into account the analogy of Pharaoh and Moses to the *nafs* and the *'aql*. Similarly, in 20, the *nafs*, who had previously suggested approaching the Caliph, now suggests the present of the jug, which Mawlānā quickly explains is no other than the body and the senses, that is, for the most part, the *nafs*. The *nafs* is shown having its own relationship to the Creator, quite distinct from its existential warring relationship with the *'aql*. But should this put too kind a light on Pharaoh and his like. Section 13 corrects this by pointing out that Pharaoh and his kind remain in perdition because of the repulsion exerted by the hearts of the perfect saints. But the parallelism with Section 21 is not the repulsion of the saints, but their attraction, which is in parallel with the Caliph's court which draws the Arab to itself. Section 14 has both those who killed Ṣāliḥ's camel and who rejected God, and the spirit of the prophet and saint, which can be a refuge for the whole world. This is in parallel with Section 22 on how Bounty needs beggars. The correspondence between the two is in the heading of 14, about how God makes his own side appear despicable and few, if he wants them to defeat the enemies, just like Ṣāliḥ's camel, and God similarly requires all to become beggars in order to obtain His Bounty. Sections 15 and 23 are much more clearly in parallel in that both distinguish between two types of people, between the people of Fire and the people of Light in 15, and between those that are poor for God and those that are poor of God and thirsting for something other than God in 23. Sections 16 and 24 are complementary in that the first deals with the kingdom of this world, which only someone like Solomon can cope with, and that with difficulty, and the second with the Caliph's court, the spiritual world, where the husband was set free from material desire and turned toward contemplation of God. The heading to Section 16 is a warning to a *murīd*, a *salik*, not to try to do things which can be done by a saint or friend of God. Then follows the example of Solomon, to demonstrate how difficult this world is to rule. At the Caliph's court the transformation just happened through the Grace of God.

Interpretation of Discourse Eight

This discourse completes the set of discourses dealing with the *nafs-e lawwāmah*, and prepares the way for the next state of the *nafs*, *nafs-e muṭma'innah*, the selfhood at peace with God.[21] The state of the *nafs-e lawwāmah*, that of self-blaming, is, in fact, largely the result of the intellect, *'aql*, looking at the selfhood, *nafs*, and either it or the selfhood, or both, lamenting and blaming itself for what it sees. In Discourse Four, the intellect, in the form of the hare, overcame the egotistical selfhood, symbolized by the lion, by tricking it into seeing itself in the well. The hare, symbolic of the *'aql-e juzwī*, the partial intellect, admitted to receiving guidance from a higher intellect, and did not itself destroy the lion. Indeed, Mawlānā is quite explicit that only God can overcome the selfhood, certainly not the *'aql-e juzwī* on its own. In the previous discourse, the Old Harper, as a classic representative of the self-blaming selfhood, was finally told to stop his lamentation, which 'Umar told him was a self-indulgence, because it prevented direct openness to God through prolonging self-consciousness. This discourse shows the final step that needs to be taken in order to pass through the stage of self-blaming, the stage of the *nafs-e lawwāmah*.

Mawlānā himself explains that the wife is the *nafs* and the husband is the *'aql*. The Caliph is either God, the *'aql-e kullī*, or, less likely, the Perfect Man or the Shaykh/Pir. The development of the story is that the *nafs-e ammārah* is complaining to the *'aql* about its deprivations, the result of abstinence or some ascetic regime devised by the partial intellect. The complaint includes the accusation that the *'aql* is like a false shaykh, full of pretence and using God as a trap. The *'aql* urges patience but knows the *nafs* cannot understand so he has to be severe and tell her to be quiet or he will go. It is difficult to decide precisely when the transformation to the *nafs-e lawwāmah* takes place and the two come into harmony. Although they make up and the *nafs* becomes repentant and humble in block two, in his explanation of the symbolism in Section 17, Mawlānā suggests this is a typical alternative tactic of the *nafs*, and certainly the husband, the *'aql*, seems to give in to this new approach and to succumb to worldly ambition. This occupies the first half of the story.

The second half begins with an explanation of the allegory and then takes up the development of the *'aql* in harmony with what has now become at least the *nafs-e lawwāmah*. The jug is explained as the body and the briny water as worldliness. It is the *nafs* who sews it up and who prays it is delivered safely. The husband takes it to the court and, although he came for riches, he is soon lost in contemplation, so there is a further transformation. The Caliph accepts the jug and fills it with gold, clearly indicative of spiritual riches. Whereas poverty in the first half could be taken as deliberate deprivation arising from spiritual discipline, it is clear that spiritual poverty is the major feature of the second half of the story with its constant emphasis on self-effacement. Since the second half deals with matters primarily from the point of view of the *'aql*, it is never possible to say that the *nafs* has been further transformed to become the *nafs-e muṭma'innah*, the soul at peace. What the reader is told is that the *'aql* is cleansed of its worldliness, which opens the way for the contact of the *'aql-e juzwī*, which is the husband, with the *'aql-e kullī*, which is the Universal Intelligence. Crucial to the transformation of the *ʿaql* is *faqr*, spiritual poverty, so poverty in its various forms runs throughout the discourse as a leitmotif.

Also running throughout the discourse is the need for a shaykh or Pir. This is addressed to the *sālik* for whom there are various pieces of advice. First, there is a warning about false shaykhs. Then a warning that it is rare that the use of the *ʿaql-e juzwī* can accomplish the control of the *nafs*, with the clear example in the story of the *ʿaql* being taken in by the *nafs* and being infected with worldliness. Then a warning to the disciple not to try things that are beyond his powers, such as acting like a Pir or a saint. Then an entire section is devoted to the Shaykh/Pir in which Ḥusām al-Dīn is invited to add further lines as the exemplary authority. Then there is the penultimate section in which Mawlānā points out that even ʿAlī was advised by the Prophet to seek the protection of a Pir. The final section adds the further instruction to the *sālik*: to take and endure whatever rough treatment the Pir prescribes, because it is only for his spiritual benefit.

At the very center of the discourse, one looks for the main import and emphasis, and that is where the harmony of the *nafs*, the selfhood, and *ʿaql*, the intellect, is brought about. Section 17, set at the beginning of the second half, gives a very clear explanation of the purport of the discourse, so further explanation here would be otiose. It will, however, be shown later that this discourse is in parallel with Discourse Five within Book One as a whole. The obvious parallelism is that they are both Caliph stories, although there is the change of levels from the Caliph being the shaykh in Discourse Five and God in Discourse Eight. But the two spiritual themes in common are the need for a shaykh and poverty, the first discourse has the Caliph's own self-imposed poverty, the second has real poverty too, but symbolic in the first half as the deprivation imposed on the selfhood, and becoming real spiritual poverty in the second half before the spiritual power of the Divine Court.

As to what extent there are elements of autobiography, it is impossible to tell. The discourse has about it the authenticity of having been written by someone who had experienced what he was writing about, but there is no account of Mawlānā's own spiritual progress other than the fact of his transformation. At a somewhat lighter level, however, it has been seen that Mawlānā kept himself and his immediate family within fairly tight economic restraints. The dialogue between the ascetic man and his deprived wife has about it a most authentic ring, and perhaps it should not be assumed that this dialogue is entirely imaginative and allow for the possibility that reminiscence also plays a part in its composition.

Discourse Nine: The Story of the Lion, the Wolf, and the Fox

Summary of the Narrative and Thematic Content

SECTION 1 3013–3041 (29) *How the wolf and fox went to hunt in attendance on the lion.* (a) [3013–3021] A lion, a wolf, and a fox went hunting together so that together they might capture great prey. The lion was ashamed of the other two, but he did them the honor of his company for unity's sake, just as the Prophet was told by God: "Consult them" even if his own understanding was beyond theirs. The spirit had become the body's fellow traveler. (b) [3022–3025] Their hunting went well as one would expect with a lion in the lead and they brought down their prey. (c) [3026–3041] The wolf and the fox both hoped the division of the prey would be made generously by the lion to their advantage, but the lion knew what they were thinking and just kept going on smiling, though he was thinking I will show them later since they are ungrateful for the lot they have been assigned by God and want more. How they must despise me and God. Outwardly the lion smiled, but don't trust that smile. Worldly wealth is like the smile of God; it has made us drunk. Poverty and distress are better for us because then that smile removes the lure of the world.

SECTION 2 3042–3055 (14) *How the lion made trial of the wolf and said, "Come forward Oh wolf, and divide the prey amongst us."* (a) [3042–3055] The lion told the wolf to divide the prey. The wolf said the ox is yours since it is the largest; the goat is mine because it is intermediate in size; and the hare is for the fox because it is the smallest. The lion said to the wolf: "How can you speak of 'I' and 'You' in my presence? Since you are not passing away in my presence it is necessary that you die miserably." And the lion killed the

Fig. 3.12. A Synoptic View of Discourse Nine

Sec. 1	Lion, wolf and fox go hunting together and win prey; lion has outward smile
Sec. 2	The wolf divides prey up, one animal each; lion kills wolf for saying I and You
Sec. 3	The man let in who knocked on the door and when asked said "It is You."
Sec. 4	Everything is really united in spiritual realm but only here appears to be plural
Sec. 5	The lion killed the wolf for unity's sake; the fox learns from the fate of the wolf
Sec. 6	There is a lion within the fox and thousands in Noah; be respectful and selfless

wolf because anyone uttering "I" and "We" at the door of the Divine Court is turning back from the door and returning to "nonentity."

SECTION 3 3056–3076 (21) *The story of the person who knocked at a friend's door: his friend from within asked who he was. He said, "It is I" and the friend answered, "Since you are you, I will not open the door: I know not any friend that is 'I,' "* (a) [3056–3064] A man knocked on a friend's door. The friend asked who it was, and on the answer "I" said: "Go, this is no place for the raw." Only absence and separation can cook the raw, so after a year of travel and being cooked by separation the man returned and knocked again. "Who is it?" asked the friend. "It is You," replied the man. "Come in," said the friend, "for there is no room here for two 'I's. The double end of the thread is not for the needle; since you are single, pass through the eye of the needle." (b) [3065–3076] A camel cannot pass through the eye of the needle except when fined down by asceticism and works. For that the Hand of God is necessary, which makes all possible, even bringing the dead to life, and bringing nonexistence into being.

SECTION 4 3077–3101 (25) *Description of Unification.* (a) [3077–3085] You are entirely myself, come in since you are now single. Don't mistake "K" and "N" as two; they are a single entity and only appear to be in opposition. (b) [3086–3101] Each prophet has a separate way that leads to God, but they are really all one. If the waters of their words are not listened to then they are diverted back to their original stream from which they have been diverted solely for teaching. They have their own channel, and may God grant the pure soul to see the place where speech is growing without letters, so that it may fly to the ample space of nonexistence from which our being and fantasies are fed. The realm of actuality is narrower than the realm of fantasy; the realm of sense and color is a narrow prison. The cause of narrowness is compounded-ness and plurality to which the senses are drawn. The world of Unification lies beyond the realm of sense; go there if you want Unity. The Divine Command "Kun" ("Be") was a single act; the two different letters occurring only in speech. Let us return to the wolf and the lion since this discourse has no end.

SECTION 5 3102–3123 (22) *How the lion punished the wolf who had shown disrespect in dividing (the prey).* (a) [3102–3107] On account of the wolf failing to be dead in the presence of the Emir, the lion tore off the wolf's head so that duality might not remain. Then he asked the fox to divide the prey. The fox said the King should have the ox for breakfast, the goat for lunch and the hare for supper. (b) [3118–3114] The lion asked the fox where he had learned to divide like that, and the fox replied it was from the fate of the wolf. Then the lion said, since he had become the lion's, he should himself have all the prey for there was no difference. From henceforth he was not a fox but a lion. The wise take warning from the death of friends. (c) [3115–3123] The fox was greatly relieved that the lion had not asked him first or he too would have been dead. Thanks be to God that He had us born now after past generations whom He had chastised, so that we may learn from the fate of those ancient wolves the better to watch over ourselves. The wise man lays aside this self-existence and wind since he heard what had happened to Pharaoh and the like. If he doesn't, then others can take his fate as a warning.

SECTION 6 3124–3149 (26) *How Noah, on whom be peace, threatened his people saying, "Do not struggle with me, for I am (only) a veil: you are really struggling with God (who is) within this (veil), Oh God-forsaken men!"* (a) [3124–3126] Noah said I am dead to the animal soul, I am living through the Soul of Souls. Since I am dead to the senses, God has become my hearing and perception and sight. Since I am not I, this breath (of mine) is from Him. (b) [3127–3134] Within the fox there is a lion, do not be overbold in his presence. In Noah there were thousands of lions and he was like fire to an ungrateful world. Whoever is disrespectful to this hidden lion will have his head torn off like the wolf. (c) [3135–3143] Would that the blows had fallen only on the body, so that faith and the heart would be safe. Make little of your bellies, lay the whole of "I" and "We" before Him whose Kingdom it is. When you become selfless the lion and the lion's prey are yours, since He has no need of anything. (d) [3144–3149] In the presence of His Glory, watch over your hearts because He sees our innermost thoughts. If the heart has become clear of images it can be a mirror for the Invisible and He becomes aware of one's innermost thoughts because the true believer is the mirror of the true believer. When he examines our spiritual poverty He knows the difference between the true and the hypocrite.

Analysis of Discourse Nine

The discourse has six sections arranged chiasmically with parallelism. Thus Section 1 is in parallel with Section 6 through the recurrence of the lion, fox, and wolf and by the fact that Section 6 sums up the situation opened in Section 1. Section 2 and Section 5 are both concerned with the fate of the wolf and the conclusions to be drawn from it. Sections 3 and 4 are in parallel in that they are both parts of the same story of the man knocking on the door, and, since they are at the central position, they indicate that the main point of the discourse is the need to lose self-consciousness before one can enter the Divine Presence.

Interpretation of Discourse Nine

The commentators agree that in this discourse the lion is the *rūḥ*, spirit; the wolf is the *nafs*, selfhood; and the fox is *'aql*, intellect.[22] From the rhetorical structure of Book One as a whole, which will be discussed in the next chapter, it is possible to see this discourse as the first of four that deal with the *nafs-e muṭma'innah*, the soul at peace, although that stage is only glimpsed at in this discourse in the person of Noah, the greater part dealing with an important preliminary matter. Each stage in the development of the *nafs* has its own problems, and the issue here is the very major one of the sense of "I," of self-consciousness. In the parallel Lion discourse, Discourse Four, the Lion was egoism, sometimes described colloquially as "the great I am." Only when "the great I am" has been completely annihilated, even in its less strident forms such as the self-consciousness of the wailing repentant Harper, and there is no longer any sense of self-identity, is there room for God to grant the mystic his "real" identity. "I" is really a false God, a usurper who prevents God from entering. This issue is so central to the spiritual path it is worth examining carefully.

It is not difficult to confirm that, not just bodies, but every passing thought, utterance, or desire claim to be "I." More difficult to confirm, and hence more intractable to deal with, is that deep-seated egoism that has usurped the very deepest part of one's humanity, lying beyond even the subconscious drives and desires. This means that there can be people who are apparently loving, kind, in command of their bodies, mind, emotions and desires, religiously observant and even spiritually quite advanced, who deep down love only themselves, so entrenched is the egoism. Different spiritual paths have different remedies, such as, for example, the monastic ideals of poverty, chastity, and obedience, but all presuppose that the given is a strong ascetic piety, that the action takes place within a vibrant religious context with a strong sense of God, a Prophet, or a Savior to obey and imitate, and Scriptures from which to derive solace and inspiration. The person concerned has to be deeply committed to transformation, whatever it takes.

Given all of this, Sufi spirituality requires an additional crucial element, a shaykh, pir, master, or some other such Friend of God. It has been shown how Shams took this role for Mawlānā, and how he operated on two fronts simultaneously. On the one hand, he cut away all the outer and inner supports to his egoism: his learning and preaching, his teaching and disciples, his position and reputation. On the other hand, he opened Mawlānā's spiritual heart and enabled him to attain ecstasies and mystical experiences of Love and the spiritual realm of such awesome power and transcendence that he must have felt himself as nothing. It will be recalled that it reached the point where Mawlānā could scarcely distinguish between God and Shams. This was termed, in Chapter One, *fanā fi shaykh*, annihilation in the shaykh. Then Shams disappeared for nearly a year and Mawlānā suffered the extreme pain of separation which Shams had designed for his further refinement, which must have made possible the second stage of *fanā*, *fanā fi Allāh*, annihilation in God. Maybe they should both be seen as part of the same process; no one is competent to say except Mawlānā, who simply indicates in this discourse that it was during the year of Shams' absence and separation that he lost his own sense of self-identity. After the spiritual drunkenness and the annihilation of *fanā*, comes the return to sobriety and the state of *baqā*, subsistence in God, for after the obliteration comes the discovery of the real identity of the person, their existence and subsistence within God.[23]

There are more gradual and less extreme Sufi methods of approaching the problem. The use of the *dhikr* (remembrance, repetition), "There is no God but God" to awaken and purify the heart of anything other than God is a direct challenge to the ego. The heart, which is the center of spiritual consciousness, is the bridgehead of the spirit in its campaign to displace the usurping selfhood and ego. Given time such practice will make a real difference.

When in this discourse the lion is identified as the *rūḥ*, the spirit, it is necessary to remember that for Mawlānā the spiritual world is a unity, without number and individuation. That is why it would be a mistake to attempt to specify at any particular point in this discourse whether the lion was the spirit of the person for whom the selfhood was the wolf, whether it was the Perfect Man, whether the Universal Intellect or whether God. The point is not which spirit, which would be an ill-formed question given the unity of the spiritual world, it is the contrast between the spirit and the self-identity of the *nafs*. It is the *nafs*' claim to identity which provokes the lion and costs the wolf his head. The fox as the intellect (*'aql*) had the good sense to make no such claim and was rewarded with all the "food," presumably by being granted greater access to the Universal Intellect once there was no question of an identity claim which would prevent it. The gratitude of the fox is interesting, for it is expressed in terms of gratitude for the lessons provided by the mistakes of former generations, a matter Mawlānā returns to in a number of places.

The parable of the Lion, the wolf and the fox occupies three of the six sections; the two central sections, as is to be expected, contain the real inner message. The first nine verses of Section 3 contain the central message that there is no room for two "I"s. The autobiography here is striking if one reads the friend as Shams and the raw one who knocked at his door as the still self-identical Mawlānā. He was sent away for a year so that he could be cooked with the fire of absence and separation, after which he returned and these two "sincere and devoted friends" were one in spirit. Of course, this has also a wider reference than autobiography, since the Friend can also be read as God to whom there is only access for those who have obliterated their own self-identity and self-consciousness. Section 4 gives a description of the unity of the spiritual world. Finally, in Section 6, Mawlānā gives a brief description of life beyond self-identity, *baqā*, subsistence in God, put in the mouth of Noah: "I am not I: I am dead to the ego, I am living though God. Since I am dead to the senses, God has become my hearing, perception and sight. Since I am not I, this breath of mine is from Him."

Discourse Ten:
The Story of Joseph and the Mirror

Summary of the Narrative and Thematic Content

SECTION 1 3150–3156 (7) *How kings seat in front of them the Sufis who know God, in order that their eyes may be illumined by (seeing) them.* (a) [3150–3156] It is the custom of kings to have champions on their left, since that

Fig. 3.13. A Synoptic View of Discourse Ten

Sec. 1	Sufis sit facing kings to be the soul's mirror; beauty loves mirrors
Sec. 2	Joseph's friend; spirits in bodies; gift for Judgment day; *riyāḍat*
Sec. 3	Gift a mirror to show beauty; fault perfection's; conceit; Iblīs; Pir
Sec. 4	Prophet's scribe; pride and conceit; God's cure; nothing lasts long
Sec. 5	Bal'am lost to Moses from conceit; saints' Reason; you are asses
Sec. 6	Hārūt and Mārūt acted from pride; Reason directs; Reality is Allāh
Sec. 7	Hārūt and Mārūt saw sin but not their own; conceit; God's penalty
Sec. 8	Deaf man infuriates patient; much devotion like this; avoid surmise
Sec. 9	Iblīs used analogy first; saints beyond analogy; don't be egotistical
Sec. 10	Hide high state; opinion and knowledge not for God, bad; *riyāḍat*
Sec. 11	Burnish the mirror of the heart; Anatolian and Chinese painters

is the place of the heart that is endowed with courage, and on their right to have secretaries and bookkeepers, since one writes with the right hand. In front of them they put the Sufis for they are a mirror of the soul. But better than a mirror because they have polished their breasts so it is able to receive the virgin image. Whoever is born beautiful from the loins of creation should have a mirror placed before him. The beauteous face is in love with the mirror; such a face is the polisher of the soul and the kindler of the fear of God in men's hearts.

SECTION 2 3157–3191 (35) *How the guest came to Joseph and how Joseph demanded of him a gift and present on his return from abroad.* (a) [3157–3168] The loving friend, an acquaintance from childhood, was the guest of Joseph and was telling him of the injustice and envy of his brethren. Joseph said he had not complained because he was like a lion with a chain round its neck. The lion is not disgraced by the chain. In the well and prison of the world he was like the new moon, bent double, which at last becomes a full moon. Or like a grain of wheat, first buried then raising ears of corn. Then again the corn is crushed only to become bread. Again the bread is crushed when eaten. It became mind and spirit which then became lost in love and grateful for the sowing. (b) [3169–3175] Joseph asked what traveler's gift he had brought, since God will ask where is your present for the Day of Resurrection? Or did you have no hope of returning? (c) [3176–3191] Do you believe you will be His guest? Because, if you do, go not empty-handed. Refrain from sleep and food a little and bring that as a gift. Make an effort to win the senses that see the Light and go to the vast expanse the saints have entered. Now you are burdened from the senses and exhausted but in sleep you are born aloft. Regard that as the state of the saints whom God draws without their act or consciousness to good deeds on the right and the affairs of the body on the left.

SECTION 3 3192–3227 (36) *How the guest said to Joseph, "I have brought thee the gift of a mirror, so whenever you look in it you wilt see your own fair face and remember me."* (a) [3192–3199] "Come show your gift," said Joseph. The friend said he had tried everything but had found the only thing fitting, a mirror, in which Joseph could view his beautiful face and think of his friend. (b) [3200–3211] The mirror of Being is nonbeing. The poor are the mirror of the rich; the hungry man, of bread; tinder, of flint; defect, of excellence. The tailor needs unstitched garments; the woodcutter, unhewn trees; the doctor, a patient; the elixir, vileness and baseness. Defects are the mirror of perfection; each contrary manifest by its opposite. (c) [3212–3227] Whoever has seen his own deficiency rushes to perfect himself. The only reason not to run to the

Lord is supposing oneself to be perfect. There is no worse sickness than the conceit of perfection. Blood must flow to purge self-complacency, which was Iblīs's fault, but found in all. When Iblīs tests you, your water becomes muddy because, though your stream seems pure, there is mud at the bottom. Only a Pir can drain off the mud of the flesh and body; you can't do it yourself. Entrust the wound to a surgeon. Flies gather on every wound like evil thoughts on your darkened state. If a Pir puts a plaster on the wound, the pain goes at once. The ray of the plaster shone on the wound, it did not heal by itself.

SECTION 4 3228–3297 (70) *How the writer of the (Qur'ānic) revelation fell into apostasy because (when) the ray of the Revelation shot upon him, he recited the (revealed) verse before the Prophet (had dictated it to him); then he said, "So I too am one upon whom Revelation has descended."* (a) [3228–3239] A scribe used to write down the revelation from the Prophet, but a small part of the wisdom fell on him and he thought he was as illumined as the Prophet and stopped being a scribe and became the enemy of both Prophet and the religion. The Prophet was furious and said if the light had been in him how could he have sinned. His heart was darkened and he could not repent so his head was cut off. (b) [3240–3251] God created pride and reputation to be a barrier and a chain. The chain is worse than iron since iron can be cut. When stung by a wasp you can remove the sting. This sting is caused by your own self-existence so the pain continues. (c) [3252–3266] Do not despair, call on God who has a cure. The reflection of Wisdom led the scribe astray; don't be conceited because the wisdom in you comes from the saints and is borrowed, as the light in your heart is borrowed. Be thankful not vain or self-conceited. This self-assertion sets religion against religion and leads a man to think that at every station he is in Unity. The house is bright from the sun but when it sets the truth is plain. Plants say we are green and gay by nature, but the summer says just look when I am gone. (d) [3267–3274] The body boasts of its beauty but the spirit has given it life for a day or two and says: "What will happen to your pride when I take off and you are in the grave?" The beams of the spirit are speech and ear and eye and they fall on the body as do the beams of the Saint on the soul. When the Soul of soul withdraws, the soul becomes as a lifeless body. (e) [3275–3286] I lay my head humbly upon the earth in witness at the Day of Resurrection of what has passed within me. Then will the earth and rocks speak and the mystics alone will hear; not the philosopher who did not believe in the moaning pillar. He said melancholia brings fantasies but it was his own wickedness which made him think this. He does not believe in the Devil but is himself possessed, as are you. Whoever doubts is a secret philosopher; he professes firm belief but his philosophy will sometime shame him. (f) [3287–3297] Take care, Oh Faithful, in you are all seventy two sects; make sure they don't overcome you. You laughed at the Devil because you thought yourself a good man, but when the soul is revealed how many believers will say: "Woe is me"? Now everything shines like gold, but do You protect us when we are tested on the final Day. For thousand of years Iblīs was a saint but on account of pride he grappled with Adam and was shamed, becoming like dung steaming in the sun.

SECTION 5 3298–3320 (23) *How Bal'am son of Bā'ūr prayed (to God) saying, "Cause Moses and his people to turn back, without having gained their desire, from this city which they have besieged.* (a) [3298–3308] Bal'am was like Jesus, curing the sick, but he grappled with Moses out of pride and thinking himself perfect. There are thousands like Iblīs and Bal'am but God made these two notorious and publicly punished them as a warning. You are a favorite of God, but don't grapple with a greater favorite. These signs of God's punishment are evidence of the might of the Rational Soul. (b) [3309–3320] Kill all animals for the sake of man; kill all men for the sake of Intellect. Intellect is the quality of a saint endued with the Universal Intelligence. Partial intellect is intellect too but infirm. Wild animals are inferior to man and may be killed because they are not human and hostile to humanity. What of you who have become like timorous wild asses? The ass is useful but when it turns wild may be killed, since the Lord does not excuse it. How much the less shall man be excused if he becomes wild to Intellect? His blood may be shed for his is an intellect that flees from the Intellect of intellect and is transported from rationality to animality.

SECTION 6 3321–3343 (23) *How Hārūt and Mārūt relied upon their immaculateness and desired to mix with the people of this world and fell into temptation.* (a) [3321–3329] Divine wrath smote Hārūt and Mārūt because of their arrogance; they thought they who were buffaloes could contend with a lion. The Ṣarṣar wind uproots trees but makes the leaves look beautiful; it has pity on the grass for its weakness. The ax smites thick branches but not the leaf. (b) [3330–3343] What is form when confronted with reality? Intellect directs and the wind and breath and the sky act from their reality. Reality is Allāh says the Shaykh. All the tiers of heaven and earth are but straws in the Sea of Reality.

SECTION 7 3344–3359 (16) *The rest of the story of Hārūt and Mārūt, and how an exemplary punishment was inflicted on them, even in this world, in the pit of Babylon.* (a) [3344–3349] They looked down from Heaven and saw sin and wickedness but they did not see their own fault. When the self-conceited see the sins of others they are outraged but do not see their own soul of arrogance. This is not the Defense of Religion, which has a different character. (b) [3350–3354] God said to them: "Do not scorn the sinners; give thanks you are free from lust and sexuality. Let me impose that nature on you and heaven will accept you no more. The preservation against sin you have from my protection. Beware lest the Devil prevail against you." (c) [3355–3359] This is what happened to the Prophet's scribe who thought Wisdom resided in himself. If you imitate a nightingale, how will you know its feelings toward the rose? Only from analogy and surmise as a deaf man reads lips.

SECTION 8 3360–3395 (36) *How the deaf man went to visit his sick neighbor.* (a) [3360–3369] A wealthy man told a deaf man he should visit a neighbor who was ill but the deaf man knew he would not understand what he said so he decided to surmise and give some conjectured answers that he rehearsed, then went to see the invalid. (b) [3370–3375] He asked how he was; the patient said: "Dying." but the deaf man said; "Thanks be to God." He asked him what he had drunk; the patient said: "Poison." but the deaf man said: "May it do you good." He asked which doctor was attending; the patient said: "The angel of death." but the deaf man said: "Be glad." Then he left. (c) [3376–3383] The patient was furious and abusive. "Since the purpose of visiting the sick is to produce tranquillity, then this man must be my mortal enemy," he thought. (d) [3384–3395] Many works of devotion are like this, since what the pious person thinks is pure is really foul, just like the kindly deaf man who destroyed ten years of friendship by kindling the fire of resentment. Avoid analogical reasoning, especially if the senses draw analogies about Revelation, for the sensuous ear cannot understand and the spiritual ear is deaf.

SECTION 9 3396–3425 (30) *The first to bring analogical reasoning to bear against the Revealed Text was Iblīs.* (a) [3396–3399] Iblīs was the first to bring analogies to bear regarding God's work when he said he was of fire and better than Adam of earth; he of light, Adam of darkness. But God said that the only way to preeminence was to be through asceticism and piety, not through one's relationships. (b) [3400–3406] This is a spiritual heritage not an earthly one based on relationships; the devout inherit from the Prophets but Noah's son lost his way and Abū Jahl's son became a true believer. God said to Iblīs: "The children of Adam became illumined like the moon; you are the child of fire, go in disgrace." The wise man used reason to identify the *qibla* at night, but when the Ka'ba is visible before you, don't pretend you can't see it and avert your face because you have reasoned. (c) [3407–3413] A cheep from the

Bird of God you hear and learn by heart, then construct analogies and make your imagination substance. But the saints have inner expressions you do not know and you upset their hearts as the deaf man did the patient through your analogies built only on the sound of the Bird's language, and you are proud of your success. The Prophet's scribe supposed he was the Bird's equal and the Bird killed him. (d) [3414–3425] God said: "Do not you Hārūt and Mārūt, superior to all the angels, fall from the dignity of heaven. Have mercy on wickedness and do not cleave to egoism and self-conceit lest Divine jealousy destroy you." Although they said that God's protection was their security, desire in them sowed self-conceit and they said they would come down and spread justice, peace, and security on earth. But there is a real difference between the state of heaven and earth.

SECTION 10 3426–3466 (41) *Explaining that one must keep one's own (spiritual) state and (mystical) intoxication hidden from the ignorant.* (a) [3426–3429] Ḥakīm Sanā'ī said, lay your head in the same place where you have drunk the wine. When a drunken man leaves the tavern, he becomes the laughingstock of children and fools who know nothing of his intoxication or the taste or wine. (b) [3430–3441] All mankind are children, except those intoxicated with God or freed from sensual desire. This world is play and you are all like children; only adults have purity of spirit. Lust here is like the sexual intercourse of children, wars are fought with wooden swords and riders are really on hobby horses. Wait till the hosts of heaven come galloping by. You are all pretending to ride. (c) [3442–3453] Opinion is a bad steed and imagination and reflection is like a child's play horse. The mystic's sciences are good steeds but those of sensual man a burden. Knowledge not from God is burdensome, but if you carry the burden well you will be released from it and gain spiritual joy. Do not carry it for selfish reasons, but mortify yourself so that the burden will drop. How will you, who are content with only the names of things, be freed from sensuous desire, except by the actual cup of Hū? (d) [3454–3466] What is born from name and attribute? Fantasy. Is fantasy to show you the way to union? Have you ever seen something named without a reality, go seek the thing named. But if you seek to pass beyond name and letter purge yourself of self. Become in your discipline like a mirror without rust so that you can see all sciences without a book, as the Prophet said there are some who see him as he sees them, without any *ḥadīth*.

SECTION 11 3467–3499 (33) *The story of the contention between the Anatolians and the Chinese in the art of painting and picturing.* (a) [3467–3482] The Chinese and Anatolians disputed over who were the better painters. The

Sultan put them to the test and two adjoining rooms were given one to each group. The Chinese used many colors but the Anatolians went on burnishing. When the Sultan saw the Chinese room, he was amazed by the pictures; but when the curtain was pulled back from the Anatolians' room, the Chinese pictures shone in reflection on those pure walls more beautifully than in the other room. (b) [3483–3499] The Anatolians, Oh Father, are Sufis who have burnished their breasts from greed and avarice. That purity of mirror is the heart that can receive all images as Moses holds the form of the Unseen in his heart. The mirror of the heart is unbounded and here the understanding becomes silent because the heart is He and every image shines unto everlasting without blemish. They that burnish their hearts have escaped from color and scent and see only Beauty; they have relinquished knowledge and gained certainty; given up thought and gained light. Death has no hold and none can overcome their hearts. They have let go of grammar and gained self-effacement and spiritual poverty. Their hearts are receptive of a hundred impressions that are the very sight of God.

Analysis of Discourse Ten

This discourse comprises eleven sections, ten of which are arranged chiasmically and in parallel, and one, Section 6, the central section with the inner emphasis, standing alone. This is, analytically, a particularly interesting discourse, because it combines the theme of mirrors and reflecting back with a beautifully conceived spatial image in its construction. The mirrors are the parallelism found in the first and last sections, the mirrors of the heart and soul which reflect back the beauty of God. It is as if they look inward to the center, and in the center, in Section 6, is the phrase quoted from the Shaykh, "The Reality is Allāh." In the two outermost sections, Sections 1 and 11, there are positioned the mirrors of the heart and soul, which constitute the parallelism between the two sections. The next two parallel sections, Section 2 and 10, both urge *riyāḍat*, ascetic discipline: in Section 2, as a Resurrection Day gift "in order that you may be given the senses which behold the Light," and in Section 10 "make yourself wholly purged of self, . . . become in your ascetic discipline like a mirror without rust." Section 3 deals with fault being the mirror of perfection and the worst fault that prevents one from rushing to God is the conceit that one is perfect, which was the fault of Iblīs. This is in parallel with Section 9, which is precisely about Iblīs and his fault. Sections 4, about the scribe, and 8, about the deaf man, Mawlānā himself states to be parallel in Verses 3355–3359: Section 4, because the scribe imagined the "Wisdom and

Original Light to be residing in himself," Section 8, similarly through analogy, surmise, and conjecture, rather than through direct perception. Section 5 about Bal'am and Section 7 about Hārūt and Mārūt are parallel through the two themes of pride and punishment. This leaves Section 6 as the central section within which is stated that Reality (*ma'nī*) is God, as the Shaykh said. This is the centrality both of the discourse and of the universe, and this section elaborates the last line of Section I, in which the beautiful face in love with the mirror is not just the polisher of the soul but also the kindler of the fear of God in men's hearts.

Interpretation of Discourse Ten

This is the second discourse to deal with the *nafs-e muṭma'innah* and the specific problems that need to be resolved prior to its attainment.[24] But there is a strong sense in which this discourse is about practice; the cleansing of the heart and its use as a mirror to reflect Divine Beauty is the spiritual practice needed to reach this final stage of the *nafs*' transformation, and the problems dealt with are those attendant on this practice. Unlike the previous discourse, there is in Discourse Ten a large amount of direct and explicit exhortation to the *sālik*. The diagram and analysis above reveal the beautifully conceived spatial extension of this discourse. The mirror of the Sufi's soul in Section 1 and the mirror of the heart in Section 11 both pointing inward, positioned to reflect Reality, which is Allāh, in the central section. In Sections 2 and 10 the theme of *riyāḍat*, here discipline as the polishing and burnishing of the soul and heart, is situated so that it clearly emphasizes the need to cleanse the mirror and keep it clean. Between the mirrors and their wiping and the Reality of God, are a number of specific defects that prevent the mirrors from reflecting Reality: conceit, pride, and arrogance, on the one hand, and analogy, surmise and opinion, on the other. The pride and arrogance here are different in kind from their manifestation in the *nafs-e ammārah*, they are the more intractable problems of egotistical or spiritual pride, the conceit of perfection, and so on, to which, as Mawlānā's examples demonstrate, not even the angels are invulnerable. The second set of problems and defects that cloud the mirror and prevent the reflection of Reality, are analogy, opinion, and surmise. If you give somebody an important book to read and they come back saying: "It reminds me of Plato's dialogues," or if you takes them to your most cherished view or landscape and they say: "It reminds me of Bournemouth," you know they have not had a direct encounter with either the reality of the book or the reality of the view. Instead of a direct contact, they have seen both the book and the view through the fog of their own preexisting associations and memories and come up with analogies and secondhand responses, instead of a response of their own produced by a direct encounter with reality. Similarly, preexisting opinions, or guesses in the case of the deaf man, prevent a direct contact with reality, because they too produce a fog through which the reality is distorted. Although analogy, opinion, and surmise would not usually be thought of in the same category as pride arrogance and conceit, for the would-be *nafs-e muṭma'innah*, they produce the same result, an inability to have a direct contact with reality, an inability of the heart and soul to reflect back the Reality and Beauty of God. All of this is expressed "spatially" by the rhetorical structure of this discourse.

Since most of the discourse is explicit and clear, there is no need to add further to this interpretation. The rationale is perfectly articulated in the rhetorical structure. It might be helpful, however, to recall the spiritual and experiential context. The major transformation which has taken place must leave the spiritual traveler in an unfamiliar and vulnerable state. The old sense of self has gone to be replaced by a new sense of subsisting in God and being centered in the heart. The aim of the spiritual travelers at this point, the ideal to be placed before them, is so to burnish the heart it reflects back to God the beauty of the spiritual world, as a returning traveler's gift for the Day of Resurrection. New problems arise, new vulnerabilities. The worst one highlighted in this discourse is the conceit of perfection; another is the failure to recognize that all the newly discovered spiritual powers and experiences are simply borrowed for a while, or are just the reflections of another's spiritual glory. But the positioning of analogy, conceptualization and surmise as parallel with the faults of fallen angels would not be expected, certainly not from Sufi theory, as hazards at this stage. It seems most likely, therefore, that it derives from Mawlānā's personal experience and should be regarded as autobiographical. Of all the sections in this discourse, the one that does not derive from scripture or some other such source, and at least feels as if it has the authenticity of everyday life, is the brilliantly told episode of the deaf man, which deals with surmise.

Sufi theory distinguishes between *'ilm-e huṣūlī*, conceptual knowledge, and *'ilm-e huḍūrī*, direct knowledge. It is the nature of the human mind to conceptualize and to think analogically, and it is the nature of the human understanding to surmise, to draw inferences. These natural processes cannot be regarded as "sinful"; but when used inappropriately, however natural or well-intentioned, the result must be to produce the first type of knowledge rather than the second, direct, type. Mawlānā's powerful imagery and his use of analogy, as they are encountered in his poetry, feel as though they are expressive of direct knowledge, so striking are their effect. It may well be, however, that these poetic powers were at first a hindrance rather than a facility, and that they too needed to be transformed by Mawlānā before his vision could become clear. He gives the ideal situation in the final section: "They that burnish (their hearts) have become free from scent and color: they behold immediate Beauty every moment. They have let go of the form and husk of knowledge and have raised high the banner of the eye of certainty. Thought is gone and they have gained light. . . . Their hearts receive a hundred impressions from the empyrean and the starry sphere and the void: What impressions? Nay, it is the very sight of God."

Discourse Eleven: The Story of Zayd's Vision

Summary of the Narrative and Thematic Contents

SECTION 1 3500–3583 (84) *How the Prophet, on whom be peace, asked Zayd: "How art thou today and in what state hast thou risen?" and how Zayd answered him saying, "This morning I am a true believer, Oh Messenger of Allāh."* (a) [3500–3505] The Prophet asked Zayd how he was and was told he was a true believer. He asked what his token was from the garden of faith, and Zayd replied he had been filled with love day and night and gone beyond them both to where thousands of years are but an hour. (b) [3506–3526] When the Prophet asked for the traveler's token, Zayd continued that he had seen the seven Hells and the eight Paradises and knew the difference between the blessed and the damned and how, when the spirits were born in the next life, the blessed carried off the blessed, and the damned the damned. In this world you cannot tell Hindu from Turk but I was seeing all as on the day of

Fig. 3.14. A Synoptic View of Discourse Eleven

Sec. 1	Zayd tells Prophet his vision; who lost or saved; Prophet stops him
Sec. 2	Luqmān's innocence shown; Judgment Day; each gets like for like
Sec. 3	God wants it hidden for fear or hope; silence best service to Unseen
Sec. 4	Prophet got light from Sun, but others couldn't bear it, even Zayd
Sec. 5	Zayd is gone; Resurrection; Water of Life; fire of lust; fear of God
Sec. 6	Fire destroys city; water won't work; it's God's fire; be generous

Resurrection. (c) [3527–3542] Oh Prophet, shall I make manifest the Resurrection and pull back the curtains on Paradise, Hell, and the intermediate state for the unbeliever to see? Shall I tell of the pleasures of Paradise and the cries of woe from the damned? I would tell all but I fear to offend the Messenger of God. (d) [3543–3557] "Hold back," said the Prophet, "because when the reflection of God strikes the heart all shame goes. The mirror has shot out of its case and the mirror and balance cannot lie. If you ask them to conceal the truth they would say you should not expect them to deceive because God has made them to reveal the truth. Put the mirror back in its case if illumination has lit up your breast." "How can the Sun of eternity be contained in a case?" said Zayd. The Prophet replied that if you put a finger on the eye you can obscure the sun and a fingertip can veil the moon. That is a symbol of God's covering, that a whole world may be hidden by a single point." (e) [3558–3565] Look at the sea; God made it subject to man, as he did the four rivers of Paradise, and just as the two flowing eyes are subject to the heart and spirit. As the heart dictates they turn to poison or edification, to the concrete or the abstract, to universals or particulars. (f) 3566–3577] Likewise the senses obey the dictates of the heart. The foot dances or flees, the hand writes. Sometimes the hand is a friend, sometimes an enemy. The heart speaks to all the members of the body; it is a wonderful hidden link. The heart must have the seal of Solomon over all the senses and limbs. (g) [3578–3583] Oh heart since you are a Solomon, take control over the demons, since if you are free from deceit, the demons cannot take the seal from your hand. But if you have deceit then your kingdom is past. If you deny your deceit, how will you escape from the mirror and the balance?

SECTION 2 3584–3608 (25) *How suspicion was thrown upon Luqmān by the slaves and fellow servants who said that he had eaten the fresh fruit which they were bringing (to their master).* (a) [3584–3597] Luqmān was an ugly slave and despised. Their master used to send them to the garden to fetch him fruit but out of greed they ate it all and blamed Luqmān. The master was angry but Luqmān suggested he give everyone hot water to drink and made them run till they were sick, which would show who had eaten the fruit. The master did so and from Luqmān there came only pure water. (b) [3598–3607] If Luqmān's wisdom can do this, consider the Lord's wisdom, since one day all the veils will be lifted and everything revealed. The fire of Hell is the torment of infidels because it is the test of stone, and their hearts are stony. Bad treatment is for bad people; ugly mate for ugly mate. If you wish for the light make ready to receive light; if you wish to be far from God be self-conceited. If you wish to find a way out of this prison, bow in worship to the Beloved.

SECTION 3 3608–3655 (48) *The remainder of the story of Zayd (and what he said) in answer the Prophet, on whom be peace.* (a) [3608–3617] "Arise, Zayd, and restrain your rational spirit which exposes faults, for God now requires concealment so that no one should refrain from worship. His mercy is universal and He wishes prince and captive both to be hopeful, fearful, and afraid. Hope and fear are behind the veil so they can be fostered. When you rent this veil, what becomes of fear and hope?" (b) [3618–3627] A man by the river thought a fisherman was Solomon, but wondered why he was in disguise. He was still in two minds when Solomon became King again and the demon fled. Then the man saw Solomon's ring and all doubt departed. Anxiety exists when the object sought is hidden. The searching is for the unseen. When he was absent, imagination was strong; when present, imagination left. (c) [3628–3640] God wants us to believe in the unseen, which is why He has shut the window on the fleeting world in order that they may make their efforts in darkness. For a while things are reversed and the thief tries the magistrate and the Sultan becomes a slave of his own slave for a while. Service performed in absence, like protecting a border far from the Sultanate, is worth far more than service performed in the presence. (d) [3641–3643] "Since the unseen, the absent and the veil are better; it is best to close the mouth. Refrain from speech; God Himself will make manifest what is needed. Witness for the sun is its face, but the greatest witness of all, is God." (e) [3644–3655] "Speak I must since God and His angels and men of knowledge bear witness that there is no Lord except Him who endures forever. The angels are associated with the testimony because unsound eyes cannot stand the radiance of the sun and lose hope like the bat. The angels are helpers in this testimony, each with its rank and worth, reflected in three or four pairs of luminous wings. Each human is associated with that angel who shares the same dignity."

SECTION 4 3656–3667 (12) *How the Prophet said to Zayd: "Do not tell this mystery more plainly than this, and take care to comply (with the religious law)."* (a) [3656–3667] The Prophet said his companions were like stars, a candle for travelers and meteors to be cast at devils. No moon or stars would be needed as witnesses if everyone had an eye that could look at the sun. He, the moon, said he was just a man but it was revealed to him that God is One. "I was as dark as you but the sun gave me this revelation. I am dark in relation to spiritual suns but light with regard to human darkness. I am dark so you can bear my light. I am mixed like honey and vinegar to cure the sickness of the heart; now you have recovered from your illness, drink only the honey." If the heart is restored to soundness and purged of sensuality, then thereon God is seated. He controls the heart directly. But where is Zayd that he can be counseled not to seek notoriety?

SECTION 5 3668–3706 (39) *The return to the story of Zayd.* (a) [3668–3670] You will not find Zayd now for he has gone. Not just you, Zayd could not find himself; he is without trace like a star in the Milky Way. (b) [3671–3684] Senses and rational thought are obliterated in the knowledge of the King but when night comes the stars have to work and God restores the senses to the senseless, and dancing and waving they praise God for having brought them to life. At Resurrection, both the thankful and the ungrateful rush from nonexistence to existence. Why do you pretend not to see? You have been dragged into existence by the Lord. Nonexistence is the slave and is always trembling in fear of being brought into existence. (c) [3685–3694] You seek the world out of fear of the agony of spirit. Agony of spirit is everything, however pleasing, other than the love of God; it is to face death without the water of life. People look at earth and death and doubt about the water of life. Reduce doubt; go toward God in the night for the water of life is the mate of darkness. But don't sleep because when the merchant sleeps the night-thief gets to work. Your enemies are those made of fire. (d) [3695–3706] Fire is the enemy of water and water the enemy of fire, which it kills. The fire is lust, the root of evil, and brings you to Hell. It is not quenched by water but from light, the light of God. Lust is not reduced by indulgence but by restraint; don't feed the fire. Why should the fire of lust blacken the soul that has in it the fear of God?

SECTION 6 3707–3720 (14) *How a conflagration occurred in the city (Medin*(a) *in the days of 'Umar.* (a) [3707–3720] In the time of 'Umar a fire caught half a city and water was afraid of it. People threw water on it but it increased, fed from beyond itself. The people went to 'Umar and said water will not work. He replied that the fire was their own wickedness, forget water and give out bread in charity. Cease to be avaricious. They said they have been bountiful, generous and opened their doors but 'Umar said they had done so for ostentation and rule and habit not from fear and piety and supplication. Distinguish the friend of God from the enemy of God; sit with the man who sits with God. Everyone shows favor to his own kind and thinks he has done really good work.

Analysis of Discourse Eleven

This discourse is in six sections. Section 1 introduces Zayd, who had a vision in which he saw the true nature of people, who were virtuous and who were sinners, on the Day of Judgment. The primary parallelism with Section 1 is Section 5. Section 5 completes the story of Zayd, which Section 1 begins, and the major theme of both is the Day of Resurrection, Judgment Day. Whereas Section 1 shows how it will be, Section 5 offers advice to the reader or spiritual traveler as to how they can and should prepare for it. Section 2 is in parallel with Section 6, first, because they are both about a Perfect Man other than Zayd, Luqmān in 2 and 'Umar in 6; second, because they are both concerned with distinguishing the good from the evil; third, because of the motif of fire, which is described as the test for the stony-hearted in 2, and demonstrated as such in 6. Sections 3 and 4 are parallel in that they are both about Zayd, and in both the Prophet explains the reasons why Zayd should not speak of what he had seen. This has been shown above in the diagram as the primary rhetorical structure.

There are also secondary parallelisms between Sections 1 and 6, and Sections 2 and 5. Sections 1 and 6 both have examples of people who have cleaned the mirrors of their hearts and can see people's real natures and motives, Zayd and 'Umar, and both are about distinguishing between the friends of God and the enemies of God. Sections 2 and 5 are parallel through water, which reveals Luqmān's virtue in 2 and the Water of Life in 5. There is also a parallelism through the Day of Resurrection in both sections.

Interpretation of Discourse Eleven

From a synoptic point of view, this is the third discourse dealing with the preparatory stages and the attendant problems that arise prior to the stage of the *nafs-e muṭma'innah*, the selfhood at peace with God.[25] Zayd's problem, although he doesn't see it as a problem, is that he has received illumination, but he is not spiritually mature enough to know what to do about it. Fortunately the Prophet is able to instruct him as to what he can and should do, and what he shouldn't do, although what the final outcome is not known

The first section gives the vision of Zayd, that he saw the inner spiritual state of each person as it will appear on Judgment Day, who damned and their fate, who blessed and their good fortune. This is a grace apparently given to those who can see with the eye of certainty, the *'ayn al-yaqīn*, also generally referred to by Mawlānā as the eye of the heart. The Prophet's reaction is to restrain him, pointing out that he is being headstrong and that when the reflection of Reality hits a person, shame leaves; that the mirror cannot be expected to lie, but it can be, and should be, put back in its case. There then follows a wonderful description of how all the organs, powers and parts of a person who is transformed are under the control of the heart and subject to the command of the spirit. The implication is that Zayd has only to ask inwardly and he won't see such things; his mirror will be sheathed.

The story of Luqmān's use of water to distinguish the good from the bad at once appears as a legitimate demonstration of fault and innocence and also as a metaphor for Judgment Day when God will reveal the inner nature of each and the fate of each according to that nature. It ends with the admonition not to be self-conceited and not to turn away from the Beloved. But the central message of this discourse is contained in the two innermost sections, 3 and 4. God wishes for this concealment, first, in order to allow full scope to fear and hope; second, because it would be too easy to believe in what is seen and God wishes that "they believe in the unseen," since it is more worthy to serve the unseen. Therefore it is better not to speak since God will make known what is necessary through angels and prophets. Although God is the only real Witness to Reality, these intermediaries are needed because their reflection of God's Light is more bearable than the direct Light of God. But the message concludes: "When the throne of the heart is restored to soundness and purged of sensuality, thereon 'The Merciful God is seated on His Throne.' After this, God controls the heart without intermediary, since the heart has been given this direct relationship." [Verses 3665–3666]. This is the ultimate ideal station for the mystic, where God is enthroned within and in control of his heart and all that his heart controls. Mawlānā has done here what he did in Discourse Nine, he has slipped into a fairly spectacular episode, almost unobtrusively, the central inner message of the discourse about that most longed-for mystical grace, the enthronement of God within. The reader's attention can be so taken with the episode of Zayd, which is really the outer story, that the inner message can be missed. Similarly in Discourse Nine, it is easy to think that the point is that there is no room for two "I"s and to miss the almost unobtrusive verse about the year of suffering in separation, which was the very means of Mawlānā's own transformation.

For God to take control it is necessary for the person to disappear, like Zayd in Section 5, who has become invisible like "a star on which the sun shone." But when night comes, "the stars, which had become hidden, go to work again." Although this is portrayed as the Day of Resurrection, Nicholson rightly suggests it also refers to the return to consciousness after a transcendent mystical state.[26] In the mundane state, portrayed as the darkness of night, the spiritual traveler is advised to follow the darkness-consuming *'aql-e kullī*, the Universal Intellect, and grasp the Water of Life, the mate of darkness, which can put out the fire of lust. It is religion and the Light of God which can kill the fire, since what carries the water to the fire is the fear of God in men's hearts. The reason the charity was insincere and provoked the fire in the final section was because it did not derive from piety and fear, but from self-interest.

Discourse Twelve: The Story of 'Alī and the Infidel Knight

Summary of the Narrative and Thematic Content

SECTION 1 3721–3772 (50) *How an enemy spat in the face of the Prince of the Faithful, 'Alī, may God honor his person, and how 'Alī dropped the sword from his hand.* (a) [3721–3726] 'Alī, the Lion of God, was empty of deceit. One day, in battle with unbelievers, he had overcome a knight and was about to slay him when the knight spat in his face. He immediately threw his sword away and the knight was astonished at this display of mercy and forgiveness. (b) [3727–3733] The Knight said, "What did you see that was more interesting than killing me, that caused your anger to abate, that was better than life so that you gave me mine? In bravery you are a Lion of the Lord, in generosity the cloud of Moses." (c) [3734–3738] Moses' cloud gave cooked and sweet food in the desert for forty years unceasingly until the vile people of Israel demanded leeks, green herbs and lettuce. (d) [3739–3744] Oh people of the Prophet, that food is spiritual food, which will continue till the last day. Accept the Prophet's saying that "He gives me food and drink" as meaning spiritual food, without any false interpretation—which is really rejection—since false interpretation derives from faulty understanding. Since the Universal Intellect

Fig. 3.15. A Synoptic View of Discourse Twelve

Sec. 1	Learn *ikhlāṣ* from 'Alī; 'Alī not killing enemy who spat; knight asks why
Sec. 2	Knight asks the reason and seeks to know how the sun transforms
Sec. 3	'Alī not slave of body but of God, no self-interest on his part
Sec. 4	'Alī not angry with his future murderer; contraries; Divine decree
Sec. 5	Need for humility; prayer to God for His grace without which nothing
Sec. 6	'Alī not angry with his murderer; death is life; a return to the Unity of God
Sec. 7	'Alī not killing murderer; not written; not body's slave but master of spirit
Sec. 8	Prophet and 'Alī as Perfect Men; no interest in worldly dominion
Sec. 9	'Alī not killing since not fully Will of God; conversion; end of book; patience

is the kernel and our reason the rind, alter yourselves and not the traditions of the Prophet. (e) [3745–3751] "Tell what you have seen, Oh 'Alī, for these are God's mysteries. Your eyes saw the Unseen while the bystanders saw nothing." (f) [3752–3756] One sees the moon plainly, one sees only the dark, while a third sees three moons. They are all alert in their senses but not everything is accessible to every eye. (g) [3757–3765] "Reveal the mystery, Oh 'Alī, of whom God approves, or I will tell you how it seems to me. You are giving off light like the moon, but it would be better if the moon comes to speech. You are the Gate of Mercy to the City of Knowledge, be open, Oh Entrance to God. Every atom is a viewpoint of God, but only when it is opened." (h) [3766–3772] Until the Watcher opens a door, the idea does not dawn; but when the door is opened then the person is amazed to discover what he had been searching fruitlessly for years. Opinion never gets further than its own nostrils. Can you see anything other than your own nose? How will it be with your nose turned up in conceit?

SECTION 2 3773–3786 (14) *How that infidel asked 'Alī, saying "Since you were victorious over such a man as I am, how did you drop the sword from your hand?"* (a) [3773–3782] "Speak Oh 'Alī, that my soul may stir like the embryo." The embryo cannot stir when it is under the control of the stars, so it turns toward the sun which endows it with spirit. How does the sun do this? It has many hidden ways whereby it transforms natures. (b) [3783–3786] "Tell it forth, Oh royal falcon, wherefore this mercy in place of vengeance?"

SECTION 3 3787–3843 (57) *How the Prince of the Faithful made answer (and explained) what was the reason of his dropping the sword from his hand on that occasion.* (a) [3787–3809] "I wield the sword for God. I am not the servant of my body but the servant of God. I am the Lion of God not the Lion of my passions. I am as the sword and the wielder is the Sun. I have removed the baggage of self and deemed that which is other than God to be nonexistence. I am the shadow, my Lord is the Sun. In battle I make men living, not dead. I am a mountain of mercy, patience, and justice; how could the wind of passion carry off a mountain? Only rubbish can a wind carry off. I am a mountain and only stirred by love of God. Anger is king over kings but to me is a slave. Since the thought of something other than God intervened, I sheathed my sword that everything I do, loving, hating, giving, withholding, may be only for God's sake. I am God's entirely and what I do for God's sake is not from opinion, or fancy, or conformity, but from intuition since I have tied my sleeve to the skirt of God. I am the moon and the Sun in front of me is my guide. (b) [3810–3812] I have to speak according to the understanding of the audience, there is no other way as the Prophet showed. I am free from self-interest; hear the testimony of a freeman for that of a slave is worth nothing." (c) [3813–3824] In religious law the testimony of a slave is worthless, and in God's sight that of the slave of lust is the worst. Only God's favor can redeem such a slave. The only approved witness is he who is not the slave of sensuality, so in the Warning in the Qur'ān the witness was the Prophet who was free from creaturely existence. (d) [3825–3830] "Since I am free how can anger bind me. There is nothing here but Divine qualities, come in. God has made you free, you have escaped, come in. You are I and I am you; how could 'Alī kill 'Alī? You committed a sin better than any act of piety." (e) [3831–3840] How fortunate was the sin, like that of 'Umar against the Prophet or the magicians of Pharaoh. Disobedience becomes obedience despite the slanderous devils who seek to make a sin of it. God's act of mercy has driven them away in envy. (f) [3841–3843] "Come in, for I open the door for you. You spat and I gave you a present. If I give this to the sinner, I give treasures and kingdoms to the righteous."

SECTION 4 3844–3892 (49) *How the Prophet said in the ear of the stirrup holder of the Prince of the Faithful ('Alī), may God honor his person, "I tell you, 'Alī will be slain by your hand."* (a) [3844–3853] "I am so merciful I was not even angry at my own murderer. The Prophet told my servant that one day he, my servant, would kill me. My servant told me to kill him so it would not happen but I said this is Divine Ordainment; I do not hate you because you are God's instrument and I must not attack the instrument of God." (b) [3854–3858] "When then is retaliation allowed?" asked the Knight. 'Alī replied: "It is from God too and it is a mystery. He takes offense at His own act since in mercy and vengeance He is One. If He breaks His own instrument, He mends what He has broken." (c) [3859–3876] Every law that God has canceled He has replaced with a better, as night cancels day and day then night, for contraries are manifested by means of contraries. In the black core of the heart he places the light of love. The Prophet's warring caused peace in a later age. He cut off thousands of heads that the whole world might be secure, as the gardener lops off a branch or pulls up weeds and the dentist pulls out bad teeth. Many advantages are hidden in defects; for martyrs there is life in death. (d) [3877–3892] How long will you be attached to white bread for which you have lost your honor? Although white bread has broken your fast, He alone can mend what has been broken. He knows how to tear and how to sew, how to ruin a house and how to make it habitable, how to cut off a head and how to restore a hundred. Had He not ordained retaliation then no one would dare to retaliate, because everyone whose eyes God had opened would know that the slayer was subject to Divine predestination, even if he had to kill his own child. Go, fear God, and do not rail at the wicked. Know you own helplessness before the snare of the Divine decree.

SECTION 5 3893–3923 (31) *How Adam marveled at the perdition of Iblīs and showed vanity.* (a) [3893–3898] Adam looked with contempt and scorn on Iblīs, he behaved with self-conceit and became self-approving; he laughed at the plight of the accursed Iblīs. The jealousy of God cried out against him: "Adam you are ignorant of inner mysteries. If God should choose to He could put to shame a hundred Adams and bring forth a hundred Devils newly converted to Islam." Adam said, "I repent of this look; I will not be so disrespectful again." (b) [3899–3923] Oh Help of those that cry for help, lead us aright. There is nothing worse than separation from You. Possessions and our bodies destroy our spirituality and no one can save his soul without Your security. Even if one could save his soul he would still be miserable separated from You. You have the right to upbraid Your creatures because You alone are perfect and brought the nonexistent into existence. You can make grow and then destroy, and then, having destroyed, restore again. Since You made us, we should only be humble and content, but since we are engaged with the flesh, unless You call us, we are devils. If we are delivered from the Devil, it is only because You have delivered us. You are the Guide without whom we are blind. Excepting You everything destroys us and becomes fire for us. Everything but God is empty; truly the grace of God is a cloud pouring abundantly and constantly.

SECTION 6 3924–3937 (14) *Returning to the story of the Prince of the Faithful, 'Alī—may God honor his person—and how generously he behaved to his murderer.* (a) [3924–3929] Returning to 'Alī and his murderer, 'Alī said: "I see him day and night but am not angered by him because death has become sweet for me. It is death outwardly but life inwardly; what seems an end is really permanence. (b) [3930–3937] Since I long for death the prohibition not to cast oneself into destruction is meant for me. Slay me my friends for in death is my life. How long shall I be parted from home? If I was not separated from God, why else would He say: "Verily we are returning to Him?" He who returns flees from the revolution of Time and approaches Unity.

SECTION 7 3938–3947 (10) *How the stirrup holder of 'Alī, came (to him), saying, "For God's sake kill me and deliver me from this doom."* (a) [3938–3947] The murderer begged me to kill him, saying he would make it lawful, but I told him it was not possible for it had been written. He should not grieve for I am his intercessor. I am the spirit's master not the body's slave. Without my body

I am noble and death will be my banquet. How could someone who treats his body like this covet the Princedom and the Caliphate. Only outwardly does he strive for power, in order to show princes the right way, to give another spirit to the Princedom, and fruit to the palm-tree of the Caliphate.

SECTION 8 3948–3974 (27) *Explaining that the motive of the prophet in seeking to conquer Mecca and other (places) than Mecca was not love of worldly dominion, inasmuch as he has said "this world is a carcass," but that on the contrary it was by the command (of God).* (a) [3948–3955] How can you think that the Prophet sought to conquer Mecca out of love for the world? He cared only for God rather than the treasures of the Seventh Heaven. If these treasures were worthless to him, what then of Mecca, Syria, and 'Iraq? (b) [3956–3963] This is the thinking of a hypocrite who judges from the analogy of his own worthless soul. Iblīs saw the dust and said how can this offspring of clay be superior to me of the fiery brow? Such a view which regards the holy Prophets and saints as men is the inheritance from Iblīs. (c) [3964–3974] I am the Lion of God who has escaped from phenomenal form and seeks freedom and death, not the lion of this world who seeks prey and provision. Desire for death became a criterion for the Jews in the Qur'ān; if they were the chosen people they would have wished for death to enter paradise, but they didn't and became tax payers asking the Prophet not to shame them."

SECTION 9 3975–4003 (29) *How the Prince of the Faithful, 'Alī—may God honor his person—said to his antagonist, "When you spat in my face, my fleshly self was aroused and I could no longer act with entire sincerity (toward God); that hindered me from slaying thee."* (a) [3975–3979] 'Alī said to the knight that when he spat in his face his fleshy self was aroused and half of his fighting was for God's sake and half from passion; since partnership with God is not allowed he did not finish him. He, the knight, was made by God and you can only break God's image by the command of God. (b) [3980–3989] When the infidel heard this he repented and sought to become the slave of that Lamp which lit the light of 'Alī. He asked for the Muslim profession of faith and fifty of his tribe accepted Islam. By the sword of mercy 'Alī saved so many from the sword of iron. (c) 3990–4003] Now a morsel of bread has broken the flow. When bread was spirit it was inspirational, now it has become form it leads to disbelief. The words are coming forth earth-soiled; the water is turbid; stop up the mouth of the well so God may again make it pure and sweet, that He who made it turbid may again make it pure. Patience brings the object of desire, not haste. Have patience—and God knows best what is right.

Analysis of Discourse Twelve

The form of this discourse is identical to that of Discourse One with which it is clearly in parallel. It is formally A, B, C, D, E, D*, C*, B*, A* with the emphasis on Section 5, which is a direct prayer to God. Sections 1 and Section 9 are in parallel in that narratively they represent the beginning and the conclusion of the story in that Section 1 gives the sparing of the Knight and Section 9 his conversion. Thematically, they are paralleled by the concept of *ikhlāṣ*, purity and total surrender to God in act, the word that occurs in the first line of the story and is repeated as the theme of sincerity in the heading of the last section. Section 2 and Section 8 are parallel in that Section 2 introduces the concept of the sun as the Perfect Man who transforms the embryonic *sālik's* nature, and Section 8 presents the Prophet and 'Alī as Perfect Men. Narratively the question asked in 2 as to why mercy in place of vengeance is answered in 8 by the title, the example of the Prophet, and 'Alī's insistence that he too is not interested in worldly dominion. Sections 3 and 7 are parallel in that in both 'Alī states he is not the servant of his body but the servant of God and master of the spirit, and in both sections he refrained from killing because it was not ordained. Sections 4 and 6 are parallel in that they are both concerned with 'Alī's murderer, and the fact that 'Alī was not angry with him. In thematic terms, Section 4 introduces the contraries, and God in multiplicity, as well as God replacing one thing with another, whereas in 6, this is developed into seeing death as life and a return to God as Unity. This leaves Section 5, which stands as the central emphasis. This begins with an anecdote on the need for humility and is followed by a direct prayer to God requesting His Grace and Love without which we are nothing.

Interpretation of Discourse Twelve

This discourse is the climax of the development of the *nafs-e muṭma'innah*, which culminates in the state of *ikhlāṣ*, sincerity, total submission to God's Will, without any trace of self-interest.[27] It is also the culmination of the Sufi Path, the *sulūk*, the spiritual journey from the perspective of the selfhood, and the conclusion of Book One of the *Mathnawī*. The preparatory stages in the development of the *nafs-e muṭma'innah* have been: in Discourse Nine, dying to self and self-consciousness (*fanā*); in Discourse Ten, the purification and burnishing of the heart so that it reflects Reality and the Beauty of God; in Discourse Eleven, the enthronement of God within the heart; now, in

Discourse Twelve, living and acting in total obedience and surrender to God's Will, *ikhlāṣ*. This is the model the spiritual traveler, *sālik*, needs to hold before him or her self, and the final stage is exemplified here in 'Alī. But *ikhlāṣ* is not the only element of the ideal placed before the *sālik* in this discourse: indeed, it is the outer message, in the sense that it is contained in the two outermost sections. Since this discourse is the culminating discourse of Book One, the ideal is a composite one that sums up in a sense the whole book. This discourse is in parallel with Discourse One and the elements of the parallelism are examined in the next chapter, but it is also in parallel with the first discourse in Book Six where one of the major themes is the "temptation of free-will," temptation because what is sought for ideally at this stage is not free will but God's Will. This is a conclusive correspondence between the two discourses, and hence between the two books.

Proceeding synoptically, the first two sections to consider are the outermost two, Sections 1 and 9. Section 1 has the knight being spared after he had spat in 'Alī's face and his questioning 'Alī as to why. Section 9 gives the answer that because he became angry he couldn't kill him, since half of the action would have been from God and half from his own anger. Since in God's affairs partnership is not allowed, he was spared. The knight is so impressed he asks to be converted to Islam. At which point Mawlānā, who had just taken two mouthfuls, finds that to be enough to stop the flow of his thoughts and composition and brings the book to an end, urging patience on the reader.

Coming to the next pair of sections inward, Sections 2 and 8, Section 2 repeats the knight's question about why mercy instead of vengeance, but adds the comment: "that my soul may stir within my body like the embryo." The point here is that the embryo was thought to be affected by the influences of Saturn, then Jupiter, then Mars during the first three months of pregnancy, and in the fourth month it came under the influence of the sun which breathes into it the spirit of life. Spiritually the knight was asking for his soul to be awakened by the "sun," that is, the Perfect Man, here 'Alī, but, at a more general level, maybe this is a reference also to Shams. In Section 8 comes the answer, that the Perfect Man, here the Prophet, is interested only in God, the Beloved, above even the delights of Heaven, so his conquests were only at God's Command and not for worldly domination. To think otherwise would be to judge from analogy with oneself, a practice deriving from Iblīs. 'Alī was the Lion of God, seeking freedom and death, not the worldly lion seeking prey and provision. The two messages from this parallelism are first that the Perfect Man, whose eye has seen the Friend, quickens the soul as the sun does the embryo; and second, that only the children of Iblīs judge the saints and the prophets from the analogy of their own wicked souls, as indeed the knight had judged ʿAlī and was surprised in consequence to be still alive. Both could be seen also as messages deriving from Mawlānā's own experience with Shams and the judgment some of the disciples made about Shams.

Coming further in still, Section 3 could be said almost to list the ideal qualities the *sālik* should aim for: to be the Lion of God, not of the passions; to have removed the baggage of self; to deem what is other than God to be nonexistence; to be a shadow, with God as the sun; to be united with God, to make men living not slain; to have anger as one's slave, not vice versa; to be free from self-interest. In the parallel Section 7 the list continues: not to attempt to act against what is written; to be the spirit's master, not the body's slave; to deem the body to be of no value. "Given all this," asks ʿAlī, "how could one covet Princedom?"

Coming even closer to the central inner purport are the two flanking sections, Sections 4 and 6, which deal with ʿAlī and how he behaved to his future murderer. This episode is well known and certainly germane to the overall narrative, and needs no further justification, but since an autobiographical resonance has been raised with regard to Section 2, there is possibly here a suggestion of a parallel situation concerning Shams and his fate, although this is pure speculation, since some of the disciples were certainly murderous, even though the idea that they murdered Shams has been rejected. The central theme of Section 4 is God's Ordainment, and how it is a hidden mystery. How when God breaks he really mends, is one of the contraries which is part of His mystery. The narratively parallel Section 6 is also thematically parallel in that one of the great spiritual contraries is here illustrated, that what is death outwardly is life inwardly. Here is the ideal given to the *sāliks* who have attained to this stage of the *nafs-e muṭmaʾinnah*, that for them death should become sweet, and that like ʿAlī they should wonder how long they will be parted from home and a return to Unity. It is only safe to reach this stage if it is coupled with a total acceptance of God's Ordainment, lest they seek death before the ordained time. Mawlānā emphasizes this point by the parallelism, as well as by the warning given in verse 3930.

Finally there is the central section, Section 5, which contains the main inner message of the discourse. This begins with the episode of Adam's look of contempt for Iblīs, which an outraged cry from God quickly corrects and leads to Adam's repentance. The word Mawlānā uses for the fault that produced Adam's look, is *ʿujb*, which Nicholson translates as vanity, but it covers pride, haughtiness, conceit, superiority, indeed all the opposites of humility. It means to think highly of oneself. God's response was that, should He wish, he could shame a hundred Adams and produce a hundred Devils newly converted to Islam. Adam was properly put in his place, and the message for the *sālik* is clear, that lack of humility is a particular problem for the *nafs-e muṭma'innah.* This episode is followed by a most wonderful prayer which should be read in its entirety, since it is the inner summit of Book One. It is a prayer for help, a prayer for humility, a reminder that even evil is ordained, and much more besides. It concludes with a final verse in Arabic:

Everything except Allāh is empty and vain;
The Grace of Allāh is a cloud pouring abundantly and continually.

Chapter Four

Book One as a Whole and as a Part

The previous chapter has shown how it is possible to read all the sections of Book One synoptically as being grouped into twelve discourses, with three link sections. This was done by recognizing that the organization of sections into discourses makes use of the principles of parallelism and chiasmus. This chapter is concerned with the organization of Book One as a whole, and also whether Book One is a carefully integrated part in a larger whole, the *Mathnawī* itself. It is recognized that the material advanced for the latter proposal can only be provisional and suggestive at this stage in the absence of further additional analyses for each of the other books of at least a similar depth to that conducted in Chapter Three. But it is with an analysis of Book One as a whole that this chapter begins.

The Synoptic Analysis of Book One as a Whole

The synoptic analysis in Chapter Three now makes it possible to examine Book One as a whole, using the discourses identified as the parts of that whole. The formal structure is set out in fig. 4.1, which shows that the twelve discourses are arranged chiasmically and in parallel. The first and twelfth discourses both have nine sections and the sixth and seventh, separated by a highly significant link section at the very center, both have twelve sections. There is confirmatory symmetry in the patterning of the discourses, which have odd and even numbers of sections, giving Odd, Even, Odd, Even, Even, Even, (center) Even,

Even, Even, Odd, Even, Odd. Further clear evidence of the emergent rhetorical structure is given by the fact that Discourse Four, a Lion story, is in parallel with Discourse Nine, another Lion story, the combined total of their sections being forty. Discourse Five, a Caliph story, similarly is in parallel with Discourse Eight, another Caliph story, and again the combined total of their sections is forty. When looked at as two halves, both halves show a link section between the first and the second discourses. It is here argued that such formal symmetry could never have arisen accidentally, as the result of spontaneous inspiration; it must have been the outcome of very careful planning by Mawlānā, probably before even a line was composed. The symmetry is too perfect, and the numerology too significant, for it to have happened in any other way.

The addition of the number of sections in discourses that are in parallel is particularly interesting. First, Discourses One and Twelve each have nine sections, and the sum of these is the extremely important Mevlevi number of eighteen. Discourse Two and Discourse Eleven have together thirty sections, that is, five times six, as opposed to three times six for the preceding couple. Discourses Three and Ten again have eighteen sections when added together, again three times six. As has been pointed out above, Discourses Four and Nine, the two parallel Lion discourses, and Discourses Five and Eight, the two Caliph discourses, have, for each pair, forty sections. Forty is not divisible by six, but it does not need to be because it is a very important Sufi number in its own right, as for example in the *chilla*, the forty days and nights of *khalwah*, seclusion, retreat, which is a practice observed by a number of Sufi Orders. Finally there are Discourses Six and Seven, both of twelve sections. Twelve is clearly important to Mawlānā in that there are twelve discourses in Book One. The sum of two twelves is twenty-four, that is, four times six. The six pairs therefore produce the following sequence: Three time six, five times six, three times six, forty, forty, four times six. The importance of the number six is, of course, confirmed by the fact that the Mathnawī itself has six books. Numerologically, six is symbolically important because God created the universe in six days; because in Islamic culture there are six directions: left, right, in front, behind, below, and above; and because numerologically six is the first Pythagorean perfect number. Any one of these or a combination could have been influential in Mawlānā's choice of six, or he might simply have been following the example of Farīd al-Dīn 'Aṭṭār in the *Ilāhī-Nāmeh*. Whatever the case, for present purposes it is enough to have identified the numerical symmetry of Book One, and to have shown that this symmetry relies on taking as pairs the chiasmically organized parallel discourses. In fig. 4.1 below, the number of sections in each discourse is shown in square brackets.

Fig. 4.1. A Synoptic View of Book One

Discourse One	The King and the Handmaiden [9]
Link	The Greengrocer and the Parrot [1]
Discourse Two	The Jewish King who for Bigotry's sake used to Slay Christians [24]
Discourse Three	Another Jewish King who tried to destroy the religion of Jesus [7]
Discourse Four	The Lion, the Beasts, and the Hare [34]
Discourse Five	The Caliph 'Umar and the Ambassador of Rūm [8]
Discourse Six	The Merchant and the Parrot [12]
Link	Explanation of the tradition: *"Whatever God Wills Comes to Pass"* [1]
Discourse Seven	The Story of the Harper [12]
Link	The Two Angels [1]
Discourse Eight	The Caliph, the Arab of the Desert, and his Wife [32]
Discourse Nine	The Lion, the Wolf, and the Fox [6]
Discourse Ten	Joseph and the Mirror [11]
Discourse Eleven	The Vision of Zayd [6]
Discourse Twelve	'Alī and the Infidel Knight [9]

It is now important to examine the parallelism between discourses in the same way that, in the previous chapter, the parallelism between sections was analyzed. The thematic structure confirms and further elucidates the formal structure. Particularly strong is the parallelism between Discourse One and Discourse Twelve. Both share the same internal structure A, B, C, D, E, D*,C*, B*, A*, which places a special emphasis on E. When the King greets the Divine Physician in Discourse One, he addresses him as "the Chosen One, the Approved One," using the epithet *murtaḍā*, which is a title applied to 'Alī. This is then followed by words attributed to 'Alī. This permits a provisional identification of the Divine Physician, which is confirmed in the parallel Discourse Twelve which is explicitly about 'Alī as the Perfect Man, and in which the epithet *murtaḍā* is also used of him. Narratively the parallelism between the two stories is that the first is about killing when it is the Will of God, while the second is about not killing when it is not the Will of God. But within the book as a whole, which deals with the *nafs*, Discourse One gives the beginning of the way, the *sulūk*, with the *nafs* falling in love with the world and having to be weaned off it by the Divine Physician and Love. Discourse Twelve can be considered as the completion of the way and perfect action, illustrated in the total surrender and obedience to the Will of God exemplified by the *ikhlāṣ* of 'Alī.

There are many other parallelisms between these two discourses: both place emphasis on patience, self-control, *sabr*; the maiden's love of this world is in contrastive parallelism with 'Alī's love of the next world in the final discourse; the first begins with things turning out worse than was hoped for when the maiden fell ill and the doctors failed because they did not say "If God Wills," while the final discourse begins and continues with things turning out better than could be expected, especially for the Knight and 'Alī's future murderer, because of 'Alī acting from *ikhlāṣ* and obedience to God's Will; both end with the contrastive parallelism of the rightness of killing in the first and the rightness of not killing in the second; both have at their center a major passage, the first on Love, human and divine, the Perfect Man and mention of Shams, the second on the need for humility and a great prayer to God for help without which nothing is possible. Between these two major passages comes the link section between Discourse Six and Discourse Seven on the tradition "Whatever God Wills comes to pass" which is similarly majestic and magisterial in tone and style and completes the structural and thematic symmetry. There are so many parallelisms of various kinds between these two discourses that it is difficult to chose a single phrase to encapsulate them all but perhaps "The Will of God and pure and impure love and action" comes closest. There is also clearly a strong autobiographical element in Discourse One, especially in Section 5, but also in the totality. It is not unreasonable, therefore, to expect a similar autobiographical element in the parallel Discourse 12. One speculative autobiographical possibility was suggested in the Interpretation of that discourse, but Section 5 could well have a biographical resonance for Mawlānā in the crucial importance of humility, a quality hard to retain, by all reports, as one's spiritual state advances.

The parallelism between Discourse Two and Discourse Eleven is equally complex but could be best expressed as that of "vision." The Jewish King is squint-eyed; he sees double and cannot see that Moses and Jesus are one. His vizier confuses the Christians by producing a multiplicity of conflicting doctrines and appointing twelve different successors so the Christians end up killing each other. This multiple vision is in contrastive parallelism with Discourse Eleven about the pure vision of Zayd. Zayd's asceticism and self-discipline has been rewarded with a vision of people's natures and fates as seen on the Day of Judgment and he wishes to speak about it. The Prophet of the Lord of both worlds, tells him not to speak, since these are things that God wishes to remain hidden. It is important that it is Muḥammad who instructs Zayd. In Discourse

Two, Moses is the symbol of plurality and this world, Jesus of unity and the next world, and Muḥammad, whose name was a refuge for the Christians who survived the slaughter, the symbol of unity in diversity and diversity in unity and of both worlds. Discourse Two ends with the question: "If the name of Aḥmad can become an impregnable fortress, what of the essence of that trusted Spirit?" Discourse Eleven answers this by showing Muḥammad as the Perfect Man. In the first discourse, the Christians, as the spiritual powers, are shown as divided, deceived and with distorted vision. In the second, all the spiritual powers and the faculties are described as united under the control of the heart which when ready will accept God's enthronement. Thus vision, Muḥammad and living in both worlds constitute the main parallelism between the two discourses. Again it was suggested that there was a strong autobiographical element in Discourse Two. Equally, therefore, it might be expected that Discourse Eleven has an autobiographical element, and from poems in the *Dīwān-e Shams* it is apparent that Mawlānā had many high spiritual experiences and raptures. While, however, these states are described in general terms, the contents rarely are, and it must seem likely that he too was reined back and told not to speak of things which are meant by God to be hidden.

Between Discourse Three and Discourse Ten, the parallelism can be summed up as "reflection back and return to one's origin." In Discourse Three, the King sets up an idol of the *nafs* and if the Christians, the spiritual travelers on the way, don't bow down to it they are thrown into the fire. The Christians, following the child, all entered the fire (of asceticism) and obtained *fanā*, annihilation of selfhood. The King's wickedness was reflected back to him by their state and actions and he was shamed. Finally the fire blazed up and killed the Jews. The Jews were born of fire and returned to fire since everything returns to its own congener, every particular to its own universal. Discourse Ten also deals with these two themes, the mirror being a central image, especially the mirror of the heart or soul that needs to be cleansed by ascetic disciplines. The return to one's source in this discourse is the return to God with the mirror of the heart polished so that it reflects back God's Beauty. The use of the Sufis as mirrors to reflect back the nature of the king in front of whom they sat is described in Section 1 of Discourse Ten. This is paralleled by the shaming of the king by a similar reflection back in Discourse Three.

Discourses Four and Nine are clearly narratively parallel in that they are both Lion stories, but they are also thematically parallel in that they both deal with the self: the first with egoism, pride, and selfishness, and the second with selflessness and the loss of the sense of "I." In the first story the selfhood wants control and is killed at the end of the story. In the second story, the selfhood is killed at the beginning and the Lion acts to ensure the freedom of the animals.

Discourse Five and Discourse Eight are both Caliph stories and the theme that makes them parallel is that of *faqr* or spiritual poverty. In the first story the ambassador, who is by definition rich and a Christian, expects the Caliph 'Umar to have a palace and is surprised by his "poverty." The ambassador can be said to represent the traveler at the very beginning of the way when he first meets his shaykh, 'Umar. In Discourse Eight, the Arab himself already is a *faqīr* and the story shows the various stages on the way as he obtains harmony with his *nafs*, his wife. In addition, then, to poverty, the stories are made parallel with the further themes of the stages on the way and the importance of the shaykh or pir. There is one further parallelism, which is the development of the role of the Caliph. In Discourse Five he is the shaykh but in Discourse Eight he is God.

Discourse Six and Discourse Seven are parallel through the theme of Voice. In the first story, the parrot is in the cage because of his voice and he only becomes free when he makes himself as if dead. He starts the story in the cage and ends the story free. There is much explicit instruction about speech and its dangers in Discourse Six. Discourse Seven starts at the universal level with the Voice and Breathings of God and the particular story of the Harper comes in the second half. He too has been led astray by his voice throughout his life and now he repents in his old age and God grants him riches and the transformation of his *nafs*. The two stories show a clear development from the voice of the parrot, which keeps the parrot in the cage, to the voice of God, which sets the spirit free. In both of these discourses, it is the cage of "reputation," *jāh*, in which the voice keeps both the parrot and the Harper. It is tempting to wonder just how much of these two discourses is autobiographical given Mawlānā's poetical voice and his formidable reputation. That Mawlānā also experienced the Voice of God must be apparent to everyone who has read the *Mathnawī*. In Mawlānā's usage of twelve-term structures, there is nearly always a crux, a crisis, a transition to be made, between 6 and 7. It will be recalled that the comment on the central Link Section dwelt at length with the crucial role played by *faqr* and *niyāz*, not only as the key to unlock the cage, but as the key to entering the second half of the book, with its depiction of higher spiritual states. Was this too a hard-earned lesson learned by Mawlānā, which he passes on to every reader or hearer of his *Mathnawī*, and to every disciple in his circle. Of course such a suggestion is speculative and quite unprovable, but there is such authenticity in the telling that it is better the question is left open.

The Rationale of Book One as a Whole

Having examined the parallelism between the chiasmically arranged discourses, it is now necessary to look at the discourses sequentially, to identify the rationale that determines what comes where. It is possible to say that the first four discourses display the negative aspects of the *nafs*, the *nafs-e ammārah*, the self which commands to evil; the next four show the situation changing as the *nafs* becomes the *nafs-e lawwāmah*, the self that blames itself; the last four show the positive and developed *nafs*, the *nafs-e muṭma'innah*, the self at peace. This is a formal thematic structuring, in that it divides Book One into three blocks, each of four discourses. That is why, in the diagram above, there is a space between Discourses Four and Five, and between Discourses Eight and Nine. It is also a demonstration and confirmation of the proposal that the identification of the rhetorical structure will reveal the rationale of Book One. There was already the expectation that Book One dealt with the *nafs*, because that is the characteristic of the first of the King's sons in the *Ilāhī-Nāmeh* of Farīd al-Dīn 'Aṭṭār which Mawlānā has followed in assigning the overall subjects of each of the six books, but nowhere has it been suggested that Mawlānā went further and made the Qur'ānic threefold typology of the *nafs*, the basis of the organization of Book One. Each block, each stage of the selfhood, will now be considered in turn.

In the first block of discourses, Discourse One sets the scene and states the problem: the *rūḥ*, the spirit, symbolized by the king, has acquired a handmaiden, the *nafs*, who quickly falls ill within this new association, because she is already in love with the world, as symbolized by the goldsmith. This is the starting point of Book One, of the *Mathnawī* itself, and of the Sufi Way. The problem is resolved only by the intervention of the Divine Physician, who could be all or any of Love, the Perfect Man, the advanced Sufi Shaykh, or several other possibilities. Discourse Two shows how certain properties of the *nafs-e ammārah*, such as anger, jealousy, or bigotry produce double vision, and how the *nafs* deceives, confuses, and divides, and can spoil even the most cherished devotional and spiritual practices through its cunning. Discourse Three presents the choice of worshiping the *nafs* or taking on the fire of asceticism that leads to *fanā*. It is the fire of lust that destroys the *nafs* worshiper. In the next discourse, the Lion is pride and egoism, which destroys itself, having been outwitted by the Hare, *'aql*, intellect, which has access to the *'aql-e ma'ād*, Universal Intellect. In these four discourses, first the goldsmith, then the vizier, then the Jewish King, and then the lion are all killed, but, in fact, each has, either directly or indirectly, brought about their own destruction. Each of these four discourses displays certain aspects of the *nafs-e ammārah*: the falling in love with the world, pride, jealousy, anger, bigotry, worship of the self, and egoism, for example. Each also offers a different solution: Divine intervention and being cleansed by Love; the prophets, and particularly the Name of Aḥmad; asceticism or self-denial; and the intellect. There is no time scale for these first four discourses, but they all seem to belong to the *Jāhiliyya*, the pre-Islamic period of ignorance, appropriately, since they deal with the *nafs-e ammārah*.

Looking at the second block of four discourses, Discourse Five brings about the beginnings of a change due to the first meeting with a pir who explains about *ḥāl* and *maqām* and why the spirit is combined with matter. Discourse Six shows the merchant as the *nafs-e lawwāmah*, the *nafs* that blames itself, distraught, thinking he has killed his spirit through what he said and reported. At the end, the parrot of the spirit flies off, having given the merchant spiritual advice, so the merchant ends up wiser, but not yet transformed. Discourses Seven and Eight give further examples of this form of the *nafs* in the persons of the Harper and the Wife of the Arab. These last two stories see the *nafs-e lawwāmah* moving, at least in a temporary *ḥāl*, state, to the next stage, the *nafs-e muṭma'innah*. As with the first block of four discourses, this second block similarly shows four stages in the development of the second type of selfhood, the self that blames itself. The first shows the *nafs* in the form of the unbelieving ambassador, who is in the grip of the worldly assumptions of *māl o jāh*, wealth and rank, being awakened to spiritual things. The second shows the *nafs* in the form of the merchant regretting bitterly having killed the spirit through what he said and repeated, but ending up wiser but not transformed. Then comes the turning point of the book, with the central Link section on "What God Wills, comes to pass," which explains that the pretended death of the parrots symbolized *niyāz*, supplication, self-naughting, and which also speaks of spiritual resurrection. The third discourse is in the second half of Book One, and tells of the Voice and Breathings of God permitting the repentant *nafs* in the form of the Harper to transform further, but only when it gives up lamentation, the self-indulgence of the *nafs-e lawwāmah*. Finally, the entire process of transformation is exemplified in the Arab, who symbolizes *'aql*, intelligence, and his wife, the *nafs*, whose eventual harmony permits the *nafs* to move to the final stage of its transformation.

The final set of four discourses all have to do with the *nafs-e muṭma' innah*, the self that believes and is at peace with God. Strictly speaking, only the very last discourse portrays the full *nafs-e muṭma'innah*, but each of the other three discourses deals with one or another property which pertains to the *nafs-e muṭma'innah*, so they are related to this stage if only preparatory. They deal respectively with selflessness, polishing the heart to be a mirror for God, spiritual vision and *ikhlāṣ*, pure action from the Will of God, sincerity and total submission. All of these states are necessary for the *nafs* to be transformed into *nafs-e muṭma'innah*, each is a sequential development towards this final state of the self. Each state of the *nafs* has its problems, which each discourse illustrates: "I" consciousness in the first; the dirt on the mirror in the second—that is pride, conceit, and arrogance, on the one hand, and analogy, opinion, and surmise, on the other—the danger of speaking of things that should remain hidden, in the third; the danger of acting not wholly from the Will of God but also from self-interest in the fourth, which also places particular emphasis on the need for humility.

This exposition of the different stages in the development of the *nafs*, is the main rationale of Book One, but it is not the whole of it: sometimes hidden, sometimes explicit, there is in every discourse, instruction to the *sālik*, the traveler on the Sufi Path. In fact, the expositions of the Sufi path and that of the three stages of the *nafs* are fully integrated to form one single rationale, although one that has, rhetorically at least, both an outer, *zāhir*, side, the stages of the *nafs*, and an inner, *bāṭin*, side, the Sufi spiritual path. It is now proposed to trace this spiritual path through the twelve discourses.

Discourse One is foreshadowed in the last line of the Proem as providing "the very marrow of our inward state." This discourse is both a general introduction to the book and to the Sufi path. It start its instruction to the *sālik* with that most crucial quality to be cultivated, *adab*, which Nicholson translates as seemliness, but which has, of course, a much wider and more significant import than this word conveys. It involves at all times proper behavior and attitude to God, and then to all creation, including other people, and especially toward one's shaykh. *Ṣabr*, patience, self-control, restraint, is another quality emphasized and illustrated. There are a number of pointers to other aspects of the Sufi path: the importance of dreams as the mode of contact with the spiritual world; the giving and keeping of promises; the keeping of secrets; *muḥāsibah*, self-investigation; *khalwah*, seclusion; the central importance of prayer and the shaykh, saint, or Perfect Man; but above all the crucial role of Love—"Love, human or divine, both lead us yonder." Discourse One is Mawlānā's Sufi manifesto, it proclaims the Mevlevi path to be the Path of Love, but as the first book is seen from the perspective of the *nafs*, then it is Love as the cleanser of the *nafs* that is highlighted. As Mawlānā says in the Proem: "He (alone) whose garment is rent by a (mighty) love is purged of covetousness and all defect." It is Love and *'irfān*, gnosis, which is the poison used slowly to undermine the goldsmith and thus free the *nafs* from its love of the world. In this way, the first discourse can be seen as a general statement of Mawlānā's particular Sufi Path of Love.

Discourse Two brings the *sālik* face to face with the deviousness and thorough nastiness of the *nafs-e ammārah*, the self that commands to evil. Much of the message for the *sālik* is contained in the explicit story and the warnings about the damage that jealousy and envy can do; specifically Mawlānā shows how the *nafs* is so clever it can undermine and utilize almost everything the *sālik* might do on the spiritual path: prayer, virtuous action, seclusion, silence, and so forth, and it can destroy his inner togetherness, his *jam'iyat.* Discourse Three presents the dilemma starkly: submit to the *nafs*, or follow the way of discipline and self-mortification. But in the central inner section, there is first the warning to the *sālik* not to ridicule the shaykh or it will rebound on himself, and then the advice to learn how to weep, through being merciful to the weak and those that weep, because weeping attracts the Mercy of God. Discourse Four begins with the debate about the respective merits of relying on Destiny to provide, *tawakkul*, or on work and effort. It was pointed out in the Interpretation of this passage that, whatever the strengths and weaknesses of the arguments, every *sālik* is likely to experience the whole gamut of attitudes and arguments within himself in his early years on the spiritual path. At the very center of this discourse, the subject emphasized is the keeping of secrets, but this is contained within an exposition of *'aql*, intellect, both particular and Universal. It is the potential access that a cleansed heart can have to the Universal Intelligence, which offers a way to the *sālik*, the way of catching an objective glimpse of himself, as the lion did when he saw his own reflection in the bottom of the well, and of not liking what one sees. But Mawlānā is careful to insist, in the final section of Discourse Four, that particular intelligence, *'aql-e juzwī*, cannot itself defeat the *nafs*, only God can.

Discourse Five is generally accepted by the commentators as being about the first meeting with one's shaykh or pir. The Interpretation of this discourse should be consulted here, since it gives ample evidence of the correctness of this proposal. The shaykh, 'Umar, found the potential *sālik*, the ambassador, eager and of good potential, and begins to instruct him and finally induces in him a transformation and a yearning for God. Discourse Six is notable for a significant contrast between the training of the *sālik* in the first half of the discourse and that in the second half. As stated in the Interpretation, in the first half the *sālik* is urged "to prefer silence and watch his speech very carefully. Abstinence is required and the avoidance of self-indulgence. He requires a master and needs a pattern to follow: to wear the dervish frock, to weep in private, to eat and follow only what is lawful, to recognize he is imperfect and not to strive beyond his limitations out of conceit." Then comes the pretended death of the parrot which Mawlānā explains as *niyāz*, self-abasement, and *faqr*, spiritual poverty. Then, in the second half, the training of the *sālik* consists of awakening love for God within his heart by means here of wonderful flights of mystical love poetry from Mawlānā. It would be a mistake to take the two halves sequentially, since clearly both types of training took place concurrently, with *niyāz* and *faqr* at the interface between the two.

At the interface between the first half of the book and the second half, comes the wonderful central Link section which can be read again and again, and probably was. It marks a major transition to a higher level, which seemingly only someone in whom some degree of transformation had already taken place, could hope to reach. The first half of Discourse Seven, which begins Book One, is devoted to the Universal spiritual world, only descending to the particular in the story of the old Harper, possibly personifying a reminiscence of Mawlānā, in the second half. The Harper provides the ideal here for the *sālik:* the gratitude he expresses for God's Favors, his repentance, his dedication of himself to God, his poverty, and his self-abasement. Prayer in the graveyard is also another specifically Sufi practice, and, throughout this discourse, a constant theme is that of resurrection, both as spiritual rebirth, and as the ever-present reminder of the coming Day of Judgment. But the overall message of this discourse for the *sālik* is the encouragement it gives for him to participate in the commerce and traffic between the two worlds, especially through dreams. The two twists in this discourse are both instructive for the *sālik.* The first twist relates to the special spiritual rain which can make people unaware of God, so that this world can continue to function, since it relies on the motive power of selfishness. Such a perspective provides a valuable corrective to any feeling of spiritual superiority in the *sālik.* The second twist is when it is revealed that excessive lamentation is the self-indulgence of the *nafs-e lawwāmah*, since it contains the very self-consciousness that inhibits further progress.

The final discourse dealing with the *nafs-e lawwāmah*, is Discourse Eight. It has two halves, the first showing how the *nafs*, protesting to the *'aql* about the deprivation it is suffering as a result of a regime of asceticism, changes direction and wins the *'aql* over by a different strategy; the second showing how the two working together in harmony allow the soul to reach the Caliph's court where there is a transformation to a higher spiritual level, and a cleansing of worldliness. Crucial to this discourse are the two main themes: spiritual poverty, and the need for a pir. Even 'Alī needs a shaykh, as the Prophet advised. The message for the *sālik* here is that, when he has a shaykh, he must endure whatever harsh treatment the shaykh dispenses, since it will be for his eventual spiritual benefit.

Discourse Nine is short and contains general Sufi instruction, foreshadowed in the previous discourse, about the need to lose "I" consciousness. Easy enough to say but it is the most intractable problem for anyone on the spiritual path. One the one hand, it requires a lion to remove one's head, on the other it requires a year of suffering the pain of separation. Discourse Ten is more elaborate and concentrates of those defects which prevent the *sālik* from polishing his heart and soul to reflect the Reality and Beauty of God. These are first: spiritual pride, conceit, and a sense of superiority; and second: analogy, opinion, and surmise. Again *riyāḍat*, discipline, is given as a necessary requirement for the *sālik* to effect such a cleansing. The discourse also gives the *sālik* a wonderful analogy as the ideal to hold before himself, that of the cleansed heart and soul as the traveler's gift of a mirror which he could take back to God on his return so that it reflects back to God, His own Beauty. Discourse Eleven makes a very strong explicit case for not speaking about high spiritual experiences and the things that are shown, since God wishes that people should use hope and fear and should believe in the unseen since that is more meritorious. Almost hidden in this discourse is the guidance about the heart, that it controls all the bodily, psychic, and spiritual functions at this stage and awaits only the enthronement of God in the heart. Had that been attained by Zayd he would not have even wished to speak. Finally, Discourse Twelve presents the *sālik* with the spiritual ideal: to be totally surrendered to the Will of God, without any self-interest. *Ikhlāṣ* is so much more than "sincerity"; it is total purity of action and full surrender to God in every possible respect. If this were not a sufficient ideal for the *sālik*, other qualities of the Perfect Man mount up: to be a lion of God, not of the passions; to have removed the baggage of self; to regard anything other than God as nonexistence; to be united with God and deem the body as of no value; to accept God's Ordainment, even though death is considered preferable to life. Right at the very center comes Mawlānā's great prayer to God for help, and the great emphasis given by Mawlānā to the need for humility. In the ideal of 'Alī as the Perfect Man, the *sulūk* finds its culmination.

The Linear and the Nonlinear Ordering of Book One

Finally, it is possible to show both ordering principles, the sequential and the synoptic, working together, with the themes that connect the discourses in parallel. The difference between the two sides, between the first six discourses and the last six discourses, can be described as "un-transformed" and "transformed," which will convey the development from the left-hand side to the right-hand side. Figure 4.2 below also shows the sequential movement down, the turning point of *niyāz*, self-abasement, and the movement of resurrection and spiritual rebirth up again. This is not an altogether satisfactory representation, since the twelve discourses start from the low point and rise progressively as the *sālik* develops. The true descent is the reed-pipe's lament in the Proem, the journey from God, and this book describes the beginnings of the journey back, at least from the perspective of the *nafs*. Allowance must be made for this inadequacy in the diagram. There are then two systems of ordering: the sequential and the nonlinear parallelism of the synoptic. It is here argued that, in order to exemplify formal, narrative, thematic and spiritual integration so beautifully within a single structure, the whole book must have been planned very carefully, as will be argued in the concluding chapter. The diagram below attempts to show the two systems of ordering as they are integrated in the structure of Book One.

FIG. 4.2. THE SEQUENTIAL AND CHIASMIC STRUCTURES OF BOOK ONE

Un-transformed		**Transformed**
nafs-e ammārah ↓		↑
Discourse One	Pure and impure love and action; Will of God; 'Alī	**Discourse Twelve**
Discourse Two	Vision; two worlds; Muḥammad	**Discourse Eleven**
Discourse Three	Reflection back; return to one's origins	**Discourse Ten**
Discourse Four	Lions; egoism and selflessness	**Discourse Nine**
Nafs-e lawwāmah		*Nafs-e muṭma'innah*
Discourse Five	Caliphs; spiritual poverty; the shaykh	**Discourse Eight**
Discourse Six	Voice; imprisonment and freedom	**Discourse Seven**
↘	**Link:** "Whatever God Wills comes to pass"	↗

Book One as a Part

The synoptic approach to each of the twelve discourses separately and then to Book One as a whole, has demonstrated how tightly organized at least this book is. The final proposal that needs to be demonstrated is whether Book One is a part in the larger whole of the *Mathnawī* itself, and whether the work itself has its own overarching level of organization. What evidence might there be for this? First, there is the claim that in the division into six books, each book has a subject represented by one of the six sons in the *Ilāhī-Nāmah* of Farīd al-Dīn 'Aṭṭār. This gives an overall plan to the work, although this must remain tentative prior to detailed analyses of all of the books. Second, there is the love story that extends from Book Three into Book Four. Functionally this story acts as a hinge, a binding, which connects the first half of the work with the second half. If then the work is thought of as a hinged mirror, Books One, Two, and Three will be reflected in Books Six, Five, and Four. This is the right order because chiasmus is a mirror image. Here, in a most provisional way, and without the depth of analysis of Book Six that has been presented in Chapter 3 for Book One, some attempt will be made to test the hypothesis that Book One and Book Six are chiasmically parallel. Everything that has been seen so far in this analysis suggests that this could well be the case.

Book One has as its subject the *nafs*. As the selfhood is the instrument given to enable human kind to exist and operate in this world, its view of the world is essentially sensual and phenomenological and pluralistic. Its instinct is to see the part and not the whole. The literary mode most in keeping with such a perspective would be one of separateness, to have clearly identifiable discrete parts, narratively and thematically distinct. This has been shown by analysis to be the case, since there was little problem in identifying the separate discourses, in spite of Mawlānā's reluctance to mark them. Book Six, however, has a quite different subject, that of *tawḥīd*, Unity. This requires a different literary mode from Book One, one in which everything appears interconnected. Such, indeed, is the case in Book Six, where one discourse appears to merge with the next, and there seem to be few obvious borders. If the world of form is exemplified in Book One, in Book Six it is the world of formlessness that is exemplified. Nonetheless, it is possible to identify areas that are thematically related, and, although no attempt is made here to identify the discourses of Book Six, in a general way it will be shown that there is evidence of intertextual parallelism and chiasmus between the two books, certainly enough to justify a deeper examination.

The first discourse of Book One is the story of the King and the Handmaiden, which needs no further description here. The essence of the human state is that the spirit, *rūḥ*, which has come from the spiritual world of Formlessness and No Place, is in association with a selfhood, *nafs*, which is tied to the phenomenal world. The final "story" in Book Six, that of the three princes, is similarly concerned. Nicholson writes, in his commentary: "Its subject is the soul's descent into the world of forms and the subsequent experiences of the "traveler" (*sālik*) in quest of Reality." That Mawlānā not only intended these two discourses to be in parallel, but intended that they should be known to be so, is made clear by the reference to the story of the King and the Handmaiden of Book One in Verse 3666 of Book Six, early on in the final discourse. The occasion for this mention is the failure of the three princes to utter the saving clause, *istithnā*, "If God Will," in the same way that the physicians in the first story of the *Mathnawī* failed to cure the girl because they too neglected to utter the saving clause. Mawlānā devotes a number of scathing verses in Book Six to the mistaken underlying attitude of the physicians that led them to neglect the *istithnā*, associating the reader too with the same lack of understanding. But the parallelism does not stop here: it was shown how ʿAlī, as an exemplar of the Perfect Man, was a common element in the parallelism between Discourse One and Discourse Twelve in Book One. In Book Six, there is in this final story an entire section devoted to the tradition that Muḥammad said: "When I am the protector of any one, ʿAlī too is his protector." There are also abundant examples of the crucial role played by the *walī*, the saint or Perfect Man, in both stories. But above all else, it is the role of Love that provides the conclusive correspondence between these two discourses. In the opening discourse of the *Mathnawī*, in the crucial central section, it was said: "Love, human and Divine, both lead us yonder." In the concluding discourse in Book Six, there are plenty of examples of precisely this. In Book One, Love is the great physician, the cleanser of the *nafs*; in this part of Book Six, Love is the great universal power of which even Hell is afraid: "For this reason, Oh sincere man, Hell is enfeebled and extinguished by the fire of Love" (Verse 4608). It is not uncommon for an author to conclude his work by a reference back to its beginning, so parallelism between the beginning of a work and its end is not conclusive evidence of the hypothesis advanced here. Nonetheless, it is the first step, and there is encouragement from the fact that other commentators have noted the parallelism just discussed.[1]

Discourse Two in Book One and Discourse Eleven in Book Six (Book Six: Verses 3014–3582) are the next discourses that will be in parallel if the hypothesis is correct. It will be recalled that the first of these discourses had as major themes: seeing double, jealousy and envy, deception and cunning, multiplicity and the loss of togetherness, the Prophets Moses, Jesus, and Muḥammad, a king, and a vizier. It was also suggested that there was a strong autobiographical element to this discourse, possibly relating to the jealousy that arose among the disciples of Mawlānā when he began his close association with Shams, which led to a breakdown in the togetherness of the disciples, both outwardly and inwardly, and possibly to the ultimate disappearance of Shams. Discourse Eleven in Book Six is about a poor dervish who was heavily in debt but unworried, because he knew he could rely on the generosity of a certain Khwaja in Tabriz. He goes to Tabriz only to find the Khwaja had died, at which he was devastated. The bailiff arranges for a collection to be made to meet his debts, but it is not enough. They visit the Khwaja's tomb together, return to the bailiff's house, and fall asleep. In a dream, the Khwaja tells the bailiff that he had provided for the dervish and explains where he had buried the riches. It is not difficult to find in this story a continuation of the autobiographical element in Discourse Two of Book One, since Mawlānā himself must have been in just this situation after the disappearance of Shams. If this is speculative, more certain parallelisms are to be found. The second section of Discourse Eleven in Book Six is about a king seeking advice from his vizier while under attack in his fortress from Ja'far who had ridden out alone. The vizier says the king should surrender, since Ja'far was clearly Divinely aided and had a great collectedness in his soul derived from God. The fifth section contains a parable about a man who sees double. The seventh and eighth sections are about envy and jealousy, initially for a horse, which Khwarizmshah was talked out of by the chief minister, but then about God's Jealousy if one pays attention to anything other than God. God is not only the source of all jealousy, but also the source of all deception and cunning. All the main themes of Discourse Two in Book One are taken up and developed in Discourse Eleven of Book Six.

Between Discourse Three of Book One and Discourse Ten of Book Six, the parallelism is the theme of *jinsiyyat*, how everything is drawn to its own congener. It is the major theme of both discourses, although Discourse Ten illustrates, in the story of the frog and the mouse, the consequences of association with someone other than one's own congener, as foreshadowed toward the end of Discourse Three.

Between Discourse Four of Book One and Discourse Nine of Book Six, the parallelism is the theme of sharing or not sharing food, and who should eat what. In Book Six, to the wonderful story of the Muslim, the Christian, and the Jew and who ate the halwa, is appended a fifth section about Dalqak from which the moral is that one should pause and reflect before entering upon precipitate action. If the messages of Book Six were applied to Book One, the egotistical lion would simply have eaten the hare the moment he turned up, and he would have thought hard and long before ever jumping into the well.

Of course, there is the deeper level that both discourses share: that of seeing situations directly, and what prevents one from doing so. "Know that (true) knowledge consists in seeing fire plainly, not in prating that smoke is evidence of fire" (Book Six: Verse 2505). "(All this) noise and pompous talk and assumption of authority (only means) 'I cannot see: (kindly) excuse me' " (Book Six: Verse 2509). In this way, it is possible to regard the intertextual chiasmic parallelisms between Book Six and Book One as a sort of commentary on the themes and situations of Book One, but from the perspective of Unity.

Any further exploration of this hypothesis must await the full analysis of Book Six. Over half of the verses of Book Six have been examined and within them the parallelism with Book One has been found to be both striking and considered. There is, therefore, no reason to think that the other half of Book Six will be any different. Brief and unsatisfactory as this short examination has been, it has demonstrated, albeit in a preliminary way, that the hypothesis is correct, and that there is an even higher level of organization than that of the book, namely, that of the Mathnawī as a whole. A great deal more work, both of analysis and reflection, will be required before the full extent and depth of this overarching organization can be revealed. Meanwhile, as Mawlānā himself says when explaining the lengthy interval between the appearance of Book One and that of Book Two, time is needed to allow the blood to turn into milk.

Chapter Five

Conclusion

The last two detailed analytical chapters, Chapter 3 and Chapter 4, have, it is hoped, successfully demonstrated both the validity of the description of the design of the *Mathnawī* given in the Introduction, and also the merit of adopting a synoptic rather than a sequential reading. What has been shown is that Mawlānā's masterpiece is highly structured both in form and content and uses parallelism and chiasmus to organize the higher levels of the work. This concluding chapter looks at some of the conclusions to be drawn from this discovery.

How Mawlānā Composed the *Mathnawī*

The first thing that needs to be considered is just what is the beautifully symmetrical and numerologically precise design revealed in Chapter 4 and shown in fig. 4.1. At one level, it has to be regarded as the author's plan, almost certainly preexisting the actual verses of the *Mathnawī*. It is too specific, too precise, to have arisen accidentally, as the result of some creative outpouring of extempore poetry. If that is the case, then it means that Mawlānā must have planned the *Mathnawī* in advance, at least to as far down as the level of the section headings. There are a sufficient number of cases in which the section headings seem almost at odds with the content of the verses that follow, to suggest that the section headings came first. This would imply that Mawlānā went into the creative composing sessions he reportedly had with Ḥusām al-Dīn, his amanuensis, with a very clear idea of what was to be achieved in each section. The verses within a section flow naturally and logically, moving seemingly effortlessly from one theme to the next. Occasionally he soars on some particular subject and then apologizes to Ḥusām al-Dīn for keeping him up all night. There is no contradiction, then, between the preplanning of the *Mathnawī*, on the one hand, and the spontaneity of Mawlānā's creativity on the other; they are not mutually exclusive. Any constraint the plan placed on creative spontaneity must have been more than compensated for by the provision of subject, context and direction. The *Mathnawī* was preplanned down to the level of section headings, and spontaneous and extempore in the outpouring of the verses within each section. This suggested mode of composition is implicit in the discovery.

This conclusion might cause some initial disappointment for appearing to compromise the inspirational and spontaneous property many find in the *Mathnawī*, but it should not. On visiting a particularly fine building, one doesn't say the builders were inspired; rather one attributes the inspiration to the architect. Mawlānā himself speaks in several places of an architect receiving a design in the imaginal domain that is later actualized in a building. Design is as much open to creativity and inspiration as composition is. But the process suggested above as the most likely method of composition allows for both the planning of the *Mathnawī* and also the composition of its verses to be inspired, thus widening the scope for inspiration rather than narrowing it.

Mawlānā's Hidden Organization as the Writer's Plan

That Mawlānā planned the *Mathnawī* is apparent from the elaborateness, symmetry, and numerical precision of Book One. How would he have done it? There were before him the exemplars of Sanā'ī, Aṭṭār, and Nizāmī, so the literary genre of the *mathnawī* was an obvious choice. From 'Aṭṭār's *Ilāhī-Nameh*, it has been suggested, he derived the overall plan, that there should be six books, each devoted in subject to one of the king's sons in that work, namely: the *nafs*, or selfhood; the Devil, or Iblīs; *'aql*, or intellect; *'ilm* or knowledge; *faqr*, or spiritual poverty; and *tawḥīd*, or Unity. How far and in what manner he kept to this scheme will only be known when further work is done on the other books, but certainly this first book can be said to have the *nafs* as the overall subject. The work would be divided into two halves, each of three books, hinged in the middle with a story that connected Book Three and Book Four. Since the central theme of the *Mathnawī* is Love, that would be concentrated around the very center of the work. Love might appear in other places, such as in Book One, but there it would be seen from the perspective of the *nafs*, as the great purifier of covetousness and worldliness, for example. In the central position, Love would be treated in its own right. It is the hinge in the middle that creates the chiasmus and places, for example, Book One, on the *nafs*, in parallel with Book Six, on *tawḥīd*. This provides the opportunity to present themes, viewed first from the perspective of the *nafs* in Book One, and again viewed from the perspective of *tawḥīd* in Book Six, but in reverse order. That then is the overarching master plan of the *Mathnawī*. From the very start he must have decided to use parallelism and chiasmus, although whether he found it initially in Niẓāmī or in 'Aṭṭār or in Sanā'ī or in someone else has yet to be ascertained. He must also have decided at the outset the extraordinary scale of what he was proposing: that each book should be around four thousand lines of verse. It is also likely that he decided from the beginning that each book should ideally have twelve discourses, but again confirmation of this will have to wait for further analysis of the other books, although it is certainly the case in the first three books. He must also have determined at this point that these discourses should be unmarked following the pattern of the *Asrār-Nāmeh* of 'Aṭṭār.

Coming down to the next level, the level of the book, it seems chronologically unlikely that Books One and Six were planned in detail at the same time, nor would it have been necessary. Once Book One was written, it would have been easy enough to write Book Six when the time came, simply by reflecting some of the situations or features of Book One but in reverse order. Against this, however, it does seem that the story of the frog and the mouse in Book Six might have been foreshadowed at the end of the Discourse Three in Book One. It could be that in writing Book One, Mawlānā already had in mind some of the possible themes and subjects of Book Six, even if it had not been planned in detail.

When it came to the detailed planning of Book One, the specification was settled: to plan twelve discourses on the different stages and characteristics of the *nafs*, while at the same time showing the different stages along the Sufi Path. The traditional Qur'ānic division of the progression of the *nafs* into the three stages of *nafs-e ammārah*, *nafs-e lawwāmah* and *nafs-e muṭma'innah*, would have been an obvious choice as the organizing principle at this point, which meant that there would be four discourses for each stage, although it has been seen that with regard to the final stage only the last discourse is fully the *nafs-e muṭma'innah*, the other three discourses being preliminary and preparatory to that one. This further provided the opportunity to use the two halves of the book to show the untransformed selfhood in the first half, and the transformed selfhood in the second, with the point of transition at the exact rhetorical middle as chiasmus requires, with the *nafs-e lawwāmah* appropriately straddling the central position, where *niyāz*, self-abasement, and *faqr*, spiritual poverty, are made the key to further progress. A further specification was that the discourses themselves should be in parallel chiasmically, so a communality of theme was required between the six parallel pairs of discourses as was shown in fig. 4.1 in Chapter 4. Maybe it was at this stage too that Mawlānā imposed on himself the further specification of the numerological symmetry, in terms of how many sections any particular pair of parallel discourses should have. Already, this has become more that just a writer's plan, although it is that too. It is both an author's specification of how it has to be written and also the beginnings of a hierarchical organization of what has to be written, the content of the spiritual life. It is hierarchical because there are already three levels of organization: the level of the work with its six chiasmically parallel books, the level of Book One with its twelve chiasmically parallel discourses, and the level of the discourses with the chiasmically parallel sections that have yet to be determined. The overarching plan of the work provides both the subject of Book One and the context of the book; the rationale of Book One, which was revealed in Chapter 4, provides the thematic subject of each discourse and the context of that discourse; and the rationale of each discourse provides the thematic subject of each section and the contexts of each section.

Nowhere is Mawlānā's inspired architectonic creativity more apparent than in the designing of the discourses. As has been shown in Chapter 3, each discourse is a work of art in its own right. Each has its own unique structure and rationale; even those with the same number of sections manage to use them in its own unique way to produce its own particular distribution of emphasis. Consider, for example, the parallel pair of discourses, Discourse Six and Discourse Seven. Both have twelve sections, both make use of the division into two halves, but they each do it in a different way as the analyses and interpretations have shown. It is worth pausing at this point to reflect on the various considerations that must have been before Mawlānā when he came to design the discourses. The two major considerations must have been content and structure. The organization of the subject of the *nafs* was already specified, with four discourses to each stage in the development of the *nafs*. It seems most likely that Mawlānā referred to the *Ihyā 'Ulūm al-dīn*, "The Vivification of the Religious Sciences" (c. 1106), by Muḥammad al-Ghazzālī for help in deciding the distribution of features of the *nafs-e ammārah*, and, to a lesser extent, of the later stages too. This work is very systematic in dealing with the various aspects of the spiritual life, and is replete with anecdotes and examples. But the greatest source, indeed the criterion for deciding which features to place in which discourse, was Mawlānā's own experience, his own biography, which is what gives the work such authenticity. The identification of the features to be demonstrated and the spiritual points to be made in each discourse then must have raised the question of what would be the most effective vehicles to accomplish this. Mawlānā had a huge repertoire of sayings, anecdotes, parables, stories and fables available to him. Nicholson has said that Mawlānā has borrowed much but owes little, thereby indicating the extent to which he made everything his own and often changed a narrative to suit his own thematic and educational purposes. The two parallel discourses concerned with the shaykh or pir are Five and Eight, and these were natural candidates for Caliph discourses, since in Mawlānā's view the shaykh is the deputy of God for a disciple. Similarly those dealing with pride and ego and with selflessness, Discourses Four and Nine, were good candidates for lion stories. There is great narrative variety in the *Mathnawī*, and Mawlānā was a superb storyteller, but it is also apparent that it is the thematic and symbolic content which determines the narrative, as his adaptations of his sources demonstrate.

Having considered the question of content, that is, of themes and narratives, there was then the question of structures. A primary issue was that of the number of sections for each discourse. The analysis in Chapter 4 has shown that, in Book One, there was a numerologically precise determination of the number of sections based on the sum of the sections in parallel discourses, giving 18, 30, 18, 40, 40, 24. What matters in this consideration of the planning of discourses is that it is a further factor that was required to be taken into account. Eighteen is an important Mevlevi number, an importance emphasized by Mawlānā's use of it in the first half of the Proem to Book One. That being the case it is unsurprising that the first and the last discourses should each have had nine sections. It was also necessary to Mawlānā that the two central discourses should have the same number of sections, since the same feature appears in Book Two. Order, proportion, and symmetry, like beauty and sublimity, are self-authenticating in a work of art and require no further hermeneutic, but for the poet the numerology represents a further self-imposed constraint.

But in fixing on a shape and structure for a discourse, the themes to be dealt with, and the narrative lines, the real demand on Mawlānā must have been the self-imposed requirement of parallelism. Parallelism can be thought of as both a curse and a blessing for a poet. It is a curse because it places yet another constraint on a writer, in the same way that the meter and the rhyme does. It is a blessing because it offers the opportunity of making a point in two different ways, of being more explicit, of developing an emphasis, of going beyond a single verbal assertion to presenting a shape, a relationship, an opening of the understanding which can be transforming. In Book One there are eighty-five pairs of parallel sections, and Mawlānā uses parallelism in many different ways, as has been seen. Many sections, for instance, deal with a number of different points, and the parallel sections are able to define which point is central. But not all of Mawlānā's parallelisms are semantic, there are some which are simply aesthetic, such as when both sections take the form of question and answer. This is a subject that will require a major study when all six books have been analyzed.

In designing his discourses, Mawlānā displays astonishing versatility and originality: as in the use of blocks of sections; the different treatment of one half as opposed to the other half in, for example, Discourse Seven, where the first half is nonchiasmic and the second half is chiasmic; and in the spatial usage in both Discourse Seven and Discourse Ten. There is nothing mechanical in his structures; constantly he does the unexpected. It is as if Mawlānā had encountered parallelism, chiasmus and ring-composition, mastered it and had made it his own. When many more studies have been done of synoptically structured works it is quite possible that Mawlānā will come to be regarded as one of the few great masters of these techniques in world literature, so accomplished is his craftsmanship.

When Mawlānā had selected his themes and narrative vehicles, factored in the numerology, fixed on the shape and structure of each discourse making use of ring composition, parallelism, and chiasmus together with his own innovations, he was then able to write down the section headings and the plan of the whole of Book One was in place. It was an extraordinary feat to have achieved given the self-imposed constraints, the complexity of the subject matter and the sophistication of the structuring. The plan of Book One was an inspired and creative vision. Its outcome, the section headings and all that they implied, then enabled Mawlānā to exercise his equally creative and inspired poetic gifts in the company of Ḥusām al-Dīn and give birth to the poetic text of his masterpiece, the *Mathnawī*.

This account of the factors and processes involved in the planning of Book One which resulted in the section headings, can then be seen as the production of the writer's plan following which Mawlānā was able to give free rein to his poetic creativity within the further constraints of meter and rhyme. But it is also much more than Mawlānā's writer's plan, for why else would he have left his discourses unmarked and further obscured the organization of the work by using parallelism and chiasmus. To answer this it is necessary to reflect again on Mawlānā's grand design of the *Mathnawī*.

The Design of the *Mathnawī*

As has been said before, design combines the notion of structure with that of purpose. Enough has been shown about Mawlānā and his attitudes to dismiss at once any idea that the *Mathnawī* was written for his own greater poetic glory. The project was too vast, too demanding in the skills and years required for its completion, for it to have been undertaken from any motive other than a most powerful and sustained inner imperative. Given that Mawlānā had been transformed inwardly and sought to follow a higher will than his own, it seems best to assume that he was spiritually required to write it. In fulfillment of this imperative, what was Mawlānā's purpose in creating the *Mathnawī*? Almost certainly it was to effect the spiritual transformation of his hearers and readers. He was a superb poet who had such control he could produce almost any effect that he wished. He was also a very experienced spiritual teacher with a profound understanding of human nature and spiritual psychology. Finally, he was a true friend of God, to whom had been granted many transcendent spiritual experiences, as is apparent from his writings and his biography. These three qualities he brought together in his major project of producing the *Mathnawī*, the hearing, reading, and pondering of which was his chosen means of passing on to others the way of inner transformation and the experience and understanding of this mundane world and the spiritual world that he had been granted. The road not taken by Mawlānā, as was suggested in Chapter 1, was to establish his circle of disciples as a Sufi Order. Through the *Mathnawī* he was able to reach a far greater audience, perhaps more intimately, while at the same time avoiding the many hazards attendant on institutionalization.

The *Mathnawī* is not one thing, it is many, as Mawlānā makes clear in the Preface to Book One: a curer of hearts, a spiritual resting place, an expounder of the Qur'ān, a consoler and purger of grief, a source of abundant gifts, a confounder of unbelief and a purifier of dispositions. In another sense, it is a *dhikr*, a remembrance and recollection of God, as the first line of the poem tells: "Listen to the reed-pipe as it tells its story, complaining of separation." The reed-pipe, the *nay*, was reportedly Mawlānā's favorite instrument, which was used prominently in the *samā'*, the Mevlevi collective *dhikr*, with its plaintive flights expressive of the laments of the spirit, removed from God, suffering its love in separation and longing to return. This is the standpoint, the viewpoint, of the *Mathnawī*, that of the spirit, lovelorn and yearning, separated from the Beloved, trapped in existence, and forced to suffer its association with the selfhood. The notes of the *nay* are poignant and evocative; as with all music their effect is direct, unmediated by meanings, since, as Mawlānā says in the very last half-line of the *Mathnawī*: "For there is a window open from heart to heart."

Having looked at the multiple purposes of the *Mathnawī*, there is now the question of its structural design. For the details of its three levels, their literary forms, their requirements for readers and their possible effects, the reader is referred to the very full description given in the Introduction. Here there are a number of general points that need to be addressed, beginning with the use of ring composition, parallelism and chiasmus. Since Mawlānā has used this literary technique to hide the spiritual world, which, as he has made explicitly clear in Discourse Eleven, God requires to remain unseen, the conclusion must be that ring composition, parallelism, and chiasmus did not constitute a familiar literary genre in Mawlānā's time, in spite of its use by Nizāmī. The silence of commentators and the absence of any mention of it in contemporary works on poetics and rhetoric appear to confirm this conclusion. His decision to follow 'Aṭṭār's example in the *Asrār-Nāmeh*, of not marking where a discourse began and ended, greatly helped in his concealment of both the spiritual world and of his use of these techniques. The moment that one recognizes the beginning and end of a discourse, the internal organization of the discourse becomes apparent together with its use of these literary principles. The combination of these two factors has proved to be brilliantly successful in concealing what Mawlānā has done. Although, however, Mawlānā has deliberately and successfully hidden the beautiful order and organization of his great work, he must have had some expectation of it being uncovered by suitable equipped individuals. Although there is nothing in writing, it would be absurd to imagine that nobody else has realized what Mawlānā had done over the last seven centuries.

The consequence of using the synoptic principles of parallelism and chiasmus is to produce a text that sequentially is subject to sudden discontinuities, unexpected digressions, un-bridged transitions, and repetitions, in short to appear plan-less. The self-presentation of such works has, therefore, somehow to justify the uneven and disorganized sequential surface appearance of their texts. The *Mathnawī* is probably best thought of as addressed mainly to the *sālik*, the spiritual traveler, and to the disciples in Mawlānā's circle to whom passages were read aloud. There are, though, continual changes of voice and of addressee. Largely, however, it presents itself, not as a product, but as the record of an oral process, the process of spiritual instruction, training, and teaching through parables. Mawlānā uses himself superbly as "speaker." The reader or hearer, treated as a *sālik* under instruction, is sometimes addressed as "you" and is subjected to the same diagnosis, and given the same, often abusive, treatment as the *sālik.* In addition, Mawlānā sometimes presents himself as the poet, carried away with some theme, having to return to some story he was in process of telling before he was diverted. Both modes, the occasion by occasion direction of the *sālik* by a shaykh, or the poet inspired by some theme, are used to cover, to some extent, the somewhat awkward sequential appearance of the text and its seeming lack of direction, indeed, they almost make a virtue of it. The *Mathnawī* presents itself as unrehearsed, as moving spontaneously, as wandering into digressions, as subject to sudden changes of direction and sudden leaps of thought, and yet with the assurance that it is guided and protected by God, and a place of refuge and refreshment for the spiritual traveler. This is its self-presentation, of spontaneous extempore outpouring, written down by Ḥusām al-Dīn, his long-suffering amanuensis. This is Mawlānā as speaker, as superb poet, as a hugely entertaining yet profoundly wise and inspired spiritual adept. It is the excellence of the poetry, the insights and the incidents, the flights of mystical imagination, and the depth of human understanding that take the edge off the criticism directed at the *Mathnawī* for being random, lacking in order or structure, and being generally plan-less. Yet it would not have been Mawlānā's purpose entirely to disguise this seeming lack of order, since he had to leave his readers somewhat dissatisfied or they might never see the need to search deeper and further.

The first level, the surface verbal level, which has been termed here the self-presentation of the *Mathnawī,* can be said to utilize two main lines of approach: exposition and edification on the one hand, as befits an experienced Muslim preacher and spiritual teacher, and poetic effect on the other, as befits a master poet. Both lines of approach combine to create an immediacy, a directness, a compelling engagement with the reader or listener. It needs to be remembered here that very few cultures can match the culture of Persian-speakers with regard to the refinement and responsiveness of their poetic sensibilities. Not only is there a rich and powerful poetic literature, but poetry for Persian speakers remains a natural and highly potent mode of expression that can evoke a response that seems to reach to the very core of their cultural roots and being. This needs to be understood because it is so different from the place of poetry in contemporary Western culture. A well-chosen line of verse can settle a dispute, dispensing with the need for further reasoning or argument, indeed, bypassing argument and reason altogether. If, as Mawlānā declares, there is a window open between heart and heart, Persian poetry can certainly pass through it, although, in the context of the quotation, he was speaking about the even deeper language of silence, which is why the *Mathnawī* ends where it does. If Persian poetry in general can have this effect in a Persian speaking culture, how much the more does mystical or spiritual Persian poetry, since spirituality, like poetry, also has a very major place in Persian culture. With some people, the effect of even a single line of the *Mathnawī* is able to trigger a shift from their everyday selves to their spiritual natures, so widely and well is it known, and so potent is its effect. To a large extent this type of effect relies on the formative role which the *Mathnawī* has played in the development of Persian spiritual and literary culture, but it could never have attained this power without the receptivity of Persian speakers' poetic and spiritual sensibilities.

To readers coming to the *Mathnawī* from other cultures, of course, the situation is quite different. Nonetheless, even in translation, there is still sufficient poetic effect to affect the readers, although they may have to rely more on the authenticity and sublimity of the content rather than the poetic medium through which it is expressed. The immediacy and urgency of Mawlānā, the striking imagery, the penetrating parables and metaphors, the instruction and advice, the prayers and piety, the soaring passages of mystical imagination, the humor and the human comedy, all of this comes through even in translation. The non-Persian speakers may lose the poetic effect of the surface level, but they are rewarded by its edification as much if not more than the Persian speakers who have to balance the power of the poetry with the seriousness of its content.

The second level is the hidden inner Sufi level. Of course, there is much in the first level that is explicit instruction to the spiritual traveller, the *sālik*, but a large component of the spiritual content of the *Mathnawī* is hidden. Mawlānā has used several means to hide this content. The first way accords with the rhetorical question of Chesterton's fictional detective Father Brown, who asked himself: "Where would a wise man hide a leaf?" His answer was: "In the forest." The *Mathnawī* is a long work and sometimes crucially important spiritual points are made in lines that would pass almost unnoticed except by those who are most alert to such matters. In Book Two, Mawlānā is launched into an explanation of Divine Unity when he suddenly stops claiming to be interrupted by the readers or hearers who are dying to know what happens next in the story he was telling. There are a number of places where he relies on the reader's interest in the narrative to hide important spiritual truths, which he slips in almost unnoticed. One of the most crucial spiritual events in his own development was the year when Shams left for the first time and Mawlānā had to endure the transforming suffering of separation. This is dealt with in Discourse Nine in the section that tells the anecdote of the man who knocks at the door and answers: "It is I," only to be told he cannot come in because there was no room there for two "I"s. This is such an important issue, pregnant with meaning at every level, and strikingly told in this anecdote, that the reader is fully satisfied that he has got the point and, in consequence, misses the crucial part that the man was sent away for a year to suffer burning separation for his development. Many of the sections contain several themes and make a number of points so it is easy for Mawlānā to hide things in this way.

A second way is the use of Sufi symbolism. Mawlānā in this followed 'Aṭṭār, who makes great use of this technique using stories, parables and allegories to put over spiritual matters. Usually the shape and form of the story has applications on several levels so these symbolic stories are multivalent. So that things do not become too fixed, sometimes the symbolic role of a particular character changes even within the same story. Often the falcon is the symbol for the spirit in a person, but a duck can be both a symbol of greed, waddling along totally focused on possible food, or a person able to operate both on land, this world, or in water, the spiritual world. There are a number of occasions where Mawlānā explains the symbolism himself, for example in Discourse Eight, or in explaining that the pretended death of the parrots in Discourse Six was symbolic of *niyāz*, self-abasement, in the Central Link section. The potency of this form of symbolism is considerable, and the message for the readers is that they will have to work and be intelligent to capture the various levels of symbolic meaning hidden in these stories.

The use of Sufi symbolism was well-established and familiar, even expected, so Mawlānā went even further than his predecessors in seeking to hide his inner, spiritual organization. The third way, as has been shown already, is his use of the literary principles of parallelism and chiasmus to order his masterpiece and to hide its rationale, and, in order further to obscure what he had done, there is his decision not to mark the discourses. Additionally, he was inventive in his structuring so that not all discourses were necessarily chiasmic, and he introduced the notion of blocks of sections. He did the unexpected so that everything has to be approached anew without presupposition or assumption. As with the symbolism, the structuring requires the reader to work hard and to be intelligent, in essence, to search. The spiritual seeker must seek. As has been shown, the unsatisfactory ordering of the *Mathnawī* at the surface level, demands this search, this seeking.

In the search for what is going on, parallelism, the use of correspondences and analogies, is a valuable aid. It is not just the author whose creativity is reined back by parallelism, the reader too faces the problem of his own creative imagination and enrichment, which parallelism can help to solve provided the reader knows that it is there. In a literary culture in which analogy and symbolism abound, it is particularly important to be able to define the level at which something is to be taken. Take, for example, Discourse Four in which the lion, out of pride and egoism, jumps into the well and is destroyed. Some readers and commentators expect in a mystical work every death to be really symbolic of *fanā*, the annihilation of self, and are unwilling to let anyone just die a normal death. But here, once the rationale of Book One is understood, it is clear that the death of the lion is an example, not of *fanā*, but of how the *nafs-e ammārah* destroys itself and egoism is weakened when it is shown its own reflection. It is in the second parallel lion discourse, Discourse Nine, where the need for *fanā* is emphasized. This is an example of how the rhetorical structure, through the organisation of contexts, is able to set limits on a reader's enrichment and add clarity and definition to meanings. Parallelism is also valuable in establishing where Mawlānā has placed his emphasis in sections covering a number of themes, since the sections in parallel will revert to the main theme emphasized.

It must not be thought that the uncovering of the rationale of Book One has revealed any great spiritual or theological mystery: the threefold division of the states of the *nafs* and the different properties of each had already been discussed at length by a number of prestigious authors long before Mawlānā's time. Similarly the Sufi spiritual Path had been the subject of a number of different systematizations prior to Mawlānā. The notion of searching for "deeper" meanings, which suggests digging a pit ever deeper in search of buried treasure, is perhaps not the most appropriate way to approach the *Mathnawī*, even though, he himself gave the analogy of roots. What is interesting, and why the notion of "deeper" is found inappropriate, is that the hidden organization that this study has identified is not underground at all, it is the superstructure of the work itself. It towers above the surface text like Sinan's Selimiyeh Cami Mosque at Edirne, ever thrusting upward to the heavens. Each of the twelve discourses in Book One can best be thought of as a beautifully proportioned building with rooms interconnecting through the intricate system of correspondences that parallelism makes possible. These are to be explored and experienced, the connections and correspondences weighed and pondered, the shapes and situations, the perspectives and analogies, allowed to enter to awaken and to transform the understanding and aspirations of the reader.

It is worth reflecting at this point on Mawlānā's pragmatic design. The *Mathnawī* models its author's experience of reality. There are three levels: the surface text reflecting this world, the unseen overarching organization by ring composition reflecting the spiritual world, and between the two is the symbolic hidden level of the Sufi path. In so far as the reader is taken to be the spiritual traveler, the *sālik*, it is clear that Mawlānā locates his ideal reader in this intermediate level. Further, the presumed spiritual status of the reader/spiritual traveler would be within the range of the selfhood which blames itself, the *nafs-e lawwāmah*, since the selfhood that commands to evil would not want to read the *Mathnawī*, and the selfhood at peace with God would not need to. The arena of encounter between Mawlānā and the *sālik* is the discourse, a structured present moment much larger than the "passage" of the sequential reader. This is where the readers/spiritual travelers have to search, work, and struggle, since each discourse requires that they interrogate not only the text but themselves as well. As has been said before, the discourse has to be identified, its structure fathomed, its symbolism understood, its parallelisms explored, and the present moment of the reader has to be stretched to embrace the whole with its multiple modes and levels of experiencing. To do all this it is necessary to connect the two worlds by continually reaching down to the text and up to the overarching organization above. While with effort it is possible to stretch the present moment to embrace the whole of a discourse, it is not possible to do so for the whole of a book, let alone for the entire work. There has therefore to be an acceptance of one's own smallness, that one's present moment is contained within larger present moments, and that even to contemplate this induces that most important initial mystical state, bewilderment. The *Mathnawī* in this way is not just about the nature of reality, it is a concrete demonstration of it, and a practical way of training spiritual travelers for its attainment.

The third level, that of the deepest roots and of the spiritual world, has been interpreted as *Ḥaqiqah*, Reality, but here it is necessary to be careful. For Mawlānā, as for all Muslims, only Allāh is real, hence an alternative name for Allāh is Al-Ḥaqq, the Real. Allāh transcends both the mundane and the spiritual worlds, while yet being intimately near to both. Something in this physical world is less real than its counterpart in the spiritual world, since the spiritual counterpart is its real nature, its *ḥaqq*, as seen by Allāh. This can also be expressed by saying that the reality, *ḥaqq*, of an entity is that part of it that looks to Allāh and says, "*Yā Hū*," "Oh He." Since that part is the spiritual component of the entity concerned, it is reasonable to call the spiritual world "reality," which it is compared to, and seen from, this world. When, however, the spiritual world is seen in relation to Allāh, it is not reality, for only Allāh is Real.

It is much too soon to speak of this level of the spiritual world in the *Mathnawī*. Only when the remaining five books have been thematically mapped and fully analyzed as has been done here for Book One will it be possible to see precisely what Mawlānā has done in this regard. From what has been seen here, it can be said that there is an unseen organization of the whole work, hidden by ring composition, which means the whole *Mathnawī* is a unity, is interconnected, and is beautifully symmetrical and structured. This organization contains the rationale of the whole and of the separate books and discourses and hence is the primary cause and purpose of what appears in the text. In this way, and in other ways too, it conforms to what Mawlānā describes as the spiritual world, and it functions as the spiritual world for the poem. For the reader it is enough for now to know that it is there and that it is the real guide to reading the text. Rather than speculate further about this, it is now time to turn to the reader.

It will be recalled that Mawlānā distinguishes between *taqlīd*, imitation, where everything one learns is borrowed and secondhand, and *taḥqīq*, verification, realization, where everything is encountered directly and met in its reality, its *ḥaqq*. For the readers and *sāliks*, the first thing is to read and reread and make both the explicit and symbolic material of each discourse, with its structures and correspondences, their own, and to verify it in their own experience. Then, in a nonprogrammatic way, realization dawns; bits and pieces suddenly fall into place as part of the reader's reality, maybe while bathing, maybe triggered by a situation at work, maybe when catching an unexpected reflection of themselves in a mirror in a shop and not recognizing who it is. Nobody can force this kind of realization, it will happen when it will, when the situation is propitious. Certainly it has nothing to do with the intellectual search for "deeper" meanings, which Mawlānā might have described as looking for truffles in the mud. Realization is about finding, not searching with the mind, and the place in which realization dawns, as Mawlānā constantly stresses, is in the heart and not the head, so for it to happen there has to be a shift in one's center of gravity from head to heart. But this kind of realization is, if you like, the lesser realization: the greater realization, *taḥqīq*, is for the *sālik* to realize their own reality, to realize *Ḥaqq*, Almighty God, within themselves, about which the later books of the *Mathnawī* also have much to say. This then is Mawlānā's mystical design, and every one of the many aspects of Book One that has examined in this work is subordinated to that overarching purpose.

Finale

There is much more that requires to be done: there are five more books to analyze and reflect on, five more rationales to identify, and then the rationale of the *Mathnawī* itself. Studies need to be made of Mawlānā's discourse structures, of his use of parallelism, of the antecedents to his macro-compositional style, and of his numerology. But all of these are for another day, for the present there is just one more issue to confront: if Mawlānā has hidden this inner world, for whatever reason, what right have the present authors, like Zayd in Discourse Eleven, to proclaim it aloud. Will not the disclosure frustrate Mawlānā's purpose, and spoil the *Mathnawī* for many readers? There are reasons for hoping this will not be the case.

The first reason is that, although Mawlānā has clearly deliberately hidden the beautiful order and organization of his great work, he must have done so in a time when he had some expectation of it being uncovered by somebody. But what is certain, for various reasons, is that now it is even less likely that anyone, let alone the modern reader, will discover for themselves what Mawlānā has hidden, especially as the scholarly consensus is that there is no organization, hidden or otherwise. Further, the current popularity of Rūmī can only serve to muddy the water even more, through the proliferation of mistaken views and through the presentation of bits of the *Mathnawī* in anthology form, which further obscures the rhetorical structure wherein lies the organization of contexts and significance. Earlier, what has been discovered in this study was likened to a map; the modern reader needs such a map for the *Mathnawī* and a map has never ruined the view or spoilt the walk.

There are two more positive reasons for not being concerned. First, what has been discovered here greatly enhances the *Mathnawī*. It reveals that the work has far greater richness and heights than had hitherto been suspected, and that Mawlānā is an even more considerable literary and spiritual figure that even his present reputation allows. Second, it shows the mystical and spiritual world to be highly rational and intelligent, not at all the preserve of the woolly minded who find mystery in muddle and the irrational. One could, however, be concerned for those who derive great comfort and inspiration from the *Mathnawī* as they have always read it, and for whom these discoveries might appear to constitute a threat or, worse, a claim to ownership of something precious of their own. Let them be reassured; this study has added nothing to the *Mathnawī*, it has projected nothing on to the *Mathnawī*, it has simply shown what Mawlānā has done at the macro-compositional level. It is still wholly Mawlānā's; speaking to whoever can hear, and the present study constitutes no threat, nor does it undermine what anyone holds most precious, nor does it make any claim to superior understanding. For those Iranians, however, whether expatriate or not, who mistake the cultural comfort they derive from the *Mathnawī* with spiritual comfort, Mawlānā himself has a parable in Book Two, which has been explained here already in Chapter 1, of a peasant going out in the dark to stroke his ox in a stall, little realizing that what he is stroking is the lion who has eaten his ox. Everyone must decide for themselves whether 'their' *Mathnawī* is a familiar, comforting ox being stroked with *taqlīd*, or whether it is a lion encountered firsthand and directly through the process of *taḥqīq*.

This leads to the final and most significant reason for not being concerned. Although this work has provided a map of Book One from the synoptic point of view, it is still required that the readers of the *Mathnawī* grapple with the hidden structures, forms, and meanings to make them their own. All of this searching still remains for the readers to do, as do the rewards of realization that await them in consequence. The most we can hope for is that this work has made their task a little easier. As Mawlānā puts it in Book Two, Verse 1796:

Chand gū'ī chūn ghiṭā bar dāshtand *Kīn nabūdast ānki mī pandāshtand*

How many times will you say, when the veil is lifted,
Things were not as they were thought to be.[1]

Notes

Chapter One. Contextualizing the *Mathnawī*

1. The sources for the study of Mawlānā's Life have recently been reexamined and thoroughly analyzed by Lewis in his excellent work, *Rumi: Past and Present, East and West* (Lewis, F. L., 2000). The outline of Mawlānā's life given here, which is provided to contextualize the *Mathnawī*, accords with many of his conclusions, but, for a fuller examination and discussion of the sources and their analysis, the reader must have recourse to Lewis's work. As a piece of scholarship, exhaustive in its scope and penetrating in its analysis, it is a major advance for which all Rumi students must be grateful, and it is here strongly recommended to the reader.

2. It was under Fakhr al-Dīn's patronage that the poet Niẓāmī of Ganja (1141–1209) had written his didactic spiritual *mathnawī*, the *Makhzan al-Asrār*, The Treasury of Secrets, a work of importance among the antecedents of Mawlānā's *Mathnawī*.

3. See Lewis, F. D. (2000), p. 153, and Chittick, W. C. (2004), p. 179.

4. There are, however, recorded accounts of how somebody whose heart is already awake and constantly filled with love can open another's heart to love. See, for example, Markides, K. C., *Riding with the Lion* (New York: Penguin Arkana), 1996, pp. 302–303. For the various methods used by different Sufi orders to purify and awaken the heart see Mir Valiuddin, *Contemplative Disciplines in Sufism* (London: East-West Publications), 1980. For an account of what it can be like to be on the receiving end of such spiritual training and awakening of the heart, see Tweedie, I., *Daughter of Fire* (Nevada City: Blue Dolphin Publishing), 1986.

5. See Lewis, F. D. (2000), p. 163.

6. See Lewis, F. D. (2000), p. 180.

7. This has been recently translated into English and annotated by Chittick, or as much of it as could be translated, since it is an uncommonly problematic text. He calls the work *Me and Rumi; The Autobiography of Shams-e Tabrizi*, and it was published by Fons Vitae in 2004. This is a crucially important text and should be read by any serious student of Mawlānā.

8. See Lewis, F. D. (2000), p. 182.

9. These brotherhoods belonged to the *futuwwa* or "youngmanliness" tradition, and they each had initiatory rituals, hierarchies, and codes of conduct and ethics. In a sense they competed with the Sufi orders for members.

10. For an account of this see Chittick, W. C. (1983), pp. 5–6.

11. Forūzānfar, B. (ed.), *Kulliyāt-e Dīwān-e Shams* (Tehran: Tehran, Intishārāt-e Nigāh), 1995.

12. Nicholson, R. A., *The Mathnawī of Jalālu'ddīn Rūmī*, Edited from the oldest manuscripts available with critical notes, translation, and commentary, 8 volumes (London: Luzac & Co.), 1925–1940.

13. Forūzānfar, B. (ed.), *Fīhi mā fīhi* (Tehran: Amir Kabir), 1981.

14. Subhānī, T. (ed.), *Majālis-e sab'ah* (Tehran: Kayhān), 1994.

15. Subhānī, T. (ed.), *Maktūbāt-e Mawlānā Jalāl al-Dīn Rūmī* (Tehran: Markaz-e Nashr-e Daneshgahi), 1992. The observation by Chittick is made in Chittick, W. C. (1983), p. 7.

16. See, for example, Pocock, D. F., *Mind, Body and Wealth* (Oxford: Basil Blackwell), 1973, p. 95.

17. "The embellishment of tomb and sepulchre,
Is not from stone or wood and plaster;
Rather inter your self in purity,
Burying 'I' in the 'I' of the Almighty,
Become His dust, entombed in His concern,
That God's Breath may refresh your own.
A fancy tomb, with domes and battlements,
Is out of place for spiritual attainments." (Book III: Verses 130–133)

18. Lewis, F. L. (2000), p. 424.

19. This image is taken from the "dead parrot" story in Book One, which will be examined later.

20. See, for example, Arberry, A. J. (1961), p. 21, which is his English translation of Mawlānā's Discourses, where he spells out with force and clarity the dangers to the spirit of this kind of association.

21. Lewis, F. D. (2000), p. 426.

22. For a full account of Mawlānā's theological and spiritual thought see: Schimmel, A., *The Triumphal Sun* (London: Fine Books), 1978 (especially Chapter 3); and Chittick, W. C., *The Sufi Path of Love* (Albany: SUNY Press), 1983.

23. *Mathnawī*, Book II: Verses 503–512.

24. See Katz, Steven J., "The 'Conservative' character of Mysticism," in Katz, S. J. (ed.), *Mysticism and Religious Traditions* (Oxford: Oxford University Press, 1983), pp. 3–4.

25. Ibid, pp. 18–19.

26. Ibid, p. 19.

27. For a general overview of this subject, see: Arberry, A. J., *Classical Persian Literature* (London: George Allen and Unwin), 1958; Baldick, J., "Persian Sufi Poetry up to the Fifteenth Century," in Morrison, G. (ed.), *History of Persian Literature* (Leiden: Brill), 1981; De Bruijn, J. T. P., *Persian Sufi Poetry* (Richmond: Curzon), 1997.

28. The word *mathnawī* derives from the Arabic word for two, and came to mean a poem written in doublets or couplets. A line of verse (in Persian, *bayt*) in a *mathnawī* consists of two halves that are called *miṣrā'* or hemistichs. The two halves rhyme, so that the rhyme is internal to the verse. This gives a rhyme scheme of aa/bb/cc/ and so on, with the rhyme changing for each *bayt*, verse.

29. For scholarship on Sanā'ī see: De Bruijn, J. T. P., *Of Piety and Poetry: The Interaction of Religion and Literature in the Life and Works of Ḥakīm Sanā'ī of Ghazna* (Leiden:

Brill), 1983; Lewis, F. D., *Reading, Writing and Recitation: Sanā'ī and the Origins of the Persian Ghazal*, Doctoral Thesis, University of Chicago, 1995.

30. There is an accurate translation of this work into English: Darab, G. H., *The Treasury of Mysteries* (London: Luzac), 1945.

31. *Nizami Ganjavi, The Haft Paykar; A Medieval Persian Romance*, translated with an Introduction and Notes by Julie-Scott Meisami, Oxford World's Classics (Oxford: Oxford University Press), 1995. For further study of this work by Meisami, see also Meisami, J-S, *Medieval Persian Court Poetry* (Princeton: Princeton University Press), 1987.

32. The major study of the poetry and spirituality of 'Aṭṭār is Ritter, H., *Das Meer der Seele. Mensch, Welt und Gott in den Geschichten des Farīduddīn 'Aṭṭār* (Leiden: Brill), 1955 (reprinted 1980). An English translation has recently been published: *The Ocean of Soul: Men, the World and God in the Stories of Farid Al-Din 'Attar* (Handbook of Oriental Studies: the Near and Middle East) by Hellmut Ritter, translated by John O'Kane (Leiden: Brill), 2003. For a recent collection of essays on 'Aṭṭār see Lewisohn, L. and Shackle, C. (eds.), *Farid al-Din 'Attar and the Persian Sufi Tradition, The Art of Spiritual Flight* (London: I. B. Tauris), 2006.

33. Of these four, two, The Parliament of the Birds and The Book of the Divine, have been translated into English as follows: Afkham Darbandi and Dick Davis, *The Conference of the Birds* (London: Penguin Books), 1984; Boyle, J. A., *The Ilāhī-Nāma or Book of God* (Manchester: Manchester University Press), 1976.

34. De Bruijn, J. T. P., *Persian Sufi Poetry* (Richmond: Curzon), 1997, pp. 109–110.

Chapter Two. Reading the *Mathnawī*

1. The fact that a manuscript is the earliest extant, however, does not necessarily mean it is the most authentic, since it could belong to a variant tradition of the text. It might be, in that case, that the most authentic belongs to a tradition represented by later manuscripts. Nicholson was well aware of this and writes in the introduction to his edition of Books One and Two: "for the maxim *seniores priores* is one which no editor ought to believe till he has verified it." Nicholson did not have access to the oldest Konya manuscript when he edited Book One, but he has noted its variants from his own text in an appendix to the translation of Books Three and Four. He notes that the Konya manuscript omits five of the headings he established in his edition of Book One, three from the first story—at Verses 78, 101, and 222—and two later headings at Verses 1427 and 3077. The fact that three are omitted in the first story suggests that the scribe did not attach much importance to the headings and had begun to leave them out until a supervisor of some kind told him to keep them all in. Later, when the full design of Book One has been identified, it will be shown that rhetorical symmetry and numerology require the first and the last story to have the same number of sections, that is nine, so the rhetorical design prefers Nicholson's text, which is largely based on the manuscript British Museum, Or. 6438, to the early Konya manuscript in this regard. The other two headings omitted seem to be simply carelessness since the surrounding text clearly marks these points as transitions where a heading would be expected.

2. Browne, E. G., *A Literary History of Persia*, Vol. II (Cambridge: Cambridge University Press), 1951, p. 520.

3. Chittick, W. C., *The Sufi Path of Love* (Albany: SUNY Press), 1983, p. 6.

4. Arberry, A. J., *Tales from the Masnavi* (Richmond: Curzon Press), 1993, p. 11.

5. Quoted in Lewis, F. D., *Rumi Past and Present, East and West* (Oxford: One World Publications), 2000, p. 542, quoting from the first edition of the *Encyclopaedia of Islam.*

6. Rypka, J., *History of Iranian Literature* (Dordrecht: D. Reidel Publishing), 1968, p. 241.

7. Schimmel, A., *The Triumphal Sun* (London: Fine Books), 1978, p. 35.

8. Nicholson, R. A., *The Mathnawī of Jalālu'din Rūmī*, Vol. VI (Cambridge: E. J. W. Gibb Memorial Trust), 1926, p. viii.

9. Ibid., pp. viii–ix.

10. The second of Richter's lectures is concerned with the *Mathnawi*, and it is this that the Institute of Islamic Studies–London has had translated into English and published in the journal *Transcendent Philosophy*, Vol. 2, No. 3, September 2001, pp. 15–34.

11. Lewis, F. D., *Rumi Past and Present, East and West* (Oxford: One World Publications), 2000, p. 560.

12. Ibid., p. 561.

13. Representative of Persian scholarship are the following: "It is true to say that the *Mathnawi* has no plan or pre-arranged scheme of chapters. The sequence of its contents is determined by the flowing outpouring of the speaker's mind, and Rumi has composed the *Mathnawi* in accordance with the needs of his audiences and the demands of the occasion." 'Abd al-Husayn Zarrinkub, *Sirr-i Ney* (Tehran: 'Elmi), 1985, p. 47; "The *Mathnawi* is the outpouring of Mawlana's unfettered mind. There is no affectation, formality or prior consideration in its creation; Mawlawi's speech is delivered naturally like a fountain gushing out from the heart of the earth. It is extempore improvisation." 'Abd al-Karini Sorush, *Qomar-i 'Ashiqaneh*, Tehran. 1990, p. 32; "Maulawi composed the *Mathnawi* extemporaneously," Badi' al-Zaman Foruzanfar, *Resale-yi tahqiq dar ahwal wa zindigani-yi Mawlana*, rev. ed. (Tehran: Zawwar), 1954, p. 108; "The great difficulty in the study of Rumi results from his manner of exposition. In his *Mathnawi*, the threads of various motifs cross one another and are interwoven into such a confused fabric that one requires a good deal of patience to follow him. On the feeble thread of an insignificant story, he strings the beads of his ideas and feeling without any system." 'Abd al-Hakim Khalifa, *The Metaphysics of Rumi* (Lahore: Institute of Islamic Culture), 1965, p. 3; "This book is a chain of stories which are the narration of life, and accompanying them there comes some guidance and deliberations; and they have no order." Muhammad 'Ali Islami Nadushan, *Bagh-Sabz-i 'Ishq*, Tehran, 1988, p. 110.

14. Baldick, J., "Persian Sufi Poetry up to the Fifteenth Century," in *Handbuch der Orientalistik*, Erske Abteilung, Der Nahe und der Mittlere Osten, Von Spuler (ed.), Iranistik Zweiter Abschnitt Literatur, Liefering 2 (Leiden: Brill), pp. 113–132.

15. Ibid., p. 126.

16. Some examples are: Whitman, C. H., *Homer and the Homeric Tradition* (Cambridge, Mass.: Harvard University Press, 1958); Stanley, K., *The Shield of Homer: Narrative Structure in the Iliad* (Princeton: Princeton University Press), 1993; Beck, I., *Die Ringkomposition bei Herodot* (= Spudasmata 25 Hildesheim), 1971; Katicic, R., "Die Ringkomposition im ersten Buche des Thukydideishen Geschichtswerkes," *Wiener Studien* 70, 1957; Richardson, L., *Poetical Theory in Republican Rome* (New Haven: Yale University Press, 1944); Brooks Otis, *Virgil: A Study in Civilized Poetry* (Oxford: Oxford University Press), 1964; Tatum, J., *Xenophon's Imperial Fiction* (Princeton: Princeton University Press), 1985;

Craven, T., *Artistry and Faith in the Book of Judith*, Society of Biblical Literature Dissertation, Series 70 (Chico, Cal.: Scholars Press), 1983; Fowler, A., *Triumphal Forms* (Cambridge: Cambridge University Press), 1970; Dainon, P., "The Middle of Things: Narrative Patterns in the Iliad, Roland, and Beowulf," in Niles, J. D., (ed.), *Old English Literature in Context* (Cambridge: Cambridge University Press), 1980; McMahon, R., *Augustine's Prayerful Ascent* (Athens and London: University of Georgia Press), 1989; Weightman, S. C. R., "Symbolism and Symmetry: Shaykh Manjhan's *Madhumalati* Revisited," in Lewisohn and Morgan (eds.), *The Heritage of Sufism*, Vol. III (Oxford: One World), 1999; Duckworth, G., *Structural Patterns and Proportions in Virgil's Aeneid: A Study in Mathematical Composition* (Ann Arbor: University of Michigan Press), 1962.

17. Douglas, M., *Leviticus as Literature* (Oxford: Oxford University Press), 1999.

18. Douglas, M., *In the Wilderness*, Journal for the Study of the Old Testament Supplement Series 158 (Sheffield: Sheffield Academic Press), 1993.

19. Douglas, M., Ibid., p. 118–119.

20. See Cassuto, U., *A Commentary on the Book of Genesis* (original Hebrew 1947), part 2: *From Noah to Abraham*, English translation Israel Abrahams (Jersualem: Magnes Press), 1964.

21. See Fox, J. J., "Roman Jakobson and the Comparative Study of Parallelism," in *Roman Jakobson: Echoes of His Scholarship* (Lisse: Peter de Ridder Press), 1977, pp. 59–90.

22. See Andersen, G. W., "Characteristics of Hebrew Poetry," in *The New Oxford Annotated Bible with the Apocrypha* (Oxford: Oxford University Pres), 1977, pp. 1523–1528.

23. Quoted in Douglas, M., *In the Wilderness*, Journal for the Study of the Old Testament Supplement Series 158, (Sheffield: Sheffield Academic Press), 1993, p. 106, from Milgrom, J, *Numbers. The JPS Torah Commentary* (Philadelphia: The Jewish Publication Society), 1990, p. xxii.

24. Schmidt's publications relevant here are: "Die Komposition von Yasna 49," in Heesterman et al. (eds.) *Pratidānam: Studies presented to F. B. J. Kuiper* (The Hauge: Mouton), 1968, pp. 170–192; "Associative Technique and Symmetrical Structure in the Composition of Yasna 47," in Frye, R. N. (ed.), *Neue Methodolgie in der Iranistik* (Festschrift fur Wolfgang Lentz) (Wiesbaden: Harrassowitz), 1974, pp. 306–352; and, with contributions from W. Lentz and S. Insler, "Form and Meaning of Yasna 33," in *American Oriental Society Essay Number 10* (New Haven: American Oriental Society), 1985. Schwartz's relevant publications are: "Sound, Sense and Seeing in Zoroaster: The Outer Reaches of Orality," in *International Indo-lranian Congress Proceedings* (Bombay: K. R. Cama Oriental Institute), 1991, pp. 127–163; and "The Ties that Bind: On the Form and Content of Zarathushtra's Mysticism," *Proceedings of the First Gāthā Colloqium*, W. Z. O. Croydon, 1998, pp. 127–197.

25. Schwartz, M., "Sound, Sense and Seeing in Zoroaster: The Outer Reaches of Orality," in *International Indo-Iranian Congress Proceedings* (Bombay: K. R. Cama Oriental Institute), 1991, p. 131.

26. Schwartz, M., "The Ties that Bind: On the Form and Content of Zarathushtra's Mysticism," *Proceedings of the First Gāthā Colloquium*, W. Z. O. Croydon, 1998, p. 197.

27. Schwartz, M., "Sound, Sense and Seeing in Zoroaster: The Outer Reaches of Orality," in *International Indo-Iranian Congress Proceedings* (Bombay: K. R. Cama Oriental Institute), 1991, p. 131.

28. Schwartz, M., "The Ties that Bind: On the Form and Content of Zarathushtra's Mysticism," *Proceedings of the First Gāthā Colloquium*, W. Z. O. Croydon, 1998, p. 196.

29. Douglas M., *In the Wilderness*, Journal for the Study of the Old Testament Supplement Series 158, (Sheffield: Sheffield Academic Press), 1993, p. 101.

30. Hintze, A., "On the Literary Structure of the Older Avesta," in *BSOAS*, *65*, 1. London, 2002, pp. 31–51.

31. Meisami, J. S., *Medieval Persian Court Poetry* (Princeton: Princeton University Press), 1987. Meisami has also translated the whole of the *Haft Paykar* into English in the Oxford World's Classics series published by the Oxford University Press in 1995. Not only is this translation probably the finest verse translation of any work of Persian literature, but the introduction also contains important matters that are not dealt with in the study of the poem in her *Medieval Persian Court Poetry*.

32. Meisami, J. S., ibid., p. 208.

33. Meisami, J. S., *Haft Paykar: A Medieval Persian Romance*, Oxford World's Classics (Oxford: Oxford University Press), 1995, p. xxvi.

34. Meisami, J. S., ibid., p. xxvi.

35. Meisami, J. S., ibid., p. xxvi.

36. Meisami, J. S., ibid., p. xxvi.

37. As has been noted above, the choice of subject for each of the six books appears to have been made as an intertextual act of homage to the great Persian spiritual poet Farīd al-Dīn 'Aṭṭār, in whose work the *Ilāhī-Nāmeh* the first of the King's six sons is representative of the selfhood, the *nafs*.

38. A thorough and systematic treatment of how all these, and many other, matters are dealt with and understood by Mawlānā is found in Chittick, W. C., *The Sufi Path of Love* (Albany: SUNY Press), 1983. Useful too here is Schimmel, A., *The Triumphal Sun* (London: Fine Books), 1978, especially Chapter 3.

Chapter Three. A Synoptic Reading of Book One of the *Mathnawī*

1. Nicholson, R. A., *The Mathnawī of Jalālu'ddīn Rūmī*, Vol. VII, Commentary on the First and Second Books (London: Luzac and Co.), 1937, p. 3. Nicholson's comments on the Arabic Preface are contained in pages 3–8 of his *Commentary*.

2. Nicholson's commentary on this Proem is to be found between pages 8–14 of his *Commentary*.

3. Meisami, J. S., *Medieval Persian Court Poetry* (Princeton: Princeton University Press), 1987, p. 50. Meisami deals with the *nasīb* extensively but *seriatim*, so there has to be recourse to the index to locate all the references.

4. Meisami, J. S., ibid., p. 49. Meisami is here quoting from Ibn Qutaibah's classic description of the genre.

5. It has been remarked that, unusually, the poem does not begin with the Arabic words for "In the name of God, the Merciful, the Compassionate," which is said or written at the beginning of any undertaking. This phrase begins with the letter "b," and has eighteen consonants in Arabic, certainly one of the reasons that eighteen is considered a significant number in Islam. The Proem also begins with "b," and has eighteen verses before the middle break, so perhaps this was Mawlānā's more extended way of committing his undertaking to God.

6. Nicholson's comments relating to this discourse are found between pages 14–28 of his *Commentary*. Relevant comments from Ānqirawī can be found in Satārzāde's Persian translation of the original Turkish commentary, Satārzāde, *Sharḥ-e Mathnawī* (Tehran: 'Ismat), 1995, pp. 55, 82, 118, 120. Sabzewārī's comments can be found in Burūjerdī, M. (ed.) Sabzewārī, Mullā Hādī, *Sharḥ-e Mathnawī* (Tehran: Sazeman-e Chap wa Entesharat-e Vezarat-e Farhang wa Ershad-e Islami), 1992, pp. 28–29. Hereafter Ānqirawī commentary will be referred to as "*Ānq*" followed by the page numbers, and Sabzewārī's commentary will be referred to by "*Sabz*" followed by the page numbers.

7. Nicholson, R. A., op cit., p. 15.

8. Nicholson's comments on this section are between pages 28–34 of his *Commentary*.

9. Nicholson's comments are found between pages 34–69 of his *Commentary*. Ānqirawī's comments are in *Ānq*, p. 172. Sabzewārī's comment on the unity of prophets and saints is in *Sabz*, p. 52. Forūzānfar's comments are in Forūzānfar, B., *Sharḥ-e Mathnawī-ye Sharīf* (Tehran: University of Tehran Press), 1967, pp. 152, 154, and 187.

10. Dabashi, H., "Rumi and the Problems of Theodicy," in Banani, Houannisian and Sabagh (eds.), *Poetry and Mysticism in Islam: The Heritage of Rumi* (Cambridge: Cambridge University Press), 1994.

11. Dabashi, H., ibid., pp. 124 and 126.

12. Nicholson's comments on this discourse are between pp. 69–75 in his *Commentary*. See also *Ānq*, p. 328, *Sabz*, 74, Furūzānfar, B, *Sharḥ-e Mathnawī-ye Sharīf* (Tehran: University of Tehran Press), 1967, p. 291, and *Sharḥ-e Bahr al-'Ulūm* (Lucknow), 1293, p. 36.

13. Nicholson's comments on this discourse are between pp. 75–104 in his *Commentary*. See also *Ānq*, pp. 567–586, and Forūzānfar, B., *Sharḥ-e Mathnawī-ye Sharīf* (Tehran: University of Tehran Press), 1967, pp. 482–490.

14. Nicholson's comments on this discourse are between pp. 75–104 in his *Commentary*. They are particularly full for the early discourses but become more sparse for later ones.

15. Nicholson's comment on Verse 1030 is excellent here: "The phenomenal world is the outward form of the Universal Reason; its essence is the Divine Knowledge that animates and rules it as the spirit animates and rules the body. Man is potentially capable of attaining this knowledge, which may be likened to the magic seal whereby Solomon exercised dominion over men and jinn and beasts and birds."

16. Nicholson's comments on this discourse are between pp. 104–112 of his *Commentary*. See also *Ānq*, pp. 576–581, 596–600, 602, 604–606, 612, 617–618, 621–624, 631, 633, and *Sabz*, pp. 107, 109–113. See also *Sharḥ-e Bahr al-'Ulūm* (Lucknow), 1293, pp. 55, 57.

17. Nicholson's comments on this discourse are between pp. 112–128 of his *Commentary*. See also *Ānq*, pp. 637, 641–644, 675, 678–679, 683–685, 689–690, 692, 697–703, 707–708, 712, 715, 722, 724–726, 730, 732–733, 744, 748, and *Sabz*, pp. 114, 120–127.

18. Nicholson's comments are on pp. 128–129 of his *Commentary*. See also *Ānq*, pp. 576–577 and *Sabz*, pp. 128–129.

19. Nicholson's comments are on pp. 129–147 of his *Commentary*. See also *Ānq*, pp. 764–774, and *Sabz*, pp. 129–146.

20. Nicholson's comments on this section are between pp. 145–147 of his *Commentary*.

21. Nicholson's comments on this discourse occupy pp. 147–183 of his *Commentary*. Also see *Ānq*, pp. 880–1106 and *Sabz*, pp. 146–173.

22. Nicholson's comments on this discourse are in pp. 183–189 of his *Commentary*. See also *Ānq*, 1132–1160, and *Sabz*, pp. 174–184.

23. Chittick writes of this: "All of man's character traits and habits, everything that pertains to his individual existence, must become completely naughted and "obliterated" (*maḥw*). Then God will give back to him his character traits and everything positive he ever possessed. But at this stage he will know consciously and actually—not just theoretically—and with a true and thorough spiritual realization, that everything he is derives absolutely from God. He is nothing but the ray of God's Attributes manifesting the Hidden Treasure." Chittick, W. C., *The Sufi Path of Love* (Albany: SUNY Press), 1983, p. 179.

24. Nicholson's comments on this discourse are on pp. 189–204 of his *Commentary*. See also *Ānq*, pp. 1161–1268, and *Sabz*, 187–193.

25. Nicholson's comments on this discourse are on pp. 294–213 of his *Commentary*. See also *Ānq*, pp. 1271–1343, and *Sabz*, pp. 194–295.

26. Nicholson, op cit., pp. 211–212.

27. Nicholson's comments on this discourse are on pp. 213–226 of his *Commentary*. See also *Ānq*, pp. 1346–1435, and *Sabz*, pp. 206–222.

Chapter Four. Book One as a Whole and as a Part

1. See, for example, 'Alī al-Ḥusayn Zarrinkūb, *Sirr-e Nay* (Tehran: Elmi), 1985, pp. 63–64.

Chapter Five. Conclusion

1. This verse has been beautifully elaborated by the artist and calligrapher Mohammad Saeed Naghashian on the cover of this book. At the bottom of the calligraphy this verse, expressive of our inability to see reality, is written out in isolation. Above it the same verse is written twelve times, six times from right to left and six times from left to right and upside down. Above it is the single word for God and Reality. This strikingly illustrates Mawlānā's design in Book One of the *Masnawī*, to pass from our inability to see reality, through the twelve discourses arranged chiasmically representing the twelve stages of the spiritual path, toward Divine Reality above.

Glossary of Persian Words

adab	seemliness, courtesy, propriety, respectfulness, reverence
aḥwal	squint-eyed, seeing double
ʿālamayn	the two worlds
ʿālam-e mithāl	the world of similitudes, the imaginal world
al-bāṭin	the Inward
Al-Ḥaqq	The Real, Almighty God
ʿālim	learned divine
Allāh	Almighty God
al-ẓāhir	the Outward
ʿaql	intellect, intelligence
ʿaql-e faʿʿāl	intellect in man open to the Universal Intellect
ʿaql-e juzwī	partial intellect, human reason
ʿaql-e kullī (also *ʿaql-e kull*)	Universal Intellect, Universal Reason
ʿaql-e maʿād	transcendental intellect, Universal Reason
ʿaql-e maʿāsh	empirical intelligence, discursive reason
ʿārif	mystic, gnostic
ʿāshiq	lover
ʿayn al-yaqīn	the eye of certainty
az bālā	from above
baqā (properly *baqāʾ*)	eternal subsistence in God
bayt	a line of verse, a verse
bī adabī	disrespect, discourtesy, ingratitude, lack of restraint
chillah (also *chilla*)	a forty day and night period of seclusion and solitude
dhikr	repetition, remembrance of God, invocation, prayer
dīw	a devil, demon
dunyā	the world

fanā (properly *fanā'*)	annihilation, passing away
fanā' fī Allāh	annihilation in God
fanā' fī shaykh	annihilation in the spiritual guide
faqīr	poor, possessing spiritual poverty, hence, a dervish
faqr	spiritual poverty
ghazal	a lyric
gūsh	ear
ḥadīth	tradition, saying of the Prophet
ḥāl	a temporary spiritual state, mystical state
Ḥaqīqah (also *Ḥaqīqat*)	Reality
ḥaqq	reality of something
ḥasad	envy, malevolence
Ḥikmat	Wisdom, theosophy
ḥiqd	hatred, malevolence
Iblīs	Satan, the Devil
ikhlāṣ	sincerity, purity, total submission to God's Will
Ikhtiyār	choice, authority, will, free-will
'ilm	knowledge
'ilm-e ḥuḍūrī	direct knowledge or experience of
'ilm-e ḥuṣūlī	conceptual knowledge
insān al-kāmīl	or *insān-e kāmīl* saint with highest level of human perfectibility, Perfect Man
'irfān	gnosis, mystical experiencing
'ishq	love
'ishq-e ḥaqīqī	real love, Divine Love
'ishq-e majāzī	metaphorical love, human love
istithnā	The saving clause, "If God Wills"
jabbārī	Almightiness, despotism
jabr	compulsion, predestination
jāh	position, reputation
jamāl	beauty
jam'īyat	togetherness, collectedness
jāmi'īyat	generality, multiplicity in unity and unity in multiplicity
jihād	waging war, a crusade
jins	kind, congener, someone or thing having the same nature

jinsiyyah	correspondence of kind, homogeneousness
jism	body
kathrat	plurality, multiplicity
khalīfa	designated successor, Caliph
khalwah (also *khalwat*)	solitude, seclusion
khar	donkey
khargūsh	hare
khashm	anger, rage
khayāl	phantom, apparition, imagination, idea, thought, fancy
kibr	pride, arrogance
Kun	"Be," the utterance by which God launched Creation
ladhā'idh-e dunyawī	worldly attractions, worldly pleasures
luqmah	a morsel, piece of food
maḥw	self-effacement, effacement of self and absorption in God
makr	deceit, cunning, deviousness, plotting, fraud, guile
makr-e nafs-e ghūl	deceit of the ghoul-like selfhood
māl o jāh	wealth and rank, status
ma'nī	meaning, spirit, reality,
maqālah	a discourse
maqām	a permanent spiritual station or transformation
mathnawī	an internally rhyming verseform, a narrative poem of such verses
Mathnawī-ye Ma'nawī	Spiritual Couplets, The *Mathnawī*
Mawlānā	Our Master Jalāl al-Dīn Rūmī
Mawlawī	My Master Jalāl al-Dīn Rūmī
muḥāsabah	examination, self interrogation
murīd	disciple, pupil, novice
Murshid-e kāmil	The Perfect Guide
murtaḍā	The Chosen One, the Approved One, (title applied to 'Alī)
nā'ib	deputy
nafs	selfhood, egoism, carnal or fleshy self
nafs-e ammārah	the selfhood that commands to evil
nafs-e lawwāmah	the selfhood that blames and reproaches itself
nafs-e muṭma'innah	the selfhood at peace with God
nafs-e sabu'ī	the wild animal selfhood

naghmah	a musical sound, note, musical tone
naḥw	grammar
nasīb	the opening exordium of an ode or elegy
nay	a reed pipe producing a particularly poignant sound
nifāq	hypocricy
niyāz	neediness, needfulness, self abasement, supplication
pīr	spiritual guide, shaykh, elder
pokhtah	cooked, raw, mature, transformed
qaḍā	decree, predestination, fate, accident, chance
qaṣīda	an ode
qiblah	the direction of Mecca needed for doing the prayers
quṭb	the leading saint present in the world at any time
Rabb al-ʿālamayn	Lord of both worlds
rāzdārī	the keeping of secrets
riyāḍat	spiritual discipline, asceticism
rūḥ	spirit
ṣabr	patience, self control, self discipline
sālik (pl. *sālikān*)	spiritual traveler, aspiring Sufi
samāʿ	mystical dance, collective remembrance with music, dance and verse
shahādah	Muslim Affirmation of Faith
Sharīʿah	Divine law, Islamic cannon law
shawq	longing, yearning
shaykh	spiritual guide
shayṭān	Satan, the Devil
sulūk	traversing the spiritual path
taḥqīq	realization, knowing the reality of something for oneself directly
tajallī (pl. *tajalliyāt*)	manifestation, epiphany
tanzīl	transmitting downwards
taqlīd	blind imitation, second hand acquisition
Ṭarīqah	Spiritual path, the Way
Taṣawwuf	Sufism, Islamic mysticism
tawakkul	total trust in God to provide, leaving everything to God
tawbah	repentance
tawḥīd	Divine Unity, Divine Uniqueness, Unicity
taʾwīl	spiritual exegesis
ʿujb	haughtiness, conceit, superiority, vanity, pride
ʿunwān	heading

waḥdat	unity
waḥy	inspiration, Divine Inspiration, revelation
Walī	saint, friend of God
Yā Hū	Oh God, Oh my Lord
zuhd	asceticism

Select Bibliography

Primary Sources

Este'lāmī, Muḥammad, edited with commentary, *Masnavī-ye Jalāl al-Dīn Moḥammad Balkhī*, 7 volumes (Tehran: Zavvar), 1987.

Facsimile of the 677/1278 manuscript from Konya (Ankara: TC Kultur Bakanligi), 1993.

Forūzānfar, Badī' al-Zamān, edited, *Fīhi mā fihi az goftār-e Maulānā Jalāl al-Dīn* (Tehran: Amir Kabir), 1983 (first published 1951).

Forūzānfar, Badī' al-Zamān, edited, *Kolliyāt-e Shams yā Dīvān-e Kabīr*, 9 volumes (Tehran: Amir Kabir), 1977 (first published University of Tehran Press 1957–1967).

Khorramashāhī, Qawwām al-Dīn, edited, *Mathnawī-ye ma'nawī* (Tehran: Amir Kabir), 1996.

Movahhed, Muḥammad 'Alī, edited, *Maqālāt-e Shams-e Tabrīzī*, vol. 1 (Tehran: Aryamehr Polytechnic University), 1977, vol. 2 (Tehran: Khwarazmi), 1990.

Nicholson, R. A., *The Mathnawī of Jalālu'ddīn Rūmī* (Cambridge: E. J. W. Gibb Memorial Trust), from 1925:

Volume I	The Text of Books One and Two (1925)
Volume II	Translation of Books One and Two (1926)
Volume III	The Text of Books Three and Four (1929)
Volume IV	Translation of Books Three and Four (1930)
Volume V	The Text of Books Five and Six (1933)
Volume VI	Translation of Books Five and Six (1934)
Volume VII	Commentary on Books One and Two (1937)
Volume VIII	Commentary on Books Three, Four, Five and Six (1940).

Purjawādī, Nasrollāh, edited, *Mathnawī-ye Ma'nawī-ye Jalāl al-Dīn Moḥammad-e Balkhī*, 4 volumes, Tehran, 1984.

Ṣobhānī, Taufīq, edited, *Maktūbāt-e Maulānā Jalāl al-Dīn Rūmī* (Tehran: Markaz-e Nashr-e Dāneshgāhī), 1992.

Ṣobhānī, Taufīq, edited, *Majāles-e Sab'a* (Tehran: Kayhan), 1994.

Sorūsh, 'Abd al-Karīm, *Mathnawī-ye Ma'nawī*, 2 volumes (Tehran: Enteshārāt-e 'Elmī wa Farhangī), 1996.

Commentaries and Reference Works

ʿAbd al-ʿAlī Moḥammad ibn Niẓām al-Dīn, *Sharḥ-e Baḥr al-ʿOlum*, Lucknow, 1293.

Ānqirawī, Ismāʿīl, *Sharḥ-e Mathnawī (Mesnevi-i serif serhi)*, translated from Turkish into Persian by Satarzāde (Tehran: ʿIsmat), 1995.

Ayyūb, Khwājā, *Asrār al-Ghuyūb (Sharḥ-e Mathnawī-ye Maʿnawī)*, edited by Sharīʿat, Moḥammad Jawād, Tehran, 1998.

Forūzānfar, Badīʿ al-Zamān, *Sharḥ-e Masnavī-ye sharīf* (Tehran: Tehran University of Tehran Press), 1967–1969.

Gauharīn, Ṣādeq, *Farhang-e loghāt va taʿbīrāt-e Masnavī*, seven volumes (Tehran: Tehran University Press), 1975.

Golpinarli, ʿAbd al-Baqi, *Mesnevi: tercemesi ve serhi*, 6 volumes (Istanbul: Inkilap ve Aka), 1981–1984 (translated into Persian by Ṣobhānī, Taufīq, 2nd ed., Tehran, 1995).

Kāshefī, Mullā Husayn, *Lobb al-Lobāb-e Mathnawī* (Tehran: Taqawī, Naṣrollāh), 1996.

Sabzewārī, Mullā Hādī, *Sharḥ-e Mathnawī*, edited by Borūjerdī, Moṣṭafā (Tehran: Sāzmān-e Chāp wa Enteshārāt-e Vezārāt-e Farhang wa Ershād-e Islāmī), 1992.

Shahīdī, Seyyed Jaʿfar, *Sharḥ-e Mathnawī*, 10 volumes (Tehran: Enteshārāt-e ʿElmī wa Farhangī), 1996.

Zamānī, Karīm, *Sharḥ-e jāmʿe-ye Masnavī-ye maʿnavī* (Tehran: Ettelāʿāt), 1993–1995.

Zarrinkūb, ʿAbd al-Husayn, *Sirr-e Nay* (Tehran: ʿElmi), 1985.

Zarrinkūb, ʿAbd al-Husayn, *Baḥr dar kūze* (Tehran: ʿElmī), 1987.

Translations

Arberry, A. J., *Discourses of Rumi* (Richmond: Curzon Press), 1993 (first published 1961).

Arberry, A. J., *Tales from the Masnavi* (London: George Allen and Unwin), 1961.

Arberry, A. J., *More Tales from the Masnavi* (London: George Allen and Unwin), 1963.

Arberry, A. J., *Mystical Poems of Rumi* (Chicago: University of Chicago Press), 1968.

Arberry, A. J., *Mystical Poems of Rumi*, 2: Second Selection (Chicago: University of Chicago Press), 1979.

Chittick, W. C., *Me and Rumi: The Autobiography of Shams-i Tabrizi* (Louisville, Kentucky: *Fons Vitae*), 2004.

Mojaddedi, Jawid, *Rumi, The Masnavi, Book One*, Oxford World's Classics (Oxford: Oxford University Press), 2004.

Nicholson, R. A., *Tales of Mystic Meaning, Being Selections from the Mathnawi of Jalal-ud-Din Rumi* (London: Chapman and Hall), 1931.

Nicholson, R. A., *Selected Poems from the Diwan-i Shams-i Tabrizi* (Cambridge: Cambridge University Press), 1898.

Thackston, Wheeler, *Signs of the Unseen* (Putney, VT: Threshold Books), 1994.

Williams, Alan, *Rumi: Spiritual Verses* (London: Penguin Classics), 2006.

General Works

Aflākī, Aḥmad, *Manāqeb al-ʿArefin*, edited by Yazici (Tehran: Donyā-yi Kitāb), 1983.

ʿAlavī, Mahvash, *Mawlānā, Khodāwandegār-e Ṭarīqat-e ʿIshq* (Tehran: Enteshārāt-e Sūrah), 1998.

Baldick, J., "Persian Sufi Poetry up to the Fifteenth Century," in *Handbuch der Orientalistik*, Erske Abteilung. Der Nahe und der Mittlere Osten, Von Spuler, Iranistik Zweiter Abschnitt Literatur, Liefering 2 (Leiden: Brill), 1981, pp. 113–132.

Browne, E. G., *A Literary History of Persia*, Vol. II (Cambridge: Cambridge University Press), 1951.

Behl, A., and Weightman, S. C. R., *Madhumālatī*, Oxford World's Classics (Oxford: Oxford University Press), 2000.

Cassuto, U., *A Commentary on the Book of Genesis* (original Hebrew 1947), part 2: *From Noah to Abraham*, English translation Israel Abrahams (Jersusalem: Magnes Press), 1964.

Chekowski, P. (ed.), *The Scholar and the Saint: Studies in Commemoration of Abu Rayhan al-Biruni and Jalal al-Din Rumi* (New York: Hagop Kevorkian Centre for Near Eastern Studies and New York University Press), 1975.

Chittick, W. C., *The Sufi Path of Love* (Albany: SUNY Press), 1983.

Chittick, W. C., "Rumi and Waḥdat al-Wujūd," in *Poetry and Mysticism in Islam: The Heritage of Rumi*, Banani, Houannisian and Sabagh (eds.) (New York: Cambridge University Press), 1994.

Chittick, W. C., "Rumi and the Mawlawiyyah," in Seyyid Hossein Nasr (ed.) *Islamic Spirituality, Vol. II, Manifestations* (New York: The Crossroad Publishing Company), 1991, pp. 105–126.

Dabashi, H., "Rumi and the Problems of Theodicy," in *Poetry and Mysticism in Islam: The Heritage of Rumi*, Banani. Houannisian, and Sabagh (eds.) (New York: Cambridge University Press), 1994, pp. 112–135.

Darab, G. H., *The Treasury of Mysteries* (English translation on Nizami's *Makhzan al-Asrār*) (London: Luzac), 1945.

Darbandi, Afkham, and Davis, Dick, *The Conference of the Birds* (London: Penguin Classics), 1984.

De Bruijn, J. T. P., *Persian Sufi Poetry* (Richmond: Curzon), 1997.

De Bruijn, J. T. P., *Of Piety and Poetry: The Interaction of Religion and Literature in the Life and Works of Ḥakīm Sanāʾī of Ghazna* (Leiden: Brill), 1983.

Douglas, M., *Leviticus as Literature* (Oxford: Oxford University Press), 1999.

Douglas, M., *In the Wilderness*, Journal for the Study of the Old Testament Supplement. Series 158 (Sheffield: Sheffield Academic Press), 1993.

Forūzānfar, Badīʿ al-Zamān, *Resāle-ye taḥqīq dar aḥwāl wa zendegānī-ye Mawlānā*, rev. ed., (Tehran: Zawwar), 1954.

Forūzānfar, Badīʿ al-Zamān, *Maʾakhez-e qeṣāṣ wa tamsīlāt-e Masnawī* (Tehran: Majles), 1954.

Forūzānfar, Badīʿ al-Zamān, *Maʾakhez-e Aḥādīs-e Masnawī* (Tehran: Amir Kabir), 1968.

Fox, J. J., "Roman Jakobson and the Comparative Study of Parallelism," in *Roman Jakobson: Echoes of his Scholarship* (Lisse: Peter de Ridder Press), 1977, pp. 59–90.

Hintze, A., "On the Literary Structure of the Older Avesta," in *BSOAS* 65, 1, London, 2002, pp. 31–51.

Iqbal, Afzal, *The Life and Works of Muhammad Jalal-ud-Din Rumi*, 6th ed. (Lahore: Pakistan National Council), 1991.

Khalīfa, ʿAbd al-Ḥakīm, *The Metaphysics of Rumi* (Lahore: Institute of Islamic Culture), 1965.

Lewis, F. D., *Rumi Past and Present, East and West* (Oxford: One World Publications), 2000.

Meisami, J. S., *Medieval Persian Court Poetry* (Princeton: Princeton University Press), 1987.

Meisami, J. S., *Haft Paykar*, translated into English in the Oxford World Classics Series (Oxford: Oxford University Press), 1995.

Milgrom, J., *Numbers, The JPS Torah Commentary* (Philadelphia: The Jewish Publication Society), 1990, p. xxii.

Morris, J. W., "Reading the Conference of the Birds," in De Bary, W. T. (ed.), *Approaches to Oriental Classics* (New York: Columbia University Press), 1989.

Nadushan, Muḥammad, ʿAlī Islāmī, *Bagh-sabz-e ʿIshq* (Tehran: ʿElmi), 1988.

Pūrnāmdāryān, Ṭāqī, *Ramz wa Dāstānhā-ye Ramzī dar Adab-e Farsī* (Tehran: Enteshārāt-e ʿElmī wa Farhangī), 1985.

Ritter, H., *Das Meer der Seele: Mensch, Welt und Gott in den Geschichten des Farīduddīn ʿAṭṭār* (Leiden: Brill), 1955 (reprinted 1980). An English Translation has recently been published: *The Ocean of Souls: Men, The World and God in the Stories of Farīd al-Dīn ʿAṭṭār*, (Handbook of Oriental Studies: The Near and Middle East) by Hellmut Ritter, translated by John O'Kane (Leiden: Brill), 2003.

Rypka, J., *History of Iranian Literature* (Dordrecht: D. Reidel Publishing), 1968.

Safavi, Seyed G., (ed.), *Rumi's Thoughts* (Tehran: Salman Azadeh Paublication), 2003.

Safavi, Seyed G., *Love the Whole and not the Part: An Investigation of the Rhetorical Structure of Book One of the Mathnawī of Jalāl al-Dīn Rūmī* (unpublished University of London Doctoral dissertation, London), 2003.

Schimmel, A., *Pain and Grace* (Leiden: Brill), 1976.

Schimmel, A., *The Triumphal Sun* (London: Fine Books), 1978.

Schimmel, A., I *am the Wind, You are the Fire: The Life and Work of Rumi* (Boston and London: Shambhala), 1992.

Schimmel, A., "Mawlana Rumi: Yesterday, Today, and Tomorrow," in *Poetry and Mysticism in Islam: The Heritage of Rumi*, ed. Banani, Houannisian, and Sabagh (Cambridge: Cambridge University Press), 1994, pp. 5–27.

Schmidt, H-P, "Die Komposition von Yasna 49," in Heesterman et al. (eds.), *Pratidanam: Studies presented to F. B. J. Kuiper* (The Hague: Mouton), 1968, pp. 170–192.

Schmidt, H-P, "Associative Technique and Symmetrical Structure in the Composition of Yasna 47," in Frye, R. N., (ed.), *Neue Methodolgie in der Iranistik* (Festschrift fur Wolfgang Lentz) (Wiesbaden: Harrassowitz), 1974.

Schmidt, H-P, with contributions from W. Lentz and S. Insler, "Form and Meaning of Yasna 33," in *American Oriental Society Essay Number 10* (New Haven: American Oriental Society), 1985.

Schwartz, J. V. L., "Sound, Sense and Seeing in Zoroaster: The Outer Reaches of Orality," in *International Indo-lranian Congress Proceedings* (Bombay: K. R. Cama Oriental Institute), 1991, pp. 131–165.

Schwartz, M., "The Ties that Bind: On the Form and Content of Zarathushtra's Mysticism," *Proceedings of the First Gatha Colloquium*, W. Z. O., Croydon, 1998, pp. 127–197.

Sorūsh, ʿAbd al-Karīm, *Qomar-i ʿĀshiqāneh* (Tehran: ʿElmi), 1990.

Sorūsh, 'Abd al-Karīm, *Qesse-ye Arbāb-e Ma'refat* (Tehran: 'Elmi), 1994.

Turkmen, Erkan, *The Essence of Rumi's Mathnawi Including His Life and Works* (Konya: Eris Booksellers), 2004.

Weightman, S. C. R., "Symbolism and Symmetry: Shaykh Manjhan's *Madhumālatī* Revisited," in Lewisohn and Morgan (eds.), *The Heritage of Sufism*, Vol. III (Oxford: One World), 1999 pp. 464–492.

Zarrinkūb, 'Abd al-Husayn, "*Jostojū dar Taṣawwof*" (Tehran: Amīr Kabīr), 1990 (first published 1978).

Index

16783174R00170

Printed in Great Britain
by Amazon